Tuning a Harpsichord,
FROM A PICTURE IN THE POSSESSION OF
JOHN BROADWOOD & SONS.

LONDON; ROBERT COCKS & CO. NEW BURLINGTON ST. REGENT ST. W.
PIANOFORTE MANUFACTURERS AND MUSIC PUBLISHERS, BY SPECIAL WARRANT TO
HER MOST GRACIOUS MAJESTY QUEEN VICTORIA,
AND TO HIS IMPERIAL MAJESTY THE EMPEROR NAPOLEON III.

THE PIANOFORTE,

ITS ORIGIN, PROGRESS, AND CONSTRUCTION;

WITH SOME ACCOUNT OF INSTRUMENTS OF THE SAME CLASS WHICH PRECEDED IT; VIZ.

THE CLAVICHORD, THE VIRGINAL, THE SPINET, THE HARPSICHORD, ETC.

TO WHICH IS ADDED A SELECTION OF INTERESTING

SPECIMENS OF MUSIC

COMPOSED FOR KEYED-STRINGED INSTRUMENTS,

BY BLITHEMAN, BYRD, BULL, FRESCOBALDI, DUMONT, CHAMBONNIÈRES, LULLY, PURCELL, MUFFAT, COUPERIN, KUHNAU, SCARLATTI, SEB. BACH, MATTHESON, HANDEL, C. P. EMANUEL BACH, ETC.

BY

EDWARD F. RIMBAULT, LL.D.

MEMBER OF THE ROYAL ACADEMY OF MUSIC IN STOCKHOLM, ETC. ETC.

LONDON:

ROBERT COCKS AND CO. NEW BURLINGTON STREET, REGENT STREET, W.

MUSIC PUBLISHERS TO HER MOST GRACIOUS MAJESTY QUEEN VICTORIA,
AND HIS IMPERIAL MAJESTY NAPOLEON III.

1860.

Edward F. Rimbault

The Pianoforte, its Origin, Progress, and Construction.

Facsimile of 1860 edition.

First published by Robert Cocks in London, 1860.

Republished Travis & Emery 2009.

Published by
Travis & Emery Music Bookshop
17 Cecil Court, London, WC2N 4EZ, United Kingdom.
(+44) 20 7240 2129
neworders@travis-and-emery.com

Hardback: ISBN10: 1-906857-41-5 ISBN13: 978-1-906857-41-7
Paperback: ISBN10: 1-906857-42-3 ISBN13: 978-1-906857-42-4

Edward Francis Rimboult. (1816-1876). Organist and Musicologist.

He studied under his father and then Samuel Wesley. His career was centred on London, where he started as Organist of the Swiss church, Soho.

More details available from
- Stanley Sadie: The New Grove Dictionary of Music and Musicians.

This book is scarce in its original edition.

© Travis & Emery 2009.

TO

HENRY E. DIBDIN, ESQ.

(OF FLODDEN LODGE, MORNINGSYDE, EDINBURGH)

I DEDICATE THIS VOLUME,

NOT ONLY BECAUSE I ESTEEM HIM AS

A VALUED FRIEND,

BUT BECAUSE

TO HIS GRANDFATHER IS DUE THE MERIT

OF HAVING

FIRST INTRODUCED THE PIANOFORTE TO PUBLIC NOTICE

IN ENGLAND.

PREFACE.

AMONGST the entire range of musical instruments, there is not one, in our day, that possesses so many claims to notice as the Pianoforte—the "household orchestra" of the people. Although it was the birth only of the last century, there have existed, for hundreds of years, instruments which, under different appellations, resembled the Pianoforte in the more important features of construction. Those instruments are but little known to the artist; scarcely, if at all, to the public. But the spirit of enquiry which marks the present age demands some explanation of those musical fabrics upon which so many of our eminent musicians exercised their mechanical skill, and for which they composed strains which are listened to with pleasure, even in these days of improvement.

The history of the Pianoforte has never been attempted on any scale at all commensurate with its interest or importance. Brief, unsatisfactory, and incorrect notices are indeed to be found; but these have only served to lead the enquirer into a net of inaccurate data, or a maze of wild conjecture.

Nevertheless, some articles are to be found which must, to a certain extent, be exempt from the general stigma; and amongst them the following, all of which have been used in the course of the following pages.

M. Fétis's *Sketch of the History of the Pianoforte and of Pianists*, originally printed in the *Révue Musicale*, and afterwards partly translated (the translation was left unfinished) in *The Harmonicon* for 1830-1, a valuable periodical, edited by the late Mr. W. Ayrton.

The late Professor Fischhof's *Versuch einer Geshichte des Clavierbaues*. Vienna. 8vo. 1853.

Thalberg's Remarks on Pianofortes, printed in the *Jury Report* of the Great Exhibition of 1851.

Mr. W. Pole's *Musical Instruments in the Great Industrial Exhibition of 1851*. Printed for private circulation.

I may also enumerate the valuable *Tours* in France, Italy, Germany, &c. by Dr. Burney; together with his articles in Rees's *Cyclopedia*. I have derived much curious and minute information from these sources, which cannot be too highly commended for their intelligence, learning, and accuracy. I accord this praise to Burney, because it is the fashion of the present age to speak slightingly of his labours.*

The task of writing the history of the Pianoforte was one of no small difficulty; the materials being widely scattered, and, in some cases, almost inaccessible. The amount of miscellaneous reading, too, required was almost enough to deter the most ardent explorer after hidden treasure from pursuing his labour; and when I present the following pages to the public, it is not without some misgiving that the result will be found to be far, very far short of what might have been expected. But, perhaps, if my work cannot be received as a complete history of the subject of which it treats, it may be regarded as a diligent collection of facts and opinions, illustrating the origin, progress, and construction of that delightful instrument the Pianoforte.

The materials are divided into three parts; viz.
    I. The History of the Pianoforte.
    II. The Construction of the Pianoforte.
    III. The early Composers for Instruments of the Pianoforte Class.

---

* My friend Mr. Charles Salaman's Lectures on the Pianoforte are deserving of especial notice, for the care with which they have been prepared. The information they contain has been gleaned from authentic sources, and reflects much credit on the industry and talent of their compiler.

In the first part of the work, I have given an account of the early keyed-stringed instruments which preceded the invention of the Pianoforte; i. e. the clavicytherium, the clavichord, the clarichord, the virginal, the spinet, and the harpsichord; tracing, as far as possible, their origin and progress.

And here I may remark, that a much greater antiquity is assigned to instruments of this class than has hitherto been ceded to them; although I do not go the length of the learned Abbate Pietro Gianelli, who, in the article *Cembalo*, in his *Dizionario della Musica*, says, " that King David knew something of this instrument is apparent from the 130th Psalm, where occurs the expression, ' *Laudate eum in cymbalis jubilationis*';" which is, of course, to suppose that King David wrote and spoke the Latin language; for *cymbalum* is but the vulgate translation of a Hebrew term!

I have also treated of various instruments in use by the Hebrews, the ancient Egyptians, the Greeks, &c. Perhaps some of my readers may deem this portion of my volume irrelevant to the purpose; but it seems to me absolutely necessary to trace briefly, as I have done, the progress of the lyre, the harp, the psaltery, the dulcimer, and many other of those instruments which preceded the invention of the key-board. Besides, it must be remembered that the noble works of Sir J. Gardner Wilkinson, Dr. Layard, Rosellini, &c. throw new lights on the manners and customs of those ancient nations which I have named, clearing up many doubts and difficulties which puzzled our older musical historians.

The origin of the Pianoforte is now, it is hoped, satisfactorily cleared up, by the republication of Scipione Maffei's interesting account of Bartolomeo Cristofali and his discoveries. The claims which have been set up for various ingenious men—Schröter, Marius, Silbermann, &c. now fall to the ground; and it is a source of no small gratification to me to be enabled to present a literal translation of this highly valuable document, setting forth as it does so minutely the claims of an ingenious artisan to the honor of the invention of the Pianoforte.

The list of patents appertaining to the Pianoforte, copied from the books of the Great Seal Patent Office, must be welcomed as a valuable and faithful record of the progress of the instrument. All doubts as to the various claimants for the honor of *discoveries* may be solved by referring to this list. It would doubtless have been desirable to have examined the specifications themselves, and to have recorded more minutely the particulars of each invention; but this could hardly have been done in the present instance; not solely on account of the additional labour, but because the volume already extends considerably beyond the limits proposed.

The second part of the work treats *generally* of the construction of the Pianoforte, without descending too minutely into the technicalities of the manufactory.

It is arranged under three heads: i. e.—1. The Framing. 2. The Stringing. 3. The Keys, and Machinery attached for striking the Strings, technically called the "Action." Under these divisions, all that relates to the manufacture of the Pianoforte, of whatever shape, "grand," "square," or "upright," has been carefully considered, and the various improvements and inventions duly chronicled.

And here I must express my obligations to Mr. Pole's valuable labours, as set forth in his volume already mentioned. The author is not only a *musician* in the proper sense of the word, but a gentleman of highly scientific attainments. His observations are of the utmost possible value; and whatever merit may be due to this portion of my work, it must be shared with Mr. Pole.

My notices of the improvements in the mechanical details of the Pianoforte close with the year 1851—the year of the Great Industrial Exhibition. Had they been carried down to the present time, several manufacturers would have received attention whose names do not occur in the index. Amongst them I may mention the spirited publishers of the present volume, in whose establishment an excellent class of instruments is produced, well deserving the notice of the public.

This division of the volume also contains a chapter on the " Various Mechanical Contrivances applied to keyed-stringed instruments in order to obtain sustained Sounds"—a subject which has occupied the attention of the philosophic mind for a period of nearly three centuries.

The " melographic," " mechanical," and " transposing" Pianos have also received due attention ; so also have the " Statistics of Pianofortes and Pianoforte Manufacturing as an Article of Trade ;" the " Materials used in the Construction of Pianofortes," &c.

The third portion of the work consists of an interesting collection of specimens of ancient music for keyed-stringed instruments, ranging over a period of two centuries. They have been taken from rare books and manuscripts in the possession of the author, and have been selected from a large mass of material, chiefly with a view to show the gradual progress of what may be termed the art of Pianoforte-writing.

Many old-fashioned *stereotyped* notions will be disturbed by a careful perusal of these specimens. Frescobaldi, the famed Italian organist, will be pronounced vastly inferior to our John Bull; whilst Henry Purcell, the great English musician, falls far short of his German and French cotemporaries in the art of *harpsichord*-writing. Couperin, the renowned *clavecin* writer, sinks into insignificance when compared with his predecessor in the French Court, Jean Baptiste Lully, whose harpsichord works betray a genius for which he has not hitherto received credit.

The sonatas of Handel and Scarlatti, printed for the first time in the following pages, shine forth with redoubled lustre when compared with the duller satellites by which they are surrounded.

Some of the more technical portions of my material have been thrown together in an Appendix, where, under the heads of " Hints to those who have the Care of Pianofortes," " The Mode of Tuning," and " How to regulate Defects in the Mechanism of the Pianoforte," a variety of information may be gleaned by all who need it.

I have also added to the Appendix " A Glossary of the principal Terms used in the Manufacture of the Pianoforte," which might have been indefinitely extended, had the prescribed limits (already much exceeded) of the work allowed.

Before concluding these prefatory remarks, I have one duty left, which affords me much pleasure—the offer of my sincere thanks to those gentlemen who have so kindly assisted me in carrying out my enquiries during the progress of the following pages.

And first, to my friend W. Chappell, Esq. F.S.A. who kindly translated, at my request, Scipione Maffei's Italian description of Cristofali's Pianoforte. To Thomas Jones, Esq. B.A. the learned librarian of the Chetham Library, Manchester, for the transcripts of two important documents preserved in that repository. To Mr. Murray, the eminent publisher, for permission to copy several wood-cuts from Sir J. Gardner Wilkinson's *Manners and Customs of the Ancient Egyptians*. To Robert Hendrie, Esq. for calling my attention to the monk Theophilus's curious notice, *De Mensura Cymbalorum*, and for permission to use his translation of the same. To Count Pepoli, for his kind letter (printed in the *Additional Notes and Illustrations*) respecting Marco Jadra, the early virginal-maker. To F. W. Fairholt, Esq. F.S.A. for pointing out several early representations of musical instruments. To H. E. Dibdin, Esq. for many valuable hints, and for extracts and drawings from Prætorius's *Syntagma Musicum*, in the University Library, Edinburgh. To the Messrs. Broadwood, for permission to copy the portrait of Tschudi, the founder of their firm, engraved as the frontispiece to the book. To Mr. Thomas Eastman (a gentleman on the Publishers' Staff), who kindly read over the proof sheets during the progress of the work through the press, and favoured me with his valuable observations; and also for the note on the meaning of several Hebrew terms used in the Psalms, inserted on pages 12, 13.

To Professor Fischhof, of Vienna (now, alas! no more), I acknowledge myself indebted for many valuable communications; as also to my late lamented friend, Mr. J. P. Barratt, for most valuable assistance in many technical portions of the work, especially in that portion devoted to a consideration of the causes of defects in Pianofortes, and the method of remedying them. Mr. Barratt's extensive knowledge of everything relative to the Pianoforte, and his readiness in communicating that knowledge, are well known to all who enjoyed his friendship. This acknowledgment is due from me to the memory of a truly deserving artist and a good man.

EDWARD F. RIMBAULT.

29, St. Mark's Crescent, Gloucester Road,
    Regent's Park,
       February 10, 1860.

ERRATA.

PAGE 13, line 8, read עֲשׂוֹר, עָ Ain, not צָ Tsaddi (with Kamets).
—— 13, foot-note, 2nd column, line 5, for "or," read "on."
—— 19, last line but one in the text, for "Musicá," read "Musicâ."
—— 19, foot-note, 2nd column, line 8, for "præseus," read "præsens."
—— 33, foot-note, 2nd column, line 10, for "sub-silentia," read "sub-silientia."
—— 47, foot-note, for "Fishof's," read "Fischhof's."
—— 64, foot-note, for "Arlington House," read "the Mulberry Garden."
—— 74, line 8, for "Rucker," read "Ruckers"; the same in the foot-note.
—— 77, line 18, for "Podini," read "Todini."
—— 91, line 20, for "son," read "nephew."
—— 129, foot-note, 1st column, for "Fischoff," read "Fischhof."
—— 155, line 33, for "James," read "John."
—— 156, paragraph 13th, read "SAMUEL THOMAS CROMWELL."
—— 190, line 1, for "George," read "James."
—— 208, foot-note, for "partée," read "portée de tout le monde."
—— 217, No. 28, for "Peachy," read "Peachey."
—— 218, In the italics at the head of the columns; for "*Cutalogue*," read "*Catalogue*"; for "*Grund*," read "*Grand*."
—— 218, in the division at foot of page (Belgium), for "Entwerp," read "Antwerp."
—— 220, for "*Ne. iu*," read "*No. in*."
—— 224, line 10, insert "from" before "the court or palace."
—— 229, line 17, for "1591," read "1587."
—— 233, line 29, for "born about 1591; died in 1640 read "born in 1587; died about 1654."

CONTENTS.

PART I.

THE HISTORY OF THE PIANOFORTE.

Chapter	I.	Some of the Stringed Instruments of the Ancients.	1
		The Lyre	2
		The Harp	7
		Stringed Instruments, the particular Names of which are unknown..	12
		Recent Discoveries at Nineveh	15
Chapter	II.	The Medieval Instruments that preceded the Invention of the Key-board.	17
		The Psaltery, or Psalterium	18
		The Dulcimer	23
		The Citole	25
Chapter	III.	The First Instruments of the Pianoforte Class	28
		The Clavicytherium	28
		The Clavichord	29
Chapter	IV.	The Virginal	48
Chapter	V.	The Spinet	67
Chapter	VI.	The Harpsichord	71
Chapter	VII.	The Claimants to the Invention of the Pianoforte	94
Chapter	VIII.	The Progress of the Pianoforte on the Continent	112
Chapter	IX.	The Introduction and Progress of the Pianoforte in England	130
Chapter	X.	The Progress of the Pianoforte in the Nineteenth Century	149

PART II.

THE CONSTRUCTION OF THE PIANOFORTE.

Chapter	I.	The Framing	162
Chapter	II.	The Stringing	175
Chapter	III.	The Action	184

CONTENTS.

CHAPTER IV. VARIOUS MECHANICAL CONTRIVANCES APPLIED TO THE PIANOFORTE IN ORDER TO OBTAIN SUSTAINED SOUNDS 197

CHAPTER V. MELOGRAPHIC, MECHANICAL, AND TRANSPOSING PIANOS 205

CHAPTER VI. STATISTICS OF PIANOFORTES AND PIANOFORTE MANUFACTURING AS AN ARTICLE OF TRADE; MATERIALS USED IN THE CONSTRUCTION OF PIANOFORTES; &c. ... 209

PART III.

THE EARLY COMPOSERS FOR INSTRUMENTS OF THE PIANOFORTE CLASS...... 223

A COLLECTION OF SPECIMENS ILLUSTRATING THE PROGRESS OF MUSIC FOR KEYED-STRINGED INSTRUMENTS 237

1.	Gloria Tibi, Trinitas	William Blitheman	237
2.	Sellenger's Round	William Byrd	241
3.	The King's Hunting Jigg	Dr. John Bull	245
4.	Les Buffons	Ditto	248
5.	Courante Jewell	Ditto	253
6.	Capriccio del Soggetto sopra l'Aria di Roggiero	Girolamo Frescobaldi	257
7.	Suite de Pièces	H. Dumont	262
8.	Suite de Pièces	Chambonnières	265
9.	Suite de Pièces	J. B. Lully	268
10.	Prelude and Airs	Henry Purcell	278
11.	Variationes super Cantilenam	F. X. A. Mürshhauser	284
12.	Sonata	Johann Kuhnau	292
13.	Suite de Pièces	John Mattheson	299
14.	Sonata in A minor	Domenico Scarlatti	306
15.	Sonata in G	Ditto	310
16.	Suite de Pièces	François Couperin	316
17.	Capriccio	J. Sebastian Bach	332
18.	Capriccio in G	Handel	340
19.	Fantaisie	Theofilo Muffat	344
20.	Air	Ditto	348
21.	Allemand	Ditto	350
22.	Introduction and Toccata	De Mondonville	351
23.	Rondo in E flat	Carl Philip Eman. Bach	357
24.	Fantasia	Ditto	363

ILLUSTRATIONS. XV

APPENDICES.

APPENDIX I.	HINTS TO THOSE WHO HAVE THE CARE OF PIANOFORTES	369
APPENDIX II.	ON TUNING	372
APPENDIX III.	HOW TO REGULATE DEFECTS IN THE MECHANISM OF THE PIANOFORTE	380
APPENDIX IV.	A GLOSSARY OF THE PRINCIPAL TERMS USED IN THE MANUFACTURE OF THE PIANOFORTE	387
	ADDITIONAL NOTES AND ILLUSTRATIONS	398

LIST OF WOOD-CUTS AND DIAGRAMS.

1.	Figure of a Hebrew playing on the Lyre	3
2.	Representation of an Egyptian Lyre in the Berlin Museum	5
3.	Lady playing on the Lyre, from a Theban Tomb	5
4.	Female Figure playing on the Lyre, from a Vase found at Herculaneum	6
5.	Male Figure, ditto	6
6.	Bow-shaped Harp preserved in the Museum at Florence	8
7.	Egyptian Figure with small bow-shaped Harp	8
8.	Ditto, larger	8
9.	Ditto, still larger	8
10.	Drawings of Bruce's Harps in the Tombs of *Bibán el Molóók*	10
11.	Female Figure playing on the triangular Harp	14
12.	Male Figure, ditto	14
13.	Egyptian Instrument of the Harp Class, in the Museum at Florence	14
14.	The Cithara of the Middle Ages	19
15.	The square Psalterium	20
16.	The triangular Psalterium	20
17.	The Psaltery or Nabulum of the Fourteenth Century	21
18.	Drawing of a grotesque Performer on the Psaltery of the Fifteenth Century	21
19.	The *Hackbret* or Dulcimer, as given by Luscinius	24
20.	Figure of a Lady playing on a Citole	25
21.	Drawing of the Clavicytherium	29
22.	Ditto of the Clavichord	30
23.	Diagram of the Mechanism of the Clavichord	31
24.	Drawing of the Clavicymbal	33

ILLUSTRATIONS.

25.	The Simicum, as depicted by Galilei	35
26.	The Cymbal, as represented by Grassineau	39
27.	Drawing of the Manichord	46
28.	Representation of a Lady playing on the Virginal	49
29.	The triangular Virginal from Prætorius's *Syntagma Musicum*	50
30.	The upright Virginal	53
31.	Diagram of the 'Jack' Action of the Virginal	57
32.	The Virginal of the Seventeenth Century	64
33.	Drawing of a Lady playing on the Spinet	67
34.	Representation of a Spinet made by Joseph Baudin, in 1723	69
35.	The Harpsichord, from Father Mersennus's *Harmonicorum*	72
36.	Representation of an Italian Concert in 1634	79
37.	A Spanish Harpsichord	84
38.	Diagram of the Mechanism of Cristofali's Pianoforte	99
39.	Diagram of Marius's "Harpsichord with Hammers"	104
40.	Ditto, showing a different Mechanism	105
41.	Ditto, showing the Mechanism of the upright Harpsichord	106
42.	Ditto, showing a Harpsichord with Hammers and Jacks	107
43.	Drawing of a Pianoforte in the Palace at Potsdam	119
44.	Diagram of the Mechanism of the Pianoforte as improved by Mason	137
45.	Diagram of the Framing of the modern upright Pianoforte—front view without the strings	169
46.	Ditto—back view, showing the bracings	169
47.	Diagram of the Action of the modern upright Pianoforte when the key is at rest	187
48.	Ditto, when the key is pressed down	187
49.	Diagram of the Action of the modern square Pianoforte	188
50.	Diagram of the common Grand Pianoforte Action	189
51.	Diagram of Broadwood's old Grand Action	189
52.	Ditto, with the Improvements of W. Southwell	189
53.	Diagram of Collard's Patent Grand Action	190
54.	Ditto of Erard's Patent Grand Action	190
55.	Ditto of Wornum's Grand Action	190
56.	Ditto of Zeitter's Grand Action	191
57.	Ditto of Wornum's Unique Action	191
58.	Ditto of Wornum's Double or Piccolo Action	191

PART THE FIRST.

THE HISTORY OF THE PIANOFORTE.

PART I.

THE HISTORY OF THE PIANOFORTE.

CHAPTER I.
SOME OF THE STRINGED INSTRUMENTS OF THE ANCIENTS.
INTRODUCTION.

MUSICAL Instruments with stretched strings—the first principle of the pianoforte—existed in the remotest ages of antiquity; but it is almost lost time to seek for their origin. "Shadows, clouds, and darkness" rest upon their first beginnings; and the names of their inventors, with their personal histories, are obscured by fables and traditions.

We can well imagine, that when the father of these instruments—

> ———————— " struck the chorded shell,
> His listening brethren closed around,
> And, wond'ring, on their faces fell,
> To worship the celestial sound:
> Less than a God they thought there scarce could dwell
> Within the hollow of that shell,
> That spoke so sweetly and so well."

The Egyptians are generally looked upon as the fountain from whence the arts and sciences were diffused over the greater part of Europe; and, from the wondrous records that have been handed down to us, this seems more than probable.

The ancient history of this extraordinary people is so entangled with tradition that it is impossible to unravel it. That there were extant at one period records extending up to its earliest existence is highly probable: but these were destroyed by Cambyses, who, about 525 B. C. subdued Egypt, overthrowing the temples in which the records were deposited, and slaying the priests. In the absence of written authorities, all tradition points to Ham, or one of his sons, as the first who led a colony into Egypt; and some writers suppose that Noah reigned there, identifying that patriarch with Osiris, to whose secretary, Hermes Trismegistus, is ascribed the invention of music.

THE LYRE.

Apollodorus* gives the following account of the circumstance which led to the discovery of this enchanting art; and, although the art itself certainly did not owe its origin to the encounter of Hermes with the shell of the tortoise, it is not improbable that the invention of the lyre may be attributed to some such adventitious cause: "The Nile," says the writer, "having overflowed its banks at the periodical season for the rise of that wonderful river, on its subsidence to its usual level, several dead animals were left on the shores, and amongst the rest, a tortoise, the flesh of which being dried and wasted in the sun, nothing remained within the shell but nerves and cartilages, which, being tightened and contracted by the heat, became sonorous. Mercury (Hermes), walking along the banks of the river, happened to strike his foot against the shell, and was so pleased with the sound produced, that the idea of the lyre suggested itself to his imagination. The first instrument he constructed was in the form of a tortoise, and was strung with the sinews of dried animals†." Assigning the discovery to some human being, this story has so much probability as can be

---

* *Bibliotheca*, lib. ii.

† The lyre was called, by the Greeks, *chelys* (χέλυς); and by the Romans, *testudo;* that is, *tortoise*. It seems that in these the *magas* or concavity formed towards the base of the instrument, to augment the sound, was really formed of the shell of the tortoise; for Pausanias speaks of a breed of tortoises on Mount Parthenius, excellently suited to furnish bellies for lyres. *Paus. Græc*, lib. ii, lib. viii. *Arcad.* The variations in the forms of lyres, as exhibited in ancient sculptures and paintings, are so numerous as to defy any attempt at classification. The earliest found were without the *magas*, or any contrivance to assist the sound. It is also remarkable, that, although the tradition assigns the invention of the lyre to Egypt, none of the instruments which their paintings exhibit are of the tortoise kind. The Egyptian lyre was generally held horizontally by the players, not perpendicularly, as by the Greeks and Romans. Sir J. G. Wilkinson says, they were *always* held horizontally. But this statement is contradicted by drawings in his own work.

afforded by the fact that many figures of ancient Greek lyres do actually bear the figure of a tortoise.

The lyre, in its various modifications of form, seems to have been the most common stringed instrument of all ancient nations. It possessed various forms, and various names—*lyra, chelys, testudo, cithara, barbitos,* &c., by which its principal varieties were distinguished. It seems certain, also, that the Hebrew כנור *Kinnór*, was a form of lyre, a representation of which is here copied from the curious tomb at Beni Hassan. The entire painting is supposed to represent the arrival of Jacob's family in Egypt, and is cotemporary with that event. Sir J. G. Wilkinson, from whose valuable work on the *Manners and Customs of the Ancient Egyptians* (vol. ii, p. 296) our figure is taken, says, "The lyre is rude, and differs a little in form from those generally used in Egypt; but its presence here, and in others of the oldest sculptures, amply testifies its great antiquity, and claims for it a rank among the earliest stringed instruments."

The question as to the number of strings in the original lyre of Hermes, has been a subject of much discussion; some writers assuming that it had only three, corresponding to the seasons of the year which the Egyptians recognized; *i. e.* winter, spring, and summer*. These three strings produced an acute, a mean, and a grave sound—the grave answering to winter, the mean to spring, and the acute to summer. Others contend that the lyre had four strings; the interval between the first and fourth being an octave; the second, a fourth from the first; the fourth, the same distance from the third; and that from the second to the third was a tone. Others again contend that the Hermean lyre had seven strings; but this discrepance is very likely to have arisen from confounding the lyres of the Egyptian and Grecian Hermes, or from adverting to the state of the instrument at different periods.

---

* Not only the Egyptians, but the ancient Greeks, divided their year into three seasons, which were called *hours*. Thus Hesiod:

"The *hours* to Jove did lovely Themis bear,
Eunomia, Dice, and Irene fair:
O'er human labours they the pow'r possess,
With *Seasons* kind the fruits of earth to bless."
Theogony.

THE LYRE.

Many of the Egyptian lyres were of considerable power, having five, seven, ten, and even eighteen strings. They were usually supported between the elbow and the side, and the mode of playing them was generally with the hand, and not, as in Greece and Rome, with a *plectrum**. This custom, however, observes Sir J. G. Wilkinson, was also adopted by the Egyptians; and as it occurs in sculptures of the earliest periods, it is evident they did not borrow it from Greece; nor was it unusual for the Greeks to play the lyre with the hand without a plectrum; and many instances of both methods occur in the paintings of Herculaneum.

There is as little agreement amongst ancient writers with regard to the form of the lyre, as there is respecting the number of its strings. There are drawings of it, and remains of sculpture, in which its figure exists in various shapes; some resembling the front part of the head and horns of a bull, others the shell of the tortoise. Some were ornamented with the head of a favourite animal, carved in wood; as the horse, ibex, or gazelle; and others were of a more simple shape. The strings were fastened at the upper end to a cross bar connecting the two sides, and at the lower end they were attached to a raised ledge, or hollow sounding-board, about the centre of the body, which was of wood, like the rest of the instrument. The Berlin and Leyden Museums possess lyres of this kind, which, with the exception of the strings, are perfectly preserved. That in the former collection is ornamented with horses' heads; and, in form, principle, and the alternating length of its strings, resembles one painted on the walls of a Theban tomb; though the

---

* "This implement seems to have been generally a piece of ivory, polished wood, or metal, in the form of a quill. Other forms are preserved, some of which seem to have been too clumsy to extract from the lyre tones of much sweetness or delicacy. Hawkins says that the lower joint of a goat's foot was sometimes employed. It appears that the plectrum was only used with the larger species of the lyre. When employed, it was held in the right-hand; and while the player struck the chords with it, the *fingers* of the left-hand also touched the strings. When the fingers only were used, those of both hands were generally employed: but some ancient lyrists were celebrated for their performances with one hand, and that too sometimes the left-hand. Josephus says that the *Kinnorim* of the Temple were played with the plectrum: and this may have been, although it appears from Scripture that the common lyres were played with the hand."—*Pictorial Bible*, ii, 574. The quill plectrum was used in the earliest keyed-stringed instruments.

It may be remarked, in passing, that, in the classical writings, a distinction is observed between the *Pecten*, with which the strings were fretted as with the ends of the fingers, and the *Plectrum* (from $\pi\lambda\eta\tau\tau\omega$, to strike) with which they were struck—the latter term including, as is assumed, all instruments of the bow kind.

board to which the strings are fastened is nearer the bottom of the instrument, and the number of strings is thirteen instead of ten.

We have here an engraving of both, thus affording an opportunity of comparing a real Egyptian lyre, with the representation of one drawn by a Theban artist more than three thousand years ago.

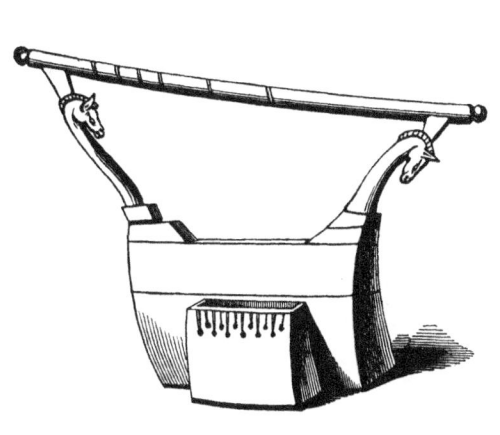 

The body of the Berlin lyre is about ten inches high, and fourteen and a half broad, and the total height of the instrument is two feet. It is entirely of wood, and one of the sides, as of many represented in the sculptures, was longer than the opposite one; so that the instrument was tuned by sliding the strings upwards along the bar.

The Greek lyres were similar to those of Egypt, sometimes imitating the shape of the head and portion of the horns of a gazelle, and other elegant forms: the strings too were as varied in number as those of the Egyptians. In Greece, the instrument had at first only four strings, till an additional three were introduced by Amphion*; who, as Pausanias seems to hint, borrowed his knowledge of music from Lydia, and was reputed to have been taught the use of the lyre by Mercury.

Seven continued to be the number of its strings, until the time of Terpander, a poet and musician of Antissa, near Lesbos (670 B. C.), who added several other strings; but many instruments were still made with a more limited number; and although

---

* Pausanias, lib. ix. The scattered notices of music preserved by this writer are very valuable.

lyres of great power had long been known, and were constantly used, many Greeks and Romans contented themselves with, and perhaps preferred, those of a smaller compass. The lyres in the paintings of Herculaneum vary in the number of their strings, as much as those in the Egyptian frescos; and we there find them with three, four, five, six, seven, eight, nine, ten, and eleven strings.

We give representations of two ancient lyres, drawn from the vases found at Herculaneum. The female figure seems to be in the act of tuning the instrument. The male, who is about to perform on a square-shaped lyre, has in his right-hand the plectrum.

There is every reason to believe that the musical instruments used by the Greeks and Romans came from the East, and were originally the same as those used by the Egyptians, Chaldeans, Phœnicians, and Syrians. The learned editor of the *Pictorial Bible* (the late Dr. Kitto) remarks: " It is, therefore, not impossible to recover, through the representations left by the Greeks and Romans, forms of lyres and other instruments nearly approximating to, if not identical with, those used by the Jews and other Orientals. The Greeks, always vain, and always jealous of their own glory, asserted that most of the musical instruments used by them were the invention of their gods or ancient poets. So they said of most inventions in science and art. But in the present instance, the Scripture alone suffices to overthrow such pretensions, since it mentions some of the instruments thus claimed as existing in times long anterior to even the ages of Greek fable. The Romans derived many of their instruments, and the traditions connected with them, from the Greeks; but their writers intimate that additions were made to them from Syria: their musical instruments came from the East. Thus Juvenal* sneers at the influx of Syrian customs and musical instruments; and Livy† mentions the great number of instrumental performers which came to Rome from Syria, after the wars between the Romans and Antiochus the Great.

"But even the Greeks are not consistent in their tales, being sometimes obliged to recur to the true source of most of their musical instruments: and this is always in the East; in some instances, Phrygia or Lydia; in others, Egypt, Syria, or Persia. As for the Hebrews, we need not suppose that they were themselves the inventors of the instruments they employed. They do not appear to have been ever remarkable for invention; and the instruments of neighbouring nations are in general so similar, that it is not necessary to seek anything peculiar in them. They were probably supplied from the same sources which supplied Greece and Rome: the Chaldeans, from among whom their fathers came; the Egyptians, among whom they so long lived; the Arabians, Syrians, and Phœnicians, by whom they were surrounded; probably furnished them with the models of most of the instruments they possessed."

THE HARP.

One account of the origin of the lyre, and consequently of all stringed instruments, attributes it to an observation made by Apollo upon the twanging of a bow-string. It might, therefore, be inferred that the earliest instruments founded on this idea would bear the form of a bow. Yet this does not appear (as far as it has been observed) from any Greek or Roman monuments; whilst *all* the harps of Egypt are more or less of the bow shape, so that the idea of such an origin would be suggested even were there no tradition to support it. The engravings, which we have selected from the perusal of a large number of Egyptian frescos, will trace the progress of the idea from the simplest modification of the bow-form to the large and magnificent bowed harp.

---

* Sat. iii.   † Lib. xxxix.

THE HARP.

The most simple application of the bow formed into a harp appears to be that afforded by the instrument represented in our first engraving: it is given by Rosellini, as copied from a real instrument preserved in the Museum at Florence.

From the number of the pegs, the strings seem to have been four in number; and which appear to have been conducted through a box  or belly, framed at one extremity of the arc, in order to strengthen the sound.

The second engraving exhibits another instrument of the same kind, with the four strings stretched over a box.

This figure is further interesting, as showing the manner in which the instrument was played, by carrying it upon the shoulder.

The next is another and rather larger instrument of the same description. It is not portable while played, but rests rather awkwardly upon the ground, without any base for its support.

The fourth figure shows a larger instrument of the class, and which has the same number of strings that Josephus gives to the Hebrew *nebel*.

All the Egyptian harps, according to Sir J. G. Wilkinson, have a peculiarity for which it is not easy to account; the absence of a pole, and, consequently, of a support to the bar, or upper limb, in which the pegs were fixed; and it is difficult to conceive how, without it, the strings could have been properly tightened, or the bar sufficiently strong to resist the effect of their tension, particularly in those of a triangular form.

The strings of the Egyptian harp were of catgut; and some of those on the harp discovered by Sir J. G. Wilkinson at Thebes, in 1823, were so well preserved, that they emitted a sound upon being touched, although they had been buried in the tomb probably three thousand years. This length of time would appear incredible, if we had not repeated instances of the perfect preservation of numerous perishable objects, even of an older date, in the sepulchres of Egypt.

The oldest harps found in the sculptures, are in a tomb, near the pyramids, of Geezeh, between three and four thousand years old; but perhaps the most interesting are those described by Bruce, in one of the tombs called Bibàn el Moloók (where the Kings of Egypt were interred), of the time of Rameses iii, B. C. 1235.

Bruce was the first to describe these representations, in a letter to Dr. Burney, which the latter printed in his *History of Music*. He also gave a drawing, engraved in that work, which was intended to represent one of the harps painted in these tombs. It is, however, so different in form and principle, as to leave no doubt that it was drawn from recollection*. Denon afterwards gave, in a rude sketch, a more correct representation, preserving the arc form which Bruce had destroyed. Then came the great French work on Egypt†, which gave a more finished and correct drawing; as also of one of the other harps, which appears to be larger, and more wonderful than that attempted by Bruce. Some serious errors have been committed in the descriptions of both these harps. According to Rosellini, the second harp contains *thirteen* strings, not *eighteen*, as stated by Bruce, nor *twenty-one*, as in the French work. But Sir J. G. Wilkinson, whose authority cannot be questioned, shows

---

* This distinguished traveller committed many mistakes, through his zeal and enterprise. But the mature investigations of the present quarter of a century have amply vindicated his character.

† *Description de l'Égypte, ou Recueil des Observations*, &c. published at Paris by order of Napoleon. See the second tome, pl. xci.

that it had only *twelve* strings. The accompanying engraving of both these harps is copied from the latter gentleman's *Manners and Customs of the Ancient Egyptians*, &c., and may be depended on for general accuracy and minuteness of detail.

Bruce, as we have said, made a fundamental error in the *form* of the first harp, and in the number of its strings. He also made another error, which has never yet been pointed out. After describing the player, he says, " To guess by the detail of the figure, the painter should have had about the same degree of merit with a good sign-painter in Europe; yet he has represented the action of the musician in a manner never to be mistaken. His left [right] hand seems employed in the upper part of the instrument among the notes in *alto*, as if in an *arpeggio ;* while, stooping forwards, he seems with his right [left] hand to be beginning with the lowest string, and promising to ascend with the most rapid execution; this action, so obviously rendered by an indifferent artist, shows that it was a common one in his time; or, in other words, that great hands [*sic*] were then frequent, and consequently that music was well understood and diligently followed. If we allow the performer's stature to be about five-feet ten-inches, then we may compute the harp, in its extreme length, to be somewhat less than six feet and a half. It seems to support itself in equilibrio on its foot, or base, and needs only the player's guidance to keep it steady. It has thirteen [ten] strings, and the length of these, with the ease and liberty with which they are treated, show that they are made in a very different manner from those of the lyre."

This description of the manner in which the performer's hands are placed upon the instrument, is calculated to give us too exalted an idea of the state of music in Egypt more than three thousand years ago. The Greeks, and other ancient nations, certainly knew nothing of the *accordance* of sounds, which we call harmony; and it is not more likely that the Egyptians were acquainted with an art, the discovery of which belongs to the medieval period*. The performers on " Bruce's harps" are simply playing *single notes in octaves:* the " arpeggios," and " rapid execution," are purely the invention of our imaginative traveller.

Bruce further adds, " Besides that, the whole principles upon which the harp is constructed are rational and ingenious; the ornamental parts are likewise executed in the very best manner: the bottom and sides of the frame seem to be veneered, or inlaid, probably with ivory, tortoiseshell, and mother-o'-pearl; the ordinary produce of the neighbouring seas and deserts. It would be even now impossible to finish an instrument with more taste and elegance." Dr. Burney himself has some interesting remarks on the same subject†, liable however to the correction necessary, from his having been in some respects misled by Bruce's drawing.

When, a few years after his letter to Dr. Burney, Bruce published his own work, he gave a representation of the second harp, which he had overlooked on the previous occasion; and which, although considerably modernized and *improved*, is far more faithfully copied than the other. With reference to both, he says, " These harps, in my opinion, overturn all the accounts hitherto given of the earliest state of music and musical instruments in the East; and are altogether, in their form, ornaments, and

---

* Whether the ancients had any knowledge of music in parts or counterpoint, is a subject that has given birth to a variety of disquisitions and disputes. The authorities in favour of the hypothesis, are Gaffurio, Zarlino, G. B. Doni, Isaac Vossius, Z. Tevo, the Abbé Fraguier, &c. Those who deny the ancients this knowledge, are Glareanus, Salinas, Bottrigani, Artusi, Cerone, Kepler, Mersennus, Kircher, Claude Perrault, Dr. Wallis, Bontempi, Buretti, Bougeant, Padre Martini, Marpurg, Rousseau, &c. The prevailing opinion among scientific men is, that the ancients were totally unacquainted with harmony in our acceptance of the term; but those who feel disposed to learn more upon the point, are referred to Dr. Burney's *History of Music*, vol. i, p. 112, where they will find the matter very ably discussed.

† Vol. i, p. 213, *et seq.*

12   THE HARP.

compass, an incontestable proof, stronger than a thousand Greek quotations, that geometry, drawing, mechanics, and music, were at the greatest perfection when this instrument was made; and that the period from which we date the invention of these arts, was only the beginning of the æra of their restoration. This was the sentiment of Solomon, a writer who lived about the time when these harps were painted: 'Is there,' says Solomon, 'any thing whereof it may be said, See, this is new! It hath been already of old time which was before us.'"

STRINGED INSTRUMENTS, THE PARTICULAR NAMES OF WHICH ARE UNKNOWN.

Much light might be thrown on the names of the various harps, lyres, and other musical instruments of Egypt, if those mentioned in the Bible were more accurately defined. But, as Calmet truly observes, "There is no subject in Scripture which has been so little understood as the nature of the Hebrew musical instruments*. The various translators of the Bible all differ as to the meaning of the terms applied to these instruments in the sacred volume; and the rabbins themselves know no more of the matter than those least acquainted with Jewish affairs. They enumerate no less than thirty-four different instruments, as used by the ancient Hebrews; supposing that the titles of several psalms, viz. *Michtam, Sigaion, Sheminith*, &c. indicate the names of particular instruments to be used in performing them. But of this there is scarcely any authority, excepting for the latter†.

---

* Those who are desirous to obtain knowledge on this subject, may read with advantage the curious investigations of Padre Martini, in the first volume of his History of Music: those of the Abbe Mattei in various dissertations with which he has illustrated his elegant translation of the Psalms in Italian verse; P. Philip Bonanni's *Gabinetto Armonico*, 1722; and the Latin dissertation of Francisco Blanchini, *De tribus generibus instrumentorum Musicæ Veterum Organicæ*, 1742.

The Padre Martini's History of Music, unfortunately, was never completed. The learned father began his work on so large a scale, that, though the chief part of his life seems to have been devoted to it, only three volumes were published before his decease in 1783. The first volume, which is wholly confined to Hebrew Music, appeared in 1757. The second and third volumes, which treat of the music of the ancient Greeks, appeared in 1770 and in 1781.

† According to the Rev. J. Jebb, *Michtam* signifies "A Psalm composed or written by David;" *Sigaion* (or *Shiggaion*), "A wandering Song;" and *Sheminith*, "a Harp of eight strings."—*A Literal Translation of the Book of Psalms*, ii, 140, 148, 157.

Mich-tam מִכְתָּם—according to the Targum, "Sculp-

THE HARP. 13

Mersennus, and, after him, Kircher*, have indeed undertaken to describe these instruments; the latter professing to have derived his information chiefly from the rabbinical writers and commentators on the Talmud. These are bad authorities; and it would only perplex the question still more to wade through their elaborate details. It is to the wonderful discoveries in Egypt that we must chiefly look for information upon this subject, and there our enquiries are more profitably rewarded.

Much confusion exists between the *cithara* or *kitarus*, the *ashúr* (*'asór*, according to the Masoretic pointing, עָשׂוֹר), the *sambuc*, the *nabl* (*nebel*), and the *kinour* (*kinnór*): nor can the various kinds of drums, cymbals, or wind instruments of the Jews be more satisfactorily ascertained. "The difficulty of identifying them is not surprising," says Sir J. G. Wilkinson, "when we observe how many names the Greeks had for their stringed instruments, and how the harps and lyres represented in the Egyptian sculptures approach each other in principle and

---

tura recta Davidis;" according to the Septuagint, "Tituli Inscriptio (στηλογραφία) ipsi David"—which seems to signify "a memorial of honour to David."

Shigga-jón שִׁגָּיוֹן " Ode erratica Davidis; i. e. varia."—*Bythner's Lyra Prophetica*. It is otherwise explained, "Occupatio aut Studium;" again, "Delectatio, lætitia, jucunditas."

Hash-sheminith—הַשְּׁמִינִית—The Sheminith "Instrumentum octo chordarum," from the numeral שְׁמֹנֶה octo.

* As these two writers will frequently be mentioned in the course of the following pages, we shall here briefly notice their biography. MARIN MERSENNUS was born at Oyse, in the province of Maine, in 1588. He was educated in the College of Sorbonne, and afterwards received the habit of the Minims. He was a great Hebrew scholar, and possessed of deep learning and research. He had also a correct and judicious ear, and was a passionate admirer of music. These gave direction to his pursuits, and were productive of numerous experiments and calculations, tending to demonstrate the principles of harmony, and to prove that they had their foundation in nature, and in the original constitution of the universe. His principal work is entitled, *Harmonicorum Libri XII in quibus agitur de Sonorum Natura, Causis et Effectibus, Generibus, Modis, Cantibus, Compositione, Orbisque totius harmonicis Instrumentis;* folio, Paris, 1636. The most material contents are dissertations on the nature and properties of sound; on strings; on consonances and dissonances; or ratios, proportion, and the division of consonances; on the modes and genera of the ancients; on singing and the human voice; on composition; and on musical instruments. This great scholar died in 1648.

ATHANASIUS KIRCHER, a jesuit of Fulda, was an able mathematician and a profound scholar. He was a professor at Wurtzburgh, in Franconia, from whence, on the entrance of the Swedes into Germany, he retired into France. He afterwards went into Italy, where he died in 1680, aged 79. He was the author of many learned works, and, among others, of the *Musurgia Universalis,* in two volumes, folio, 1650. He has been severely censured, by Meibomius and others, for his barbarous Latin, and unclassical ideas of ancient music, as well as for his credulity and want of taste in selecting his facts and materials. His *Musurgia*, however, contains much curious and useful information, for such as know how to sift truth from error, and usefulness from futility.

form; and we sometimes hesitate whether to ascribe to them a place among the former or the latter." It is among the instruments of this class, the genus of which is undecided, that we must seek for an explanation of many of those mentioned in the Scriptures.

Perhaps, among the most singular of these instruments, are those of a triangular form, two of which are here copied, as given by Rosellini, from tombs at Thebes and Dakkeh.

The first instrument has nine oblique strings, and is probably supported by a belt from the shoulders of the performer. The second instrument is a larger one of the same kind with perpendicular strings. It is held by pressing it between the side and elbow, and is played on with both hands, by one of those monsters which the Egyptian mind was so prolific in producing. From their peculiar character and form, no instruments of the kind claim a more attentive consideration.

To the same class essentially belongs another Egyptian instrument, of a very simple construction, and which is given by Rosellini, not from a painting, but from a real instrument found in Egypt, now deposited in the Museum at Florence.

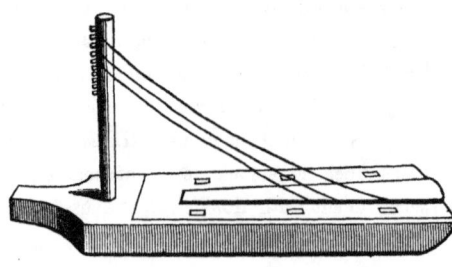

In this, the strings (originally ten in number, as appears from the pegs) form a triangle, by their extension from the upper end of a piece inserted at right angles into a large harmonical body of wood, with which the strings are at the other extremity connected; as shown in our engraving. Portions of the strings still remain, and appear to have been formed from the intestines of animals. Remembering that Solomon obtained wood for his *psalteries* by distant commerce, it is remarkable that the wood of this instrument is what Rosellini calls " a mahogany (*swietana*) from the East Indies;" and which the Egyptians must have obtained through commercial channels. Comparing the delta form, which the old authorities assign to the nabl or psaltery, with the number of the strings, Rosellini himself suggests that the present instrument has probably some resemblance to the נבל עשור, " the ten-stringed nabl " of the Hebrews*.

The instruments above represented are very similar in principle, however different their tones and powers may have been; but still they must be considered distinct from the harp, lyre, and guitar : and they may, perhaps, bear some analogy to the nabl, the sambuc, and the ten-stringed *ashúr* of the Jews.

RECENT DISCOVERIES AT NINEVEH.

The sculptures discovered by the enterprising Dr. Layard, in the ruins of Nineveh, contain representations of a musical instrument very similar to the triangular one above described. It occurs in three different places in the series of slabs now deposited in the *Nimrúd* room at the British Museum. Two of these represent processions, in which the king, returning from hunting, is met by five figures, the two last being musicians, standing side by side, and playing upon the instruments referred to. In the third slab, representing the Assyrian camp, a group of warriors, carrying the heads of the slain, are rejoicing, in company with two musicians, also with triangular instruments in their hands. Dr. Layard says, " It is possible that the Assyrians, like the Egyptians, had various musical instruments; only two kinds,

---

* " Owing to the obscurity which envelopes the instrumental music of the Hebrews, we cannot trust to Jewish tradition for any accurate definition of their various species. Even Josephus is not altogether accurate : since he speaks of the *nabal* or psaltery as an instrument of twelve strings (*Antiq.* vii, 13, 3); whereas, we know, from the second verse of the 33rd Psalm, that it had but ten."—The Rev. John Jebb's *Literal Translation of the Book of Psalms*, ii, 146.

however, are represented in the sculptures—a drum, and a sort of triangular harp or lyre, which is held between the left arm and the side, and apparently suspended from the neck. The strings of this harp, nine or ten in number, are stretched between a flat board and an upright bar, through which they pass. Tassels are appended to the ends of the strings, and the bar itself is generally surmounted by a small hand, probably of metal or ivory. The instrument was struck with a plectrum held in the right hand: the left appears to have been used either to pull the strings, or to produce notes by pressure. Like the Egyptian harp, it had no cross piece between the upright bar and the flat-board or base; it is difficult, therefore, to understand how the strings could have been sufficiently tightened to produce notes*."

---

* *Nineveh and its Remains*, 8vo. 1849; vol. ii, p. 412. In a note, the author adds, " There is a representation of this musical instrument in the bas-relief of the king standing over the crouching lion, now in the British Museum. See also Layard's *Monuments of Nineveh*, plate 12.

CHAPTER II.

THE MEDIEVAL INSTRUMENTS THAT PRECEDED THE INVENTION OF THE KEY-BOARD.

In reference to the stringed instruments of antiquity, but little can be said; unless we were to enumerate the various opinions at different times expressed by learned authors—a task by no means calculated to give the reader satisfaction. We are at a loss to conceive what the differences could have been between the numerous instruments of the same class to which we have referred. Montfaucon, indeed, says that he examined the representations of six hundred lyres and citharas in ancient sculpture, without coming to any conclusion*. Burney, in his "Reflections on the Construction of Ancient Musical Instruments,"† however, quotes a passage from Quintilian, which throws a gleam of light upon the subject. "Among the stringed instruments," says this authority," "you will find the lyre of a character analogous to masculine, from the great depth or gravity and roughness of its tones; the sambuca of a feminine character, weak and delicate; and, from its great acuteness and the smallness of its strings, tending to dissolve and enervate. Of the intermediate instruments, the polypthongum partakes most of the feminine; but the cithara differs not much from the masculine character of the lyre."

From this description we learn that the Greeks had two classes, as they imagined, of stringed instruments; one producing tones called masculine, the other those which were considered of a feminine character. "The Greeks, says a recent

---

* This learned antiquary says, in all the representations which he had seen, he did not find one musical instrument with a finger-board; but all had open strings, such as the harp and lyre are provided with. More recent research, however, has shown us that the ancient Egyptians were perfectly well acquainted with this important discovery.

† *History of Music*, vol. i, Appendix.

writer, " were especially distinguished by a regard to nature in all their works. To them we are indebted for the noblest specimens of architectural taste; and, if we may believe their disciples and annotators, they established the three orders from a consideration of the human figure. The Doric represents masculine strength; the Corinthian, virginal elegance and grace; the Ionic, matronal simplicity, and an avoidance of redundant ornament. So it appears, from the passage just quoted, they were accustomed to classify their instruments. There are two characters mentioned—the lyre, distinguished for its masculine tones, and the polypthongum, an instrument spoken of by Homer, for its feminine character. Between these two extremes, there were, in all probability, many varieties; the cithara, resembling the lyre; and the sambuca, having a similarity to the polypthongum."*

We do not intend to carry out our inquiries into the stringed musical instruments of the Greeks and Romans, as it would not lead to any satisfactory result. The arts and sciences of all ancient nations were in a rude and imperfect state. The perfection of the arts depends on scientific knowledge; and when we consider the uncertain state of the practical sciences at this early period, we can readily account for the imperfection of all ancient musical instruments. We shall therefore proceed to notice some of those instruments of the medieval period that more immediately suggested those of the class to which the present work is especially devoted.

THE PSALTERY OR PSALTERIUM

Enjoyed great celebrity in the middle ages. It was a stringed instrument, played with the fingers or the plectrum†, and differed from the cithara, chiefly in having its sonorous body placed at the top, instead of its being below‡.

---

* Higgins on Sound, p. 102.

† Kircher cites Suidas, to prove that the word *Psalterium* is derived from *Psallo*, to strike the strings with the ends of the fingers. *Musurgia.*

‡ " Sciendum quod Psalterio musico instrumento cithara est contraria, quæ concavitatem quam Psalterium habet superius, inferius habet." *Bedæ Op.* tom. viii, p. 311.

THE PSALTERY OR PSALTERIUM.

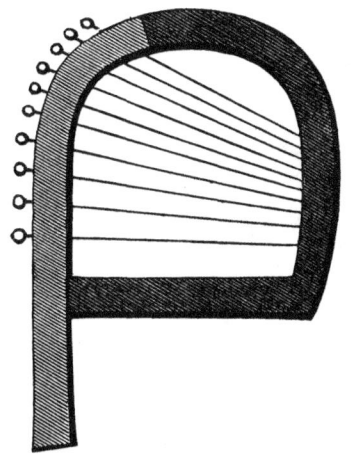

The cithara is thus commonly depicted in ancient manuscripts.

There were two forms of the early Christian psaltery—the square psalterium, and the triangular psalterium. The former had ten vertical strings. The sonorous body, which was placed at the top, according to Saints Augustine and Isidore of Seville, was of wood; or, according to St. Basil and Eusebius, of brass. Drawings of various forms of this instrument occur in a MS. of the ninth century, in the library of Boulogne-sur-Mer, and in a MS. of the eleventh century, in the Imperial Library at Paris (No. 1118)*

It is a curious circumstance, that, in manuscripts dating from the ninth to the eleventh centuries, David is always figured playing on the square psalterium, while subsequently to the twelfth century he is always depicted with the harp. This seems to show that the psalterium was, at the earlier period, considered as the nobler instrument, and more fitted to sound the praise of the Creator.

The triangular psalterium in form of a Greek Δ, resembled the cithara of the barbarians. According to Isidore of Seville, it was called *Canticum*. The Abbé Gerbert†, in his *De Cantu et Musicâ Sacrâ*, plate xxiv, has left us figures of both the square and triangular psalterium, copies of which are here given.

---

* See the *Annales Archéologiques* of M. Didron, where both are engraved. Other representations are preserved in Cotton MS., Tiberius, c. v. fol. 16, 17., Strutt's *Horda Angel-cynnan*, Carter's *Specimens of Ancient Architecture*, &c.

† The labours of this learned man are of such importance to the history of the art, that he is entitled to a passing notice. Martin Gerbert, Prince-Abbot of the convent of Benedictines, and of the congregation of St. Blaise, in the Black Forest, was born in 1720, at a small town in Austria. From his position and authority in the church, he was enabled to discover the most secret treasures of musical literature, by obtaining admittance into the libraries of convents and monasteries, closed to the ordinary enquirer. In 1762, he announced his intention of writing a history of church music, by the publication of a printed prospectus, preserved in the Critical Letters of Marpurg. He finished his noble work in six years, though, in the interval, the abbey and valuable library of St. Blaise were burnt to the ground. The full title of the work, which is in two quarto volumes, with many plates, is *De Cantu et Musicâ Sacrâ, a primâ ecclesiæ ætate usque ad præseus tempus. Auctore Martino Gerberto, Monasterii et Congregationis St. Blasii de Silvâ Nigrâ Abbate, Sacrique Romani Imperii Principe, Typis San-Blasianis*, 1774. The author divided his history of church music into three parts: the first finishes at the pontificate of St. Gregory: the second carries it on to the fifteenth century: and

THE PSALTERY OR PSALTERIUM.

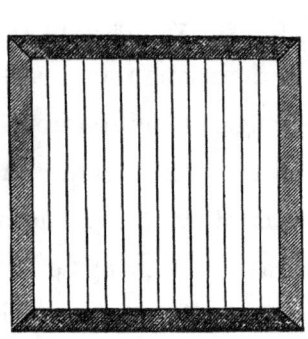 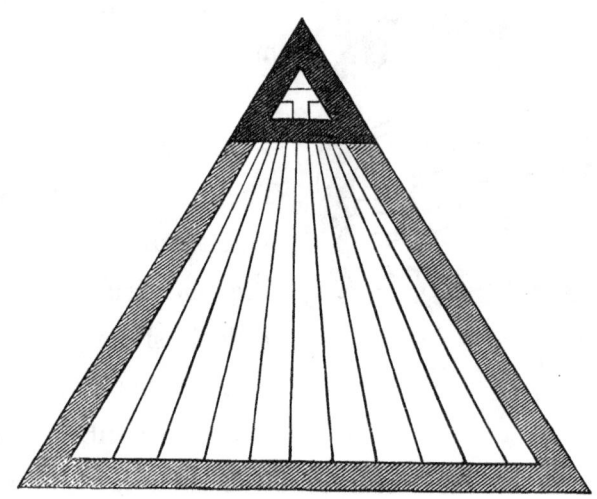

The resemblance between this instrument and the harp was probably the reason it went finally out of use. The name of psalterium or psaltery, however, was preserved, and given at a somewhat later period to a stringed instrument having some analogy to it, but more resembling the first instrument of the pianoforte class with a key-board.

Trevisa, in his translation of *Bartholomæus de Proprietatibus Rerum*, printed by Wynkyn de Worde*, gives us the following description of the latter instrument.

" DE PSALTERIO.

" The Sawtry highte *Psalterium*, and hath that name of *Psallendo, syngynge;* for the consonant answeryth to the note thereof in syngygnge. The harpe is lyke to the sawtry in sowne. But this is the dyversytee and discorde bytwene the harpe and the sawtry: in the sawtry is an holowe tree, and of that same tree the sowne comyth upwarde, and the strynges ben smytte downwarde, and sownyth upwarde; and in the harpe the holownesse of the tre is bynethe. The *Hebrewes* callyth the sawtry *Decacordes*, an instrument having ten stringes, by numbre of the ten hestes or commandementes. Stringes for the sawtry ben beste made of laton, or elles those ben goode that ben made of sylver."

---

the third to his own time. But the work which has given Gerbert the greatest distinction, is his *Scriptores Ecclesiastici de Musicâ Sacrâ potissimum. Ex variis Italiæ, Galliæ et Germaniæ codicibus Manuscriptis collecti et nunc primum publicâ luce donati, &c. Typis San-Blasianis*, 1783. This is a collection, in three volumes, of all the ancient authors who have written on music since the third century to the invention of printing, and whose works had remained in manuscript. Dr. Forkel has given an extensive analysis of it in his *Histoire de la Musique*.

* Bartholomew's singular work was written about the year 1366, and is certainly one of the most entertaining and valuable remains of antiquity. The contents are of a miscellaneous nature, and display the author's extensive knowledge of the several subjects of divinity, ethics, natural history, medicine, astronomy, geography, and various branches of the mathematics. After discussing these several topics, with great learning and ingenuity, he concludes with a very interesting dissertation on the music and musical instruments of his time.

THE PSALTERY OR PSALTERIUM.

To use more intelligible language, the instrument now called the psaltery or *nabulum*, was a stringed instrument, composed of a triangular sonorous box, one of the angles of which was often slightly flattened or rounded. The strings were placed on the upper face, sometimes perpendicular to the side opposite the flattened angle, sometimes parallel to the face opposite this flattened angle*. We have copied two interesting illustrations. The first from a MS. of the fourteenth century, in the Imperial Library at Paris; the second from a grotesque alphabet, by " the Master of 1466." †

In Wace's description of the Coronation feast of King Arthur *(Brut d'Angleterre)*, written in the twelfth century, he enumerates the various instruments used on that occasion, amongst which we have " psalterys and monochords." The psaltery was a favourite instrument of the minstrels of the middle ages, as may be gleaned from its mention in the following extracts.

---

* Grassineau, in his *Musical Dictionary*, in v. *Psalterion*, says, " It is strung with thirteen wire chords (*i. e.* strings), set to unison and octave, and mounted on two bridges, on the two sides; it is struck with a plectrum or little iron rod, or sometimes with a crooked stick (the writer here confounds the psaltery with the dulcimer, which latter was struck with a crooked stick), whence it is usually ranked among the instruments of percussion. Its chest or body resembles that of a spinet. It has its name *à Psallendo;* some also now call it *Nablum* or *Nablium.*"

† This is the instrument frequently mentioned as the *Sautry*, by Chaucer and his contemporaries.

In the *Squire of Lowe Degre*, a romance of the fifteenth century, we are told

> "There was myrth and melody,
> With harpe, getron and *sautry*,
> With rote, ribible and clokarde,
> With pypes, organs and bumbarde,
> With other mynstrelles them amonge,
> With sytolphe and with *sautry* songe,
> With fydle, recorde, and dowcemere,
> With trompette, and with claryon clere,
> With dulcet pipes of many cordes,
> In chambre revelyng all the lordes."*

Gawain Douglas, in his allegorical poem, *The Palace of Honour*, describing his visit to the Court of the Muses, says

> "In modulation hard I play and sing,
> Faburdoun, pricksang, discant, countering,
> Cant organe, figuratioun, and gemmell;
> On croude, lute, harpe, with monie gudlie spring;
> Schalmes, clariounis, portativis, hard I ring,
> Monycord, organe, tympane and cymbell;
> Sytholl, *psalterie*, and voices sweet as bell,
> Soft releschingis in dulce delivering,
> Fractionis divide, at rest, or clois, compell."†

And Holland, the author of a poem called *The Houlate*, written in 1543, enumerates the following musical instruments.

> "The *psaltry*, the citholis, the soft atharift,
> The croude, and the monycordis, the gythornis gay;
> The rote, and the recourder, the ribus, the rift,
> The trump, and the taburn, the tympane but tray;
> The lilt-pype, aud the lute, the cythill and fift,
> The dulsate, and the dulsacordis, the schalm of assay;
> The amyable organis usit full oft;

---

* Ritson's *Metrical Romances*, 1802, vol. iii, p. 189. † Sibbald's *Chronicle of Scottish Poetry*, 1802, vol. i, p. 386.

Clarions loud knellis,
Portatibis, and bellis,
Cymbaellonis in the cellis,
That soundis so soft." *

THE DULCIMER.

The psaltery or sautry gave rise to two instruments of a similar kind—the dulcimer (mentioned in some of the previous quotations), and the citole†.

The dulcimer, from *dulce melos*, sweet melody, was an instrument of a triangular form, strung with about fifty wire strings, resting on a bridge at each end, the shortest wire being about eighteen inches in length, and the longest about thirty-six. The instrument is laid out flat before the performer, and he plays on it by striking the strings with two small rods, sticks, or hammers, one held in each hand, the force of the stroke being varied according as the tones are required to be *piano* or *forte*. The psaltery appears to have been of a smaller size, and to have been provided with much fewer strings than the dulcimer. Ottomarus Luscinius, in his valuable work, *Musurgia seu Praxis Musicæ*, Strasburg, 1536‡, gives an engraving

---

* Pinkerton's *Scottish Poems, reprinted from scarce editions*, 1792, vol. iii, p. 179.

† Baretus, Minsheu, Cotgrave, Phillips, and others, speak of the dulcimer as the same with the *sambuca*: but, according to Bartholomæus, the sambuca was an instrument with hollow pipes made from the boughs of the elder tree. Leyden says, " the recorder was sometimes made of the elder bough, and denominated sambuca." (*Complaint of Scotland*, p. 150). Tyrwhitt (*Glossary to Chaucer*) makes the dulcimer the same with the *rote;* but he is clearly in error, as the latter was certainly an instrument of the bagpipe kind. The dulcimer was most probably the same with the " dulsacordis," of which we read in the earlier romances. The lexicographers have confounded the dulcimer with the *dulzain* or *dulcino*, a wind instrument resembling the tenor hautboy.

‡ This interesting and important work, which we shall have frequent occasion to quote in the course of the following pages, is in the form of a dialogue, in which the interlocutors are, Andreas Silvanus, Sebastianus, Virdung, sive malis, to use his own expression, Bartholomeus Stoflerus, and Ottomarus Luscinius. They meet by accident, and enter into conservation on music, in which Stoflerus, acknowledging the great skill of his friend in the science, desires to be instructed in its precepts, which the other readily consents to. The dialogue is somewhat awkwardly conducted; for though Stoflerus is supposed to be just arrived from a foreign country, and the meeting to be accidental, Luscinius is prepared to receive him with a great basket of musical instruments; which his friend seeing, desires to be made acquainted with its contents. The instruments are severally produced by Luscinius, and he complies with the request of his friend by a discourse, which is no other than a lecture on them. The merit of this book is greatly enhanced by the forms of the several instruments described in it, which are very accurately delineated. It is a small book, of an oblong quarto size, containing about a hundred pages.

of the dulcimer, which is here copied. It shows the instrument in its earliest stage, before it had attained its full complement of strings.

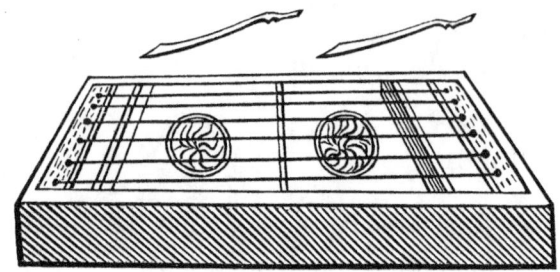

Luscinius calls it the "Hackbret," *i. e.* the Hackboard, or chopping-board, used by cooks, which it exactly resembles in shape.

"Short instruments, called dulcimers," are mentioned in the Inventory of Henry the Eighth's musical instruments, remaining in his various palaces at the time of his decease*.

Nicomachus, the Arabian, who flourished in the middle of the first century after Christ, mentions, in his curious tract on music, the trigon or *triangular dulcimer;* but we much question whether it resembled the instrument just described.

A kind of dulcimer forms a favourite instrument in Egypt at the present day. It is of a four-sided figure, with three rectangular and one sloping side. A specimen of this instrument, which Mr. Lane examined, and which is called a *ckánóon*, was about forty inches long, sixteen inches wide, and two inches deep. The face and back were made of fine deal, and the sides of beech. The sloping side of the instrument, which is made of beech, is provided with seventy-two pegs, round which are wound the ends of the same number of strings, the other ends of the strings being fastened to the opposite end of the instrument. The strings pass over a bridge; and, in order to aid the resonance, the face of the instrument is pierced in two places. The strings are made of lamb's gut, and are arranged in triplets, each note having three strings tuned in unison. The fore-finger of each hand is armed with a plectrum, made of a thin piece of buffalo's horn, kept close to the finger by a sort of thimble or sheath; and with these plectra the strings are touched. The player sits down, in the attitude customary among oriental nations, and places the instrument on his knees.

---

* Harleian MS. 1419, A. fol. 200.

THE CITOLE.

The word citole is derived from the Latin *cistella*, a little chest; and, in truth, the instrument was no other than a little chest or box upon which was stretched a series of strings. It differed from the psaltery and dulcimer in being played with the fingers, instead of plectra or small hammers. It was known in the early part of the thirteenth century, when the author of the half-historical, half-legendary history of *Fulke Fitz-Warine* mentions an outlaw " who knew enough of tabour, harp, viol, *sitole*, and jonglerie*." A drawing of the instrument is preserved in the British Museum (Bib. Reg. 20 A. 16), which is here copied.

Amongst the ancient authors who allude to the citole (besides those already quoted), are the following.

In the *Roman de la Rose*, commenced by Guillaume de Lorris early in the thirteenth century, and finished by Jean de Meun towards the end of the same, we have the following enumeration of musical instruments.

" Puis met in cymbales sa cure,
Puis prent freteaulx, et si fretele,
Et chalemaulx, et chalemelle,
Et puis taboure, et flute et tymbre,
Et *citole*, et trompe, et cheurie,
Et si psalterionne et viele ;
Puis prent sa muse et se travaille
Aux instrumens de Cornovaille,
Et espringue et sautele et bale."

Adam Davie, in his metrical *Life of Alexander*, written in the fourteenth century, describing an entertainment before the king, adds—

" At the feste was trumpyng,
Piping and eke taboryng,
Sytolyng and eke harpyng†."

---

* Wright's *Essays on the Literature and Superstitions of England in the Middle Ages*, vol. ii, p. 53. The romance has since been printed by the Warton Club.
† MS. in the Bodleian Library.

The next quotations are from the *Confessio Amantis* of the "Moral Gower."

"But thee I might knowe,
For olde men which sowned lowe,
With harpe and lute and the *citole*,
The houe dance and the carole."

*   *   *

"He taught her till she was certaine
Of harp, *citole*, and of riote,
With many a tune, and many a note." *

Chaucer, in his *Knight's Tale*, describing the statue of Venus, says—

"A *citole* in hire right hand hadde she,
And on hir heed, ful semely on to see,
A rose garland full swete, and wel smellyng,
And aboven hire heed dowves fleyng." †

In the description of King Arthur's feast, in the Romance of *Launfal*, we are told

"They hadde menstrales of moch honours,
Fydelers, *sytolyrs*, and trompours,
And elles hyt were unryght;
Ther they playde, for sothe to say,
After mete the somerys day,
All what hyt was neygh nyght." ‡

But perhaps the most curious enumeration of musical instruments of the fifteenth century is contained in Lydgate's poem entitled *Reson and Sensualité*, written about the year 1430.

"For they ronde the practyke
Of al maner of Mynstralcye,
That any mane kane specifye;
For ther wer rotys of Almayne,
And eke of Arragone and Spayne:
Songes, stampes, and eke daunces,
Dyvers plente of plesaunces,

---

* Printed by Caxton, in 1493.

† *Canterbury Tales*, edited by T. Wright, for the Percy Society, vol. i, p. 79.

‡ Ritson's *Metrical Romances*, vol. i, p. 198.

> And many unkouth notys newe
> Of swiche folkys as lovde trewe;
> And instrumentys that dyde excelle,
> Many moo than I kane telle.
> Harpys, fythels, and eke roytys,
> Wel accordyng with her notys,
> Lutys, rubibis, and geterns,
> More for estatys than taverns:
> Orgyns, *cytolys*, monacordys;
> And ther wer founde noo discordys
> Nor variaunce in ther souns,
> Nor lak of noo proporsiouns." *

"Citolers" are mentioned among the musicians in the establishment of King Edward the Third. See also, besides the above passages, Du Cange, in v. CITOLA; and M. de la Ravaliere, *Poesies du Roy de Navarre*, tom. i, p. 248.

---

* MS. Fairfax, No. 16, Bodleian Library.

CHAPTER III.

THE FIRST INSTRUMENTS OF THE PIANOFORTE CLASS.

It is generally asserted, by those who have treated of the origin of stringed instruments with key-boards, that no traces of their existence are to be found anterior to the sixteenth century. M. Fétis, indeed, goes farther back, adding, "From all that we can learn by tradition, it seems probable that the clavichord was invented by the Italians about the year 1300, and that it was afterwards imitated by the Belgians and Germans*."

But a much greater antiquity may be ascribed to instruments of this class, and the period of their invention may probably be fixed about the beginning of the twelfth century. The *clavier* or key-board was invented at the close of the eleventh century, when it was applied to the organ† ; and we cannot suppose that much time would be lost in adapting this important improvement to stringed instruments.

THE CLAVICYTHERIUM.

The first stringed instrument to which the key-board was applied, was probably the clavicytherium, or *keyed-cithara*. In its early stage, it was a small oblong box, with the strings arranged in the form of a half-triangle. The strings, which were of catgut, were sounded by means of quill-plectra, attached in a rude way to the ends of the keys. Luscinius and Mersennus have each treated of this primitive instrument, but in such a vague manner, that it is impossible to form any correct notion of its mechanism.

---

* *A Sketch of the History of the Pianoforte and of Pianists*, translated from the *Révue Musicale*, and printed in the *Harmonicon* for 1830 and 1831. We shall have frequent occasion to notice this article in the course of these pages. It is lamentably deficient in antiquarian research, but seems to be the only work (brief as it is) claiming to be a *history* of the instrument of which it treats.

† See *The Organ; its History and Construction;* by Dr. Rimbault and E. J. Hopkins. Recently published by Messrs. Robert Cocks and Co. *Historical Section*, p. 31.

The idea of the Clavicytherium was of course suggested from the lyres, citharas*, and other instruments, the strings of which were snapped with a quill or with a piece of tortoiseshell. The thought of employing mechanical contrivances had the advantage of offering means of combining a greater extent of sounds than could 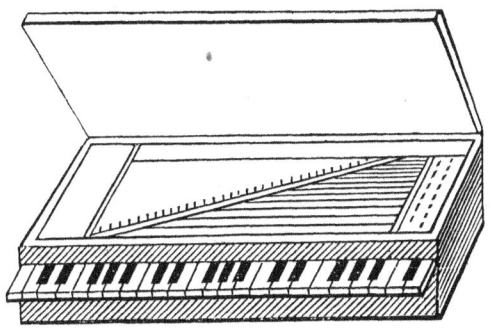 be done on any of the numerous varieties of the harp kind. The clavicytherium assumed different shapes; but the earliest delineation of its form handed down to us, is the wood-cut we have copied from Luscinius's *Musurgia, seu praxis Musicæ*, Strasburg, 1536.

THE CLAVICHORD.

The next instrument on record, to which the key-board was attached, was the monochord, clavichord, or clarichord; for it was called by all three appellations. As the

---

* The cithara was a particular species of harp or lyre; but its precise structure does not appear to be distinctly known. We have given one form of it, on p. 19; but it varied at different periods. The ancients describe it as triangular, in the form of a Greek delta; and the poets ascribe its invention to Apollo. Bartholomew, in his *De Proprietatibus Rerum*, has the following curious passage on the subject.

" *De Cithara.*

" The harpe hyghte cithara, and was fyrst founde of Appollin, as the Grekes wene; and the harpe is like to a mannys breste, for lyke wyse as the voyce comyth of the breste, soo the notes cometh of the harpe, and hath therefore that name Cithara, for the breste is callyd *Thorica Thicariuz*. And afterwarde some and some, came forth many manere instrumentes thereof, and hadde that name cithara, as the harpe, and sawtry, and other such. And some ben foure cornerde, and some thre cornerde; the strynges ben many, and specyall manere thereof is diverse. Men in olde tyme callyd the harpe Fidicula, and also Fidicen, for the strynges thereof accordyth as well as some men accordyth in Fey. And the harpe had seven stringes, and so Virgil sayth, libro septimo. Of sowne ben seven discrimina of voys, and ben as the next strynge therto. And strynges ben seven, for the fulleth all the note. Other for heaven sownyth in seven menyngs. A strynge hyghte corda, and hathe the same name of corde, the herte; for as the puls of the herte is in the breste, soo the puls of the strynges is in the harpe. Mercurius founde up fyrste suche strynges, for he strenyd fyrste strynges, and made them to sowne, as Ysyder sayth. The more drye the strynges ben streyned the more they sowne. And the wreste hyghte plectrum."

THE CLAVICHORD.

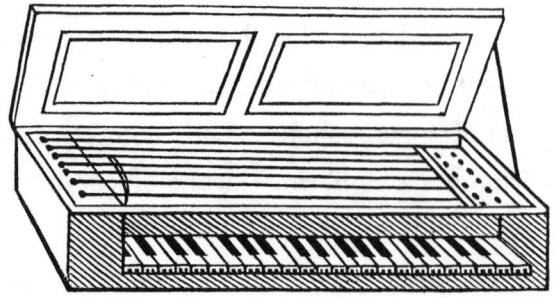

clavichord (for that is the name by which it was most commonly known) was destined to play an important part in the history of music for nearly six centuries, it is entitled to something more than a casual notice. Luscinius depicts it in this form.

Drawings or sculptures of early keyed-stringed instruments are very rare. Douce (as quoted by Sir Harris Nicolas, in the *Privy Purse Expenses of Elizabeth of York*) says, "The clavichord is frequently represented in ancient bas-reliefs, in churches, both in France and in England, which differs materially from the dulcimer." Douce must have been mistaken, as *no* such representations are to be found at the present day, nor do they exist in the numerous archeological works of France and England which we have consulted. Luscinius's engraving of the clavichord is the earliest with which we are acquainted.

It will be seen that the instrument was made something in the shape of a small square pianoforte, and was without frame or legs. Indeed, the idea of the square pianoforte was taken from the clavichord; but it retains only its shape and the disposition of the strings; their actions have no similarity. The strings of the clavichord were of brass*, and its action was simply a piece of brass pin wire, which was placed vertically at a point where it could be struck or pressed against its proper string; this pin could be held against the string as long as required by the firm pressure of the finger. It thus necessarily formed the wrest-pin for the string, which vibrated only whilst the key was held down, a close damper being fixed behind, always acting upon the string when quitted by the pin†; the string was of course, hooked upon a hitch-pin at the back, but it was tuned only after having been struck, and whilst pressed by the striking pin at the end of the key, which, in fact, formed one of the two bridges between which the string vibrated.

---

* The pandoron, a musical instrument of the lute kind, said to have been the invention of the Assyrians, had *brass* strings. Prætorius says it gave the idea of furnishing the clavichord with the same.—*Syntagma Musicum*.

† "As the clavichord was still what the Germans call '*gebunden*,' so that several keys struck a single string, it could not be perfectly tuned; people played therefore only in those modes which could be tuned with the most purity."—Forkel's *Life of Bach*, p. 24.

Some idea of the mechanism of the clavichord may be formed from the annexed diagram.

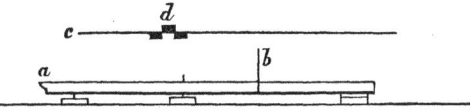

a, key; *b*, brass pin; *c*, string; *d*, cloth woven between the strings as a damper.

It is obvious that an instrument upon this construction could not have possessed much power; yet the tones are said to have been soft and melancholy, and better suited to the student, the composer, or the solitary, than for any purposes of social amusement.

Old Bach delighted in the clavichord; he considered it " the best instrument for study, and, in general, for private musical entertainment. He found it the most convenient for the expression of his most refined thoughts, and did not believe it possible to produce from any harpsichord, or pianoforte, such a variety in the gradations of tone as on this instrument, which is indeed poor in tone, but, on a small scale, extremely flexible*."

Bach's preference for the clavichord was not singular. This instrument, it will be remembered, formed part of the baggage of Mozart when he travelled; and Dr. Burney, in recording his visit to C. P. E. Bach, at Hamburgh, in 1772, says, " M. Bach was so obliging as to sit down to his *Silverman clavichord* and favourite instrument, on which he played three or four of his choicest and most difficult compositions, with the delicacy, precision, and spirit, for which he is so justly celebrated among his countrymen. In the pathetic and slow movements, whenever he had a long note to express, he absolutely contrived to produce from his instrument a cry of sorrow and complaint, such as can only be effected on the clavichord, and perhaps by himself†."

Concerning the origin of the name clavichord, and the various other appellations given to this instrument, our etymologists are not very clear. To quote a few of the most erudite:

" CLAVICORDES, an instrument having many stringes of one sound, saving that with small pieces of clothe, the sound is distinct. *Monochordium, dii neut. ge. Monochordia, orum Monochordion.*"

J. Baret's *Alvearie, or Triple Dictionarie*, 1573.

" MONOCÓRDO, an instrument with many strings of one sound, which with little pieces of cloth make distinct sounds."

Queen Anne's New World of Words, by John Florio, 1611.

---

* Forkel's *Life of Bach*, p. 28. † Burney's *Present State of Music in Germany*, &c. second edition, 1775, vol. i, p. 269.

32 THE CLAVICHORD.

"CLERICORDES, claricords or clavicórdes. *Spanish*, clavicórdias; *Latin*, clavecymbalum; *French*, clavessins, manicordion; *Italian*, clavicordio, clavicémbalo; *German*, clavicord quia eius chordæ extenduntur et circumuoluuntur clavibus (because the strings thereof are wrested up, with a wrest of iron, like a key, called, in *Latin*, clavis), vocatur etiam; *Latin*, Monochordum. It is an instrument having many strings of one sound, saving that with small pieces of cloth the sound is distinct."

John Minsheu's Ductor in Linguas: the Guide into Tongues, 1617.

"CLARICORDS. Instruments so called."

"CLARICYMBAL. See *Clavecymbal*."

"CLAVECYMBAL (Clavecymbalum). A pair of virginals, or claricords, so called, because the strings are wrested up with *clavis*, a key."

Blount's Glossographia, 1656.

"CLARICORD, or *Clericord*, a kind of musical instrument, somewhat like a cymbal."

"CLAVECYMBAL, or *Claricymbal*, a kind of instrument with wire strings; by some taken for a harpsical or virginal."

The New World of Words: by E. Phillips, 1678.

"CLARICORD. A musical instrument in the form of a spinet, containing from thirty-five to seventy strings. Florio calls it *clarigols*, and makes it synonymous with the harpsichord. He also spells it *claricoes*. See his New World of Words, ed. 1611, pp. 39, 173, 219; Harrison's Description of England, p. 238. 'Claricymballes, *cimballes*,' Palsgrave. Sir W. Leighton has *claricoales*, in his Teares or Lamentations of a Sorrowfull Soule. 4to. Lond. 1613."

Halliwell's Archaic Dictionary.

It will be observed, in the first place, that our lexicographers make no distinction between the terms clavichord and clarichord; but the one can hardly be a corruption of the other. The words suggest a totally different etymology, upon which we shall venture an hypothesis.

The word clavichord is certainly from *clavis*, a key, and *chorda*, a string; an instrument compounded of keys and strings. It seems far more likely that the *clavier* or key-board originated the name, than the key by which the instrument was tuned. Besides, the *tuning* key was not peculiar to the clavichord; it must have been used centuries before, in connection with the harp, and other similar instruments.

We learn that the strings of the clavichord were softened or deadened by slips of cloth. Now it seems probable that the clarichord was without this addition; and that the name was derived from the French *clair*, denoting a clear transparent tone, in contradistinction to the softened or muffled tone of the monochord, or clavichord. Or it may be from clarion; in low Latin, *clario*; an instrument which received its name from its shrill sounds*. We merely throw out this hint, as a likely distinction between the two instruments; in other particulars they were probably identical.

The clavicymbal differed materially from the clavichord and clarichord. It appears to have been the origin of the harpsichord, the strings being disposed " after the fashion of the harp." It was sometimes made in an upright form; sometimes in an horizontal one; its strings were of steel wire, and sounded, like the clavicytherium, by quill plectra.

The earliest drawing of this instrument exhibits it in an upright form. It is here copied from Luscinius's valuable work before mentioned†.

Julius Cæsar Scaliger, speaking of a newly-invented stringed instrument, in the first book of his *Poetics* (cap. 48)‡, has the following passage : " That new invention or contrivance was Simio's, which, from him, was called the *simicum ;* it consisted of thirty-five strings, from which is the origin of the instrument the vulgar now call monochords; in which, when in order, plectra hopping (or leaping) up, give the sounds. Moreover the points of crow-quills are added to the plectra, which elicit a more lively harmony from the brass strings. When I was a boy, it was called the clavicymbal and harpsichord ; but now, from those points, the spinet §."

---

* Menage derives the word Clarion from the Italian *Clarino,* or the Latin *Clarus ;* because of the clearness of its sound. Nicod says that the clarion, as used among the Moors and Portuguese, served anciently as a treble to several trumpets which sounded tenor and bass.

† Hawkins remarks upon Luscinius's representation of the instrument: " The clavicimbalum is no other than the harpsichord, *clavicimbalum* being the common Latin name for that instrument; the strings are here represented in a perpendicular situation; and there is good reason to suppose that the harpsichord was orginally so constructed, notwithstanding that the upright harpsichord has of late been obtruded upon the world as a modern invention. There is a very accurate representation of an upright harpsichord in the *Harmonia* of Mersennus; viz. in the tract entitled De Instrumentis Harmonicis, lib. 1, prop. xlii, and also in Kircher."

‡ Scaliger was born in 1484, and died in 1558. His *Poetics, Libri VIII,* was first printed in 1617.

§ The passage in the original is as follows :—" Fuit et Simi commentum illud, quod ab eo simicum appellatum, quinque et triginta constabat chordis, à quibus eorum origo, quos nunc monochordos vulgus vocat. In quibus, ordine digesta, plectra sub-silentia reddunt sonos. Additæ dein plectris corvinarum pennarum cuspides ex æreis filis expressiorem eliciunt harmoniam, me puero, clavycymbalum et harpichordium, nunc ab illis mucronibus, spinetam nominante."

The same words, or nearly so, are given by Prætorius, in his *Syntagma Musicum**, who adds, in a bracket, after the word monichords, *clavichordia*—the former name, as Scaliger says, "being that by which the vulgar called the instrument."

The statements of these two old writers are exceedingly valuable, as pointing out the connection between the monochord, clavichord, clavicymbal, harpsichord, and spinet.

There are no fewer than three instruments to which the name of monochord has been applied; the first and oldest is the harmonic canon of Pythagoras. It consisted of a single string; and the instrument or frame to which it was attached was marked off by sections and subdivisions corresponding with the intervals of the scale. There were three bridges, two stationary, one of which stood at each end; the other, which was placed between the two, was moveable, and, by being applied to the different divisions of the scale, showed the relation which the sounds bore to the length of the string, and in this way was useful in determining the series of intervals which it embraced. This instrument was, of course, not employed in the performance of music; but there was a stringed instrument, called a *monochord* or *unichord*, used for that purpose, not by the ancients, but by the moderns of the sixteenth and seventeenth centuries. It was sometimes called the Trumpet Marine (for what reason is not distinctly known), and was about five feet long, of a pyramidal shape, fitted up with a finger-board and bridge, and played upon like a double-bass, with a bow†.

The monochord used by our ancestors in the twelfth and following centuries was certainly not an instrument of a single string. The word is frequently spelt *monochordis*,

---

* The full title of this rare and curious book, a copy of which is preserved in the University Library, Edinburgh, is as follows:—*Syntagma musicum ex veterum et recentiorum ecclesiasticorum auctorum lectione, Polyhistorum consignatione, variarum linguarum notatione, hodierni seculi usurpatione, ipsiusque Musicæ artis observatione: in Cantorum, Organistarum, Organopœiorum, cæterorumque musicam scientiam amantium et tractantium gratiam collectum, in quatuor Tomos distributum.* Wolfenbüttel e Wittenberga, 1614, 1618.

† Representations of this instrument may be seen in the *Harmonicorum* of Mersennus, and in Bonanni's *Gabinetto Armonico*. We lately saw one of the real instruments, in excellent preservation, in the possession of Mr. Walesby, of Waterloo Place. Grassineau says, "It is the trembling of the bridge when struck, that makes it imitate the sound of the trumpet, which it does to that perfection, that it is scarce possible to distinguish one from the other, and this is what has given it the denomination of *Trumpet Marine*, tho' in propriety it be a kind of monochord."

a mode of orthography suggesting different ideas from the one-stringed instrument—in fact, a *polychord*, or instrument of many strings*.

It may perhaps be doubted whether the instrument called the monochord, the study of which was recommended by Guido in the eleventh century as the best method of teaching beginners their musical intervals, was the Pythagorean monochord above described. Guido is said to have invented the *clavier*, or key-board, and it is not at all improbable that he was the first to apply it to the medieval instrument of many strings; at any rate, the monochord seems to have been the same with the clavichord, and, as such, was the progenitor of the harpsichord, the spinet, the virginals, and the pianoforte of modern times.

With regard to the instrument called the *simicum*, Vincenzio Galilei, the father of the celebrated astronomer, in his *Dialogo della Musica Antica e Moderna*, Fiorenza, 1582, has ventured to give us a representation of it, although it may be doubted whether he had any authority from antiquity for so doing. The form which he has assigned it resembles nearly that of an upright harpsichord, without the key-board, which seems to indicate that, when played on, it was held between the legs of the performer, different perhaps from the harp, with the bass strings near, and the acute ones remote from him.

Athenæus (lib. IV) mentions the *simicum*, and the *epigonium* invented by Epigonius. "The former," he says, "had thirty-five strings; the latter, forty: the first was played with the plectrum; the latter, without it."

---

* "The term *monochord* has occasioned much perplexity to musical writers and readers by its equivocal meanings in some passages of modern authors. Sometimes it seems to signify a *one-stringed* instrument, and sometimes an instrument having several strings. In Domenico Scorpione's *Riflessione Armoniche*, published at Naples in 1701, we find, page 17, the following passage:—' Fù anco chiamato Monocordo quell' instromento che ha i tasti, come quelli del cembalo, del quale ne furone inventori gli Arabi, fù così chiamato, perchè, senza quei pannucci che s'intessono fra le corde, acciò s' oda distinto il suono di ciascuna di esse farrebbe un sol sentire, e molto confuso, e nojoso.' From this passage it appears very clearly that, in the sixteenth and seventeenth centuries, instruments having finger-keys and many strings or wires were known under the name of *Monochords*."—G. F. Graham's *Essay on the Theory and Practice of Musical Composition*; Appendix, p. 78.

THE CLAVICHORD.

These instruments, in common with many of those we have described in the previous chapter, can only be regarded as furnishing the first idea of those of the pianoforte class. The instrument to which the clavichord was much more nearly allied, was the medieval psaltery; the box of small depth, over which was stretched a set of strings.

Presuming that the monochord and the clavichord were the same instrument (which we can hardly doubt), we have evidence that it was known as early as the twelfth century, the proofs of which we shall now bring forward.

In Master Wace's *Brut d' Angleterre*, before quoted, the author mentions " psalterys " and "*monochords*;" and Ritson expressly says, in the Introduction to his *Metrical Romances*, that the musical instruments of the French minstrels at this period were " the viole, the *clavicorde*, the rote, the tabour, and others."

A very curious and important notice of this instrument occurs in the *Conseils au Jongler*, written by Giraud de Calanson, in the year 1210. Speaking of the accomplishments of the Jongleur, it is said, " he must play on the citole and the mandore, and handle the *clarichord* and the guitar*."

Of the state of music during the first half of the fourteenth century, much may be collected from the Decameron of Boccaccio, which was published in 1352, or 1353†. It is, as everybody knows, a collection of one hundred novels or tales; the author has ingeniously united them, under the supposition of a party formed during the dreadful pestilence which desolated Florence in 1348, composed of a number of cavaliers, and young, intelligent, and accomplished women, retired to a delightful part of the country, to escape the contagion. It was there agreed that each person, during the space of ten days, should narrate daily a fresh story. The company consisted of ten persons, and thus the number of stories amounted to one hundred. Each day's amusement is finished by dancing and singing; at the end of the fifth day, after a dance, the queen orders Dion, one of the gayest and most facetious of the company,

---

* See Sismondi's *Historical View of the Literature of the South of Europe*, vol. i, p. 128, Bohn's edition.

† Upon the first discovery of printing, the *Decameron* was freely circulated in Italy, until the Council of Trent proscribed it, in the middle of the sixteenth century. At the solicitation of the Grand Duke of Tuscany, and after two remarkable negotiations between this Prince and Popes Pius V and Sixtus V, the *Decameron* was again published in 1573 and 1582, "purified" and corrected.

to sing, who proposes several, at that time, well-known songs, to which the ladies offer some objection, on account of the licentiousness of the words. He tells them he would sing others, which he names, if he had a *cembalo*; "by which," says Burney, "some have imagined is meant a *harpsichord*, that instrument being now called *cembalo*, in Italian. However," continues the writer, "the harpsichord is certainly of later invention than the time of Boccaccio, who, in the passage where the word *cembalo* or *ciembalo* is used, probably meant only a kind of *tambour de basque*, or drum in the shape of a sieve, with small bells and bits of tin jingling at the sides of it; a tinkling *cymbal*, but not the modern harpsichord, nor the cymbalum of the ancients, which consisted of two parts resembling basons, which, being forcibly clashed together, marked the steps in Bacchanalian processions and the measure in singing the orgies, and which at present is in general use as a military instrument[*]."

M. Fétis, writing on the same subject, says, "some persons have expressed a doubt as to this *cembalo* being the harpsichord afterwards known under that name in Italy, and have imagined that an instrument of the same species as the cymbalum of the ancients was intended; that is to say, an instrument of percussion. This is not likely; for the use of small portable organs, and stringed instruments, had been so widely spread during the thirteenth century, as is seen in illuminated MSS., and music had made such progress in Italy in the time of Boccaccio, that it is not probable they would, under the circumstances related in the romance, have accompanied the voice with an instrument of percussion."—"If," continues the same writer, "it were permitted me to venture a conjecture in this regard, I should rather think that the instrument spoken of by Boccaccio was the *tympanum* (the *timpano* of the Italians), which is still to be occasionally seen in the hands of itinerant musicians, and which consists of a rectangular chest, in which is a sounding-board, surmounted by a bridge mounted with wire or catgut strings. The player strikes these strings with two small sticks hooked at the end, forming a harmony of two parts, and, if skilful, even executing passages of some difficulty. To the various mechanical means afterwards devised in order to

---

[*] *Hist. of Music*, vol. ii, p. 344.

obtain subsitutes for these sticks, we are doubtless indebted for the origin of stringed instruments with a key-board.*"

The instrument here described by the learned Frenchman is evidently the *dulcimer*. But we cannot help thinking that had Boccaccio intended the *timpano*, he would have spoken of it under that name. Undoubtedly the *cembalo* was a small portable clavichord or clarichord, and not the tambour de basque or the dulcimer. Both writers, however, were unacquainted with the curious passages we have adduced of its use so long before Boccaccio's period, or their ingenious conjectures would probably have been spared.

Concerning the term cembalo, it will be necessary to say a few words. The instrument called by the Italians cembalo, or clave-cymbalo, by the French clavecin, and in Latin clave-cymbalum, is always understood to be the harpsichord, or at any rate an instrument of that class, furnished with plectra, strings, and a key-board. The word *cembalo* is of ancient origin, being the cymbalon or cymbalum of the Greeks and Latins. St. Isidore derives it from *cum*, and *ballematica*, an immodest dance, usually accompanying this instrument; but it is more likely to be from *cymbos*, cavity.

The ancient cymbals were of brass or other metal, and very much smaller than those which we now call by the same name†. Cassiodorus and Isidore call the cymbal

---

Sketch of the History of the Pianoforte, in the Révue Musicale. Although differing, as we do, from many of the opinions of M. Fétis, and lamenting his want of research upon the present subject, we cannot but feel a degree of respect for his various labours in the art.

An interesting ceremony has just taken place at Brussels, in which this distinguished artist was the most prominent person. After a musical career that embraces nearly the whole of this century, the fiftieth anniversary of his marriage has been celebrated by the artists, the pupils of the Musical Conservatory, and several of the principal State functionaries of Belgium. On the day appointed, a mass was sung in the Church of the Sablon, the music of which, by the delicate attention of the ecclesiastical authorities, was of M. Fétis' own composition. After which the inauguration of his bust took place in the court of the Conservatory, in presence of a large concourse of artists and functionaries. It is a bronze cast, after Geefs, and has the inscription, "To Francis Joseph Fétis, from the Professors and Pupils of the Conservatory of Brussels." One of the expresssions of the answer of M. Fétis to the address, is characteristic of the man and his career:—" In choosing for this solemnity the fiftieth anniversary of the beginning of my domestic happiness, you become the instruments of Providence, which recompenses in a single day a life of devotion to the beautiful; for, whatever opinion posterity may form of the value of my labours, I can conscientiously say that, as artist, theorist, historian, and critic, I have struggled at first with the ardour of youth, and have been subsequently taught by the lessons of experience, to realise the triumph of the beautiful and the preservation of the soundest traditions of musical science."

† "The Cymbals (Cymbala)," says Bede, are "*small vessels composed of mixed metal, which, when stricken together on the concave side, in skilful time, produce by their delightful collision a very sharp note.*"—*Opera*, tom. viii, p. 900.

Acetabalum, the name of a cup or cavity of a bone in which another bone is articulated; and Xenophon compares it to a horse's hoof. It must, therefore, undoubtedly have been hollow. It is also certain that a handle was fastened to the exterior cavity; from which circumstance, Pliny likens it to the upper part of the thigh, and Rabanus to a phial*.

The invention of the cymbal was attributed to Cybele; on which account it was used at feasts and sacrifices. Frederic Adolph Lampe, who has written a learned work on the subject, *De Cymbalis Veterum*, 1703, gives the invention to the Curetes, or inhabitants of Mount Ida in Crete, who, as well as the people of Rhodes and Samothracia, were reputed to excel in the use of the cymbal. The Jews had their cymbal, or an instrument which translators render by that name. David, it will be remembered, in the CL Psalm, speaks of the "loud cymbals," and the "high sounding-cymbals;" and those instruments of joy and worship were early introduced into the ceremonies of the Byzantine church, where it formed a conspicuous part.

The nature of the cymbal has never been properly understood. It is generally considered as simply rhythmic, producing sounds unappreciable by the ear; but this was not the case with those of the middle ages. As we have said, the ancient cymbal was much smaller than that of the present day; and from the valuable treatise of the monk Theophilus we now learn *that they were capable of being tuned to the various sounds of the scale*. Theophilus, who flourished at the latter end of the eleventh century, has

---

* Grassineau, in his interesting *Musical Dictionary*, after noticing the ordinary cymbal, adds, "There is a kind of instrument which we likewise call a *cymbal*, which differs greatly from that above described. It consists of a frame, about four feet long and two and a half wide, along which there is a bar of wood laid straight, and a second athwart from one corner to the straight one, in this manner: ⎯⎯⎯ and a third straight, which has one like the other that meets it at one end within a little distance; so that all the bars lye thus in the frame; on each of these bars is 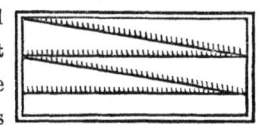 fixed an equal number of pins, about twenty-eight upon the two first, and near twelve or thirteen on those behind; which pins are not sharp, but their points are rounded; each of these supports a bar or wedge of a particular kind of metal, but chiefly a compound of bell-metal and silver, at each end, the longest whereof is about ten inches, about one and a quarter wide, and about half an inch thick, or not quite so much; these bars have a round hole about half through, to fit the pins; the sound of the longest is C, the others are diminished (in length only) according to the proportion of the intervals in music, and those of the second row answer to the flats and sharps of the spinet. There is near forty in all, so that this instrument has something more than three octaves in compass, and may be reckoned an instrument of percussion, by reason 'tis played by striking it with knobs of wood at the end of sticks. The sound it yields is very agreeable, being something exceeding soft, the low notes resembling the flute (*i.e.* the old *English* flute), but the high ones have not so much duration as these, yet their sound may be compared to that of a small flagelet."

left us a most valuable chapter on the subject of "cymbal-making for the use of the church," which we transcribe entire*.

"DE MENSURA CYMBALORUM.

"Quicunque vult facere cymbala ad cantandum rectè sonantia, ad unumquodque debet ceram dividere cum pondere, et a superioribus incipiat ut descendendo possit pervenire ad graviora. Unumquodque autem notet cum propria littera ut illud in divisione cognoscat. Imprimis faciat duas partes ceræ æquales cum libra, unam ad *a* litteram alteram ad G. Ceram *a* litteræ dividat in octo æquales partes, et tantum ad ceram G litteræ quantum est in octava parte ceræ *a*. Similiter dividat ceram G per octo et tantum det F litteræ quantum est in summa ejus, et insuper octavam ejus partem, et habebit duos tonos continuos. In illo loco semitonium † debet esse, et hoc ita inveniat. Summam ceræ *a* litteræ dividat in tres partes, ipsamque summam det E litteræ, et insuper ejus terciam partem. Deinde det tantum ceræ D litteræ, quantum est in summa *a* et octavam ejus partem. Item tantum ceræ det litteræ C quantum habet G, et mediam ejus partem, itaque haberet duos tonos post semitonium. Deinde tantum ceræ tribuat B litteræ quantum est in tota summa F litteræ et insuper terciam ejus partem, et habebit iterum semitonium; atque septem symphonias ab *a* littera usque ad B inveniat. Dyapason vero necdum haberet sine octavo cymbalo. Duplicet igitur totam ceram *a* litteræ et sic eam tribuat A litteræ, et nichil deerit. Dyatesseron, Dyapason, atque Dyapente Synemenon autem inveniat ita, tollat summam ceræ litteræ et tantum det F litteræ, et insuper medietatem ejus, ac constituat illam inter A et B. Omninò autem caveat qui cymbala formare aut fundere debet, ut de supradicta cera quæ tam cautè ponderata et divisa est, nichil mittat ad juga et spiramina, sed de altera cera faciat illa omnia. In magna providentia habeat ut, priusquam aliquod cymbalum fundatur, stagnum cum cupro misceatur, ut rectum sonum habeat. Quòd si aliter fecerit non veniunt ad tonos.

"OF THE MEASURE OF CYMBALS.

"Whoever wishes to make cymbals of proper sound for singing, should divide the wax for each one with a weight, and should begin from the highest, that by descending he may be able to arrive at the graver (cymbals). He can likewise note each one with its own letter, that he may know it in the partition. In the first place, let him make two portions of wax equal with the balance, one for letter *a*, the other for G. Let him divide the wax of letter *a* into eight equal parts, and (give) so much to the wax of letter G as is in the eighth part of wax *a*: let him similarly divide wax G by eight, and give so much to letter F as is in its total, and an eighth of its part beyond, and he will have two consecutive notes. In that place the semitone should be, and let him thus find it. Let him divide the whole of the wax of letter *a* into three parts, and give this total to letter E and beyond, the third part of it. Then let him give so much wax to letter D as is in the total *a*, and the eighth part of it. Likewise let him give as much wax to letter C as G possesses and half a part of it, and he will thus have two notes after the semitone. Then let him afford to letter B so much wax as is in the whole amount of letter F and beyond, the third part of it, and he will have the semitone again; and let him find the seven concords from letter *a* to B. The octave he cannot yet have without the eighth cymbal. Let him therefore double all the wax of letter *a*, and so give it to letter A, and nothing will be wanting: the fourth, eighth, and fifth chord let him find thus, let him take the amount of the wax of the letter and give so much to letter F and the half of it beyond, and let him establish it between A and B. He who should fashion or found the cymbals should above all take care that he puts none of the above-mentioned wax, which is so cautiously weighed and divided, to the necks and air-holes, but let him make all these from other wax. Let him have the great foresight that, before any cymbal be cast, the tin be mixed with the copper, that it may have the right sound. Because, should he have done otherwise, they are not brought to their tones. A fifth or sixth part

---

* *Theophili, qui et Rugerus, Presbyteri et Monachi, Libri III, de Diversis Artibus: Opera et Studio Roberti Hendrie.* Londini: Johannes Murray, MDCCCLVII. 8vo. Mr. Hendrie has kindly allowed us to use his translation.

† "Semitonus," *imò*.

Quinta aut sexta pars debet esse stagnum, utrumque bene purificatum priusquam permisceatur ut clarè sonent. Si autem fusa cymbala minus rectè sonuerint hoc emendetur limâ vel lapide."

"DE CYMBALIS MUSICIS.

Facturus cymbala, primum acquire tibi lectionem et secundum quod docuerit formam facito, atque ceram diligentèr pondera. Quas* cum fuderis, sicut supra dictum est, si quid per negligentiam vel incuriam de equitate tonorum defuerit, corriges. Si volueris cymbalum altiùs habere, in ora inferius limabis, si vero humiliùs, circa oram in circuitu."

should be tin, and be both well purified before they are mixed together, that they may sound clearly. Should, however, the cast cymbals sound imperfectly, this can be rectified with the file, or stone."

OF MUSICAL CYMBALS.

"Being about to make cymbals, first procure your directions, and, according to what they may have taught, make the mould, and carefully weigh the wax. When you have founded these, as mentioned above, should anything be wanting in justness of tone, through negligence or carelessness, you will correct it. Should you wish the cymbal to be higher, you will file about the mouth underneath (of the mould); but if flatter, round the rim in circumference."

The use of the cymbal in churches was discontinued upon the improvements in the construction of the organ, which instrument, however, still possesses traces of its ancient accompaniment in two of its stops, the *cymbal octave*, and the *cymbal regal*.

With the explanation we have thus been enabled to give, the ancient name of cembalo or cymbal, for a keyed-stringed instrument, does not seem so far-fetched as it has hitherto been supposed†.

To carry on our enquiries into the history of the clavichord.—There existed at Rome, about a century ago, a clavichord furnished with twenty-five keys, without any difference of form for the sharps or flats, and which had the appearance of being one of the first essays made in the fabrication of keyed-stringed instruments. It was then affirmed that it had been brought from Greece to Rome in the time of Julius Cæsar: such an opinion has no need of refutation. The author of the article *Clavecin*, in the *Encyclopédie Méthodique*‡, also speaks of another clavichord which existed in the same city; the body, table, and bridges of which were of white marble. This instrument had doubtless formed part of some monument. The date of 650 assigned it was altogether ridiculous. Zarlino speaks of a "cembalo," the relics of which existed in his time (1555), and which appeared to have been made about one hundred and fifty years previous. "The testimony of so learned a musician," remarks M. Fétis, "is undeni-

---

* Quæ?

† In the MS. romance of *Clariodus and Meliades*, we read of "The clear *cymball* with the merrie *cord*," which certainly must mean the *cembalo* or *clavicymbal*, thus bearing out our argument.

‡ M. Nicholas Joseph Hullmandel, an eminent pianist. He quitted France on the breaking out of the French Revolution, and settled in London, where he died in 1823.

G

able, and is, moreover, in accordance with what is known relative to certain celebrated artists of the fourteenth century, such as Francesco degli Organi, Nicolo del Proposto, Jacopo di Bologna, and some others, who were not only skilful organists, but also distinguished themselves on keyed instruments, as is seen in the pages of the Italian writers of the fifteenth century. Again, nothing more clearly proves the existence of the harpsichord or spinet of the fourteenth century, or, at latest, at the beginning of the fifteenth, than the manner in which they are spoken of by those who give descriptions of these instruments in the early part of the sixteenth century. They do not speak of them as new inventions; and the varieties which they mention demonstrate, in the clearest manner, that they could be the result only of multiplied essays, dating from times already long gone by. The least attention to the slow manner in which discoveries and improvements were made, in so backward a state of civilization as that of these first periods of the birth of the arts, will convince us that instruments of so complicated a kind could not start forth at once from the brain of such inventors as those described by the writers of the sixteenth century."

The popularity of the clavichord and clarichord in the fifteenth and sixteenth centuries may be illustrated by the following extracts. Caxton, in his celebrated translation of *The Knyyht of the Toure*, printed in 1484, gives us the following passage, confirming what Ritson advances relative to the common use of the clavichord by the early French minstrels. The extract occurs on sign C. 115.

"A yonge man cam to a feste, where were many lordes, ladyes, and damoysels, and arrayed as they wold have sette them to dinner, and had on hem a coote hardye, after the maner of Almayne. He cam and salewed the lordes and ladyes, and when he had done to them reverence, syre Geoffrey called hym before hym, and demanded hym where his vyell or *clavycordes* were, and that he should make his craft: and the yonge man ansuerd, Syre, I can not medle therewith. Haa, sayd the knyght, I can not beleve it; for ye be contrefaytted and clothed lyke a mynstrell."

In the accounts of the Lord High Treasurer of Scotland*, we find the instrument spoken of under the " vulgar appellation :"

"1497. Apr. 10. Item, to John Hert, for bering a pare † of monicordis of the kingis fra Abirdene to Strivelin, ix s."
"1504. Oct. 15. To the cheild [that] playit on the monocordis, be the kingis command. xviij s."

---

* Preserved in the General Register House at Edinburgh, and quoted in the Appendix to Dauney's *Ancient Scottish Melodies*. 4to. 1838.

† An ancient form of expression, meaning an instrument with more strings than one. See the term fully explained in the *Hist. of the Organ*, p. 40.

Also, in the testament of Edward Henrysoun, " Maister of the Sang Scole of Edinburgh, and Prebendare of St. Gelis Queir, quha deceist, 15 Aug. 1579." *

"Item, I leif to my sone, James Henrysoun, my gown, my coitt, my bumbasie doublet, and the bodie of poldavie, my kist, my bybill, *ane pair of monycordis*, my hat, thre of the best sarkis, ane pair of round scheittis, foure serviottis, &c."

From these extracts we might have imagined that the term monochord was used in Scotland instead of the more general name of the instrument; but this was not the case. At the marriage of James the Fourth of Scotland with the Princess Margaret, in 1503, we read that " the kyng began before hyr (*i. e.* the Princess) to play of the *clarychordes*, and after of the lute. And uppon the said *clarychorde* Sir Edward Stanley played a ballade, and sang therewith." Again, the king and queen being together, " she played upon the *clarychorde* and after of the lute, he being uppon his knee allwaies bare-headed."†

At the pageantry exhibited at Westminster Hall in 1502, on the occasion of an entertainment given to Catherine of Spain, we read that " twelve ladies had claricordis, claricymballs, and such other;"‡ and in the *Privy Purse Expenses of Henry the Seventh* § at the same period, we have the following entries:

" 1502. (Jan.) To one that sett the Kinge's *Clevechords*..............xiij s. iv. d."

" 1504. (March.) For a pair of *Clavycords*..............xx s."

Among the *Privy Purse Expenses of Elizabeth of York* ‖, Henry the Seventh's queen, we have the following :

" 1502. (August.) Item, the same day to Hugh Denys, for money by him delivered to a straungier that gave the Queene a payre of *Clavycordes*, in crownes for his rewarde..............iiij li."

This entry affords a singular instance of the queen's liberality. The " foreigner " is rewarded with *four* times the value of his gift!

Stephen Hawes, groom of the Privy Chamber to Henry the Seventh, was author of a poem called *The Pastime of Pleasure*, finished at the beginning of the year 1506. In Chapter XVI, he has the following stanza :

---

* Dauney's *Ancient Scottish Melodies*, p. 99.
† Leland's *Collectanea*. Append. iii, p. 284. edit. 1770.
‡ *Antiquarian Repertory*, vol. ii, p. 310.
§ Addit. MSS, Brit. Mus. No. 7099.
‖ Edited by Sir. N. H. Nicolas, 1830.

> " There sat dame Musyke, with all her mynstralsy
> As tabours, trumpettes, with pipes melodious,
> Sakbuttes, organs, and the recorder swetely,
> Harpes, lutes, and crouddes ryght delycyous;
> Cymphans, doussemers, wyth *claricimbales* glorious.
> Rebecks, *clarycordes*, eche in theyr degre,
> Dyd sytte aboute theyr ladyes mageste."

Among the "proverbis" that were written about the time of Henry the Seventh, on the walls of the Manor House at Leckingfield, near Beverley, Yorkshire, anciently belonging to the Percys, Earls of Northumberland, but now destroyed, were many relating to music and musical instruments. The fact of inscribing these curious rhymes on the walls, is a proof of the estimation in which the art was held at the period. Those relating to our purpose are as follows:

> "He that fingerithe well the keys of the *Claricordis* maketh a goode songe,
> For in the meane is the melodye withe a rest longe;
> If the tewnys be not pleasant to him that hath no skyll,
> Yet no lac to the *claricorde* for he doith his goode will.
> He that covytithe in *clarisymbalis* to make goode concordance,
> Ought to fynger the keyes with discrete temperaunce;
> Too myche wyndinge of the pipis is not the best,
> Which may cause them to sypher wher armoneye shoulde rest."*

Skelton, the facetious poet laureate, in one of his doggrel poems, *A comely Caystrowne*, printed by Pynson early in the sixteenth century, says of one of his characters:

> " Comely he clappyth a *payre of clavycordys*;
> He whystleth so swetely, he makyth me to swete;
> His descant is dashed full of dyscordes." †

The writer of an old poem on Music‡, in the reign of Henry the Seventh, gives the following advice:

---

* A MS. copy of these proverbs is preserved among the King's MSS. in the British Museum, Bit. Reg. 18. D. 11.

† *The Poetical Works of Skelton*, edited by the Rev. Alexander Dyce, vol. i, p. 16.

‡ " In the Fleete made by me WILLIAM CORNISHE, otherwise called Nyshewete, Chapelman with the most famous and noble King Henry the VII, his reyne the XIX yere the month of July. A Treatise between Trouth and Informacion." This curious poem, in black-letter, was printed by Wynkin de Worde. It contains a parable abounding with allusions to music and musical instruments; and seems to be a complaint of Cornishe himself, under the denomination of Musicke, against one whom, under that of Informacion, he charges with having falsely accused him.

> Who pleythe on a harp he should pley trew;
> Who syngeth a song, let his voyce be tunable;
> Who *wrestythe the Clavycorde*, mystuning eschew;
> Who bloweth a trumpet, let his wynd be mesurabyle;
> For instruments in themselves be firm and stable,
> And of trowthe (would trouthe to every man's songe):
> Tune them then trewly, for in them is no wronge."

Again he says:

> "The *clavicorde* hath a tunely kynde;
> As the wyre is wrested hye and lowe,
> So it tuneyth to the players mynde:
> For as it is wrested so must it nedes showe,
> As by this reson ye may well know,
> Any instrument mystunyd shall hurt a trew song,
> Yet blame not the *clavycorde*, the wrester doth wrong."

King Henry the Eighth, whose knowledge and love of music were very great, was a performer on the clavichord, as well as on other musical instruments. Richard Pace, in a letter to Cardinal Wolsey, preserved in the State Paper Office, says:

"The Kynge haith nowe goode passe tyme bi the newe player uppon the *Clavicordes* that M. Rochpotte haith broght wyth hym (whoo playith excellently) and like wyse bi the gentilman off Almayne whoo was wyth hys grace at Wudstoke, and hath nowe brought hydre a newe goodde and goodly instrument, and playeth ryght wele uppon the same. *Finem faciam in instrumentis Musicis, quia aliud nihil scribendum in presentia habeo.*"*

In the list of Henry the Eighth's musical instruments "remaining at Westminster in the charge of Philipp van Wilder," immediately after the king's decease, we find mention of "two payer of clavicordes."†

About the middle of the sixteenth century, an instrument called the Manichord first appeared. The writer of the article "Manicorde," in the *Encyclopédie Méthodique*, says, "it was more ancient than the harpsichord or spinet," and he presumes it to have been invented by the Germans; but it more probably first took its rise in

---

* Wolsey Correspondence, IX, art. 60. See also Sir H. Ellis's *Original Letters illustrative of English History*, Third Series, vol. i, p. 200.

† Harleian MS. No. 1419, fol. 200.

THE CLAVICHORD.

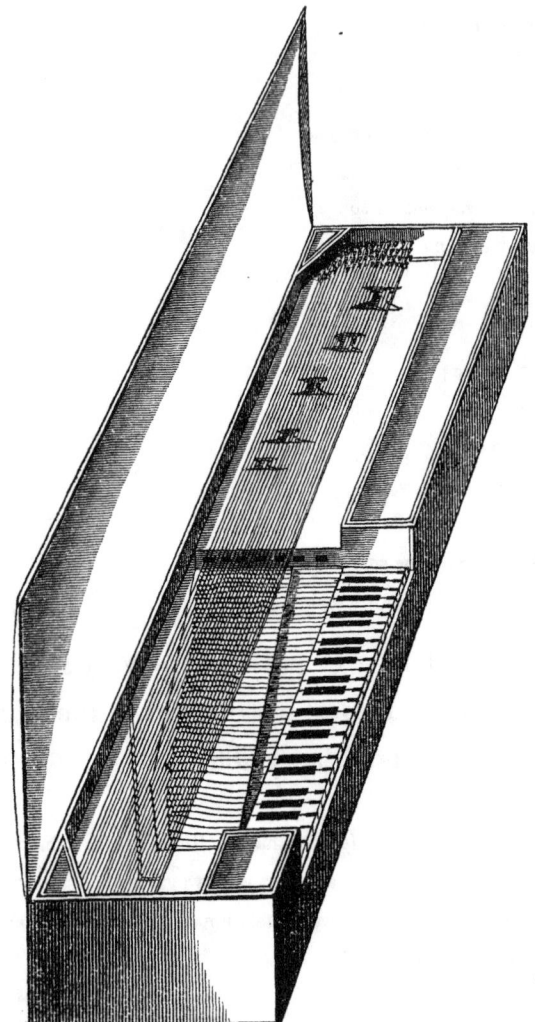

Italy. Florio has it in his *Dictionarie of the Italian and English*, 1611, and describes it as "a rigoll or claricorde." Mersennus gives us a representation of the instrument, which is here copied.

From this drawing, and the description handed down to us, the Manichord appears to have been a large and superior clavichord. It was provided with forty-nine or fifty keys and seventy strings, which rested on, or passed over, five bridges; some of the strings being in unison*. It was furnished with a kind of hammer of brass, which struck the string, and a cloth damper to stop the vibration after the note had been struck. The hammer is thus shown by the author to whom we have just referred. Mersennus also says, "It's strings, like those of the clavichord, are covered with little pieces of cloth, to deaden the sound as well as soften it; whence it is called the dumb spinet *(épinette sourde)*, and is much used in nunneries, by reason the nuns who learn may play without disturbing the silence of their gloomy cells."

This instrument exactly resembled in form the first square pianoforte. It

---

* Sir John Graham Dalzell, in his *Memoirs of the Musical Instruments of Scotland*, says, "some musicians assure me that they have seen the clavichord with more than a single string to each note. Others have described a part of the action as much resembling that of a pianoforte: that, instead of the *jack* and *quill* of the older instrument, a *stump* at the inner end of the lever struck inwards against the wires on depressing the key." This was undoubtedly the manichord.

was long and narrow; the sounding board took up half the length of the instrument, and the lid was frequently painted or inlaid with coloured woods; sometimes it was domed like the top of a hair trunk.

The clavichord, however, in almost its original form, still continued the popular instrument of Germany, and was much encouraged by the great masters of harmony. Roland von Lasz, Chapel Master to the Duke Albert of Bavaria, who died in 1594, is said to have been the first to use it in concert with other instruments.

The seventeenth century does not record any improvements in this primitive instrument; and we are told that Daniel Faber, Organist at Craylsheim in Anspach, about 1725, was the first clavichord maker who used a string for each sound!

Carl Lemme, an organist and instrument maker at Brunswick, at a somewhat later date, is said to have made "oval round clavichords with *double* sounding-boards." The clavichords of Wilhelm, of Cassel, were remarkable for their fine tone; as also were those of Vensky, Horn, and Mack, eminent makers, of Dresden.*

The last maker of the clavichord in Germany, of any note, was Krämer of Göttingen, some of whose instruments may still occasionally be met with in the old baronial residences with which that romantic country abounds.

---

* See Professor Joseph Fischof's *Versuch einer Geschichte des Clavierbanes.* Wien. 8vo. 1853.

CHAPTER IV.

THE VIRGINAL.

M. Fétis, in his *Sketch of the History of the Pianoforte*, before alluded to, has the following remarks upon the origin of this instrument:

"When the defects inherent in the construction of the clavichord were discovered, a plan was devised of striking the strings with small pieces of quill affixed to minute springs, adjusted in the upper part of small flat pieces of wood termed *jacks*. These jacks were directed perpendicularly upon the key, and when the jack had made its escape, after the string had been struck, the jack fell in such a manner as to be able to reproduce anew the sound at will. A slip of cloth applied to each side of the jack had the effect of a damper in stopping the vibration. This new invention was applied to two instruments, which differed only in form: the one was the *virginal*, the chest of which was rectangular, like that of small pianofortes; the other was the *spinnet*, which had the form of a harp laid in a horizontal position. These instruments were much in vogue towards the close of the sixteenth century, but were soon surpassed, both in respect to volume of sound and variety of effects, by the *harpsichord*."

The invention of the jack and quill had formerly been applied, although perhaps in a ruder way, to the clavicytherium. The virginal was an improvement upon that instrument, and its strings of various lengths, one to each note, were of steel and iron, instead of catgut. Sometimes latten was used; and, occasionally, for the treble notes, gold, silver, and even silk strings; but these were often affected by the weather, and less harmonious in tone.

The virginal, however, did not supersede the clavichord, which instrument, as we shall afterwards see, only fell into disuse upon the rise of the pianoforte.

THE VIRGINAL.

49

The earliest mention we have found of the virginal occurs in one of the "proverbis," as they are termed (before referred to), inscribed on the walls of the Manor House at Leckingfield, Yorkshire, in the time of Henry the Seventh*. It runs thus:

> " A slac strynge in a *Virgynall* soundithe not aright,
> It doth abyde no wrestinge it is so loose and light:
> The sound-borde crasede, forsith the instrumente,
> Throw mysgovernance, to make notes whiche was not his intente."

The virginal was also known early in the sixteenth century on the continent. Martin Agricola, in his *Musica Instrumentalis*, Wittenberg, 1529, mentions it, in company with the other keyed-stringed instruments of his time; i. e. the clavicordium, the clavicymbalum, and the clavicytherium†.

The general form of the instrument is shown by the following engraving, copied from an ancient piece of stained glass of the Elizabethan period.

---

* Bib. Reg. 18, D. 11. Brit. Mus. See Ante, p. 44.

† Among the import duties relating to music in *The Rates of the Custome House, both inwarde and outwarde, very necessarye for all Merchants to knowe, Imprinted at London, by Rycharde Kele, &c.* 1545, will be found—

" Clarycordes, the payre, 2s.; Harp Strynges, the boxe, 10s.; Lute Strynges, called Mynikins, the groce, 22d.; Orgons, the payre, *ut sint in valore;* wyer for Clarycordes, the pound, 4d.; VIRGINALES, the payer, 3s. 4d. &c.

H

THE VIRGINAL.

On the continent, the virginal was often made in a *triangular* shape. Prætorius thus depicts it, in his *Syntagma Musicum.*

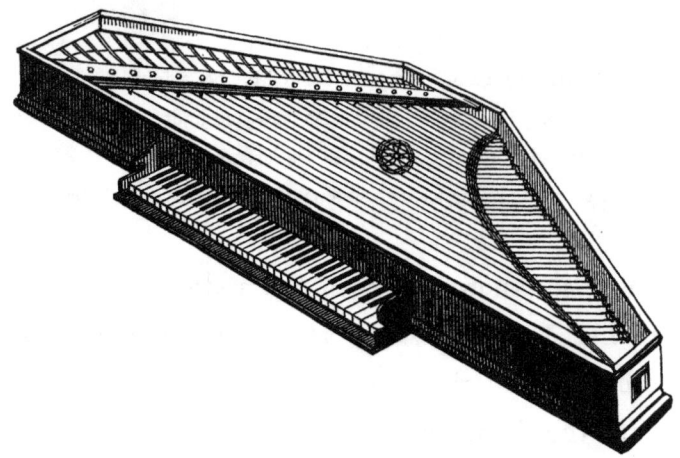

An interesting engraving of a lady playing upon the virginal is given in the series of cards so beautifully engraved by Jost Ammin, and copied in Singer's *History of Playing Cards.* Other representations of ladies performing upon this instrument occur on the title pages to the two editions of *Parthenia, or the Maydenhead of the first musicke that ever was printed for the virginalls,* 1611 and 1650*. The former is a well-executed engraving by William Hole.

Some authors have supposed that the name of this instrument was intended to convey a compliment to Queen Elizabeth—the "*Virgin* Queen;" but what we have just stated shows that the virginal was known anterior to the date of her birth. Dr. Johnson suggests that the instrument was so called " because played upon chiefly by young ladies; " and a modern writer, with better judgment, ascribes its title to its uses; and reminds us how, in the pleasant twilight of convents and old halls, it served to lead sweet voices singing hymns to the *Virgin*.

The following is what a few of our etymologists and glossarists say upon the subject:—

---

* Both editions of this rare volume are in the author's library. See a fac-simile of Hole's title-page, in the edition printed, under the author's superintendence, by the Musical Antiquarian Society.

THE VIRGINAL.   51

"VIRGINALLS. Instrumentum Musicum propriè Virginum, unde ei nomen inditum esse videtur, so called, because Virgins and Maidens play on them. *Latin*, Clavicymbalum, Cymbaleum Virginæum, fuit enim Cymbalum apud veteres Instrumentum Musicum, quod in sacris metris deorum cum Sympanis habebatur."

John Minsheu's *Ductor in Linguas, The Guide into Tongues*, 1617.

"VIRGINAL (*Virginalis*), Maidenly, Virgin like; hence the name of that Musical Instrument called *Virginals* because Maids and *Virgins* do most commonly play on them."

Blount's *Glossographia*, 1656.

"VIRGINALS (*Lat. Clavicymbalum*), a common, but noble sort of Musical Instrument, toucht in like manner as the Organ or Harpsichord, and probably so call'd, as having been thought a proper Instrument for Virgins to play on."

The New World of Words, by E. Philips, 1678.

"VIRGINAL. An instrument of the spinnet kind, but made quite rectangular, like a small piano-forte. I remember two in use, belonging to the master of the King's Choristers. Their name was probably derived from being used by young girls. They had, like spinnets, only one wire to each note. Sir John Hawkins speaks of them as being in fact spinnets, though under a different name; yet his own figures of them demonstrate a material difference in the construction. The spinnet, as many persons remember, was nearly of a triangular shape, and had the wires carried over a bent bridge, which modified their sounds; those of the *virginal* went direct from their points of support to the screw-pegs, regularly decreasing in length from the deepest bass note to the highest treble."

Archdeacon Nares's *Glossary*, in v.

The virginal, as we have seen, was known in this country in the early part of the sixteenth century, if not earlier; and one of the first patrons of the instrument was King Henry the Eighth. Hollinshed, in speaking of the removal of the court from London to Windsor, when the king was beginning one of his progresses, tells us that he "exercised himselfe dailie in shooting, singing, dansing, wressling, casting of the barre, plaieing at the recorders, flute, *virginals*, in setting of songs*, and making of ballades."

All accounts agree in describing Henry, in early life, as an amiable and accomplished prince; and the character given of him to the Doge of Venice, by his three ambassadors at the English court, could scarcely be expressed in more favorable

---

* Some of the king's own compositions are still extant. In a collection of anthems, motets, and other church offices, in the hand-writing of John Baldwin, of Windsor (the transcriber of that beautiful MS. Lady Neville's Virginal Book, in 1591), is a composition for three voices, "Quam pulchra es, et quam decora." It bears the name Henricus Octavus at the beginning, and "quod Henricus Octavus" at the end of the cantus part. The anthem, "O Lord, the maker of all things," which is attributed to him in Boyce's *Cathedral Music*, is the composition of William Mundy; the words only are taken from *Henry the Eighth's Primer*. The music of a masque, preserved in the Arundel Collection in the British Museum, is also ascribed to Henry VIII, but without sufficient authority. See Stafford Smith's *Musica Antiqua*, vol. i.

terms*. In their joint despatch of May 3rd, 1515, they say: "He is so gifted, and adorned with mental accomplishments of every sort, that we believe him to have few equals in the world. He speaks English, French, and Latin; understands Italian well; plays almost on every instrument, and composes fairly (delegnamente); is prudent and sage, and free from every vice."

In the letter of Sagudino (Secretary to the embassy), written to Alvise Foscari, at this same date, he says: "He (King Henry) is courageous, an excellent musician, plays the virginals well, is learned for his age and station, and has many other endowments and good parts." On the 1st of May, 1515, after the celebration of May Day at Greenwich, the ambassadors dined at the Palace, and, after dinner, were taken into certain chambers containing a number of organs, virginals, flutes, and other instruments; and, after having heard from the ambassadors that Sagudino was a proficient on some of them, he was asked by the nobles to play, which he did for a long while, both on the virginals and organ, and says that he bore himself bravely, and was listened to with great attention. The prelates told him that the king would certainly wish to hear him, for he practised on these instruments day and night.

Pasqualigo, the ambassador-extraordinary, gives a similar account at the same time. Of Henry, he says: "He speaks French, English, and Latin, and a little Italian, plays well on the lute and virginals, sings from book at sight, draws the bow with greater strength than any man in England, and jousts marvellously. Believe me he is in every respect a most accomplished prince; and I, who have now seen all the sovereigns in Christendom, and last of all these two of France and England, might well rest content," &c.

Upon these despatches the editor justly remarks: "As Pasqualigo had been ambassador at the courts of Spain, Portugal, Hungary, France, and of the Emperor, he was enabled to form comparisons between the state of the science in those kingdoms and our own; and, indeed, it is the universal experience of the Venetian Ambassadors, and their peculiar freedom from prejudice or partiality (no jealousy or

---

* See *Four Years at the Court of Henry VIII. Selection of Despatches addressed to the Signory of Venice,* from January, 1515, *to July* 26, 1519. *Translated by* Rawdon Brown, 8vo. 1854, 2 vols.

rivalry existing between them and England), that makes their comments on our country so valuable."

As far as our purpose is concerned, the way in which these Venetians speak of the virginal is of considerable value, as showing that the instrument was well known to them. This is obvious, also, from the fact of Sagudino, the Secretary, being able to "bear himself bravely," in his performance upon it before the courtiers.

In the *Privy Purse Expenses of King Henry the Eighth*, published by the late Sir N. Harris Nicolas, in 1827, we meet with the following entries:

"1530 (April). Item the vj daye paied to William Lewes for ii payer of virginalls in one coffer with iiii stoppes brought to Grenewiche iii li. And for ii payer of virginalls in one coffer brought to the More other iii li. And for a little payer of virginalls brought to the More. xxs............vii li."

"1531 (February). Item the xiii daye paied to Phillip of the Chambre, for William Lewes, for v payer of Virginalls.........viii li. vi s. viii. d.

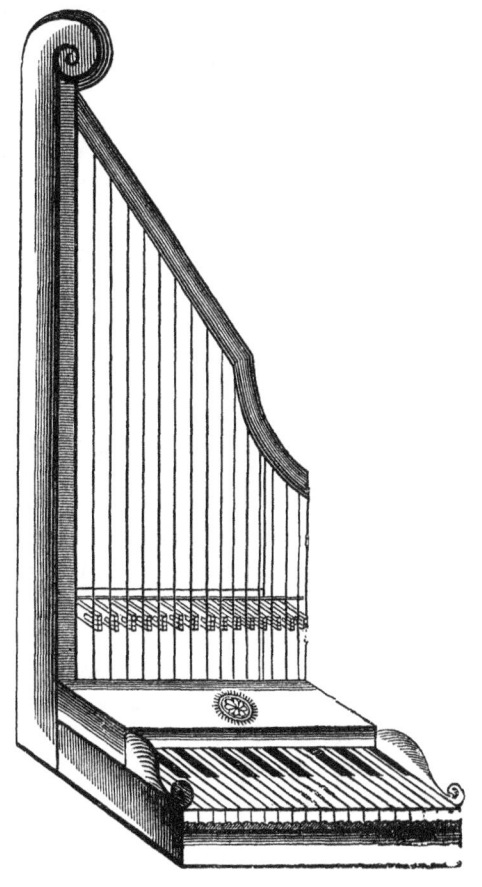

And in the inventory of King Henry the Eighth's musical instruments, taken after his death (before alluded to), we find mention of numerous pairs of virginals, both single and double. Amongst them were "Two fair pair of new long Virginalls made harp-fashion, of Cipres, with keys of ivory, having the king's arms crowned and supported by his Graces beastes within a garter gilt, standing over the keys."

The "virginalls made harp fashion" was probably an upright instrument. We give a curious drawing of an upright virginal, taken from a collection of pen-and-ink drawings of ancient musical instruments, executed about the end of the sixteenth century. It seems to have been the original from which Mersennus gave many of his engravings. It resembles the simicum (see p. 35), with the addition of a key-board and striking action.

Henry the Eighth was very solicitous that his daughters should excel in musical accomplishments, and their talents appear to have been of no mean order. Sir Frederick Madden, in his introduction to the *Privy Purse Expenses of the Princess Mary**, says, " In regard to the lighter accomplishments of music and dancing, Mary equalled, if not excelled, Elizabeth. Of the first, indeed, she appears to have been passionately fond, as intimated in the letter addressed to her from Queen Catherine Parr †. She played on three instruments, the virginals, regals, and lute, and, according to Michele ‡, excelled on the latter to a surprising degree. So early as 1525, we find particular directions given to her Governess, in regard of the Princess's occasional practice in both the above accomplishments; and in the letter of maternal advice sent by her mother after their separation, she is desired sometimes to use her virginals or lute, ' if she had any.'§ From the Expenses contained in the present volume, we learn that this monition was not disregarded; and after Mary's restoration to favour, she seems to have sedulously applied to the cultivation of music. Mr. Paston‖ is named as her teacher on the virginals, and Philip Van Wilder¶, of the Privy Chamber, as instructor on the lute. She was accustomed, it seems, to take these instruments with her wherever she removed, and items often occur of payments to a person coming from London to tune them."

These items are so interesting that we give them in *extenso*.

---

* 8vo. 1831.

† " Artem illam Musicæ, qua te simul mecum oppido delectari, non ignoro." Strype, Eccl. Mem. ii. 2. 330. The annual expense of Mary's musical and dramatic establishment, in the first year of her reign, amounts to the large sum of 2233*l*. 17s. 6d. Collier's *Annals of the Stage*, i. 165.

‡ " Intendentissima, oltre gli essercitij di donna di lavor d'ago in ogni sorte di ricamo, anco della musica, specialmente del sonar di manicordo et di leuto. In tanta eccellenza, che quando v'attendeva, la fatto maravigliare i buoni sonatorij, et per la velocità della mano et per la maniera del sonare." MS. Lansd. 840, A. f. 156.

§ Burnet, ii 2, 336.

‖ Nothing is known of this musician. He seems to have been a favorite with the Princess, who frequently made him presents. See *Household Book*.

¶ This person is often mentioned in the *Expenses of King Henry the Eighth*. In 1550, a commission was given to him by Edward the Sixth " to take to the king's use such and so many singing children and choristers as he and his deputy thought good," within any churches or chapels in England. We suspect he was the same with Phillipe de Vuildre, a motet of whose composition was printed at Antwerp in *Libro quarto Ecclesiasticarum Cantionum*, 1554. From his being selected as preceptor on the lute to the Princess, and the favour we know he enjoyed at Court, his talents appear to have been of a high order. The author is in possession of an original set of part books that belonged to the Chapel Royal in the reign of Edward the Sixth, amongst which are some interesting anthems by Philip van Wilder.

THE VIRGINAL.

"1537 (Jan.)   Item geven to one coming from London for mending of my ladys grace Virgynalls......v s."

"1537 (March).   Item geven to one Cowts for mending my ladys grace Virginalls......v s."

"1537 (March).   Item for iii y'ds of Satten geven to Mr. Paston techyng my lady of the Vyrgynalles...xxii s. vi d."

"1537 (April).   Item geven to Cowts comyng from London and mending my ladys grace Virginalls...iiii s. iiii d."

"1537 (April).   Item geven to Mr. Paston on Saynt Marke daye techyng her on the Vyrgynalles......vij s. vj d."

"1537 (May).   Item paid to the man that sett the Virginalls......vs."

"1537 (Sept.)   Item geven to one Cowts of London for mending my ladys grace Virginalls......vij s. vj d."

"1537 (Nov.)   Item geven to one Cowts of London for mending of my ladys grace Virginalls at soundry tymes......vij s. vi d."

"1538 (May).   Item geven to one Cowts mending my ladys grace Virginalls......v s."

Edward the Sixth appointed three virginal players to the court, with yearly salaries. The same musicians were retained by Mary when she ascended the throne. Their names are thus set down in a MS. in the Library of the Society of Antiquaries.

		£.	s.	d.
Players on the Virginalles,	John Heywoode*, fee	50	0	0
	Anthony Chounter, fee	30	0	0
	Robert Bowman, fee	12	3	4

Princess Elizabeth's love of music is well known, and has frequently been discanted on. Camden†, in giving an account of her studies, says, that "she understood well the Latin, French, and Italian tongues, and (was) indifferently well seen in the Greek. Neither did she neglect Musicke, so far forthe as might become a Princess, being able to sing, and play on the lute prettily and sweetly."

There is every reason to believe that she devoted much time and attention to the study of music long after she became Queen of England. Sir James Melvil‡ gives

---

* John Heywood was the only virginal player in the household of Henry VIII. His fee was £6 : 13 : 4 quarterly, but probably this was independent of board and clothing. Elizabeth and James retained three virginal players in their courts.

Heywood's ready wit and skill in vocal and instrumental music rendered him a great favourite with Henry the Eighth, and Sir Thomas More; and by the latter he was introduced to the notice of the Princess Mary, by whom he was especially patronized, rather, says Puttenham, "for the mirth and quickness of conceit than good learning that was in him." A full length wood-cut of him is prefixed to his curious work, *The Parable of the Spider and the Fly*, which has been copied by Richardson. On the accession of Elizabeth, Heywood left England and retired to Mechlin in Brabant, where he is supposed to have died in 1565.

Chounter and Bowman are unknown as musicians; they were probably merely *performers*.

† *Annales, or the History of Elizabeth, late Queen of England*. 3rd edit. 1635, p. 6.

‡ *Memoirs, now published from the original MS.* 1683, p. 50.

an account of a curious conversation which he had with this Princess, to whom he was sent on an embassy by Mary Queen of Scots*, in 1564. After her Majesty had asked him how his Queen dressed? What was the colour of her hair? Whether that or her's was best? Which of them two was fairest? And which of them was highest in stature? "Then she asked what kind of exercise she used?" I answered, says Melvil, "that when I received my dispatch, the Queen was lately come from the Highland hunting: that when her more serious affairs permitted, she was taken up with reading of histories: that sometimes she recreated herself in playing upon the lute and virginals. She asked if she played well? I said reasonably for a Queen."

"The same day, after dinner, my Lord of Hunsden drew me up to a quiet gallery, that I might hear some Musick, (but he said that he durst not avow it), where I might hear the Queen play upon the virginals. After I had hearkened a while, I took by the tapestry that hung before the door of the chamber, and seeing her back was toward the door, I entered within the chamber, and stood a pretty space hearing her play excellently well. But she left off immediately, so soon as she turned about and saw me. She appeared to be surprised to see me, and came forward, seeming to strike me with her hand; alledging, she used not to play before men, but when she was solitary, to shun melancholy. She asked how I came there? I answered, as I was walking with my Lord Hunsden, as we passed by the chamber door, I heard such a melody as ravished me, whereby I was drawn in ere I knew how; excusing my fault of homeliness, as being brought up at the Court of France where such freedom was allowed; declaring myself willing to endure what kind of punishment her Majesty should be pleased to inflict upon me for so great offence. Then she sate down low upon a cushion, and I upon my knees by her; but with her own hand she gave me a cushion, to lay under my knee; which at first I refused, but she compelled me to take it. She enquired whether my Queen or she played best. In that I found myself obliged to give her the praise."

In the dedication to Vander-noodt's *Theatre for Voluptuous Worldlings*, imprinted by Bynneman, in 1569, the author pays her Majesty the following compliment:—

---

* This unfortunate Princess, besides her personal charms, captivating powers of conversation, and knowledge of languages, had considerable taste in music.

"Your grace is expert in song and in the arte of Musicke; skilful in all kindes of musical instruments, and, according to the exact proportions of geometrie, exquisite in the measures of the dance."

Richard Mulcaster, the famous Master of Merchant Taylors' School, in some Latin verses prefixed to Tallis and Byrd's *Cantiones Sacræ*, 1575, eulogises the Queen's musical abilities in lines which are thus translated:

> "Our gracious Queen, bright glory of our age,
> The pow'r of notes harmonious can engage;
> Much joy she thence receives, but more conveys,
> While both her *voice* and *hand* the concert raise."

In a MS. note by Isaac Reed, written in a volume of old plays, we meet with the following anecdote: "When Queen Elizabeth was playing on the virginals, Lord Oxford, remarking the motion of the keys, said, in covert allusion to Raleigh's favour at court, and the execution of the Earl of Essex, 'When *jacks* start up, heads go down.'"

The jacks, as before explained, were slender pieces of wood, armed at the upper ends with quills. They were fixed on the further end of the finger-keys, and acted as plectra by impinging or twitching the strings. By the stroke of the finger, the quill was forced past the string, its own elasticity giving way, and remained above the string so long as the finger was pressed on the key, giving the string liberty to sound. When the finger was removed, the quill returned to its place, and a little bit of cloth, fixed on the top of the jack, rested on the string, and stopped its vibration, or, in other words, acted as a *damper*.

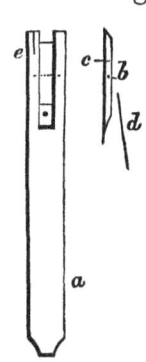

The action of these *jacks* was the constant subject of simile and pun; for instance, in Middleton's *Father Hubbard's Tales*, describing Charity as frozen, he says, "Her teeth chattered in her head, and leaped up and down like virginal jacks;" and in Dekker's *Satiro-Mastix, or the Untrussing of the Humorous Poet*, 1602,—one of the lady characters exclaims: "Lord ha' mercy on us! we women fall, and fall still; and when we have husbands, we play upon them like virginal jacks, they must rise and fall to our humours, or else they'll never get any good strains of musick out of us."

a, Jack.
b, Tongue.
c, Quill.
d, Bristle spring.
e, Cloth damper.

John Strangways, in some verses prefixed to Tom Coriat's *Crudities*, 1611, has the following lines:

> "*Kemp* yet doth live, and only lives for this
> Much famous, that he did dance the Morris
> From *London* unto *Norwich*. But thou much more
> Doest merit praise. For though his feet were sore,
> Whilst sweaty he with antick skips did hop it,
> His treadings were but friscals of a poppet;
> Or that at once I may express it all
> Like to the *jacks* of jumbled *virginall*."

Passing from these humourous notices, we must take a glance at the Queen's virginals. Several "pairs," once belonging to Queen Elizabeth, are yet extant in different parts of England. There is one, a very interesting specimen, at Helmingham Hall, in Suffolk, the ancient seat of the Tollemache family; Sir E. Bulwer Lytton is the possessor of another; the Rev. Mr. Sperling, of Kensington, is the fortunate owner of a most splendidly decorated instrument; and a fourth, certainly the most remarkable of all, is preserved at the residence of a Worcestershire esquire. It was purchased at Lord Spencer Chichester's sale, in 1805, and is of incalculable value. In the *Gentleman's Magazine* for that year, we read that "The case is of cedar, covered with crimson Genoa velvet, upon which are three gilt locks, finely engraved; the inside of the case is lined with strong yellow tabby silk; the front is covered entirely with gold, having a border round the inside two inches and a half broad. It is five feet long, sixteen inches wide, and seven inches deep, and is so lightly and delicately formed, that the weight does not exceed twenty-four pounds. There are fifty keys, thirty of ebony tipped with gold, and the remaining twenty (i. e. the semitones) are inlaid with silver, ivory, and different kinds of rare woods, each key consisting of about two hundred and fifty pieces. On one end are the royal arms, richly emblazoned; and at the other end is a symbolic and highly finished painting of a crowned dove, with a sceptre in its claw—the painting done upon a gold ground, with carmine, lake, and ultramarine.

In the Fitzwilliam Museum, at Cambridge, is preserved a small-sized folio MS. volume, in red morocco binding, elaborately tooled, and ornamented with fleur-de-lis, &c., and gilt edges, traditionally said to have been *Queen Elizabeth's Virginal Book*.

The MS. is written upon six lines, on 418 pages, throughout in the same hand. At the end of each piece of music, the arrangers' names are generally given. Among them we find, Dr. John Bull, Ferdinand Richardson, William Byrd, Thomas Morley, John Munday, Giles Farnaby, William Blitheman, Peter Phillips, Nicholas Strogers, Martin Peerson, Thomas Warrock, Thomas Tomkins, Robert Johnson, Richard Farnaby, Marchant, W. Tisdall, Hooper, Edward Johnson, William Inglott, Orlando Gibbons, Thomas Oldfield, Giovanni Pietri, Johan Pieterson Swellinck, Thomas Tallis, &c.

Dr. Burney says, " If her Majesty was ever able to execute any of the pieces that are preserved in a MS. which goes under the name of *Queen Elizabeth's Virginal Book*, she must have been a very great player; as some of these pieces, which were composed by Tallis, Bird, Giles, Farnaby, Dr. Bull, and others, are so difficult, that it would be hardly possible to find a master in Europe who would undertake to play one of them at the end of a month's practice." *

The late M. Choron expresses a similar opinion : " In every thing relating to the execution of instrumental music," says this distinguished critic, " it is of the utmost importance to dispel a very common error; which consists in believing that music was formerly very simple, and easily performed. This error arises from the circumstance of the old writers having used notes of very great value; and from its not being remembered that these notes were executed with very great rapidity, so that they had, in fact, no greater value than those in use with us at the present time. Besides, if we cast our eyes upon the collections of pieces remaining to us from former ages—upon the Virginal Book of Queen Elizabeth, for instance,—difficulties will be found which would puzzle the most able of our modern performers." †

A recent writer in *Chambers's Journal* ‡ is still "stronger" upon this point. After remarking upon the " insupportable and overwhelming difficulty " of the volume, he goes on to say, " a dozen of its pages would serve not only to crush the pretensions of any ordinary professor, but even to appal the bravest and most skilful among

---

* *History of Music*, vol. iii, p. 15.
† *Summary of the History of Music*, translated and prefixed to the first volume of the *Dictionary of Musicians*, 1827, second edit.
‡ October 27, 1855.

those spasmodic pianists who delight the concert-going public of this concert-giving age."

Opinions, such as these, regarding the extreme difficulty of the music in the Virginal Book, have become so prevalent, that it seems almost heresy to contradict them. Nevertheless, it is time the illusion should be dispelled. Of the writers above quoted, the first (Dr. Burney) is the only one worthy of notice; for he alone *saw* and *examined* the volume, and doubtless, in his time, the music possessed some claim to be considered difficult. At the present day it has no such claims. An ordinary pianist could with ease execute any of the pieces in the volume after an hour's practice.

At the end of the sixteenth century, the virginal was the popular keyed-stringed instrument in England, and was found in the house of every person of education.

In an inventory of the furniture in Kenilworth Castle, in the days of the magnificent Earl of Leicester (A. D. 1584)*, we find: "Item, an instrument of organs, regalls, and virginalls, covered with crimson velvet and garnished with goulde lace;" also, "A faire paire of double virginalls." And in the inventory of the goods and chattels belonging to Sir Thomas Kytson of Hengrave Hall, Suffolk, 1603, we have "Item, one payer of little virginalls; ditto, one wind instrument like a virginall; ditto, one great payer of double virginalls."†

In Nicholas Breton's poem entitled *A Flourish upon Fancie*, 1582, the virginal is mentioned along with other musical instruments as forming part of the ordinary stock of a gallant of those days:

"Upon an olde crackt forme,
By his bed side, there lies
Ould instruments of musick's sound
All broke in wondrous wise;
A lute, with half the strings
And all the pinnes neere out,
The belly crackt, the back quite burst,
And riven round about.
His *virginalls* with never a jack,
And scantily halfe the keyes;

---

* MS. in the possession of the writer.   † Gage's *Antiquities of Hengrave Hall*, 4to. 1822, p. 24.

> His organes with the bellows burst,
> And battred many waies.
> His fife, three holes in one;
> His harpe with neere a string.
> Great pittie, trust me, for to see
> So broken every thing."

Burel, describing the pomp and pageantry with which Queen Anne (wife of James VI) was received at her public entry into Edinburgh, May 19, 1590, mentions the virginal amongst the instruments used on that occasion:

> "Organs and regals thair did carpe,
> With their gay goldin glitt'ring strings;
> Thair was the hautbois and the harpe,
> Playing most sweet and pleasant springs;
> And sum on lutis did play and sing,
> Of instrument the onely king.
>
> "Viols and *virginalls* were their,
> With githorns maist jucundious;
> Trumpets and timbrels made greit beir,
> With instruments melodious.
> The seistar and the sumphion
> With clarche-pipe and clarion." *

Spenser has mentioned the virginal in an English *trimeter-iambic*; one of those fantastic attempts to introduce the uncongenialities of Latin versification, which the taste of the great poet soon led him to abandon. The line, however, in which the virginal is mentioned, presents a picture not unworthy of him:

> "Unhappie Verse! the witnesse of my unhappie state,
> Make thyself flutt'ring wings of thy fast flying
> Thought, and fly forth unto my Love wheresoever she be;
> Whether lying restless in heavy bedde, or else
> Sitting so cheerless at the cheerful boarde, or else
> *Playing alone careless on her heavenlie virginals.*"

---

* Watson's *Collection of Scottish Poems*, vol. ii, p. 6.

The musical instrument mentioned in one of Shakespeare's sonnets is of the same keyed family.

> "How oft when thou, my music, music play'st
>   Upon that blessed wood, whose motion sounds
> With thy sweet fingers, when thou gently sway'st
>   The wiry concord that mine ear confounds,
> Do I envy those jacks, that nimble leap
>   To kiss the tender inward of thy hand,
> Whilst my poor lips, that should that harvest reap,
>   At the wood's boldness by thee blushing stand.
> To be so tickled, they would change their state
>   And situation with those dancing chips
> *O'er whom thy fingers walk with gentle gait,*
>   Making dead wood more bless'd than living lips.
> Since saucy jacks so happy are in this,
>   Give them thy fingers, me thy lips to kiss."

Thus we have two of our great poets, Spenser and Shakespeare, showing us the delight they took in the same species of instrument which we have now, and so bringing themselves near to our pianofortes.

The first book printed in this country for a keyed-stringed instrument, appeared in the year 1611, with the following singular title:

PARTHENIA,
OR
THE MAYDENHEAD
OF THE FIRST MUSICKE THAT EVER WAS PRINTED FOR THE VIRGINALLS,

COMPOSED

By three famous Masters, William Byrde, Dr. John Bull, and Orlando Gibbons,
Gentilmen of his Majesties most Illustrious Chappell.

Ingraven

By WILLIAM HOLE;

Lond : print : for M. Dor. Evans, Cum privilegio, and are to be sould by G. Lowe, printer in Loathberry.

This work, entirely engraved upon copper plates, was again printed (from the same plates) in 1613, 1635, 1650, 1656, and 1659, and, according to Anthony a Wood, was "the prime book used by Masters in Musick for nearly half a century."

This publication was speedily followed by another of a similar kind, without date, with the following title:

PARTHENIA IN-VIOLATA,

OR

Mayden Musicke for the Virginalls and Bass Viol,

Selected out of the Compositions of the most famous in that arte,

By ROBERT HOLE,

And consecrated to all true Lovers and Practisers thereof.

All you professors of this arte divine,
So strive your earthly accents to refine
To Angell's ayres, and Saynts most holy skill,
As all your musique sound your Maker's will.

Then is there true composure of the parts,
When there's an equall harmony of hearts:
And that the sacred concords be so even
As here on Earth you strike the same wth Heaven.

Printed at London for John Pyper, and are to be sould at his Shopp at Pauls' gate, next unto Cheapside at the Crosse Keies. Cum privilegio.

Shortly after the restoration, John Playford, the ingenious publisher, put forth, without date, his work entitled

MUSICKS HAND-MAID,

New Lessons and Instructions

FOR THE

VIRGINALS OR HARPSYCHORD.

In his introduction, the author says, "The Virginals, according to the ancient standard, were made to contain 29 keys (with the half-notes 48 keys), but of later times they add to that number both above and below."

The two famous English virginal-makers of the latter half of the seventeenth century, were John Loosemore and Stephen Keen. Playford, at the end of his *Introduction to the Skill of Musick*, edit. 1672, advertises, "Mr. Stephen Keen,

Maker of Harpsycons and Virginals, dwelleth now in Threadneedle Street, at the sign of the Virginal, who maketh them exactly good, both for sound and substance."

A small virginal of this period is copied in the following wood-cut *:

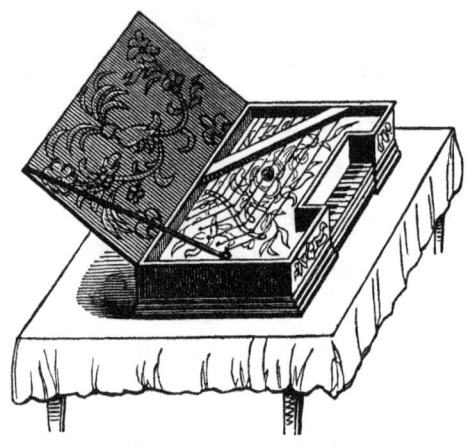

Self-acting virginals were known as early as the seventeenth century. On the 27th of August 1623, a license was granted to Bartholomew Cloys, with three assistants, to make show of a Musical Organ, with divers motions in it; to make show of an Italian Motion; to show a Looking-glass; the Philosopher's Stone; and a Virginal with machinery."† And at a later period, on the occasion of the *Fireworks to be presented in Lincoln's Inn Fields on the 5th of November* 1647, we hear of self-acting virginals, or, as the writer expresses it, " musically playing of themselves." ‡

The virginal became so common in England in the seventeenth century, that old Pepys, that entertaining gossip, describing the flight of the inhabitants by water at the time of the great fire, says, " I observed that hardly one lighter or boat in three that had the goods of a house in, but there was a paire of virginals in it."§

---

*Thomas Mackinlay, Esq. F.S.A. of Soho Square, possesses two interesting virginals of the latter part of the seventeenth century. One, made by John Loosemore, bears the date 1655. The other, made shortly after the restoration of Charles, has a curious painting on the inside of the lid, showing the Mall in St. James's Park, with a distant view of Arlington House.

† The Office-Book of Sir Henry Herbert, Master of the Revels to James the First.

‡ A rare broadside in the British Museum. See also Brayley's *Londiniana*, vol. iv, p. 56.

§ *Diary* (Sept, 2, 1666), edit. 1848, vol. iii, p. 271.

This instrument continued in general use until the beginning of the eighteenth century. One of the latest notices of it occurs in the *London Post* of July 20, 1701: " This week a most curious pair of virginals, reckoned the finest in England, were shipped off for the Grand Seigneur's Seraglio."

In addition to the specimens of this instrument still remaining, and which we have noticed in the course of the preceding pages, we may add that many others may be found in the nooks and corners of old houses, in various stages of dilapidation. Sometimes, indeed, these old " crackt " instruments are still made to " play their part ;" and we cannot conclude this chapter with a more characteristic anecdote than the following from *The Professional Life of Mr. Dibdin*. Speaking of his engagement as composer of the music to David Garrick's theatre, he says, " I was summoned to Hampton to take instructions for the *Christmas Tale;* many of the songs had been previously written, by fits and starts, and I had set some of them two or three times over; but now we were to go to work in earnest; and as he could not be easy without me, for his muse was very often in want of obstetrick assistance as to songs and choruses, however easily he might bring forth prologues and epilogues, so was I either obliged to sit up after the family, or get up before them, to lend musical aid to bits and scraps of which nobody could guess either the drift or meaning ; and all this music was to be extracted from an old *virginal*, with half the strings broke, a prodigious fine antique, which graced Mr. Garrick's beautiful drawing-room, with much about the elegance and embellishment as a spot of rust upon a polished register-stove. I used to tell him, I hoped he would bequeath it to the Antiquarian Society,"

CHAPTER V.

THE SPINET.

The spinet (*spinetto*, Ital. *épinette*, Fr.) is so called from *spina*, a thorn or quill[*]; the tone of the instrument being produced by a crow's quill inserted in the tongue of the little machine (before explained) called a jack.

The spinet, we are told, consisted of " a chest or belly, made of the most porous and resinous wood to be found, and a table of fir fastened on rods, called the sound-board, which bears on the sides: on the table were raised two little prominences or bridges, in which are fixed as many pins as there were strings to the instrument."

Mersennus[†] compares the structure of the spinet to that of the human body; he says that " the sounding-boards are the muscles; the cross bars the bones; and the strings the organs of speech." But what is more valuable, he adds; "the spinet had ordinarily, forty-nine strings, of which the lower thirty were made of latten, because that was strongest and deepest, and the higher ones, nineteen in number, were of steel and iron * * *. There were but six or seven sizes of strings; but if the spinet were made in real perfection, there would be strings of different sizes, suited purposely to every note. Even in the length of string the makers are careless, and everything depends upon the tension."

The difference between the virginal and spinet is said to have been this: " the spinet was always of a triangular shape, and had the wires carried over a bent bridge, which modified their sounds; those of the virginal, went direct from their points of support

---

[*] Florio, in his *Queen Anna's New World of Words*, 1611, p. 524, has the following:

"Spinetta, a kind of little *Spina* * * also a paire of Virginalles.

Spinetteggiare, to play upon Virginalles.

Spinetto, a thicket of brambles or briars."

[†] *Harmonicorum*, Paris, 1636; frequently quoted in our earlier pages.

to the screw-pegs, regularly decreasing in length from the deepest bass note to the highest treble." We have not been able to make out this distinction; in all the virginals and spinets which we have examined, their internal construction was the same.

The date of the invention of the spinet is not ascertained. According to Clement Marot, it was in common use among the French ladies in the reign of Francis the First (A. D. 1515, 1546). In the dedication of his version of the Psalms to his fair country-women, he tells them, that he hopes, divine hymns will supersede love-songs, and fill their apartments with the praises of Jehovah, in accompanying them on the spinet.

> " Et vos doigts sur les Espinettes,
> Pour dire Sainctes chansonnettes," *

We have copied an interesting representation of the spinet from Father Bonanni's *Gabinetto Armonico*, 4to, Rome, 1722.

According to Artusi's *Imperfettioni della moderna Musica*, printed at Venice in 1600, the spinet was known in Italy early in the sixteenth century: and Pietro della Valle, in his *Discourse on the Music of his own time*, 1640†, tells us, the first opera

---

* *Œuvres de Clement Marot*, à Lyon, 1551. 12mo. p. 192.

† Printed in the works of Battista Doni, at Florence, 1763, tom. ii.

or musical drama performed at Rome, took place in a cart, on which occasion, "Il Cavalier Leuto played wonderfully on the spinet."

Zarlino, the celebrated theorist, had a spinet, with quarter tones, made at Venice[‡]. Burney saw it, in the course of his travels, at Florence, and says it was afterwards sent to England; but we have been unable to trace it.

The family of the Ruckers, of Antwerp (of whom we shall have occasion to speak presently), were famous makers of spinets in the seventeenth century, as also were their successors, Couchet and Jean Dennis: the latter was a Frenchman, and resided for many years in Paris.

The Hitchcocks and Haywards, fathers and sons, were the great makers of spinets in London, in the first three quarters of the seventeenth century. John Hitchcock made these little instruments of a compass of five octaves. Several specimens still exist bearing dates between 1620 and 1640. The keys are of ebony, having ivory fronts; the flats and sharps inlaid with narrow slips of ivory. Charles Haward, or Hayward, is mentioned as a celebrated maker, in Salmon's *Vindication of an Essay, &c.* 1672, p. 68.

Queen Anne had, among her musical instruments, a spinet by Hayward, the loudest and perhaps the finest that was ever heard; and which she highly valued. Her Majesty, just before the period of her decease, gave especial direction that this instrument should go to the master of the children of the Chapel Royal for the time being, and that it should regularly descend to his official successors. Accordingly it passed first into the possession of Dr. Croft, and afterwards into the hands of Dr. Nares, from whom it descended to Bernard Gates, and the late Dr. Ayrton. Mr. Hawes was the next master, and when the writer last heard of Queen Anne's spinet, it was consigned to the cock-loft of that gentleman's house in the Adelphi Terrace, where, in all probability, it still remains.

[‡] In a letter to Mason the poet, dated Florence, Sept. 1770, Burney says, "This instrument was invented by Zarlino, in order to give the temperament and modulation of the three *genera*, the diatonic, chromatic, and enharmonic. It was made under Zarlino's direction in the year 1548, by Dominico Pesarese: it is now in the possession of Signora Moncini, widow of the late composer, Piscetti." In a subsequent letter, he says, "Zarlino's spinet or small *harpsichord* is now in London."

The later makers of spinets, of eminence, were Keen, Slade, Player*, Fenton, Baudin, &c. A fine specimen of the latter maker is in the possession of the writer. It has this inscription in front:

"Josephus Bavdin, Londini, Fecit. 1723;"

and its general appearance may be imagined from the following engraving.

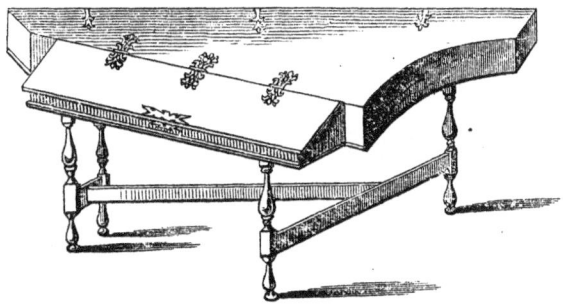

Burney, writing at the beginning of the present century,† says, "As the spinet rivalled the virginal, the small piano-forte has supplanted the spinet in public favour; and we believe that very few have been made since the middle of the last century."

---

* This maker is mentioned in Ambrose Warren's *Tonometer*, 1725, p. 7, as having made spinets with quarter tones.

† Rees's *Cyclopedia*, in v. Spinet.

CHAPTER VI.

THE HARPSICHORD.

The form of the harpsichord is precisely the same as that of the grand horizontal pianoforte. Its origin was evidently suggested by the harp, from which instrument it received its name.

Papius, and after him Du Cange, derive the name of harp from the *Arpi*, a people in Italy, who they say, erroneously, were its first inventors. Menage derives the word from the Latin, *harpa*, and that from the German, *herp* or *herpff*; others bring it from the Latin *carpo*, because it was touched or thrummed with the fingers. Dr. Hickes derives it from *harpa* or *hearpa*, which signifies the same thing; the first in the language of the Cymbri, the second in that of the Anglo-Saxons.*

Galilei† in his *Dialogo della Musica Antica e Moderna*, Firenze, 1581, has a very interesting passage respecting the harp, which we shall translate literally:

"Among the stringed instruments now used in Italy, we have, in the first place, the harp; which is in fact nothing but the ancient *cithara*, with a great number of strings, differing somewhat in form, but that chiefly owing to the taste of the artists of those times, the number of strings and their degree of tension; the extreme highest and lowest

---

* "From the Teutonic derivation of the harp, it is easy to account for its becoming the national instrument of the English. The Anglo-Saxons were of German race, and introduced the harp into Britain. Inflamed with a thirst of conquest, and eager to possess alone that fertile Isle, they almost exterminated the natives, and totally erased every vestige of Roman and British civility. The gentler modulations and softer harmony of the crwth were equally despised with its performers and admirers: this instrument was banished to Wales, Cornwall, and Armorica; in the last country, Venantius found it in the 6th century.

"The Roman Missioners kept alive and augmented the enmity between the Britons and Anglo-Saxons: the former would not adopt Popery or its superstitions, to which the latter were devoted: every temporal and spiritual motive which theological malignity could invent, was conjured up to make the resentment of both people implacable and perpetual, and with too good success. Hence the triumph of the harp over the crwth, and its general use among all ranks of people until the Norman invasion." Walker's *Historical Memoirs of the Irish Bards*, Appendix, p. 7.

† A Florentine nobleman, and father of the great astronomer, Galileo Galilei.

comprising upwards of three octaves. This very ancient instrument was brought to us from Ireland (as Dante has recorded) where they are excellently made, and in great number; and the inhabitants of which island have practised on it for many and many centuries; its being also the particular badge of the kingdom, and, as such, frequently painted and sculptured on their public edifices and coins, the people alleging, as the cause of it, that they are descended from the Royal prophet David. The harps used by them are much larger than ours, and they are usually mounted with strings of brass and some of steel, in the acute part, of the same kind as the clavichord. The performers upon them are wont to let the nails of both their hands grow to a considerable length, trimming them with great care in the manner we see the quills on the jacks of the spinnets. The number of strings are 54, 56, and as far as 60; whereas we read, that among the Jews, the *cithara*, or *psalterion* of the Prophet, had only 10 strings. The distribution of the strings of one of these harps (which I obtained a few months ago, by means of a very obliging gentleman of Ireland), I found, on careful examination, to be the same as that of *the harp with a double row of strings*, which was a few years ago introduced into Italy; although some (without a shadow of reason) assert that they have lately invented it, endeavouring to persuade the vulgar that none but themselves can play upon it, or understand its temperament, which they hold in such great estimation, that they have ungratefully denied it to many; in spite of whom, however, I will here describe it for the sake of those who may desire it. The 38 strings, which are mounted on the harp, contain four octaves and one tone; not major or minor, as some have imagined, but of the measure which I have above said to be contained in a key'd instrument. The lowest string, therefore, as well for a sharp as for a flat, is double C; and the highest string is D in alt: when they are to be tuned for B flat, the 16 lower strings on the left side are to be distributed according to the nature of the common diatonic, and the 14 that are in the opposite row to these, that is, on the right side (leaving apart the unison of D and A), must give, as we may say, the chromatic kind, agreeable in its nature to the said diatonics. The 15 that follow next, ascending the scale, are to be tempered diatonically, according to the mode of the 16 lower ones on the left side. The 13 that follow next above the first 16, are now to do the office of the lower ones on the right, as may be seen in the example.* If then you want to play in B natural, let the flats of each diatonic be altered, and tuned in one or the other of the chromatic, instead of the B flat; and let these be arranged in the place of those in the diatonic, both on the right, and the left. This mode of proceeding was so ordered by its author for the convenience and facility of the fingers of both hands, particularly in making diminutions, and lengthening sounds. We find thus among the said strings; five times C, five D, four E, four F, four G, four A, four B flat, and four B natural. Four unisons of D, four unisons of A. Four sharps of *c*, four sharps of *f*, four sharps of *g*, and the four flats of *e;* which in all make the number of 58 strings. But there are wanting, for the perfection of the diversity of harmony, the four sharps of *d*, and the four flats of *a;* for which, in those modes, or melodies, where these strings occur, their unisons which are among the chromatic strings, are accommodated to them; which unisons produce a great facility in the diminutions, as appears manifestly in practice; which facility is the cause that they are generally distributed in the manner I have mentioned.

"The harp is so similar to the *epigonium* and the *simicum*, that it may with reason be said to be one of them;

---

* In the plate, a scale of the strings of the harp, referred to by Galilei, it has twenty-nine strings in each of the two rows; that is, D at top, and DD at bottom, in the right-hand row; and C at top, and CC at bottom, in the left-hand row. It seems they were tuned in different keys, as occasion required them; and part of one row, and part of the other, served for the accidental flats and sharps; the remainder were unisons in both the rows.

THE HARPSICHORD.

nor do I think he would be much mistaken, who should maintain, that the strings were tuned in the same manner and proportion in the one as in the other instrument, seeing that these instruments were not introduced till after they began to play in consonant parts; and what distribution is best adapted to this, has been fully explained.

"Returning now to the invention and origin of modern instruments, I say, that (on account of the agreement of the name, of the form, and of the number, disposition and matter of the strings, although its professors in Italy say, that they have invented it;) from the harp, most probably, *the harpsichord had its origin;* which instrument is nothing but a horizontal harp: and from it, may be derived the key'd instruments of touch."

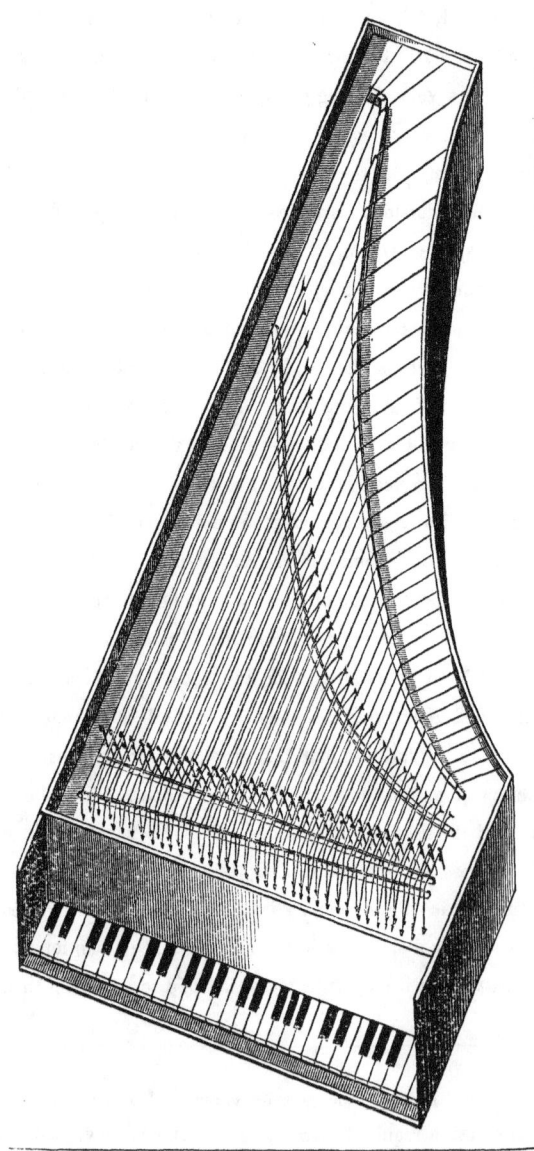

The harpsichord was, in fact, only a large-sized spinet. In the spinet and virginal, however, there was but one string for each tone; another was added to the harpsichord, the form of which, as we have said, was precisely the same as that of our grand horizontal pianofortes. In Germany this instrument was called *Flügel,* from its resemblance to the shape of a *wing.*

We give an engraving of the harpsichord from the valuable work of Father Mersennus, so often quoted in our pages.

The mechanism of the jack remained the same in this instrument as in the older virginals and spinets*. Hans Ruckers of Antwerp was the first maker who effected an important reform in the construction of the harpsichord. He was originally a joiner; but, quitting that business, devoted himself entirely to the manufacture of keyed-stringed musical instruments, and gained a reputation which was surpassed by no other. He gave his harpsichords a more powerful and con-

---

* "The action of the harpsichord was simply a key and what was called a jack, which was a piece of pear-tree with a small moveable tongue of holly, through which a cutting of crow-quill was passed to touch the string when the jack was in action." Burney, in Rees's *Cyclopedia.*

nected tone, by joining to the two strings in unison a third range of shorter and finer strings, tuned to the upper octave of the others, and which could be entoned at pleasure, either together with them, or separately. He mounted his harpsichords partly with catgut strings, and partly with steel wire. In imitation of the organ, he added a second key-board to his instruments, the object of which was to allow three strings to be heard at once, or only a single one at pleasure. In fine, he extended the compass of his harpsichord to four complete octaves (from C to C), by adding four grave sounds to the forty-five which existed before.

It was towards the close of the sixteenth century, about 1590, that Hans Ruckers first began to manufacture his harpsichords. This artist and his two sons, Jean and Andreas, who rivalled their father in ability, sent a prodigious quantity of their instruments into France and Germany.

Burney, in his entertaining sketches of *The Present State of Music in Germany, the Netherlands, &c.**, has left us an account of these artists and their successors, which it is worth while to extract. Speaking of the city of Antwerp, the Doctor says—" The famous harpsichord-makers, of the name of Ruckers, whose instruments have been so much and so long admired all over Europe, lived in this city: there were three, the first, and the father of the other two, was *John Ruckers*, who flourished at the beginning of the last century. His instruments were the most esteemed, and are remarkable for the sweetness and fulness of their tone. On the left hand of the sound-hole in the bellies of these instruments may be seen a large H, the initial of Hans, which, in the Flemish Language, means John. *André*, the eldest of John's sons, distinguished his work by an A in the sound-hole. His large harpsichords are less esteemed than those made by any one of that name; but his small instruments, such as spinets and virginals, are excellent. *Jean*, the youngest son's harpsichords, though not so good as those of the father, are very much esteemed for the delicacy of their tone; his instruments may be known by the letter I in the sound-hole. The harpsichord-maker of the greatest eminence, after them, was J. Dan. Dulcken; he was a Hessian. At present there is a good workman at Antwerp, of the name of

---

* 2nd edit. vol. i, p. 47.

Bull, who was Dulcken's apprentice, and who sells his double harpsichords* for a hundred ducats each, with only plain painted cases, and without swell or pedals ; the work too of Vanden Elsche, a Flamand, has a considerable share of merit ; but, in general, the present harpsichords made here after the Rucker model are thin, feeble in tone, and much inferior to those of our best makers in England."†

Handel possessed a fine Rucker harpsichord, which he left by will to his friend and amanuensis, Smith. Coxe, in his *Anecdotes of Handel and Smith*, speaking of Handel's original MSS., which Smith presented to King George III, adds, "The harpsichord so remarkable for the ivory being indented by Handel's continued exertions, and on which, as has been already related, the far greater part of his music had been composed, and the bust, by Roubilliac, he sent afterwards to Windsor Castle."‡

The Messrs. Broadwood possess an instrument by Ruckers, which they conceive to have been Handel's, but its geneology will not bear examination. It is, however, a very interesting instrument, and merits a brief description. It is inscribed, " Ruckers, Antwerpia, 1651." The case and lid are painted black, with ornaments in gold and colour, a sort of lacquer-work. The sound-board is ornamented also, to the great risk of its sonority. Upon a ground of pale green are arabesques, among which sit half a dozen monkeys executing a concert. The lid is inscribed upon the under surface, in letters of gold, *Sic transit gloria mundi*, a legend which is often to be met with upon spinets and harpsichords, and which doubtless signifies that the glory of the world vanishes as sound and space. On that part of the lid which turns back when the harpsichord is opened, is *Musica donum Dei* (Music is the gift of God), also written in gold letters, upon a black ground §.

---

* A *single* harpsichord of two unisons and one set of keys was, in effect, a double spinet or virginal. A *double* harpsichord had two sets of keys and three strings, two unisons and an octave, to each note.

† Rucker harpsichords, about 1760, were in such high estimation that they frequently sold for more than a *hundred* pounds each; but before the beginning of the present century, pianofortes became so prevalent throughout Europe, that the finest Rucker harpsichord would not produce more than ten pounds.

Many instruments by these eminent makers are still occasionally met with in out-of-the-way corners of our old mansions. Mr. Twining, of the eminent firm of that name in the Strand, possesses a fine *single* harpsichord by Andreas Rucker, 1640.

‡ Roubilliac's bust of Handel is still preserved at Windsor Castle; but the harpsichord cannot be found.

§ For this description we are indebted to M. Victor Schœlcher's elaborate *Life of Handel*, lately published.

It was anciently the fashion to ornament the cases of old virginals, harpsichords, and spinets with inscriptions and paintings, many specimens of which have come down to our time. An ancient sounding-board, formerly belonging to a small virginal, now in the writer's possession, has the following curious inscription upon its upper surface:

> "I once was livinge in the woods,
>   But now I am cut downe
> By stroke of cruell axe, indeed,
>   But yet to my renowne:
> For while I liv'd, I spake nought else
>   But what the boistrous winde
> Compel'd my murmuringe straines unto;
>   But beinge dead I please ye minde
> And eares of such as heare me singe,
>   So pleasant is my musickes ringe."

Among the most interesting painted instruments, we may point out the virginal of Mary Queen of Scots, still preserved in the north of England. It is made of oak, inlaid with cedar, and richly ornamented with gold. The cover and sides are beautifully painted with figures of birds, flowers, and leaves, the colours of which are still fresh and undecayed. On one part of the lid is a grand procession of warriors, whom a bevy of fair dames are propitiating by presents or offerings of wine and fruits.

The old painters were proverbially fond of adorning their harpsichords. An exquisite little painting, by Annibal Caracci, of Silenus, teaching Apollo to play the pan-pipe (mentioned as being in the British Gallery), is said to have formed one of the compartments of an instrument belonging to that great painter. The story too of Salvator Rosa and his harpsichord ought not to be omitted. Happening one day to be found by a friend in Florence in the act of modulating on a very indifferent old harpsichord, he was asked how he could keep such an instrument in his house! "Why," said his friend, "it is not worth a scudo." "I will lay you what you please," said Salvator, "that it shall be worth a thousand before you see it again." A bet was made, and Rosa immediately painted a landscape with figures on the lid, which not only was sold for a thousand scudi, but was esteemed a "*capo d'opera.*" On one end of the harpsichord he also painted a skull and music books.* Both these pictures were exhibited at the British Institution in the year 1823.

Burney, in his amusing *Tour in France*, after describing his visit to the church of St. Rocque "to hear the celebrated M. Balbastre, organist of that church, as well as of Notre Dame and the Concert Spirituel," adds, "After church, M. Balbastre invited me to his house, to see a fine Rucker harpsichord which he has had painted inside and out with as much delicacy as the finest coach or even snuff-box I ever saw at Paris. On the outside is the birth of Venus; and on the inside of the cover the story of Rameau's most famous opera, Castor and Pollux; earth, hell, and elysium are there represented: in elysium, sitting on a bank, with a lyre in his hand, is that celebrated composer himself; the portrait is very like, for I saw Rameau in 1764. The tone of this instrument is more delicate than powerful; one of the unisons is of buff, but very sweet and agreeable; the touch very light, owing to the quilling, which in France is always weak."†

The harpsichord had arrived at considerable excellence in Italy very early in the sixteenth century. In the account of a banquet given by the magnificent Cardinal, Andrea Cornaro, to the Venetian ambassadors in 1522, we read, that after dinner "There was music of every sort that could be found in Rome. Excellent fifers played continually; *harpsichords* also were there, with most wonderful sounds in them; lutes with four strings; harps and songs outside the room and inside; one music after another."‡

The author of a rare volume published at Bologna in 1590, under the title of *Il*

---

* Lady Morgan's *Life of Salvator Rosa*.

† This instrument was afterwards brought to London, when it became the property of the late James Goding, Esq. That gentleman had so little veneration for the work of Rucker, that he caused the "inside" of the harpsichord to be taken out, and a modern pianoforte substituted in its room! At the sale of Mr. Goding's musical instruments, by Christie and Manson, February 20, 1857, the instrument was thus described: "A MAGNIFICENT GRAND PIANOFORTE CASE: the top and sides beautifully painted with classical subjects, by Boucher: the inside, with a large subject of the performance of a masque by the Royal Family, exquisitely painted by Le Prince, on a superbly carved and gilt stand. The instrument, 6½ octaves, by Zeitter." It sold for seventy guineas. When Zeitter took out the old sounding-board, he caused it to be made into a handsome music box, preserving the inscription, "Johannes Ruckers me fecit Antwerpæ," at the back. This box is now in the writer's possession.

‡ *The Girlhood of Catherine de Medicis*, by J. A. Trollope, 8vo. 1856, p. 50. The author does not enable us to give the passage in the original language.

Desiderio, mentioning some curious instruments in the Palace of the Duke of Ferrari, says, " there was a harpsichord, invented by Don Nicola Vincentino, surnamed *Arcimusico*, in the year 1555. It had *six* rows of keys, comprehending in their division the three harmonic genera." He adds that the multitude of strings in this astonishing instrument rendered it very difficult to tune, and more so to play; and that, for this latter reason, the most skilful performers would seldom use it: nevertheless, he continues, " Luzzasco, the chief organist of his highness, who it is supposed must have understood and been familiar with the instrument, was able to play on it with wonderful skill." He says that this instrument, by way of pre-eminence, was called the *Archicembalo;* and that after the model of it, two organs were built; the one at Rome, by order of the Cardinal of Ferrari; and the other at Milan, under the direction of the inventor.

Father Bonnani, in his singular collection of engravings of musical instruments, entitled *Gabinetto Armonico*, 4to, Rome, 1722, gives a representation of an organ, harpsichord, two spinets, and a virginal, so contrived that they may be used separately, or *together*. This " prodigious artifice," as the monk calls it, was contrived by Michele Todino, of Savoy, for Signor Verospi, of Rome. Dr. Burney in his *Tour in France and Italy*, says, " I went this morning to visit the famous Podini gallery, in the Verospi palace. All the accounts of Rome are full of the praises of this music gallery; or, as it is called, gallery of instruments; but nothing shows the necessity of seeing for one's self, more than these accounts. The instruments in question cannot have been fit for use these many years; but, when a thing has once got into a book as curious, it is copied into others without examination, and without end. There is a very fine harpsichord, to look at, but not a key that will speak; it formerly had a communication with an organ in the same room, and with two spinets and a virginal; under the frame is a violin, tenor, and base, which, by a movement of the foot, used to be played upon by the harpsichord keys. The organ appears in the front of the room, but not on the side, where there seems to be pipes and machines enclosed; but there was no one to explain it, the old *Cicerone* being just dead."

Giovanni Maria Artusi, in his interesting work, *Delle Imperfettioni della Moderna Musica*, Venice, fol. 1600, gives a curious account of the state of instrumental music in his time, and in describing a grand concert that was made by the nuns of a convent at Ferrara, in 1598, on occasion of a double wedding between Philip the Third, King of Spain, with Margaret, Queen of Austria, and the Archduke Albert with the Infanta Isabella, the king's sister, he enumerates the several instruments that were employed, and points out their excellencies and defects. Among these the harpsichord is honoured with particular attention both as to its construction and use.

Ottavio Rinuccini's drama of *Eurydice* was set to music by Jacopo Peri, and performed at Florence in 1600, on occasion of the marriage of Mary of Medicis to Henry the Fourth of France. In Peri's preface to the printed copy of the music, he tells us that "behind the scenes, Signor Jacopo Corsi played the *harpsichord*; Don Garzia Montalvo the chitarone or large guitar; Messrs. Giovanni Battista dal Violino the lira grande; and Messer Giovanni Lapi, a large lute."

In the Oratorio entitled *Dell' Anima e del Corpo*, performed in the oratory of the church of Santa Maria della Vallicella at Rome, in 1600, the *clavicembalo* or harpsichord formed one of the instruments of the orchestra; and in Monteverde's opera of *Orfeo*, performed at the Court of Mantua in 1607, amongst the instruments used we read of "Duoi Gravicembani."*

The "orchestra" of this period is well exhibited in the following wood-cut, copied from a scarce work entitled, *Festa, fatta in Roma, Alli 25 di Febraio* 1634, *e data in luce da Vitale Mascardi*. Rome, 4to, 1634. The entire engraving represents one of those magnificent entertainments in which the cardinals and other dignitaries were so often wont to display the enormous riches of the church. The group of musicians appears at one corner. The "maestro" is seated at the harpsichord, by the side of which is the vocal choir. He is assisted by two instrumentalists; one of whom is playing upon the viol da gamba, the other upon a large lute, or perhaps the "lira grande."

---

* Hogarth, in his *Memoirs of the Musical Drama*, vol. i, p. 17, edit. 1838, says, speaking of this opera, "Th Genius of Music, who speaks the prologue, is accompanied by two *gravicembani*, probably misprinted for *clavicembali*, or harpsichords."

For a long period, according to M. Fétis, the Italians did not avail themselves of the improvements made in the harpsichord, and continued to construct these instruments with two strings only to each note, and with a single key-board. The best manufacturers, at the beginning of the seventeenth century, were a Venetian priest named Zanetti, Crotone, and Farini. The latter conceived the idea of mounting his harpsichords entirely with catgut strings instead of wire, which gave them a more mellow and soft quality. To this kind of instrument he gave the name of *Clavicitherium*—the name of an older instrument, then out of date. Farini's example was followed shortly after by several German makers.

About the year 1620, Rigoli, of Florence, invented the vertical harpsichord, taking the idea from the earlier clavicymbal, which has since been imitated in a variety of the pianoforte. Near the same period, Richard, a French artist, acquired great and merited reputation for the excellence of his harpsichords. He was the first who conceived the idea of substituting small slips of cloth in the place of the quill, for producing the sound; by this means he succeeded in obtaining tones more agreeable, and yet without any diminution of power. Richard formed several distinguished artists, who necessarily perfected different details in the manufacture of the instrument.

The need of improvement in the quality of the tone of the harpsichord, which had always been harsh and disagreeable to delicate ears, led artists to attempt to disguise at least a defect like this by artificial means. Instruments were accordingly constructed with more than twenty different modifications, to imitate the tones of the harp, the lute, the mandolin, the bassoon, the flageolet, oboe, violin, and other instruments. The sounds discovered in the course of these experiments, and in which no analogy could be discovered to those of any other known instrument, were honoured with new and fantastic names, such as *jeu céleste, angélique, &c.*

A good illustration of this point is afforded by the following hand-bill, copied from the original, which appeared about the middle of the eighteenth century:

"HARPSICHORD IMITATING FOURTEEN WIND AND CHORDED INSTRUMENTS.

"THE SIEUR VIRBES, Professor of Music, and Teacher of the Harpsichord, from Paris, most respectfully acquaints the Nobility, Gentry, and Public, in general, that he is lately arrived in this Capital, with a most extraordinary Harpsichord, of a mechanism sufficiently simple, but so curious withal, as to deserve the attention of all connoisseurs, on account of the effects it produces, and its additional improvements. The very flattering reception he met with, on his first voyage here, from the Royal Society, and the most eminent artists, has encouraged him to give a new degree of perfection to that instrument, and offer it as a tribute of gratitude to this nation, whose suffrages he will be ever proud to deserve. He may be heard every day in the week, Sundays excepted, from twelve until three o'clock. To begin on this day, the 20th instant, No. 40, Suffolk street, Charing-cross.

"Admittance, a crown each person.

"He is in possession of the certificate from the Royal Academy in Paris, which testifies, that his new-invented Harpsichord imitates in nature the fourteen following instruments:—The Lute, Harp, Harmonica, German Guitar, Italian Mandoline, Hautboy, Tabor and Pipe, Tabor and Galoubet of Provence, Sistrum, Bassoon, Clarinets, Martial Kettle Drums, and celestial Harmony. The latter produces the most pleasing sensation, and cannot be compared in its grateful sound to any instrument hitherto known.

"The certificate may be seen, and an English translation of the same to be had of the inventor, as above."

In order to produce these different effects, new rows of jacks were added, which were furnished with materials of the softest kind, and most conducive to expression. The performer could produce these different effects either together or separately, by means of springs acted upon by the knees, or by pedals: sometimes, in order to facilitate these combinations, a third key-board was added to the two former. And yet, with all this complication, the grand secret, the real shading of the *piano* and *forte*, was wanting still; nothing better was devised for augmenting or diminishing the sound, than to put in motion different rows of jacks, so as to withdraw them from, or approximate them to, the strings at pleasure.

The result of these various experiments led to the invention of the *stops*, as they were termed, of which there were three kinds: the *forte* stop, which raised the dampers; the *soft* stop, which partly stopped the vibration of the strings; and the *buff* stop, which interposed a layer of cloth or soft buff leather between the jacks and the strings.

These stops seem to have been the origin of the pedals. They were used in the "middle age" of pianoforte-making as well as in the earlier harpsichords.

About the middle of the eighteenth century, Godfrey Silbermann, of Freyberg, and Blanchet, of Paris*, made several very important improvements in the details of the harpsichord, and particularly in the key-board, to which they gave a lightness unknown in former instruments. These makers added new key-boards, and extended the compass, of a large number of instruments made by the Ruckers.

Paschal Tasquin, "keeper of the musical instruments to the King of France," the celebrated pupil and successor of Blanchet, first used buff leather as a substitute for quill, in the year 1768. He also invented several ingenious pieces of mechanism in connection with the harpsichord, a detailed account of which may be seen in the *Encyclopédie Méthodique (Arts et Métiers Mécaniques*, tom. iv. pt. 1.)†

Schobert, an ingenious mechanic and an elegant composer of music, was the inventor of a harpsichord with a double bottom, in which was placed, above the first sounding-board, a range of strings of two octaves, of considerable size and length, to strengthen the bass. These strings were sounded by a piece of mechanism brought into action by a range of pedals. Harpsichords of this description were constructed by Silbermann of Strasburg, and by Perronard of Paris.

---

* The family of the Blanchets are well remembered in France as celebrated *clavier* makers. François Etienne Blanchet flourished in 1750. His grandson Armand (born 1763) succeeded to his business, and died in 1818. The firm of Blanchet and Roller still occupy a prominent position among the pianoforte makers of Paris.

† M. Trouflant, canon and organist of the cathedral at Nevers, addressed a letter to the *Journal de Musique*, 1773, on the inventions of M. Paschal Tasquin. See also the report of Baron de Dietrick to the Académie des Sciences, cited in the *Encyclopédie Méthodique*, 1791, art. Clavecin.

Wiegleb, " an organ and musical instrument maker " of Berlin, made harpsichords and spinets in 1724, in which the strings were sounded by brass or metal tongues, instead of the bristles or crow-quills commonly used.* This idea was revived some few years later, in 1788, by a maker named Hopkinson (an Englishman), resident at Paris. Godfrey Silbermann, of Freyberg, invented a piece of mechanism similar to that of the clavichord, which struck the string at its half length, by which the harmonic sounds were heard at the same time that the whole string was sounded; the strings of this harpsichord were much longer than those in common use. This instrument was called the *Clavecin d'Amour*. There was also a double harpsichord, named by its inventor, Johann Stein of Augsberg, the *Vis-à-vis* harpsichord, because each of its extremities was furnished with a key-board, by which means two persons could play at the same time.

But, perhaps, the most extraordinary invention of the time was that of Louis Bertrand Castel, a Jesuit of Montpellier. This worthy monk whose *Physical System* ranks among the best philosophical works of the early part of the last century, and whose *Optics of Colours* is still esteemed, studied vision and the nature of colours, as blended or contrasted with each other, till, his imagination getting the better of his understanding, he confounded the eye with the ear, and associated the harmony of tints with that of sounds. Infatuated with this idea, he invented what he called an *Ocular Harpsichord*, which was strung with coloured tapes instead of wires, and being placed in a dark room, when the keys were touched, the transparent tapes, which respectively corresponded with them, became visible; and the various successions and combinations of colours, consequent to this operation, produced effects on the sight which his fancy assimilated to the impression made on the ear by melody and harmony †.

---

* " Besides arming the tongues of the jacks with crow and raven quills, several other means were tried by which to produce a softer tone, and to be more durable. As the quilling a harpsichord with three stops was nearly a day's work, leather, ivory, and other elastic substances were tried; but what they gained in sweetness, was lost in spirit."— Burney, in *Rees' Cyclopædia*.

† This instrument was publicly exhibited in London in 1757, as appears by a rare tract in the possession of the writer, entitled *Explanation of the Ocular Harpsichord, upon shew to the Public*. Invento exoritur docto geminata Voluptas, affinisque Sono nascitur, ecce color. Am.

London: Printed for S. Hooper and A. Morley at Gay's Head, near Beaufort Buildings, in the Strand, MDCCLVII (pp. 22).

Varieties of the harpsichord were multiplied as fancy suggested, but the result of the greater part of these experiments was similar to many that have since been made on the pianoforte; they amused for awhile, but were never generally adopted.

The Spanish harpsichords of the eighteenth century acquired considerable reputation, and were much sought after by judges. Burney, recording his visit to Farinelli at Bologna, adds his testimony to their excellence in the following words: " Signor Farinelli has long left off singing, but amuses himself still on the harpsichord and viol d'amour; he has a great number of harpsichords made in different countries, which he has named according to the place they hold in his favour, after the greatest of the Italian painters. His first favouirte is a *piano-forte*, made at Florence in the year 1730, on which was written in gold letters, *Rafael d' Urbino*, then Correggio, Titian, Guido, &c. He played a considerable time upon his Raphael with great judgment and delicacy, and has composed several elegant pieces for that instrument. The next in favour is a harpsichord given him by the late Queen of Spain, who was Scarlatti's scholar, both in Portugal and Spain; it was for this princess that Scarlatti made his two first books of lessons, and to her the first edition, printed at Venice, was dedicated, when she was princess of Asturias; this harpsichord, which was made in Spain, has more tone than any of the others. His third favourite is one made likewise in Spain, under his own direction; it has moveable keys, by which, like that of Count Taxis at Venice, the player can transpose a composition either higher or lower. Of these Spanish harpsichords the natural keys are black, and the flats and sharps are covered with mother-of-pearl; they are of the Italian model, all the wood is cedar, except the bellies, and they are put into a second case."

We are fortunately able to give an engraving of a Spanish harpsichord (probably the very one mentioned as having been made for the Queen of Spain), from the title page to a very rare work, entitled *Essercizi per Gravicembalo di Don Domenico Scarlatti, Cavaliero di S. Giacomo e Maestro de Serenissimi Prencipe e Prencipessa delle Asturie*, &c. folio oblong, no date or imprint. The shape of the frame-work and legs upon which the instrument stands is exceedingly graceful, far superior to the English and German harpsichords of the same date.

THE HARPSICHORD.

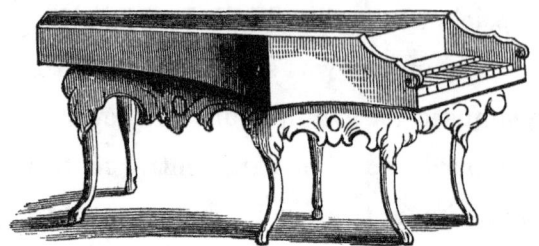

We see, from the foregoing extract, that transposing instruments are no new invention, although recently imposed upon the public as such. The keyed instrument in the possession of Count Torre Taxis, of Venice, was made under the direction of the King of Prussia in 1760. "It is in shape," says Burney, "like a large clavichord, has several changes of stops, and is occasionally a harp, a harpsichord, a lute, or piano-forte; but the most curious property of this instrument is that by drawing out the keys the hammers are transferred to different strings, by which means a composition may be transposed half a note, a whole note, or a flat third lower at pleasure, without the embarrassment of different notes or clefs, real or imaginary."

The harpsichord does not appear to have been commonly used in England before the latter half of the seventeenth century; it was then called the *harpsicon*, and the *harpsical*. John Playford, in the second book of his *Select Ayres and Dialogues*, folio, 1669, advertises, "If any person desire to be furnished with good new virginals and *Harpsicons*, if they send to Mr. Playford's shop, they may be furnished at reasonable rates to their content."

In the Harleian Collection, No. 5936, is preserved a curious hand-bill of the worthy Thomas Mace, "one of the clerks of Trinity College, Cambridge." In describing his "musical furniture" which he wishes to dispose of, he adds: "There is a *Pedal Harpsicon* (the absolute best sort of *consort harpsicon* that has been invented); there being in it more than 20 varieties, most of them to come in with the foot of the player, without the least hindrance of play (exceedingly pleasant): and also a *single harpsicon.*"

In his *Musick's Monument*, published in 1676, Master Mace is very particular in his description of this instrument. The passage is so curious, that we extract it:

To the Harpsicon, yet more properly, and much better, to the Pedal, an instrument of a late invention, contriv'd as I have been inform'd, by one Mr. John Hayward of London, a most excellent kind of instrument for a consort, and far beyond all harpsicons or organs that I yet ever heard of (I mean either for consort or single use); but the organ is far beyond it for those other performances before-mentioned.

"Concerning this instrument (call'd the Pedal because it is contrived to give varieties with the foot), I shall bestow a few lines in making mention of it, in regard it is not very commonly used or known, because few make them well, and fewer will go to the price of them, twenty pounds being the ordinary price of one; but the great patron of musick in his time, Sir Robert Bolles (whom, in the University, I had the happiness to initiate in this high art) had two of them, the one I remember at 30*l.* and the other at 50*l.* very admirable instruments.

"This instrument is in shape and bulk just like a harpsicon, only it differs in the order of it, thus, viz. There is made right underneath the keys near the ground, a kind of cubbord, a box, which opens with a little pair of doors, in which box the performer sets both his feet, resting them upon his heels (his toes a little turning up) touching nothing, till such time as he has a pleasure to employ them; which is after this manner, viz. there being right underneath his toes four little pummels of wood, under each foot two, any one of these four he may tread upon at his pleasure; which by the weight of his foot drives a spring, and so causeth the whole instrument to sound, either soft or loud, according as he shall choose to tread any of them down: for without the foot so used nothing speaks.

"The outside of the right foot drives one, and the inside of the same foot drives another; so that by treading his foot a little awry, either outward or inward, he causeth a various stop to be heard, at his pleasure; and if he clap down his foot flat, then he takes them both, at the same time (which is a third variety and louder).

"Then he has ready, under his left foot, two other various stops, and by the like order and motion of the foot, he can immediately give you three other varieties, either *softer* or *louder*, as with the right foot, before-mentioned, he did.

"So that thus you may perceive he has several various stops at pleasure, and all quick and nimble, by the ready turn of the foot.

"And by this pritty device, is this instrument made wonderfully rare and excellent; so that doubtless it excels all harpsicols or organs in the world, for admirable sweetness and humour, either for a private, or a consort use."

The harpsichord was used in our public theatres in the latter half of the seventeenth century. When Shakespeare's *Tempest*, as altered by Dryden and Davenant, was played at the Duke's Theatre, in Lincoln's Inn Fields, in 1667, it seems probable that the band was for the first time placed between the audience and the stage. The following is part of the introductory description: "The front of the stage is opened, and the band of twenty-four violins with the *harpsicals* and theorbos, which accompany the voice, are placed between the pit and the stage."

The chief harpsichord-makers in England at this time were Charles and John Hayward, and John Hitchcock, some of whose instruments are still occasionally to be met with in our old country mansions.

These artists were succeeded by Keen, Slade, Player, Fenton, Baudin and John Harris; the last-named was the son of the celebrated organ-builder, Renatus Harris;

and he claims the distinction of having taken out the first patent in this country for an "improvement" in the construction of the harpsichord. This patent bears date Oct. 22, 1730, and is clearly described in the following advertisement, preserved in the curious collection of proclamations, broadsides, &c. presented to the Chetham Library, Manchester, by James O. Halliwell, Esq. F.R.S. (No. 830.)

"TO THE NOBILITY, GENTRY, AND OTHERS, THAT ARE LOVERS AND JUDGES OF MUSICK.

"Tho' many of the Quality and Gentry, &c. read the News Papers, 'tis believed there are but Few that regard the Advertisements; so that tho' the Advertiser is at considerable Expence to have his Affair made known to them, 'tis of little Service to him: I therefore beg leave to use this Method, and hope those Honourable Persons to whose Hands these Papers are humbly presented, will be pleased to read them, their Benefit being designed by

Their most obedient humble Servant,

JOHN HARRIS.

" His Majesty has been graciously pleas'd to grant to John Harris, his Letters Patent, for the making of an Harpsichord with two Sets of Strings, on which may be performed, either One Unison, or Two; or Two Unisons and an Octave together; and the Forte's or Piano's, or Loud, or Soft, or the contrary, may be executed as quick as Thought: And double Basses may be also expressed by touching single keys; so that here, Divisions may be played well, without the Thumb and little Finger together, which could not be well done otherwise; and Shakes may be here performed, which cannot be done by the Thumb and little Finger together.

"All Persons that shall make any of these Instruments, or in any respect imitate them in their extraordinary Performances, shall be prosecuted according to Law, and whoever will discover any one that (without my License) shall do so, shall, upon Conviction, be well rewarded by John Harris.

"N.B. These instruments are now made in Perfection; and Mr. Harris will (at a very reasonable Expence) make double basses, to either single, or double key'd Harpsichords, which are already made by other Persons, which will give a Fulness and Nobleness to the Instrument, that the best of other Harpsichords have not; and is very useful in playing a Thorough Bass, or other Musick, for the Parts are expressed in a double Manner, when you please. This Performance will not in the least injure the Tone or Sound of any instrument; nor make it go sooner out of Tune, than it would do without it, and the Touch will be very good when the double Basses are used, and also when they are not.

" Mr. Harris (Organ, Harpsichord, and Spinnet Maker) lives within three Doors of Bedford Court, in Red Lyon Street, Holborn, London."

In 1730, one William Barton, of whom nothing is known, took out a patent for his "new invention of pins of silver, brass, steel, and all other sorts of metals, to improve the use of harpsichords and spinnets, which will improve the tone of the said instruments, and last many years without amendment; crow and raven's quills, of which they are now made, requiring frequent change and trouble in repairing."

In 1741, Rutgerus Plenius, an ingenious harpsichord-maker, issued the following curious broadside, which is transcribed from a copy of the original in the Chetham Library (Halliwell's Coll. No. 772).

"ACTA VIRUM PROBANT.

"HARPSICHORDS, With a Stop that imitates ye Welch Harp Having Quils that (tho' daily used) will last many years without breaking, they being chemically prepar'd, and all cut of equal Length to a Hair's Breadth, in an Engine invented for that Purpose which with Six other visible improvements are made by Virtue of His Majesty's Royal Letters Patent By the Inventor only, RUTGERUS PLENIUS; Who begs leave to acquaint all Gentlemen and Ladies, Lovers of Harmony, and Encouragers of industrious Artists, that He, after Ten years indefatigable Researches to bring this noble Instrument to ye highest Degree of Perfection, has made more than Twenty essential Improvements in the Said Instrument, tho' many of them can't immediately fall under the Cognizance of every Spectator, yet ye hand in playing will virtually feel their good Effect. And He humbly presumes that ye Boldness of ye Instrument united to the Delicacy of it's sound, as well as distinct Expression of every Single Tone, free from ye Confus'd jumble of Sounds often heard in many Harpsichords, will most agreeably touch ye Ear of every Auditor, it having already met with universal Applause, particularly from ye most eminent Masters of Musick in England: The Truth of these Assertions, with a further Detail of the whole, He is ready, at all Hours, to make appear to ye Curious, who shall honour him with their Presence.

"BY HIS MAJESTY'S ROYAL LETTERS PATENT, GRANTED TO RUTGERUS PLENIUS, HARPSICHORD MAKER; For the sole Making, Use & Benefit of a New invented musical Instrument, called a Lyrichord. Which imitates a Violin, Violoncello, & Double Bass; but when play'd Full, it resembles a perfect Organ of a most delightful Tone, altho' by Catgut Strings only, without Pipes. It admits of playing Forte & Piano; as also of swelling any Single Note (or many Notes ad libitum) on ye same Key, by ye simple Pressure of ye Fingers: But what is most surprising, & indeed incredible if not seen (yet plainly demonstrable to every one) its strings never go out of Tune, as long as ye constituent Materials of ye Instrument remain entire; a Thing which has been so long wisht for & desir'd, & in all Ages, 'till now, by every one, deem'd impossible to find out. This therefore is to inform ye Nobility, Gentry, & others, That ye aforesaid Rutgerus Plenius has now, (after Ten years painful study & Labour, accompany'd with no small Expence) brought ye above mention'd Instrument to Perfection. And he humbly presumes, that all Gentlemen & Ladies, who will do themselves ye pleasure & him ye Honour of seeing & hearing it, will be fully convinced of ye Truth of ye foregoing Assertions; & at ye same Time be agreeably diverted by ye Harmony of ye Instrument; it being esteem'd & approv'd by all that have yet seen it; particularly by ye most eminent Masters of Musick in England, who allow it to be ye most curious Piece of Workmanship & most wonderful Instrument they have ever seen or heard of. The Price of seeing & hearing it perform'd on, at any Time between ye Hours of Twelve & Four o'Clock, is Half a Crown each Person, at ye Inventor's House (ye King's Arms being over ye Door) in south Audley Street, Grosvenor Square; where a good Hand is provided for ye Entertainment of ye Audience.

"N.B. The above described Lyrichord is not (as many erroneously thought) the same which appear'd in the World Two years ago, But a Complete intirely New Piece and (in the opinion of every one who has seen them both) excels That by at least a hundred Degrees."

A few years afterwards, Plenius's Lyrichord was thus advertised in the public papers:

"TO BE SEEN AND HEARD 'TILL SOLD,

very day from eleven in the morning, 'till two in the afternoon, Sundays excepted, at the Golden-Ball, opposite the Little South door of St. Paul's, in Paul's Church-Yard, for half a crown each person.

"The Lyrychord, the most curious musical instrument ever invented; which at a very great expence of money and ime, is now brought to a great degree of perfection. It imitates the Violin, Bass-Violin, and Double-Bass, and tho' it has no pipes, yet, when played full, it resembles a perfect Organ, and is touch'd by keys, like a Harpsichord. It admits of playing loud and soft, and the close-shake, as also of swelling any single note, or many notes together, by the simple pressure of the fingers: But what is most surprising, and indeed incredible if not seen (yet plainly demonstrable to every one) it's strings never go out of tune, as long as the constituent materials of the instrument remain entire: a thing hitherto deem'd impossible to find out.

"Note. A good performer is provided to entertain the audience, during the aforesaid hours."—*The Public Advertiser*, June 12, 1755.

The last notice we have of Plenius's invention, occurs on February 11th, 1772, in the following manner:

"TO BE SOLD BY AUCTION,
By Mr. Christie,
At his Great Room, late the Royal Academy, in Pall Mall,
To-morrow and Thursday;

Fifteen fine toned Harpsichords, with double and single keys, several of which with double and single bass pedals, &c. being the stock in trade of Frederick Naubauer, Harpsichord-maker, together with a *Lyrichord*, a capital melodious instrument made by the famous Rutgerus Plenius. To be viewed this day. Catalogues may be had as above."

One of the most important harpsichord-makers of the eighteenth century was a foreigner, resident in England, named Tabel. Nothing seems to be known of his history; but in his factory two men were employed that afterwards rose to considerable eminence as makers of musical instruments—Burckhardt or Burkat Tschudi, and Jacob Kirkmann.

Tschudi was a Swiss, who came to this country about the year 1732. The authors of *The Universal Helvetian Swiss Lexicon* tell us that "he was a poor journeyman joiner who went to England and made himself known at the Court of London as an eminent clavier-maker. Besides many other famous things, he made, in 1765, an ingenious harpsichord with two manuals for the King of Prussia. He was married in London, where he died in 1775, leaving great wealth to his family." Tschudi was " harpsichord-maker to the Royal Family;" and in 1769 took out a patent for an " improvement" in the harpsichord. Burney says, " His work was extremely neat, and his tone and touch refined and delicate, while his instruments were new ; but neither so full nor durable as those of Kirkman. Snetzler, who added horizontal organs to many of his harpsichords, used to account for his instruments soon losing their perfection, by his working in a very hot room, and keeping them there, in order to give to the tone the brilliancy of old instruments; but as soon as they were removed to a cold or damp room, the wood swelled so much, as to warp, crack the bellies, and disorder all the movements; accidents which we never remember to have happened to the excellent instruments of his worthy son-in-law and successor, Broadwood."

The same author, in his *Present State of Music in Germany*, speaking of the musical instruments in the Palace at Potsdam, thus alludes to the " ingenious harpsichord" above mentioned : " In another apartment there is a most magnificent harpsichord, made by Shudi in England; the hinges, pedals, and frame are of silver, the case is inlaid, and the front is of tortoiseshell; this instrument, which cost 200 guineas, was sent to Hamburg by sea, and from thence to Potsdam, up the Elb and the Havel, which, I was told, had injured it so much, that it has been useless ever since ; however, it is natural to suppose that some jealousy may have been excited by it, and that it has not had quite fair play from those employed to repair it; for I never heard of any one of the great number of harpsichords which are annually sent from England to the East and West Indies by sea, receiving so much damage as this is said to have done in a much shorter passage. And now I am upon the subject of musical instruments, I must observe that the Germans work much better out of their own country than they do in it, if we may judge by the *harpsichords* of Kirkman and Shudi; the *pianofortes* of Backers; and the organs of Snetzler ; which far surpass in goodness all the keyed instruments that I met with in my tour through Germany."

To this notice of Tschudi, we may add, that the Messrs. Broadwood possess an interesting portrait of the Founder of their firm in the act of tuning the King of Prussia's harpsichord.

Kirkman, whose sign of the king's arms in Broad Street, Golden Square, we are told, was as well known to the nobility and gentry as the equestrian statue of Charles at Charing Cross, was esteemed perhaps the most eminent harpsichord-maker of his day. Burney, whose valuable articles in *Rees's Cyclopædia* have been of great use in these pages, has left us the following characteristic memoir of him.

"Jacob Kirkman, an excellent harpsichord-maker from Germany, who came to England about the year 1740, and worked with the celebrated Tabel, as his foreman and finisher, till the time of his death. Soon after which, by a curious kind of courtship, Kirkman married his master's widow, by which prudent measure he became possessed of all Tabel's seasoned wood, tools, and stock in trade. Kirkman himself used to relate the singular manner in which he gained the widow, which was not by a regular siege, but by storm. He told her, one fine morning, at breakfast, that he was determined to be married that day before twelve o'clock. Mrs. Tabel, in great surprise, asked him to whom he was going to be married, and why so soon? The finisher told her that he had not yet determined whom he should marry, and that, if she would have him, he would give her the preference. The lady wondered at his precipitancy, hesitated full half an hour; but, he continuing to swear that the business must be done before twelve o'clock that day, at length she surrendered; and as this abridged courtship preceded the marriage act, and the nuptials could be performed at the Fleet or May Fair, 'without loss of time, or hindrance of business,' the canonical hour was saved, and two fond hearts were in one united, in the most summary way possible, just one month after the decease of Tabel. Kirkman lived long enough to stock the whole kingdom with his instruments, and to amass great wealth. He had no children, but as many nephews hovering over him as a Roman pontiff.

"Theodorus, the father of Isocrates, was a flute-maker, who acquired wealth sufficient, by his employment, not only to educate his children in a liberal manner, but also to bear one of the heaviest public burdens to which an Athenian citizen was liable; that of furnishing a choir or chorus for his tribe, or ward, at festivals and religious ceremonies. Each tribe furnished their distinct chorus, which consisted of a band of vocal and instrumental performers and dancers, who were to be hired, maintained, and dressed, during the whole time of the festival: an expense considerable in itself, but much increased by emulation among the richer citizens, and the disgrace consequent to an inferior exhibition. The fluctuations of trade and public favour have rendered the business of boring flutes far less profitable at present, than it was in the time of Theodorus. But our harpsichord-maker, Kirkman, who was known to be worth 90,000*l.* twenty years before he died, doubled the profits of his instruments by becoming a pawnbroker and a usurer; obliging young heirs with money as kindly and with as much liberality as a Hebrew.

"At a time when ruin stared harpsichord-makers in the face, by the rage with which musical ladies were seized for the guitar, in preference to all other instruments, Kirkman hit upon an ingenious expedient, which saved himself from bankruptcy, and restored the harpsichord to all its former favour.* He did not live to see his excellent double harpsichords of sixty or seventy guineas price sold at auctions for twelve or fourteen pounds, and the original purchasers turn them out of their houses as useless lumber. But such are the vicissitudes of this world, that our descendants will, perhaps, know as little about the pianoforte, as we do now of the lute or lyre. Kirkman is supposed to have died, in 1778, worth near 200,000*l.*"

Jacob Kirkman was succeeded in his business by his son Abraham, who ably kept up the family name by the manufacture of his instruments. He was in his turn succeeded by his son Joseph, who continued to make the best English harpsichords up to the commencement of the present century.

The harpsichord was greatly improved by that great mechanical genius, John

---

* This expedient is related by the same writer in another part of his work. (See article, GUITAR, *Rees's Cyclopædia*, vol. xvii.) "The common guitar used in England has frequently had fits of favour in this country. About fifty years ago its vogue was so great among all ranks of people as nearly to break all the harpsichord and spinet makers, and indeed the harpsichord masters themselves. All the ladies disposed of their harpsichords at auctions for one third of their price, or exchanged them for guitars; till old Kirkman, the harpsichord maker, after almost ruining himself with buying in his instruments for better times, purchased likewise some cheap guitars, and made a present of several to girls in milliners' shops, and to ballad singers in the streets, whom he had taught to accompany themselves with a few chords and triplets, which soon made the ladies ashamed of their frivolous and vulgar taste, and return to the harpsichord.

Joseph Merlin. This extraordinary artist was born at St. Peter's, in the city of Huys, between Namur and Liège, September 17, 1735. After residing six years in Paris, he came to England, on the recommendation of the Royal Academy of Sciences, in the suite of the Spanish Ambassador, Count de Firentes. He arrived here, May 24, 1760, and resided for some time with the Count, in Soho Square. In 1768, he exhibited many curious inventions at Cox's Museum, in Spring Gardens, of which place he seems to have been the director for several years. In 1774, we find him residing in the parish of Marylebone, when a patent was granted him for " his new-invented kind of compound harpsichord, in which, besides the jacks with quills, a set of hammers of the nature of those used in the kind of harpsichords called *pianoforte*, are introduced in such manner that either may be played separately or both together, at the pleasure of the performer; and for adding the aforesaid hammers to an harpsichord of the common kind already made, so as to render it such compound harpsichord."

The common harpsichords of large size had two rows of keys, and three strings to each note. Of these three, two were tuned in unison, and the third sounded an octave higher. The latter was abolished by Merlin in 1775, and replaced by another unison which left the tone equally full, and rendered the instrument less susceptible to atmospheric influences. After constructing a great variety of musical instruments, and extraordinary pieces of mechanism*, this artist died, May 1804, leaving only a small fortune, but a name unrivalled for mechanical ingenuity.

From an advertisement now before us, it appears that Merlin's musical instruments in his possession at the time of his decease were not disposed of for more than thirty years afterwards. They are described as

---

* "During the latter part of the eighteenth century, this ingenious mechanic and musical instrument maker gratified the curious and tasteful by the public exhibition of his organ, pianoforte, and other inventions, at his Museum in Princes Street, Hanover Square. Merlin's mind was adequate to the embracing the whole compass of mechanical science and execution; at least, in the articles connected with elegant and domestic amusement. One of his ingenious novelties was *a pair of skaites*, contrived to run on wheels. Supplied with a pair of these and a violin, he mixed in the motley group of one of the celebrated Mrs. Cornelly's masquerades at Carlisle House, Soho Square; when, not having provided the means of retarding his velocity, or commanding its direction, he impelled himself against a mirror, of more than five hundred pounds value, dashed it to atoms, broke his instrument to pieces, and wounded himself most severely." *Busby's Concert Room Anecdotes*, vol. ii, p. 137.

"CELEBRATED MUSICAL INSTRUMENTS

INVENTED AND MANUFACTURED BY THE LATE

MR. JOHN JOSEPH MERLIN.

To be sold by Auction by Mr. MILLS,

Friday, 21 July, 1837."

"Amongst them will be found The Celestial Harp, and full Band of Keyed Instruments. This surprizing and powerful Keyed Instrument is capable of producing all the effects of a full Orchestra, equal in power to four or six Violins, the same number of Tenors and Violoncellos, and other powerful accompaniments may be added. By means of a catgut worked by brass circles, the whole is made to sound. The performer is also enabled by one of the pedals acting as a mute to give the instrument all the effects of the Welsh Harp. As a source of profit for an Exhibition, this instrument might prove a fortune in the hands of a spirited speculator. "Also, Merlin's Original Private Harpsichord. Little remains beyond the case and a part of the action; yet enough remains to remind one of the great and talented individual."

The English harpsichords of the eighteenth century were infinitely superior to those constructed on the continent. Burney has left us an opinion upon this point, in his *Tour in France*, which is worth extracting. He says:

"To persons accustomed to English harpsichords, all the keyed instruments on the continent appear to great advantage. Throughout Italy they have generally little octave spinets to accompany singing in private houses, sometimes in a triangular form, but more frequently in the shape of our old virginals; of which the keys are so noisy, and the tone so feeble, that more wood is heard than wire. The best Italian harpsichord I met with for touch was that of Signor Grimani at Venice; and for tone, that of Monsignor Reggio at Rome; but I found three English harpsichords in the three principal cities of Italy, which are regarded by the Italians as so many phenomena. One was made by Shudi, and is in the possession of the Hon. Mrs. Hamilton, at Naples. The other two, which are of Kirkman's make, belong to Mrs. Richie, at Venice, and to the Hon. Mrs. Earl, who resided at Rome when I was there."

It is needless to follow up all the contrivances of the harpsichord-makers of this period to obtain sonority of tone, and to do away with the jarring noise produced by the action of the quill against the string; suffice it that the grand desideratum was attained, and the *hammer harpsichord* was soon to appear before the world in the shape of that charming and expressive instrument known to us all under the familiar appellation of the *pianoforte*.

CHAPTER VII.

THE CLAIMANTS TO THE INVENTION OF THE PIANOFORTE.

It was within a few years of each other, that, by a remarkable coincidence, three makers, in three different parts of the world, conceived the idea of the pianoforte. The one was an Italian, the other a Frenchman, and the third a native of Germany. Marius, the French manufacturer, and Schröter, the German organist, have hitherto had the advantage of priority of date conceded to them, whilst the claims of Bartolommeo Cristofali, of Padua, have been almost entirely overlooked.

Cristofali has an able advocate in the Count G. R. Carli, an elegant writer of the last century, who relates that he (Cristofali) invented the improvement during his stay at Florence, in the year 1718. The essay on music, which is to be found in the Milanese edition of Carli's works, published in eighteen volumes, 1784-7, contains the following spirited passage:—" From the organ we pass readily to the clavicembalo—an instrument always progressing towards perfection, and much improved by Bartolommeo Cristofori (*i. e.* Cristofali), a Paduan, who added hammers to the mechanism; of which *great invention* we are so forgetful that we have even believed it a new thing, bringing it here from Germany and England, and receiving it as an unique production of those fortunate regions which are destined to illuminate us with our own Italian lights. Thus it is that we have never known how to preserve any single thing for our own honour."

The Count's error, as to the exact date, has caused much confusion, and has led to Cristofali's claims for *priority* of invention being ignored. The discovery which the Count places in the year 1718, had been made known to the public in 1711.

Bartolommeo Cristofali was born at Padua, in 1683, and settled at Florence in

1710, as "harpsichord-maker to the Grand Duke of Tuscany." Nothing seems to be known of his career, and but for the curious account of his invention of the pianoforte in the *Giornale de' Litterati d'Italia*, Venice, 1711 (tom. v, p. 144), his name would hardly have been remembered.* The article in question was written by the celebrated Scipione Maffei,† and we feel proud in being able to present it to the reader *entire*, in the original language, and with an English translation. It is certainly a great curiosity, and will, no doubt, be read with interest.

"NUOVA INVENZIONE D'UN GRAVECEMBALO COL PIANO E FORTE; AGGIUNTE ALCUNE CONSIDERAZIONI SOPRA GLI STRUMENTI MUSICALI.	"NEW INVENTION OF A HARPSICHORD, WITH THE *PIANO* AND THE *FORTE*; ALSO SOME REMARKS UPON MUSICAL INSTRUMENTS.
"Se il pregio delle invenzioni dee misurarsi dalla novità, e dalla difficoltà, quella, di cui siamo al presente per dar ragguaglio, non è certamente inferiore a qualunque altra da gran tempo in quà si sia veduta. Egli è noto a chiunque gode della musica, che uno de' principali fonti, da' quali traggano i periti di quest'arte il segreto di singolarmente dilettar chi ascolta, è il piano, e'l fortezzo, sia nelle proposte e risposte, o sia quando con artifiziosa degradazione lasciandosi a poco a poco mancar la voce, si ripiglia poi ad un tratto strepitosamente : il quale artifizio	"If the value of inventions is to be measured by the novelty and difficulty, that of which we are now to give an account is certainly not inferior to any that has been discovered for a long time. It is known to every one who delights in music, that one of the principal means by which the skilful in that art derive the secret of especially delighting those who listen, is the piano and forte in the theme and its response, or in the gradual diminution of tone, little by little, and then returning suddenly to the full power of the instrument; which artifice is frequently used

---

* Fétis, in his *Biographie Universelle des Musiciens*, has a very meagre notice of Cristofali, whose name, he thinks, is more properly Cristofori. He also devotes an unprofitable article to this subject in the *Revue Musicale de Paris*, 1834. Fétis had evidently never seen the *Giornale de' Litterati d'Italia*. In his work called *La Musique mise à la Portée de tout le Monde*, Brussels, second edition, 1839, he says :—"As early as 1716, a manufacturer at Paris, by the name of Marius, had presented to the Academy of Sciences, for their examination, two harpsichords, in which he had substituted little hammers for the strips of wood used to strike the strings. *Two years afterwards* (?), Cristoforo, a Florentine, improved upon this invention, and made the first piano which has served as a model for those which have since been made." Although Cristofali's claim to the invention has lately been disputed, it was acknowledged by Dr. Burney, in *Rees's Cyclopedia* in v. PIANOFORTE. He says :—"There is a minute account of the invention and a description of the *pianoforte*, in the *Giornale d'Italia* (tom. v. p. 144), printed at Venice, 1711. This instrument was invented at Florence, by Bartolommeo Cristofali, harpichord-maker, a native of Padua, in the service of the Grand Duke of Tuscany." In this statement he is followed by the *Oxford Encyclopædia, Wilkes' Cyclopædia*, the fourth edition of the *Encyclopædia Britannica*, &c. &c. ; yet, with the *fact* in print, in our Encyclopedias, we find Mr. George Hogarth (*Musical World*, July 15, 1836) giving a sketch of the "History of the Pianoforte," and totally omitting the name of its inventor !

† It is referred to correctly in Forkel's *Allgemeine Litteratur der Musik*, Leipzig, 1792, p. 262; Lichtenthal's *Dizionarioe Bibliografia*, Milan, 1826, v. iv, p. 67 ; Walther's *Musicalisches Lexicon*, 1732, p. 192, &c. The article is also said to have been translated into German, by Köenig, and inserted in Mattheson's *Critica Musica*, tom. ii, p. 335.

è usato frequentemente, ed a maraviglia ne' gran concerti di Roma con diletto incredibile di chi gusta la perfezione dell'arte. Ora di questa diversità ed alterazione di voce, nella quale eccellenti sono, fra gli altri, gli strumenti da arco, affatto privo è il gravecembalo; e sarebbe, da chi che sia, stata riputata una vanissima immaginazione il proporre di fabbricarlo in modo, che avesse questa dote. Con tutto ciò, una sì ardita invenzione è stata non meno felicemente pensata, che eseguita in Firenze dal Sig. BARTOLOMMEO CRISTOFALI, Padovano, Cembalista stipendiato dal Serenissimo Principe di Toscana. Egli ne ha finora fatti tre della grandezza ordinaria degli altri gravecembali, e son tutti riusciti perfettamente. Il cavare da questi maggiore o minore suono dipende dalla diversa forza, con cui dal sonatore vengono premuti i tasti, regolando la quale, si viene a sentire non soli il piano, e il forte, ma la degradazione, e diversità della voce, qual sarebbe in un violoncello. Alcuni professori non hanno fatto a quest'invenzione tutto l'applauso ch'ella merita; prima, perchè non hanno inteso, quanto ingegno si richiedesse a superarne la difficoltà, e qual maravigliosa delicatezza di mano per comprirne con tanta aggiustatezza il lavoro: in secondo luogo, perchè è paruto loro, che la voce di tale strumento, come differente dall' ordinaria, sia troppo molle, e ottusa; ma questo è un sentimento, che si produce nel primo porvi su le mani, per l'assuefazione che abbiamo all' argentino degli altri gravecembali; per altro in breve tempo vi si adatta l'orecchio, e vi si affeziona talmente che non sa stancarsene, e non gratifice più i gravecembali comuni; e bisogna avvertire, che riesce ancor più soave l'udirlo in qualche distanza. E'stata altresì opposta eccezione di non avere questo strumento gran voce, e di non avere tutto il forte degli altri gravecembali. Al che si risponde prima, che ha però assai più voce ch' essi non credono, quando altri voglia, e sappia cavarla, premendo il tasto con impeto; e secondariamente, che bisogna saper prendere le cose per lo suo verso, e non considerare, in riguardo ad un fine, ciò ch'è fatto per un altro. Questo è propriamente strumento da camera, e non è però adattabile a una musica di chiesa, o ad una grand' orchestra. Quanti strumenti vi sono, che si usano in tali occasioni, e che non pertanto si stimano de' più dilettevoli? Egli è certo, che per accompagnare un cantante, e per secondare uno strumento, ed anche per un moderato concerto, riesce perfettamente; benchè non sia però questa l'intenzion sua principale, ma

and with marvellous effect, in the great concerts of Rome, to the incredible delight of such as enjoy the perfection of art. Now, of this diversity and alteration of tone, in which instruments played by the bow especially excel, the harpsichord is entirely deprived, and it would have been thought a vain endeavour to propose to make it so that it should participate in this power. Nevertheless, so bold an invention has been no less happily conceived than executed in Florence, by Signor Bartolommeo Cristofali, of Padua, harpsichord-player, in the service of the most serene Prince of Tuscany. He has already made three, of the usual size of other harpsichords, and they have all succeeded to perfection. The production of greater or less sound depends on the degree of power with which the player presses on the keys, by regulating which, not only the piano and forte are heard, but also the gradations and diversity of power, as in a violoncello. Some professors have not given to this invention all the praise it deserves; because, in the first place, they did not see how much ingenuity was required to overcome the difficulty, and what marvellous delicacy of hand was required to adjust it with so much nicety; and, secondly, because it appeared to them that the tone of such an instrument was more soft and less distinct than the ordinary ones; but this is a feeling produced by first impressions of the clearer sound we have on other harpichords; but in a short time the ear so adapts itself, and becomes so charmed with it, that it never tires, and the common harpsichord no longer pleases; and we must add that it sounds yet more sweet at some distance. It has further been objected to this instrument, that it has not a powerful tone, and not quite so loud as other harpichords. To this may be answered, first, that it has more power than they imagine, if any one, who wishes and knows how to use it will strike the keys briskly; and, secondly, he should consider the object, the attainment of which has been so greatly desired, and not in a point of view for which it was not intended.

"This is properly a chamber instrument, and it is not intended for church music, nor for a great orchestra. How many instruments there are, used on such occasions, which are not esteemed among the most agreeable? It is certain that, to accompany a singer, and to play with one other instrument, or even for a moderate concert, it succeeds perfectly; although this is not its principal intention, but

si quella d'esser sonato a solo, come il liuto, l'arpa, le viole di sei corde, ed altri strumenti de' più soavi. Ma veramente la maggior opposizione, che abbia patito questo nuovo strumento, si è il non sapersi universalmente a primo incontro sonare, perchè non basta il sonar perfettamente gli ordinari strumenti da tasto, ma essendo strumento nuovo, ricerca persona, che intendene la forza vi abbia fatto sopra alquanto di studio particolare, così per regolare la misura del diverso impulso, che dee darsi a' tasti, e la graziosa degredazione, e tempo e luogo, come per iscegliere cose a proposito, e delicate, e massimamente spezzando, e facendo camminar le parti, e sentire i soggetti in più luoghi.

"Ma venendo alla struttura particolare di questo strumento, se l'artefice, che l'ha inventato, avesse così saputo descriverlo, come ha saputo perfettamente fabbricarlo, non sarebbe malagevole il farne comprendere a' lettori l' artifizio: ma poichè egli non è in ciò riuscito, anzi ho giudicato impossibile il rappresentarlo in modo, che se ne possa concepire l' idea, e forza, ch' altri si ponga all' impresa, benchè senza aver più lo strumento davanti agli occhi, e solamente sopra alcune memorie fattesi già nell' esaminarlo, e sopra un disegno rozzamente da prima disteso.

"Diremo adunque primieramente, che in luogo degli usati salterelli, che suonano con la penna, si pone qui un registro di martelletti, che vanno a percuotere la corda per di sotto, avendo la cima, con cui percuotono, coperta di dante. Ogno martello dipende nel suo principio da una rotella, che lo rende mobile, e le rotelle stanno nascoste in un pettine, nel quale sono infilate. Vicino alla rotella, e sotto il principio dell' asta del martello vi è un sostegno, o prominenza, che ricevendo colpo per di sotto, alza il martello, e lo spinge a percuoter la corda con quella misura d'impulsione, e con quel grado di forza, che vien dato dalla mano; e quindi viene il maggiore o minor suono a piacere del sonatore; essendo agevole anche il farlo percuotere con molta violenza, a cagione che il martello riceve l'urto vicino alla sua imperniatura, che vuol dire, vicino al centro del giro, ch' egli descrive; nel qual caso ogni mediocre impulso fa salire con impeto un raggio di ruota. Ciò che dà il colpo al martello sotto l'estremità della prominenza suddetta, è una linguetta di legno, posta sopra una leva, che viene all' ncontro del tasto, e ch' è alzata da esso, quando vien premuto dal sonatore. Questa linguetta non posa però sopra

rather to be played alone, like the lute, the harp, viols of six strings, and other most sweet intruments. But, really, the great cause of the opposition which this new instrument has encountered, is the general want of knowledge of how, at first, to play it; because it is not sufficient to know how to play perfectly upon instruments with the ordinary fingerboard, but, being a new instrument, it requires a person who, understanding its capabilities, shall have made a particular study of its effects, so as to regulate the measure of force required on the keys and the effects of decreasing it, also to choose pieces suited to it for delicacy, and especially for the movement of the parts, that the subject may be heard distinctly in each.

"But now, as to the particular construction of this instrument. If the inventor had known as well how to describe as he has to manufacture it, it would not be difficult to explain it to the reader; but as he has not succeeded in that, so I judge it impossible for me to represent it so that a due idea may be formed of the skill of the invention, especially as I have no longer the instrument before my eyes, but only some memoranda made while examining it, and a rough model laid before me.

"I will say, then, in the first place, that instead of the usual *jacks* that produce sound by quills, there is a row of little hammers that strike the string from below, the tops of which are covered with leather. Every hammer has the end inserted into a circular but, that renders it moveable, but these buts are partially imbedded, and strung together, in a receiver. Near the but, and under the stem of the hammer, there is a support or projecting part, that, receiving a blow from below, raises the hammer, and causes it to strike the string, with whatever measure of impulse, and whatever degree of force is given by the hand of the performer; and hence the sound is greater or less at the pleasure of the player. Also, it can be made to strike with much force, because the hammer receives the blow near its axis, and therefore even a slight touch will affect it readily. That which gives the blow to the hammer under the extremity of the forenamed projection is a little tongue of wood, placed upon a lever that meets the key, and that is raised by it when pressed by the player. This little tongue, however, does not rest upon the lever, but is slightly raised and strung on two jawbone-shaped pieces that are placed

la leva, ma n'è alquanto sollevata, e si sta infilzata in due ganasce sottili, che le son poste a questo effetto una per parte. Ma perchè bisognava, che il martello percossa la corda subito la lasciasse, staccandosene, benchè non ancora abbandonato il tasto dal sonatore; ed era però necessario, che il detto martello restasse subito in libertà di ricadere al suo luogo; perciò la linguetta, che gli dà il colpo, è mobile, ed è in tal maniera congegnata, che va in su, e percuote ferma, ma dato il colpo subito scatta, cio passa; e quando lasciato il tutto, ella torna giù, cede, e rientra, riponendosi ancora sotto il martello. Questo effetto ha conseguito l'artefice con una molla di filo d'ottone, che ha fermata nella leva, e che, distendendosi, viene a battere con la punta sotto la linguetta, e facendo alquanto di forza, la spinge, e la tiene appoggiata a un altro filo d'ottone, che ritto, e fermo le sta dal lato opposto. Per questo appoggio stabile, che ha la linguetta, e per la molla, che ha sotto, e per l'imperniatura, che ha dalle parti, ella si rende ora ferma, ed ora pieghevole, secondo il bisogno. Perchè i martelli ricadendo dopo la percossa non rifavellissero, e ribattessero nella corda, si fanno cadere, e posare sopra una incrociatura di cordoncini di seta, che quetamente li raccoglie. Ma perchè in questa sorte di strumenti è necessario spegnere, cioè fermare il suono, che, continuando, confonderebbe le note che seguono, al qual effetto hanno le spinette il panno nelle cime de' salterelli; essendo anche necessario in questo nuovo strumento l' ammorzarlo affatto, e subito; perciò ciascheduna delle nominate leve ha una codetta, e sopra queste codette è posto un filare, o sia un registro di salterelli, che dal loro ufizio potrebbero dirsi spegnitoij. Quando la tastura è' in quiete, toccano questi la corda con panno, che han su la cima, ed impediscono il tremolare, ch' essa farebbe al vibrarsi dell' altre sonando; ma compresso il tasto, ed alzata da esso la punta della leva, viene per conseguenza ad abbassarsi la coda, ed insieme lo spegnitojo, con lasciar libera la corda al suono, che poi s' ammorza lasciato il tasto, rialzandosi lo spegnitojo stesso a toccar la corda. Ma per conoscere più chiaramente ogni movimento di questa macchina, e l' interno suo artifizio, si prenda per mano il disegno, e si osservi a parte a parte la denominazione di esso.

for this purpose one on each side. But as it was necessary that the hammer, having struck the string, should instantly quit it, although the key was still under the finger of the player, and the hammer should be in readiness to return to its place; therefore the little tongue that gives the blow is made moveable, and so connected that it moves up and strikes firmly; but, having struck the blow, it suddenly becomes loose—that is, it moves on; and, when entirely free, it returns to its place under the hammer.

The inventor has obtained this effect by a spring of brass wire that he has fastened in the lever, and which, distending itself, strikes with the point under the tongue, and, with some force, pushes it and holds it pressed against another brass wire, which stands erect and firm on the opposite side. By this firm support to the tongue, and by the wire which is under it, also by the balance of the whole, it becomes at one time firm, and at another pliable, just as may be required. In order that the hammers, in falling back after the blow, should not strike the string a second time, and so repeat the sound, they are made to fall and rest upon little strings of silk crossed, which receive them without noise. But because, in instruments of this description, it is necessary to stop the sound of the strings, which, by continuing to vibrate, would confuse the notes that follow, for which purpose spinets have cloth at the ends of the jacks; and it being also necessary in this new instrument to check it entirely and suddenly; therefore, each of the aforesaid levers has a little tail-piece, and on these tail-pieces a register of jacks is placed, which, from its use, might be called the damper. When the keys are at rest, these touch the string with cloth, which is on the top of them, and they prevent the vibration which would be caused by the striking of other strings; but when the key is pressed, and the point of the lever is raised, the tail-piece is consequently lowered, and with it the damper, so as to leave the string free to vibrate; but this ceases so soon as the key is quitted, and the damper again rises so as to touch the string. However, in order to understand more clearly every movement of this mechanism, and its internal contrivance, let the reader examine the diagram, and observe the accompanying description.

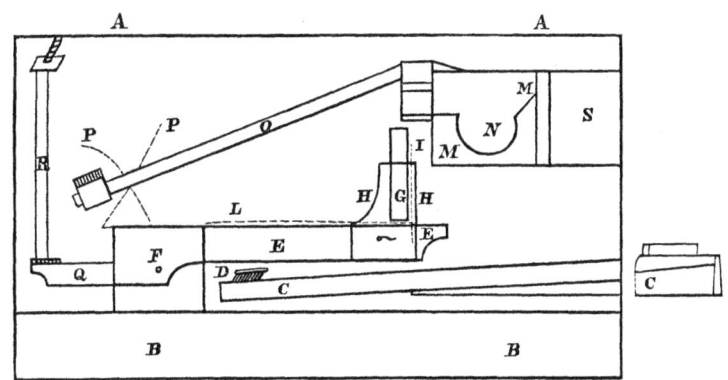

SPIEGAZIONE DEL DISEGNO.	EXPLANATION OF THE DIAGRAM.
A. Corda.	A. String.
B. Telajo, o sia pianta della tastatura.	B. Frame of the key-board.
C. Tasto ordinario, o sia prima leva, che col zoccoletto alza la seconda.	C. The key or first lever, which at its extremity raises the second lever.
D. Zoccoletto del tasto.	D. The block on the first lever by which it acts.
E. Seconda leva, alla quale sono attaccate, una per parte, le ganasce, che tengono la linguetta.	E. The second lever, on each side of which is a jawbone-shaped piece to support the little tongue or hopper.
F. Perno della seconda leva.	F. The pivot of the second lever.
G. Linguetta mobile, che alzandosi la seconda leva, urta e spinge in su il martello.	G. The moveable tongue (hopper), which, being raised by the second lever (E), forces the hammer upwards.
H. Ganasce sottili, nelle quali è impernata la linguetta.	H. The jawbone-shaped pieces between which the hopper is pivoted.
I. Filo fermo d' ottone schiacciato in cima, che tien ferma la linguetta.	I. The strong brass wire pressed together at the top, which keeps the hopper in its place.
L. Molla di fil d' ottone, che va sotto la linguetta, e la tiene spinta verso il filo fermo, che ha dietro.	L. The spring of brass wire that goes under the hopper and holds it pressed firmly against the wire which is behind it.
M. Pettine, nel quale sono sequitamente infilati tutti i martelletti.	M. The receiver, in which all the buts of the hammers rest.
N. Rotella del martello, che sta nascosta dentro al pettine.	N. The circular part of the hammers, which rests in the receiver.
O. Martello, che spinto per di sotto dalla linguetta va a percuoter la corda col dante, che ha su la cima.	O. The hammer, which, when pressed upwards by the hopper, strikes the string with the leather on its top.
P. Incrociatura di cordoncini di seta, fra' quali posano l'aste de martelli.	P. The strings of silk, crossed, on which the stems, or shanks, of the hammers rest.
Q. Coda della seconda leva, che si abbassi nell' alzarsi la punta.	Q. The end of the second lever (E), which becomes lowered by the act of striking the key.
R. Registro di salterelli, o spegnitoi, che, premuto il tasto, si abbassano, e lasciano libera la corda, tornando subito a suo luogo per fermare il suono.	R. The dampers, which are lowered when the key is touched, leaving the string free to vibrate, and then returning to their places, stop the sound.
S. Regolo pieno per fortezza del pettine.	S. Part of the frame to strengthen the receiver.

Dopo di tutto questo è da avvertire, che il páncone, dove si piantano i bischeri, o pirdi di ferro, che tengono le corde, dove negli altri gravecembali è sotto le corde stesse, qui è sopra, e i bischeri passano, e le corde vi si attaccano per di sotto, essendovi bisogno di più sito nel basso, affinchè v'entri tutta la macchina della tastatura. Le corde sono più grosse delle ordinarie, e perchè il peso non nocesse al fondo, non sono raccomadate ad esso, ma alquanto più alto. In tutti i contatti, che vale a dire in tutti i luoghi, dove si potrebbe generar rumore, è impedito con cuojo, o con panno; specialmente ne' fori, dove passano perni, è posto ha per tutto con *singolar maestri* del dante, e il perno passa per esso. Quest' invenzione è stata dall' artefice ridotta ad effetto anche in altra forma, avendo fatto un altro gravecembalo più col piano e forte, con differente, e alquanto più facile struttura, ma nondimeno è stata più applaudita la prima.

Essendo questo ingegnoso uomo eccellente anche nel lavorare gravecembali ordinari, merita di notarsi, com' egli non sente coi moderni artefici, chi per lo più gli fabbricano non solo senza rosa, ma ancora senza sfogo alcuno in tutto il casso. Non già ch' egli creda necessario un sì gran foro, come erano le rose fattevi dagli antichi, nè che stimi opportuno il forargli in quel sito, ch' è sì esposto a ricever la polvere, ma suol' egli farvi due piccoli buchi nella fronte, o sia nel chiudimento davanti, che restano occulti, e difesi; ed afferma esser necessario in alcuna parte dello strumento un tale sfogatojo, perchè nel sonare il fondo deve muoversi, e cedere; e chi il faccia, si conosce dal tremare che farà ciò che vi porrai sopra, quando altri suona; ma se il corpo non avrà foro alcuno, non potendo l' aria ch' è dentro cedere e uscire, ma standosi dura e forte, il fondo non si muove, e quindi il suono ne viene alquanto ottuso, e breve, e non risonante. Là dove fattovi un buco, vedrai tosto dar più il fondo, e restar la corda più alta, e sentirai maggior voce, e accostando le dita al predetto foro, quando altri suona, sentirai far vento, e uscirne l'aria. A questo proposito non vogliamo lasciar di dire, che ricavandosi, come è noto, bellissimi lumi per la Filosofia naturale dall' indagare le affezioni, e gli effetti dell' aria, e del moto; un fonte grandissimo, benchè finora affatto sconosciuto, di scoprimenti, e di cognizioni intorno a ciò esser potrebbe l'osservar sottilmente le diverse, e mirabili operazioni dell' aria impulsa negli strumenti musicali; esaminando la fab-

After this, it is to be observed that the plank in which the iron pins are fixed that hold the strings, and which, in harpsichords, is under the strings, is above in this, and the pins come through it, and the strings are attached to them below, there being more need of space in the bass to admit the whole of the mechanism of the key action. The strings are thicker than usual, and, in order that their tension may not injure the bottom, they are not trusted to this, but fixed somewhat higher. In all points of contact, or wherever any rattle might occur, it is prevented by leather and by cloth, especially in the holes through which the centres pass, there is placed everywhere [con singolar maestri del dante?], and the centre passes through it. This invention has also been effected in another form, the inventor having made another harpsichord, with the piano and forte, in a different and somewhat more simple shape; but, nevertheless, the first has been more approved.

This ingenious man, being also excellent in the manufacture of ordinary harpsichords, deserves notice, because he does not agree with the modern makers, who, for the most part, manufacture them not only without a *rose* in the centre, but even without any other escape for the sound throughout the case. Not that he thinks it necessary to make the hole so large as the roses of ancient manufacturers, nor does he think it desirable to make the opening in that part of the instrument, because it is exposed to dust; but he makes two small apertures in the front, so that when the instrument is closed, they are concealed and protected from it. He asserts that such apertures are necessary in some part of the instrument, because, when played on, the sounding-board ought to vibrate; and that it does so, is known by the trembling of anything you may place upon it when any one plays: but, if there were no opening, the air, not having an escape, could not yield, but would remain fixed; and hence the sound would be somewhat obtuse and short, instead of resonant. When, however, a hole is made, you will soon see the sounding-board give more, and the string remain higher, and you will hear a stronger (fuller) tone; and by placing the finger close to the aforesaid opening, you may feel the vibration and the exit of the air. I may here remark that, profiting by the investigations of natural philosophy into the inclinations and effects of air and motion, a great

brica loro, e riflettando da che nasca in essi la perfezione, o 'l difetto, e da che se ne alteri la costituzione; come, a cagion d'esempio, la variazion del suono, che succede negli strumenti, che hanno l'anima, quai son quelli da arco, se questa un pocolino si muove di sito; divenendone tosto l'una corda più sonora, al'altra più ottusa; l'alterazione, e la diversità delle armonie, che ricevono gli strumenti dalle diverse misure, e singolarmente i gravecembali dall' essere il loro fondo alquanto più grosso, e alquanto più sottile, e così di mill' altre considerazioni. Non è anche da tralasciare, che tenendosi universalmente, che siano sempre imperfetti i gravecembali nuovi, e che acquistino perfezione solamente col lungo tempo; pretende questo artefice, che si possa lavorargli in modo, che rendano subito sonora voce non meno degli strumenti vecchi. Afferma egli, che il non risonar bene de' nuovi nasca principalmente dalla virtù elastica, che per qualche tempo conservano la sponda incurvata, ed il ponte; perchè, finchè questi fanno forza sul fondo per restituirsi, la voce non vien perfetta: che però se questa virtù elastica sarà loro tolta interamente prima di porgli in opera, verrà subito a levarsi questo difetto, com' egli in pratica esperimenta. Contribuirà ancóra la buona qualità del legno; onde il Pesaro si cominciò a servisi de' cassoni vecchi, che trovavo sopra i granai di Venezia, e di Padova, e ch' erano per lo più di cipresso di Candia, o di Cipro.

Non sarà qui discaro agli amatori della musica, che alcuna cosa si dica anche d'un altro raro gravecembalo, che si trova pure in Firenze in mano del Sig. Casini, Maestro lodatissimo di Cappella. Ha questo cinque tastami, cioè cinque interi ordini di tasti, l'uno sopra l'altro gradatamente; e si può però dire strumento perfetto, essendovi divisa ogni voce ne' suoi cinque quinti; onde, che si può in esso far la circolazione, e scorrere per tutti i tuoni senza urtare in dissonanza alcuna, e trovando sempre tutti gli accompagnamenti perfetti, come fa sentire il suo posseditore, che lo ricerca eccellentemente. Gli ordinari gravecembali, come tutti gli strumenti, che hanno tasti, sono molto imperfetti, a cagione, che non essendo le voci divise nelle sue parti, molte corde vi sono, che non hanno quinta giusta, e bisogna serversi degli stessi tasti per diesis, e per b molli; per ischivare in parte il quale errore alcune vecchie spinette si vedono, massimamente dell' Undeo, con alcuni de' neri tagliati, e divisi in due, del che non comprendono

amount of knowledge might be gained by closely observing the various and wonderful effects on air set in motion by musical instruments; by examining the form of its vibrations, and reflecting whence arises the perfection or imperfection of their sounds, and how to alter them; as, for instance, the variations of sound in instruments capable of expression, such as those played with a bow, which, if the position be slightly changed, becomes in one place sonorous, and in another obtuse; also, the alteration and diversity of sound in different measurements, and especially in harpsicords, from the bottom of the case being thicker or thinner, and from many other considerations. It must not be forgotten that, the universal opinion being that new harpsichords are always imperfect, and that they acquire perfection only by age, this manufacturer pretends that he can make them in such a manner as to be immediately as sonorous as old instruments. He asserts that the want of vibration in new instruments arises principally from the elasticity of the wood, that for some time keeps the sides and the bridge uninfluenced by pressure, and that, until they press upon the frame, the sound remains imperfect; that if this elasticity be entirely taken from them before employing them in the manufacture, this defect will immediately be removed, as he finds by experience. The good quality of the wood will also contribute; wherefore Pesaro made use of old chests that he found in the granaries of Venice and Padua, which were for the most part of cypress wood from Candia and Cyprus.

It will not be here disagreeable to lovers of music to hear something of another rare harpsichord, which is in Florence, in the hands of Signor Casini, a most esteemed Maestro di Cappella. This has five key-boards—that is, five entire sets of keys, one above the other, and which may be called a perfect instrument, the five fifths in every octave being tuned perfect (instead of only one, as then the custom), so that you may modulate and run through all the keys without any dissonance, and always finding the accompaniment perfect, as may be experienced by hearing the possessor play upon it, who displays it to perfection. Ordinary harpsichords, like all instruments with fingerboards, are very imperfect; because, the tuning not being equal in all keys, there are many keys that have not a perfectly tuned fifth, and we are obliged to employ the same key for a sharp and for a flat; to avoid which defect, there

la cagione molti professori; ed è veramente, perchè dovendo per modo d' esempio dal diesis di Ge sol-re-ut, al b molle A la-mi-rè corrervi almeno un quinto di voce di differenza, v' è necessità di due corde. Ma nasce dall' imperfezione accennata, che un gravecembalo, o tiorba non si può interamente accordare con un violino, benchè sonando in concerto l'orecchio non se n' avvegga; e ne nasce parimente, che ne i più de' neri non si compone, e solo vi si va con riserva, e da alcuni Maestri, solamente quando alla parola ben conviene il falso, e 'l disgustoso della voce. Questa imperfezione degli strumenti, che hanno tasti cagiona altresì, che nell' udir sonare s' accorgeremo molte volte, quando il componimento è spostato, come parla il dialetto Fiorentino, o come dice la lingua comune, trasportato; perchè venendo a cadere in quelle corde, che non hanno quinta, la falsità del suono offende l' orecchio. Non così avverrà nel violino, che non avendo tasti, può trovar tutto a suo luogo, e in qual si sia tuono far sentir le voci perfette. Il gravecembalo adunque, di qui parliamo, oltre al diletto del perfetto suono, può esser utile a molte speculazioni su la teorica della musica; nè si credesse che troppo difficile fosse la sua accordatura, mentre anzi è più facile, attesochè procede sempre per quinte perfette; là dove ne gli strumenti ordinari, bisogna aver attenzione di far che cali la quinta, che crescano la quarta, e la terza maggiore, con più altre avvertenze.

are some old spinets, chiefly those of Undeo, with some of the black keys divided down the middle, the reason for which many professors do not understand; and it is truly because there being the fifth of a note difference between G sharp and A flat, there is a necessity for two strings.

However, owing to the before-named imperfection, a harpsichord or a theorbo lute cannot be tuned perfectly like a violin; although, when used in concert, the ear does not detect the imperfection; and hence it arises that there are no compositions in keys that require a great number of sharps or flats, that they are used sparingly, and, by some masters, only when an imperfect sound suits the expression of the words, or harshness is to be expressed by the voice. This imperfection in instruments that have finger-boards is also often perceptible, when the accompaniment is transposed; because, by changing into keys that have ill-tuned fifths, the imperfections of sound offend the ear. It will not so happen with the violin; because, not having a finger-board, the notes may be sounded in the right position, and the sound be perfect in any key. The above-named harpsichord, therefore, besides possessing the charm of perfect intonation, may be useful in many experiments on the theory of music; nor should it be supposed that its tuning is too difficult, for it is really more easy, in consequence of the fifths being tuned perfect; whilst, in the ordinary instruments, it is necessary to pay attention to the flattening of the fifths and the sharpening of the fourths and major thirds, as well as to other things.

Marius,* the French manufacturer, the next competitor for the invention of the pianoforte, submitted his instruments for examination to the Académie des Sciences in the month of February, 1716. In the *Recueil des Instruments et Machines approuvées par l'Académie Royale des Sciences*, published by this learned Society, under the year 1716, we find, in Nos. 172, 173, and 174, engraved plans of Marius's four *clavecins à maillets*, with a description of the instruments. This artist had already been known to the public, in 1700, by his harpsichords in three pieces, so constructed as to be able to shut into each other for convenience in travelling.

---

* Fétis has, singularly enough, omitted the name of this maker in his *Biographie Universelle des Musiciens*, although he refers to it under the article CRISTOFORI. The last edition of the *Encyclopædia Britannica*, in a most wretched article upon the pianoforte, speaks of Cristofali and Schröter, but makes no mention of Marius. It is much to be lamented that greater care is not bestowed upon works intended for reference.

The *clavecins à maillets* evinced considerable invention and ability. They consisted of four instruments, one in the form of the common harpsichord; another with a mechanical contrivance above the strings; the third, vertical; and the fourth, in which both jacks and hammers were used. The first differed from the clavichord only in this, that each tone of the instrument was furnished with three strings, and that the hammers, the weight of which restored the key to its position after the string had been struck, were faced with leather for the purpose of softening the tone. As for the rest, the hammer, which stood perpendicularly upon the key, was carried directly to the string by the key itself, without any intermediary aid, and without an escape-movement. In the second instrument, he approached still nearer to the desired result, by arranging the hammers in such a manner that they swung in a kind of stirrup. By this means they were independent of the keys, which, meeting them in their course, impelled them against the string; and the hammer fell after striking the string, even though the performer kept his finger upon the key. By different combinations, Marius had rendered his mechanism fit to be placed either above or below the strings. His third *clavecin à maillets* was a vertical one, in which the key impelled a rod, furnished with the hammer, directly upon the string. His last invention, as we have stated, united the two principals of the jack and the hammer.

The following are Marius's own descriptions and drawings from the *Machines et Inventions approuvées par l'Académie Royale des Sciences, depuis son etablissement jusqu'à present ; avec leur Description.* Tome Troisième, à Paris, 1735, 4to.

CLAVECIN À MAILLETS.	HARPSICHORD WITH HAMMERS.
INVENTÉ PAR M. MARIUS.	INVENTED BY M. MARIUS.

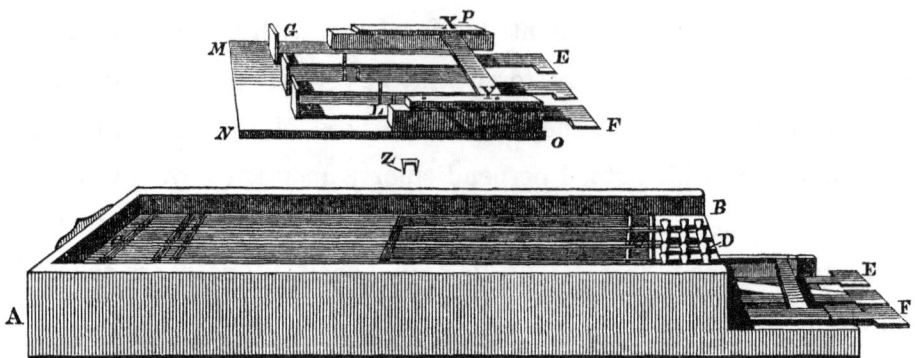

Cette methode de tirer le son du clavecin, consiste à substituer des maillets à la place des sautereaux. Le corps du clavecin est ici representé par la caisse A B ; cette caisse porte un fonds à la moitié de sa hauteur : c'est sur ce fonds que sont tendues des cordes fixées par des pointes à l'extrémité c, and bandés par des vis à l'extremité D. Là les côtés de la caisse sont coupés pour recevoir dans le fond une petite boëte M N O P, qui contient le clavier ; I O, L P, sont des bords à coulisse dans lesquels on fait entrer une barre X Y, sous laquelle se trouve le centre de mouvement des touches E F ; ces touches prolongées en dedans de la caisse, portent à l'endroit G des maillets qui répondent aux rangées de cordes posées sur la caisse. L'on voit à l'inspection de cette figure que les maillets peauvent être de différente épaisseur et doivent toujours être posées perpendiculairement aux extrémités des touches qui doivent les élever. A l'endroit I L est une rangée des chevilles fixées à chaque côté des touches, et qui servent à les tenir toujours dans leur direction verticale ; c'est autour d'un étrier tel que z que chaque touche peut s'élever et s'abaisser. On observera de tenir le maillet plus pésant que le reste de la touche, afin qu'il puisse descendre plus promptement après le choc. L'on voit le chemin et le mouvement que chaque maillet fait par la troisiéme touche du clavier de la première figure en allant de F vers E ; le maillet de cette touche est représenté frappant les cordes qui lui répondent.

This method of producing the sound from the harpsichord consists in substituting hammers for jacks. The body of the harpsichord is here represented by the case A B ; this case has a sounding-board in its centre ; it is on this sounding-board that the strings are stretched, fixed by points to the extremity c, and by screws to the extremity D. The sides of the case are cut to receive in the bottom a small box M N O P, which contains the key-board ; I O L P are the edges with grooves, in which is placed a bar, X Y, under which is placed the centre movement of the keys, E F ; these keys are prolonged beyond the case, having at the spot G hammers corresponding with the rows of strings placed in the case. On inspecting the diagram, we observe that the hammers are of different thicknesses, placed perpendicularly to the ends of the keys which lift them up. At the spot I L, is a row of pegs fixed to each side of the keys, and which serve to hold them in their vertical direction ; it is around a stirrup such as z that each key should rise and fall. Care must be taken that the hammer is heavier than the rest of the key, in order that it may descend more promptly after having struck the string. The direction and movement each hammer makes, is seen by the third key of the key-board (going from F towards E) in the above diagram : the hammer of this key is represented striking the string to which it belongs.

L'on croit que par des clavecins de cette construction, l'on pourra tirer des sons plus ou moins aigus en employant des forces connuës sur les touches suivant les différens tons et les différentes mésures indiquées par les pièces que l'on voudra exécuter.

Voici sur cette théorie différentes manières d'employer les maillets et de leur donner toutes les positions possibles.

It is thought that on harpsichords of this construction sounds more or less sharp (or acute) can be produced, even by employing the usual power on the finger-board according to the different keys and the different marks of time indicated on the pieces we wish to perform.

According to this theory, there are different modes of employing the hammers, and of giving them all possible positions.

AUTRE CLAVECIN À MAILLETS.
INVENTÉ PAR M. MARIUS.

ANOTHER HARPSICHORD WITH HAMMERS.
INVENTED BY M. MARIUS.

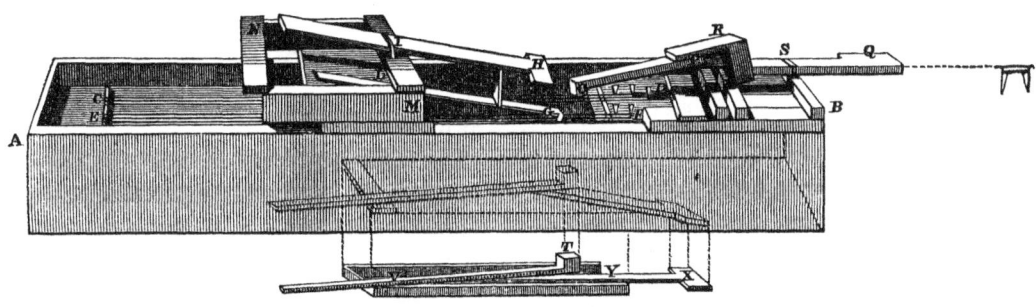

A B est une caisse qui représente le clavecin ; sur cette caisse sont deux rangs de cordes C D, E F. Les maillets sont ici représentés dans différentes positions, c'est-à-dire, placés pour tirer le son en dessus, et une en-dessous ; deux manières de le tirer en-dessus, et une en-dessous. Par exemple, le maillet G est en-dessus, et frappe sur la corde au moyen de la touche H mobile au point I ; le petit montant K est attaché à la touche H, et sert à faire frapper le marteau G, ce marteau étant attaché à l'endroit L par un petit étrier de fer, autour duquel il se meut librement. L'on peut faire regner le long du clavecin un semblable clavier, posé au-delà de ses bords sur une caisse transversale telle que M N, sur le devant de laquelle seront posés tous les maillets et toutes les touches.

Le maillet O frappe sur le rang de cordes D C ; ce maillet est aussi attaché en P par un étrier W semblable aux autres, autour duquel il se peut mouvoir, de même que la touche Q mobile au point S. Lorsque l'on pese sur la touche Q, l'extrémité R du maillet se leve, le maillet O frappe sur les cordes et en tire le son. Il faudra observer

A B is the case which represents the harpsichord ; on this case are two rows of strings C D, E F. The hammers are here shown in different positions—that is to say, some to strike down and one to strike up. For example, the hammer G is above and strikes on the string by means of the key H, which is moveable at the point I ; the small upright K is attached to the key H, and causes the hammer G to strike ; the hammer being attached to the spot L by a small band of iron, around which it moves freely. All the keys of the harpsichord may be similarly arranged on a key-board, such as M N, on the front of which the hammers and all the keys can be placed.

The hammer O strikes on the row of strings D C ; this hammer is also attached at P by a band, W, similar to the others, around which it can move, the same as the key Q is moveable at the point S. When we strike the key Q, the extremity of the hammer R rises ; the hammer O strikes the strings, and produces the sound. It must be ob-

dans la construction d'un semblable instrument, que toutes les queues des maillets soient plus pesantes que les têtes, afin que le maillet après avoir frappé, se relève de lui même et ne laisse point de tons faux.

La deuxième figure est pour faire voir comment on peut établir un clavier, à maillets pour tirer le son en-dessous. Le maillet T est mobile au point v, et la touche x mobile en Y : en ce cas il faut que la tête T du maillet soit plus pesante que la queue.

served, in the construction of such an instrument, that all the buts of the hammers are heavier than the heads, in order that the hammer, after having struck the string, may rise of itself, and leave no false tones.

The second diagram is to show how a key-board can be made with hammers to produce the sound from below. The hammer T is moveable at the point v, and the key x is moveable at Y : in this case it is necessary that the head of the hammer T should be heavier than the but.

TROISIÈME CLAVECIN À MAILLETS.

INVENTÉ PAR M. MARIUS.

THIRD HARPSICHORD WITH HAMMERS.

INVENTED BY M. MARIUS.

Ce qu'il y à de particulier dans ce clavecin est, que le sautereau comme A B porte une cheville C qui frappe les cordes en-dessous, de même que les maillets que l'on a décrits précédemment. A quelque endroit autour de la cheville est un morceau d'étoffe pour étouffer le son, comme on le pratique aux autres clavecins.

L'extremité A du sautereau est posée sur le bout de la touche E F G, dont le centre de mouvement est en F. Il

This harpsichord differs from the others, inasmuch that the jack A B has a peg, C, which strikes the strings underneath, in the same manner as the hammers which we have described in the preceding inventions. At a particular spot round the peg, is a piece of stuff to stop the sound, as in other harpsichords.

The extremity A of the jack is placed on the end of the key E F G, of which the centre of movement is at F.

est necessaire que ce centre soit le plus près qui'l sera possible de l'extrémité G, afin que le sautereau retombe avec plus de promptitude après avoir frappé les cordes ; par ce moyen on aura un son plus net. L'on voit par entre eux ces sortes de sautereaux.

L'avantage d'un clavecin construit de sautereaux semblables est, que la sujétion de les remplumer, se trouve supprimée.

It is necessary that the centre should be as near as possible to the extremity G, in order that the jack should fall with promptitude after having struck the strings : by this means a clearer tone will be produced. The jacks may be observed in the interior of the instrument.

The advantage of a harpsichord constructed upon this principle is that the jacks will not require *re-quilling*.

QUATRIÈME CLAVECIN À MAILLETS ET A SAUTEREAUX.

INVENTÉ PAR M. MARIUS.

FOURTH HARPSICHORD WITH HAMMERS AND JACKS.

INVENTED BY M. MARIUS.

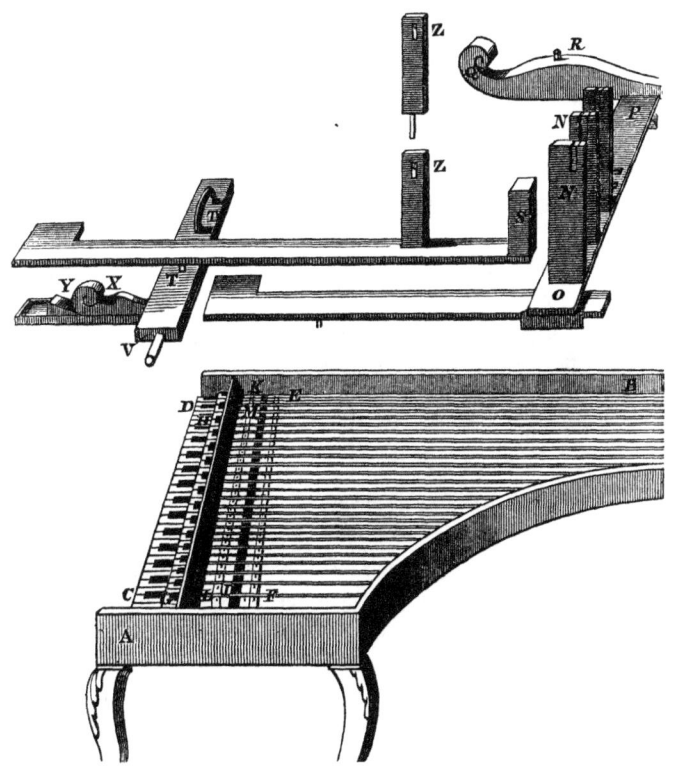

Après que M. Marius eut trouvé les maillets, il substitua à la place des sautereaux en donnant à ces maillets differentes positions, comme il vient d'être dit sur les planches précédents : il trouva aussi le moyen de placer deux jeux dans un seul clavecin, en y employant les maillets et les sautereaux, et faisant neanmoins ces deux

AFTER M. Marius had discovered the hammers, he substituted them in the place of the jacks, by giving to these hammers different positions, as shown in the preceding plate. He discovered also the means of placing two actions in a single harpsichord, by employing both hammers and jacks, and making, nevertheless, these two

jeux tout-à-fait independans l'un de l'autre; c'est-a-dire, que les maillets peuvent servir seuls, de même que les sautereaux, et tous les deux à la fois quand on le veut; ce qui s'execute en cette sorte.

A B est un corps de clavecin ordinaire; le clavier inférieur C D à rapport a la rangée de sautereaux E F, et le clavier supérieur G H fait joüer la rangée de maillets J K; la troisiéme rangée, L M, contient des espèces de sautereaux fixés sur les touches des mêmes maillets, et garnis de drap, afin d'étouffer le son après que le maillet a frappé. Les sautereaux N N passent au travers d'une planche O P posée sur des tasseaux à coulisses, dans lesquelles cette planche peut se mouvoir horisontalement suivant la largeur du clavecin, au moyen de la pièce P Q mobile au point R, de manière qu'en poussant cette pièce par son extrémité Q, l'on fait avancer les sautereaux, qui pour lors répondent au-dessous des cordes, et sont en état d'en tirer le son; et au contraire lorsque l'on ne voudra plus des sautereaux, on tirera à soi la pièce, les touches sur lesquelles elles posent sont assez larges pour leur permettre ce mouvement. Voici quel est le mouvement des maillets, pour s'en servir, et pour les supprimer.

Le maillet S est fixé sur la touche qui fait la bascule sur un étrier T fixé sur une traverse W, aux extrémités de laquelle sont des tourillons qui lui permettent de tourner; à cette traverse l'on fixe une pièce X qui s'étend à chaque côté du clavier, et sous laquelle on fait couler un coin Y pour élever ou abaisser tous les maillets ensemble; c'est-à-dire, que si on laisse la traverse dans son état naturel, les maillets toucheront les cordes, et lorsque l'on voudra les supprimer, on poussera le coin Y sous la pièce X, et pour lors les maillets braisseront et ne toucheront plus aux cordes. Le sautereau Z est posé sur la touche à quelque distance du maillet; ce sautereau doit être construit, et placé de manière qu' à l'instant du coup, il soit prêt à étouffer le son.

actions independent of each other; that is to say, the hammers could be used alone, or the jacks alone, or both together, at pleasure, which is done in this way.

A B is the body of the ordinary harpsichord; the lower key-board, C D, belongs to the row of jacks E F, and the one above, G H, moves the row of hammers J K; the third row, L M, contains a kind of jack fixed on the keys of the same hammers, and covered with cloth in order to check the sound after the hammers have struck the strings. The jacks N N pass across a plank, O P, placed on brackets with grooves, in which this plank can move horizontally (according to the size of the harpsichord), by means of the piece P Q moveable at the point K, in such a manner that, in moving this piece by its extremity, Q, the jacks are made to advance, and are thereby prepared underneath the strings, and in a state to produce the sound. When you do not require to use the jacks, draw towards you the *piece;* the keys on which they rest are large enough to allow this movement. Hence the movement of the hammers, and the mode of suppressing them.

The hammer S is fixed on the key which see-saws on a stirrup, T, fixed on a cross piece, W, at the extremities of which are pivots which allow it to turn; to this cross piece is fixed a piece, X, which reaches to each side of the key-board, and under which runs a wedge, Y, to raise or lower all the hammers together; that is to say, if the cross-piece is left in its natural state, the hammers will touch the strings, and when you wish not to use them, you push the wedge Y under the piece X, and by that means the hammers will be lowered so as not to touch the strings. The jack Z is placed on the key at some distance from the hammer; this jack should be constructed and fixed in such a manner that, the instant the blow is struck, it should be ready to damp the sound.

The remaining claimant to the invention of the pianoforte is Christopher Gottlieb Schröter. This eminent artist was born August 10, 1699, at Hohenstein, on the frontiers of Bohemia. His father, an organist and professor of music, taught him the rudiments of the science, in which he progressed so rapidly, that at the age of seven he was admitted into the Chapel Royal of Dresden. Under the able tuition of Schmidt the Chapel Master, and Behnisch the theorist, he completed his musical education. According to the wish of his mother, young Schröter next studied theology at Leipzig; but this not suiting the bent of his inclination, he took advantage of her death and returned to the study of music. Once more visiting Dresden, he became acquainted with the celebrated composer, Antonio Lotti, in whose service he accepted the post of secretary. In transcribing and studying the works of the most celebrated Italian composers, Schröter greatly improved his style and knowledge of music. Lotti returned to Italy in 1719, when the subject of our notice received the offer to accompany a German nobleman to England; this opened new fields of observation to our young aspirant, and he accordingly accepted it, returning to Dresden in 1724. He now determined to continue his researches into the science of music, which he had commenced under the able direction of Schmidt and Behnisch; and accordingly entered the University of Jena, where he completed his first work on the theory of music, which was well received by his professional brethren. After remaining about two years in that city, he obtained, without solicitation, the post of organist to the principal church at Minden; which appointment he resigned, in 1732, for that of " chief organist " at Nordhausen in Saxony. He died in the latter city, November, 1782, at the age of eighty-three.

Whilst a pupil of the School at the Holy Cross at Dresden, in 1717, Schröter is said to have constructed a model of a pianoforte, which was afterwards exhibited to the Court at Dresden. Although the Elector of Saxony then testified his approbation of the invention, Schröter received neither honour nor reward, and the new instrument remained in abeyance. Many years afterwards, in a letter, dated " Nordhausen, 22 September, 1738," printed in Lorenzo Mizler's *Musikalische Bibliothek*, vol. iii, p. 464, Leipzig, 1752, writing upon the mathematics of music, and laying down " rules on temperament for the use of organ builders and instrument makers who are ignorant of mathematics," he thus alludes to his invention: " Indeed some of these artists, who for several years have understood *one of my inventions*, have given it out as their own. In 1717, I constructed, at Dresden, after much consideration, the model of a new clavier with *hammers*, partly with, partly without springs, upon which one at pleasure might play *loudly* or *softly*."*

According to the late Professor Fischoff, the mechanism of Schröter's invention was simple. The hammer consisted of a lever of about three inches and a half in length, moving on a pivot with a leather head; the lever rested near the pivot on a pin with a leather head, screwed into the further end of the finger key; and the pin was of such a length that, when the key was slowly pressed down, the face of the hammer came within about a quarter of an inch of the string; but, when the key was smartly struck, the hammer, by the rapid motion communicated, was thrown up to give the string a blow, and, instantly recoiling, fell on the leather head of the pin and left the string free to vibrate.

In another plan of Schröter's—for it seems he constructed two models—the hammers were placed *over* the strings; but the inventor himself considered this device impracticable, "because the metal springs which should bring back the hammer after striking, did not promise to be durable."

It is singular that these three ingenious men, Cristofali, Marius, and Schröter, should have conceived the same idea, within a few years of each other, and without any apparent communication or collision. But the priority of invention is certainly due to the Italian maker, whose claims are now fully established.

The object of centuries was at length accomplished. The quill, pig's bristle, thorn, ivory tongue, leathern tongue, &c. were soon to be banished. A small hammer

---

* H. C. Koch, in his *Musikalisches Lexikon*, says, "the pianoforte was invented by J. C. Schröder, of Dresden, in Saxony, in the year 1717. He had a model made of this invention, and presented it to the Court of Dresden for inspection. The hammers recoiled, and were covered with leather. Some time after, Mr. G. Silbermann, a musical instrument maker, began to manufacture pianos, and succeeded in bringing them to a tolerable degree of perfection. It has been questioned, however, whether Schröder, or B. Cristofali, an instrument maker of Florence, had the first idea of it; but the most authentic accounts establish indisputably the claim of Schröder to this ingenious invention." Why did not this learned writer ascertain the *true* date of the *Giornale de' Litterati d' Italia?*

In Thalberg's "Remarks upon the Pianofortes," in the Great Industrial Exhibition of 1851, printed in the *Reports of the Juries*, p. 326, the name of Schröter is altogether omitted in the great pianoforte-player's brief historical sketch.

was made to strike the string, and evoke a clear, precise, and delicate tone, unheard before. The "scratch with a sound at the end of it" was doomed to a lingering fate. The harpsichord had been changed into an instrument of *percussion*, and it only remained for later manufacturers to perfect, extend, and popularize the now "worldwide" pianoforte.

CHAPTER VIII.

THE PROGRESS OF THE PIANOFORTE ON THE CONTINENT.

The pianoforte, upon its first introduction, was not successful. Nor can we wonder at this; the public is always slow at receiving innovations; "besides," as M. Fétis remarks, "the resources of the new instrument were not understood, and the keys required a greater delicacy of treatment than those of the harpsichord; in a word, it became necessary for musicians and amateurs to change their style of playing, a circumstance, of itself, sufficient to retard the success of the pianoforte."

Of Cristofali and Marius we hear nothing; their inventions seem to have been treated with neglect or indifference. Schröter was better appreciated by his fellow countrymen. Silbermann of Strasburg, Späett of Dresden, and Stein of Augsberg, followed up his discoveries; and it is to these makers that Schröter alludes, in the passage we have quoted from Mizler's *Musikalische Bibliothek*.

Godfrey Silbermann was born at Frauenstein, in Saxony, in 1684. He is sometimes called Silbermann of Freyberg, sometimes Silbermann of Strasburg; the first, from his having built the organ of Freyberg Cathedral; the second, from his having learnt his profession, and chiefly lived, in the city of Strasburg. Whether this ingenious artist had any knowledge of the inventions of Cristofali, Marius, or Schröter, we have not the means of ascertaining; certain it is that he was one of the *earliest* makers of pianos, and the *invention* is generally attributed to him throughout Germany.

Silbermann constructed two pianofortes, and submitted them for approval to the great Sebastian Bach, who is recorded to have highly praised them as ingenious pieces of mechanism, but complained of their feebleness of tone, especially in the upper octaves. Struck with the justness of this remark, Silbermann withdrew his instruments until he had found the means of remedying this serious defect. After repeated essays, and considerable expense, he was enabled to present a new instrument to Bach, who declared that *it was without fault.* From this moment the fame of Silbermann extended throughout Germany, and the first step in the *progress* of the pianoforte was accomplished.*

We must relate Forkel's account of Bach's visit to Frederick the Great, about this period, as an important event in connection with the history of the pianoforte:

"The reputation of the all-surpassing skill of John Sebastian Bach was at this time so extended, that the King often heard it mentioned and praised. This made him curious to hear so great an artist. At first he distantly hinted to his son (Charles Philip Emanuel, at that time in the service of Frederick) his wish that his father would one day come to Potsdam. But, by degrees, he began to ask him directly why his father did not come? The son could not avoid acquainting his father with these expressions of the King's; at first, however, he could not pay any attention to them, because he was generally too much overwhelmed with business. But the King's expressions being repeated in several of his son's letters, he at length, in 1747, prepared to take this journey, in company with his eldest son, William Friedemann. At this time the King had every evening a private concert, in which he himself generally performed some concertos on the flute. One evening, just as he was getting his flute ready, and his musicians were assembled, an officer brought him the list of the strangers who had arrived. With his flute in his hand he ran over the list, but immediately turned to the assembled musicians, and said, with a kind of agitation,

---

* "The pianoforte was scarcely known in the time of Bach; and from the style of his compositions, it is evident that they were the product of the harpsichord, an instrument of very limited powers; the boldest effects of which were produced by sprinkling the chords in *arpeggio*, which occasioned a disagreeable jingling. The early sonatas of Haydn also bear marks of the influence of this instrument, and possess nothing of the expression of his later works. The invention of the pianoforte has formed an era in the art. It has been the means of developing the sublimest ideas of the composer, and the delicacy of its touch has enabled him to give the lightest shades, as well as the boldest strokes of musical expression. It is the only instrument that will represent the effects of a full orchestra; and since its mechanism has been improved. Beethoven has displayed its powers in a way not contemplated even by Haydn himself." *Lives of Haydn and Mozart,* 8vo. 1817, Note, p. 106.

'Gentlemen, old Bach is come.' The flute was now laid aside; and old Bach, who had alighted at his son's lodgings, was immediately summoned to the palace. William Friedemann, who accompanied his father, told me this story, and I must say that I still think with pleasure on the manner in which he related it. At that time it was the fashion to make rather prolix compliments. The first appearance of J. S. Bach before so great a king, who did not even give him time to change his travelling dress for a black chanter's gown, must necessarily be attended with many apologies. I will not here dwell on those apologies, but merely observe, that in William Friedemann's mouth they made a formal dialogue between the King and the apologist. But what is more important than this, is that the King gave up his concert for this evening, and invited Bach, then already called old Bach, to try his *fortepianos made by Silbermann*, which stood in several rooms of the palace. The musicians went with him from room to room, and Bach was invited every where to try and to play unpremeditated compositions. After he had gone on for some time, he asked the King to give him a subject for a fugue, in order to execute it immediately without any preparation. The King admired the learned manner in which his subject was thus executed extempore; and probably to see how far such art could be carried, expressed a wish to hear a fugue with six obligato parts. But as it is not every subject that is fit for such full harmony, Bach chose one himself, and immediately executed it to the astonishment of all present, in the same magnificent and learned manner as he had done that of the King. His majesty desired also to hear his performance on the organ. The next day, therefore, Bach was taken to all the organs in Potsdam, as he had before been to Silbermann's *fortepianos*. After his return to Leipsig, he composed the subject which he had received from the King, in three and six parts, added several artificial passages in strict canon to it, and had it engraved, under the title of *Musikalisches Opfer* (Musical Offering), and dedicated it to the inventor."

In the same interesting *Life of J. S. Bach*, is another passage of importance to our subject. After informing us that Bach used " two *clavichords* and the pedal, or a *harpsichord* with two sets of keys, provided with a pedal," the writer adds: " He liked best to play upon the clavichord; the harpsichord, though certainly susceptible of a very great variety of expression, had not soul enough for him; and the *piano* was in his life-time too much in its infancy, and still much too coarse to satisfy him. He therefore considered the *clavichord* as the best instrument for study, and, in general, for private musical entertainment. He found it the most convenient for the expression of his most refined thoughts, and did not believe it possible to produce from any harpsichord, or *pianoforte*, such a variety in the gradations of tone as on this instrument, which is, indeed, poor in tone, but on a small scale extremely flexible. Nobody could adjust the quill-plectrums of his harpsichord to his satisfaction; he always did it himself. He also tuned both his harpsichord and *clavichord* himself, and was so practised in the operation, that it never cost him above a quarter of an hour. But then, when he played from his fancy, all the twenty-four modes were in his power; he did with them what he pleased. He combined the most remote as easily and as naturally together as the nearest; the hearer believed he had only modulated within the compass of a single mode. He knew nothing of harshness in modulation; his transitions in the chromatic scale were as soft and flowing as if he had wholly confined himself to the diatonic scale. His *Chromatic* Fantasia, which is now published, may prove what I here state."

John Andrew Stein, of Augsburg, by the silvery and brilliant tone which he gave his pianos, tended greatly to increase the popularity of the new instrument. He was born at Heidelstein in 1728, and was a pupil of Silbermann's. In 1758, he visited Paris, where he worked for many years, and brought his abilities as a maker of pianos to perfection.* We have already spoken of him as a celebrated maker of harpsichords (see p. 82, *ante*). He died at his native city, Augsburg, February 22, 1792. In the latter years of his life, his factory was directed by his son Andrew, and his daughter Nanette, afterwards married to Streicher of Vienna.

Mozart frequently alludes to Stein, in his very graphic and interesting letters. In one, dated "Augsburgh, October 14th, 1777," he says, "I had the honor of performing for three quarters of an hour on a good piano by Stein. I played several fantasias; and, in fine, whatever music happened to be there, *at sight;* among others, several

---

* Stein invented the keyed-instrument called the Poly-Toni-Clavichordium, an account of which may be seen in the *Augsburgischen Intelligenzblatt*, October 5th, 1769. For a list of this ingenious artist's various publications, see C. F. Becker's *Systematisch-Chronologische Darstellung der Musikalischen Literatur*, 4to. Leipzig, 1836.

pretty pieces by one Edelmann. I spoke of going to pass the afternoon with Stein, whereupon the young man immediately proposed accompanying me. I thanked him for his attention, and promised to return in two hours. I accordingly did so, and then set out, accompanied by the son-in-law, whom one would take for a student. Though I had particularly requested that my name might not be mentioned, Mr. Langenmantel had the imprudence to say to Mr. Stein, 'I have the honour of presenting to you a virtuoso on the piano.' I instantly disclaimed this quality, and stated myself to be an unworthy pupil of Mr. Sigl, of Munich. Stein made a negative movement with his head, and said, 'May I have the honour of receiving Mr. Mozart?' 'Oh no,' replied I, 'My name is Trazom, and here is a letter which I have to deliver to you.' He was about to open it immediately, but I would not give him time. 'Why will you read the letter now,' I asked; 'let us go to your music-room, I am impatient to try your pianos.' 'As you please,' was his reply, 'but I think I am not deceived.' He opened the door; I immediately ran to one of the three pianos which were in the room, and commenced playing. He could no longer resist his impatience; he opened the letter, looked at the signature, and with an exclamation, came to clasp me in his arms."

In a letter, a few days later, "Augsburgh, October 17th, 1777," he has some very interesting particulars connected with Stein's mode of manufacturing pianos. "I begin," says the great musician, "with Stein's pianos. Before meeting with them, I thought those of Spaett the best; now I give the preference to the first mentioned, for the key-board is better and more commodious than that in the pianos of the Ratisbon manufacturer. In passages that require vigorous play, I can lift the finger or leave it on the note, for the sound is not prolonged beyond the instant in which it is heard. I strike the chords as I please, and the tone is always the same: it is neither stronger nor weaker; it never shivers, and never fails to sound, as happens sometimes with other pianos. It is true that Stein never lets a piano go under three hundred florins, but one cannot sufficiently repay the trouble and zeal which he employs. His instruments have one quality found in them alone: they have all the escape-movement; it is almost impossible that a piano, without this, should render a well articulated sound. The hammers fall again as soon as they have touched the string, whether the finger be left on the key or not. When Stein has finished a piano, he plays on it passages of all sorts, and never quits it till it is capable of anything, for he labours not for his pecuniary interest, but for that of the art. He frequently says : ' If I were not myself a passionate amateur in music, my patience would long ago have failed me; but I like an instrument which assists the musician, and serves for a long time. His pianos are, in fact, very lasting. He warrants the solidity of the sounding-board. When he has completed one, he exposes it to the air, rain, sun, snow, in a word to every variety of atmosphere, that it may split: then by means of slips firmly glued in, he closes the crevices. When a sounding-board has been thus prepared, it may be regarded as safe against all accidents. He has now three pianos finished, on one of which I have been playing to day. The pedals, which are pressed by the knees, are also better in Stein's pianos than in any other. I scarcely touch it, yet the effect is palpable, and as soon as I discontinue this pressure the sound resumes its natural quality."*

---

* Mozart played upon the *new instrument* when he was a mere child. The writer of his biography says, " When Mozart, at the age of six years (*i. e.* in 1762), sat down to play in presence of the Emperor Francis, he addressed himself to his majesty, and asked, ' Is not Mr. Wagenseil here? We must send for him, he understands the thing.' The Emperor sent for Wagenseil, and gave up his place to him, by the side of the *piano*. ' Sir,' said Mozart to the composer, ' I am going to play one of your concertos, you must turn over the leaves for me.' Hitherto, Wolfgang had only played on the harpsichord, and the extraordinary skill which he displayed on that instrument seemed to exclude even the wish that he should apply to any other. But the genius which animated him far surpassed any hopes that his friends could have dared to entertain; he had not even occasion for lessons." *Lives of Haydn and Mozart*, 8vo. 1817, p. 342.

A correspondence has lately taken place in the *Neue Berliner Musik-Zeitung* respecting Mozart's piano. The result has been the publication of the following letter in its pages, which we think will be perused with interest:

"Sir,

In consequence of the question asked by some one in Vienna, and which appeared in No. 35 of the *Berliner Musik-Zeitung* for this year: " Who now possesses Mozart's piano, which the minister, Count von Rantzau, is said to have purchased in the year 1806, from Mozart's widow ?" I wrote Count Kuno von Rantzau, of Rohlsdorff, with whom I have the honour of being acquainted, and begged for information respecting the valuable relic. I have received a very comprehensive answer, the most interesting portion of which I do myself the honour of communicating to you."

" How much I am delighted " (so runs the answer), "in answer to your communication of the 25th of last month, to be able to give the information you require concerning the piano of the Great Mozart, which is in our possession at our ancestral mansion. The instrument was certainly purchased by my uncle, and in 1806 conveyed to Breitenburg, after the death of his respected friend, from the latter's widow, who lived to the end of her life on a footing of friendship with my family.

The mechanism of the key was not, in the first instance, more perfect than the construction of the sounding-board; for it consisted merely of a *pilote* attached vertically to the key, which impelled against the string a short and light hammer, suspended by a leather hinge, and guided by a thin shank which passed through its centre. Stein discovered a better process, when he devised the simple escapement, which still retains its name of *German mechanism*, and is still employed in the greater part of the pianofortes fabricated at Vienna. In this piece of mechanism, which has the two-fold advantage of great lightness and little expense, the hammer falls the moment the *pilote* of the key has described its elliptical curve, and allows the strings to vibrate at liberty, though the finger still remains on the key. Considering the fineness of the strings used in the first pianofortes, this piece of mechanism was not only sufficient, but the very best that could be devised.

At this period, the best instruments had a compass of only five octaves, were mounted only with double strings, and, instead of pedals, were furnished with two iron springs, ornamented with copper knobs, in that part of the chest nearest to the bass,

---

"The possessor of our family estates, Count Conrad of Rantzau, died in 1845, and was succeeded by my father. In order to regulate the inheritance and family property, a sale was ordered to take place, by the superior court, of the various art-treasures, etc. collected by Count Conrad, and catalogues were printed and sent out at the time, and advertisements inserted in all the principal German, French, and English papers, from which the notice in the *Berliner Zeitung*, of the 27th August, would seem to have been taken.

"I myself, during the above and following years, managed these family estates until the decease of my dear father, and the auction could not take place until 1849, at Breitenburg, in my presence.

"For works of art by Thorwaldsen, for paintings, and, also, for all kinds of fashionable rubbish, enormous prices were realised—for Mozart's piano there was not a single bid higher than the wretched price of an old mahogany box. Truly indignant at this, I at least saved from the common broker's shop this interesting relic of our greatest German musician, on which his incomparable *Requiem* was certainly composed, and from which his fingers drew forth, for the last time, those immortal tones that still re-echo on the soul of every German possessed of feeling—by order of my dear father, who retained his deep love of the sacred art of music to his 83rd year, I purchased Mozart's instrument for the castle. *It is now, since my father's death, together with the lordship of Breitenburg, in the possession of my brother, Friedrich August zu Entin, Hofchef of the Grand Duke of Oldenburg. The piano, however, stands, at present, as it has since 1806, in its place of honour in Breitenburg,* which unfortunately has not been inhabited for years."

"I hasten, honoured sir, to place this interesting account at your disposal, in order that you may use it, if you please, in your paper, and remain, with the greatest consideration,

"BEHREND, M.D."

"*Grevermühle in the Grand Duchy of*
"*Mecklenberg-Schwerin, October,* 1856."

to raise the dampers. In order to move these springs, it was necessary that the player should use his left hand, and consequently he was obliged, for a moment, to quit the key-board. Stein improved these springs by making them to act by means of knobs placed against the knees.

A rough idea of the appearance of a pianoforte of this period, may be formed from the following wood-cut, copied from a picture in the palace at Potsdam.

The chief cotemporaries and successors of Stein may be thus enumerated.

John Adam Späett, or Spaeth (mentioned in Mozart's letter), was a celebrated maker of organs and keyed-stringed instruments in the latter half of the eighteenth century. He was born at Ratisbon, in which city he built the Cathedral organ. His pianofortes obtained almost an equal reputation with those of Stein. He died, at a very advanced age, in 1816.

Christian Ernest Frederici, the favourite pupil of Silbermann, was born at Merona in Saxony, in 1712. He is said to have made the first *square* pianoforte. He spent the greater part of his life in improving keyed-stringed instruments, and was an organ-builder of no mean repute. He died in 1779. An account of some of his inventions may be seen in the *Leipzig Magazin des Buch-und-Kunsthandels*, 1781.

John Godfrey Hildebrand, the son of Zacaria Hildebrand, the eminent organ-builder, and himself a distinguished builder, settled at Berlin, about 1758, as a maker of keyed-stringed instruments. In 1782 he constructed a square pianoforte, in which the sounding-board occupied the entire length of the instrument, the hammers being placed *above* the strings. Marius and Schröter had proposed this plan as early as 1716 and 1717, but both abandoned it as impracticable. Hildebrand was not more successful. It was left for Streicher of Vienna, and Petzold of Paris, to show the *practicability* of this arrangement; and, finally, for M. Pape to bring it to perfection.

Christopher Michael Lenkler of Rudolstadt was one of the most ingenious mechanists of his time. His instruments ranked very high, and were as much sought after as those of Godfrey Silbermann. He flourished about 1760, and died before 1790.

Francis Ignace Seuffert, born at Wurzburg in 1731, was an organ-builder and pianoforte-maker of considerable eminence in his time. He was living at Wurzburg in 1807, well advanced in years. His two sons, John Philip, and Francis Martin, were also eminent manufacturers of pianos at Vienna.

John Andrew Streicher, born at Stuttgardt in 1761, was an excellent practical musician. In his visits to Augsburg, he became accquainted with Stein, and married his daughter. After his marriage, he took up his residence at Vienna, where he commenced an extensive manufactory for the making of pianos. He made many improvements in their mechanism, and improved the principle of placing the hammers *above* the strings. He died May 25th, 1833.

Dr. Burney, in his entertaining *Tour in Germany*, gives a number of interesting notices of the pianoforte, which show its gradual progress in public favour.

At Potsdam, he says, " after dinner I went to see the King's new palace (*das neue Schloss*), built since the last war. * * * * The apartments are fitted up with the utmost magnificence and taste; there is a *suite* of rooms appropriated to almost every branch of the royal family. Those of the King, of his sister Princess Amelia, and of the Prince of Prussia, are the most splendid. In each of these apartments there is a room dedicated to music, furnished with books, desks, a harpsichord, and other instruments. His majesty's concert room is ornamented with glasses of an immense size, and with sculpture, partly gilt, and partly of the most beautiful green varnish, by Martin of Paris; the whole furniture and ornaments of this room are in the most refined and exquisite taste. There is a *piano-forte*, made by Silbermann of Neuberg, beautifully varnished and embellished; and a tortoise-shell desk for his majesty's use, most richly and elegantly inlaid with silver; on the table lay a catalogue of concertos for the *New Palace*, and a book of manuscript solfeggi, as his Majesty calls them, or preludes, composed of difficult divisions and passages for the exercise of the hand, as the vocal *solfeggi* are for the throat. His Majesty has books of this kind, for the use of his flute, in the music room of every one of his palaces."

At Vienna, after recording his visit to Hasse, the Doctor says: "From hence I went to M. L'Angier's concert, which was begun by the child of eight or nine years old, whom he had mentioned to me before, and who played two difficult lessons of Scarlatti, with three or four by M. Becke, upon a small and not good *pianoforte*. The neatness of this child's execution did not so much surprise me, though uncommon, as her expression. All the *pianos* and *fortes* were so judiciously attended to; and there was such shading of some passages, and force given to others, as nothing but the best teaching, or greatest natural feeling and sensibility could produce. I enquired of Signor Giorgio, an Italian, who attended her, ' upon what instrument she usually practised at home,' and was answered, ' on the clavichord.' This accounts for her expression, and convinces me that children should learn upon that, or a *pianoforte*, very early, and be obliged to give an expression to Lady Coventry's Minuet, or whatever is their first tune; otherwise, after long practice on a monotonous harpsichord, however useful for strengthening the hand, the case is hopeless."

Speaking of the celebrated John Philip Kirnberger*, whom he visited at Berlin, in the same tour, he says: "He played, at my request, upon a clavichord some of his *fugues* and church music, which are very learned and curious; he likewise presented me with a copy of his *musical institutes,* and a short dissertation upon *tempera-*

---

* "Court musician to the Princess Amelia of Prussia, in Berlin. He was one of the most remarkable of Bach's scholars, full of the most useful zeal and general enthusiastic feeling for the art; beside the development of Bach's mode of teaching compositions, the musical world is indebted to him for the first and only tenable system of harmony, which he has abstracted from his master's practical works. He has done the first in his Art of Pure Composition (*Kunst des reinen Satzes*); and the second, in The True Principles for the use of Harmony (*Grund sätze zum Gebrauch der Harmonie*). He has, besides, been of service to the art, by other writings and compositions, as well as by teaching." Forkel's *Life of J. S. Bach.*

ment, which he has lately published, as well as of several manuscript compositions. After this he had the complaisance to go with me to the house of Hildebrand, the best maker of harpsichords and *pianofortes* in Berlin; here M. Kirnberger played again, and discovered great strength of hand, as well as knowledge in harmony and modulation."

We have now to consider the progress of the pianoforte in France. It does not appear that Marius's invention was ever adopted, or that he made any disciples by his discovery of the hammers. Fétis, indeed, says, "Marius' discovery met with *no* success in France, where custom is often seen opposed to the success of what is new." Blanchet, however, made instruments with hammers; and Paschal Tasquin, whom we have before mentioned as an eminent harpsichord maker (p. 81 *ante*), manufactured, in 1776, small square pianos in "imitation of the English;" but they were not well received. In fact, down to the year 1779, France had remained dependent on Germany and England for its instruments of this kind; nearly all those found at Paris, at this epoch, came from the manufactories of Augsburg, Ratisbon, and London. The brothers Erard were the first to free their country from this state of dependence, and manufactured small pianofortes of five octaves with two pedals, the silvery tone and perfect mechanism of which were truly remarkable for that period.

The great mechanical genius, Sebastian Erard, was born at Strasburg, April 5, 1752, and was the eldest of the four children of an upholsterer. At the age of eight years, he commenced the study of architecture, perspective, linear design, and practical geometry, in the schools of his native city; and his mind, fertile in invention, was continually suggesting to him new problems, and devising its own means of resolving them. Erard, himself, confessed that it was to his early acquaintance with drawing and the principles of mechanics that he owed his success. His father, having married very late in life, was surprised by death before his children reached an age at which they could be useful to their mother, or support themselves. Sebastian Erard became the head of a family at the age of sixteen. As his native town did not afford him the scope of which he felt the need, he set off courageously for Paris. He arrived there in 1768, and obtained employment with a harpsichord maker, whose chief workman he soon became, and whose jealousy he as quickly aroused by the superiority of his workmanship. His master, wearied by Erard's constant inquiries respecting the principles upon which instruments were constructed, and, in fact, unable to furnish the information sought for, first reproached him with wanting to know everything, and concluded by dismissing him from his service. Another celebrated manufacturer of harpsichords being called upon to make an instrument which demanded something beyond his mere every-day routine, and finding himself not a little puzzled how to answer the unusual demand, sought out young Erard, whose reputation was already budding, and proposed to him to undertake the construction of the instrument for a certain sum of money, allowing the person of whom it had been originally bespoke to affix his name to it. Erard consented, and the instrument was completed; but, when it was delivered, the purchaser, who probably had no very great confidence in the ability of the manufacturer he had employed, demanded some explanation of the mechanism; the nominal maker was forced to refer to his assistant.

This anecdote soon circulated among the musical circles of Paris, and drew attention towards the rising artist, who shortly after made himself still further known by his mechanical harpsichord, a master-piece of invention and workmanship, which produced a most lively sensation among the professors and amateurs. This remarkable piece of mechanism was constructed for the cabinet of curiosities of M. de Blancherie. The Abbè Roussier inserted a detailed description of it in the *Journal de Paris*, which was afterwards reprinted in the Musical Almanack of Luneau-de-Bois Germain, in 1776.

Sebastian Erard was hardly twenty-five years old, when his reputation was so fully established, that whoever wished to have any new ideas carried into execution applied to no one but him. He was sought out by the most distinguished men, and introduced to the Duchess of Villeroi, a lover of the arts, a protectress of artists, and, above all, passionately fond of, and having a highly cultivated taste for, music. The Duchess wished Erard to remain in her employ, and offered him an advantageous engagement; but, preferring independence, and having besides already conceived the idea of a visit to England, he declined the offer, consenting, however, to stay with the Duchess till he had executed some plans of her invention; occupying, during that time, an apartment in the Hotel Villeroi, but with perfect liberty and command of his own movements. In his old age he still delighted to recall to mind the goodness of Madame Villeroi, and express the gratitude with which she had inspired him.

It was in the Hotel Villeroi that Erard made his first piano. This instrument had been known for many years in England and Germany, but was still little used in France; and the few instruments that were to be found in Paris were imported from Augsburg, Ratisbon, or London. It was the fashion in some great houses to have these foreign instruments. Madame Villeroi asked Erard whether he could construct a piano? He had already conceived the idea of making one, and his answer was prompt and decided in the affirmative; he set immediately to work, and his first, like everything else he made, showed that it came from the hands of a man of taste and invention. It was heard in the saloon of Madame Villeroi by all the distinguished artists and amateurs of Paris. Numerous applications were made to him by the nobility for similar instruments; but finding it impossible to execute their orders, he sent for his brother, Jean Baptiste, to come to Paris and help him. Quitting the Hôtel de Villeroi, he founded his house in the Rue de Bourbon, in the Faubourg St. Germain; an establishment which the efforts of the two brothers eventually rendered one of the finest in Europe.

The *Luthiers*, or makers of musical instruments, of Paris, who carried on the trade of importing foreign pianos, found the new factory injurious to their commerce; they made a seizure in it, under the pretext that the brothers Erard were not members of the Corporation of Fanmakers, to which the Luthiers belonged. Sebastian Erard had powerful friends, however, and he obtained a brevet from Louis the Sixteenth which delivered him completely from the prosecuting corporation. This document is so highly interesting that we transfer it to our pages:

"This day, the fifth of February, one thousand seven hundred and eighty-five, the King being at Versailles informed that Mr. Sebastien Erard has succeeded by a new method of his invention to improve the instrument called a forté-piano; that he has even obtained the preference over those made in England, of which he makes a commerce in the city of Paris, and his majesty wishing to fix the talents of Mr. Erard in the said city, and to give him testimonies of the protection with which he honours those who, like him, have by assiduous labour contributed to the useful and agreeable arts, has permitted him to make, to cause to be made, and to sell in the city and faubourgs of Paris, and wherever it may seem to him good, forté-pianos; and to employ there, whether by himself or by his workmen, the wood, the iron, and all the other materials necessary to the perfection or the ornament of the said instrument without his being liable on this account to be troubled or disturbed by the guards, syndics, and adjutants of the corporations and committees of arts and trades for any cause or under any pretext whatever; under the conditions, nevertheless, by the said Mr. Erard of conforming himself to the regulations and ordinances concerning the discipline of journeymen and workmen, and of not admitting into his workshops any but those who shall have satisfied the aforesaid regulations. And for assurance of his will, his majesty has commanded me to expedite to the aforesaid Mr. Erard the present brevet, which he has chosen to sign with his own hand, and to be countersigned by me, Secretary of State, and of his commands and Finances.

(Signed) LOUIS.

LE BARON DE BRETEUIL."

Incessantly occupied with new inventions and improvements, the genius of Sebastian Erard embraced a vast variety of subjects; he invented the organized pianoforte with two key-boards, one for the piano and the other for the organ. The success of this instrument was considerable. The Queen commanded one to be made for her own use, and in the construction of it Erard introduced several novel contrivances, which, at that time, awakened much interest. The Queen's voice was of limited compass, and almost every piece was too high for her. Erard rendered the key-board of his new instrument moveable, so that by changing its position with relation to the strings, a composition might be played a semitone, whole tone, or even a minor third, lower or higher, without tasking the player's ability to transpose: for instance, according to the position of the key-board, the key D would strike any string between B natural below and F natural above its proper string. It was in the organ part of this instrument that he also made the first attempt to produce a crescendo and diminuendo by the mere pressure of the finger on the key; and this he afterwards carried into effect, on a large scale, in an organ built for the King's chapel. Gretry, in his *Essais sur la Musique*, particularly pointed out this invention to the notice of professors and to the attention of government.

The revolution now broke out in France, and Sebastian Erard determined on removing to England; not with any intention of finally abandoning his native country, to which, on the contrary, he always meant to return, but with a view of opening new channels for the sale of his instruments. In London, as in Paris, Erard filled his manufactory with instruments of his own invention. In 1794, he took out his first patent for improvements in harps and pianofortes, and his instruments soon became fashionable. In 1796, he availed himself of the altered state of affairs in France to return to Paris, and, at this period, made his first horizontal grand pianos in the shape of harpsichords after the English fashion. These instruments were the first of the kind, with escapements, that had been seen in Paris; they had the defect which formerly accompanied all similar instruments—a slowness of action in the levers and hammers. The Parisian pianoforte-players, accustomed to the easy touch of the small pianos without escapements, disliked the new invention; and it was for this reason, that, after much study and many experiments, Erard brought out, in 1808, another new species of piano, of reduced dimensions, and so more suited to the general size of Parisian rooms, and the mechanism of which acted with greater freedom and ease. Dussek played on one of these pianos with the greatest eclat at the concerts given in the Odéon by Rode, Baillot, and Lamarre, on their return from Russia. Amateurs and professsors were alike satisfied; but Erard was not: he knew that there still remained some defects; the touch, indeed, was easy, but the hammers did not act with precision. On his return from London, at a later period, we shall find him exhibiting the model of a grand piano, uniting every excellence in its mechanism of which the instrument is susceptible.

About 1808, Erard returned to London, and there crowned his reputation as a manufacturer of musical instruments, and still more as professed master of mechanics, by his invention of the double-movement harp. The success of this new harp was immense; which induced Erard to neglect the manufacture of pianos in London, and confine himself to that of harps only. Nevertheless, in all the patents he took out in England, improvements on the piano, which he meant to carry into effect in France, are mixed with those of the harp. At every exhibition his works received the prize; thrice he obtained the gold medal; and for one of his last exhibitions, the cross of the Legion of Honour was decreed him; in short, he received every honorary reward that could be bestowed on the talents of a first-rate manufacturer.

The model of his grand pianoforte with double escapement was exhibited in 1823; the mechanism was most ingenious. The point to be achieved was to unite in the same instrument all the nice shades of touch which can be produced by the simple mechanism without escapement, and at the same time all the precision in the stroke of the hammer which is the effect of the escapement.

Erard's constitution, robust as it originally was, could hardly endure his continued exertions. For many years he suffered by disease; and at length breathed his last at his country house *La Muette* near Passey, on the 5th of August, 1831. His funeral was attended by some of the most distinguished artists in Paris.

The founder of another important pianoforte manufactory in France, was the celebrated Ignace Pleyel. This artist was born in 1757, at Rupperstahl, a small village within a few leagues of Vienna. He was the twenty-fourth child of Martin Pleyel, a schoolmaster of that place, and of a lady of noble family, disinherited by her parents on account of what they deemed so imprudent a marriage: she died in giving Ignace birth. The widower again entered into the wedded state, had fourteen children by his second wife, and expired in the ninety-ninth year of his age.

The young Ignace learned, according to the German custom, his own tongue, the elements of the Latin language, and music, all at the same time. His natural disposition for the latter induced his father to give him Vanhall as a master; and at the age of fifteen he was placed under the instruction of Haydn, with whom he lived five years, at the expense of 100 louis per annum, a large sum at that period, which was defrayed by the Count Erdoedy, a wealthy Hungarian nobleman, who, struck by the talents and manners of the youth, took him under his protection. In 1777, his patron allowed him to visit Italy; and at Naples his genius for instrumental music was evinced in a set of quartets, in which were first displayed that originality of melody which is the characteristic of all his works, and a manner entirely his own.

In Italy, Pleyel made the acquaintance of the great masters then flourishing in what was at that time the " land of song," of Cimarosa, Guglielmi, and Paisiello; and his taste was much improved by hearing the most celebrated singers. Nardini, the violinist, was still living, and Pugnani, the master of Viotti, was in all his vigour. With such advantages, his improvement was rapid, and he gained much that he had failed to learn under Haydn, who, though the greatest composer of his age, was by no means a good master: indeed, it may be laid down as a general rule, says the French critic from whom we translate, that genius of a high order and the power of teaching, are rarely, if ever, united in the same person. At Naples, Pleyel was introduced to the King, who received him with much kindness, and desired him to compose an opera. His *Ifigenia in Aulide* was in consequence produced, which proved successful; but it was the first and last work of the kind from the same pen.

In 1793, Pleyel was appointed chapel master of the Cathedral of Strasburg, and composed several masses and motets, all of which, unfortunately, were destroyed in a great fire a few days after they were written. From the above period to the year 1793, he produced nearly all those works which wafted his fame into every city in Europe; scarcely any instrumental music was willingly listened to, but that which he had created. In 1791, Saloman having engaged Haydn to compose symphonies for his concerts, the managers of a rival institution, named the Professional Concert, sent for Pleyel to supply works of a similar kind. He accordingly visited London, and produced a symphony of no ordinary merit, as well as a charming concertante; but, in the contest with the father of this high class of composition, he had no chance. The concert, which was under the direction of feeble-minded persons, failed, and Pleyel did not add to his reputation by the part he had taken in it; though he was a pecuniary gainer to the amount of £1200, with which sum he purchased an estate near Strasburg.

Suspected of aristocratic opinions, Pleyel was, in 1793, denounced no less than seven times to the republican authorities at Strasburg, and at length fled, but was pursued and taken. He was severely interrogated, and protested his *civism*, though required, as a proof of his sincerity, to set the music to a kind of drama for the anniversary of the 10th of August; he of course consented, and was allowed to return home to compose the work, but under the guard of two gendarmes, and almost with the axe suspended over him. After an uninterrupted labour of seven days, the music was finished, then performed under the author's direction, and afforded so much satisfaction to the Strasburgers that the author never after was suspected of encouraging politics at all adverse to the government. Little satisfied, however, with an occurrence which had put on so threatening an aspect, Pleyel sold his estate in 1795, went to Paris with all his family, and entered into a commercial speculation, becoming publisher of music and manufacturer of pianofortes. The enterprise proved successful, and the business was afterwards carried on by his son, Camille, in conjunction with Kalkbrenner.

Although both these gentlemen were skilful musicians, they devoted themselves to trade, as a more profitable and satisfactory pursuit.*

After a laborious career, Pleyel retired to enjoy an estate, not far distant from Paris, purchased by the fruits of his talents and industry, and indulged his taste for agriculture. His happiness seemed complete, when the revolution of July alarmed a mind somewhat enfeebled by time; his fears for the security of his property agitated a frame not very strong; he became ill, his anxieties increased, and, after three months of suffering, he died on the fourteenth of November, 1831.†

Concerning the progress of the pianoforte in Italy, the country which gave it birth, we have no authentic information, although we feel assured that it was not neglected. Geronimo of Florence, and Gherardi of Parma, are said to have carried out Cristofali's discoveries; but the particulars of their labours are not recorded. Farinelli's *favorite* instrument, the " Rafael d'Urbino," it will be remembered, was a pianoforte made at Florence in 1730‡—a fact in itself alone sufficient to prove the high excellence attained by the Italians at an early period in the history of its construction.

---

* According to Professor Fischoff, Ignace Bleyel commenced musicseller at Paris in 1796; and pianofortemaker, in 1805. In 1824, Camille (his son) and Kalkbrenner joined the firm. In 1834, they employed two hundred and fifty workmen, and made 1000 pianofortes in the course of the year. The firm is now Pleyel, Wolff, and Co.

† These particulars, concerning Pleyel, are chiefly derived from a notice which appeared in 1832 in the *Revue Musicale*.

‡ Described in Burney's *Tour in Italy* (see ante, p. 83).

CHAPTER IX.

THE INTRODUCTION AND PROGRESS OF THE PIANOFORTE IN ENGLAND.

THE first pianoforte seen in this country, according to all accounts, was made by one Father Wood, an English monk at Rome, and by him sold to Samuel Crisp, Esq. a gentleman of considerable taste and learning, who sold it again to Fulke Greville, Esq. at the price of one hundred guineas.* For a long time this instrument was

---

* The two gentlemen, whose names are thus mixed up with the introduction of the pianoforte in England, are deserving of a passing notice.

SAMUEL CRISP was the intimate friend of Dr. Burney, the musical historian, and of his amiable family. In mind, manner, and habits, he was one of the most refined characters of the latter half of the last century. Madame d'Arblay says he was "a scholar of the highest order; a critic of the clearest acumen; possessing, with equal delicacy of discrimination, a taste for literature and for the arts; and personally excelling as a *dilettante* both in music and painting." He was the author of a tragedy called *Virginia*, and several poetical effusions in the magazines of the day. He visited Italy and other parts of the continent in 1757; and, upon his return to England, two or three years after, took up his residence at Hampton; where he fitted up a small house with paintings, prints, sculpture, and musical instruments, arranged with the most classical elegance. He died, April twenty-fourth, 1783, aged seventy-six, deeply regretted by all who had known him during life. His epitaph in Chesington Church, Surrey, was written by Dr. Burney.

FULKE GREVILLE, a descendant of the friend of Sir Philip Sydney, and known as the author of *Characters, Maxims, and Reflections*, was, at the middle of the last century, generally looked upon as the finest gentleman about town. "He excelled," says Madame D'Arblay, in all the fashionable exercises, riding, fencing, hunting, shooting at a mark, dancing, tennis, &c. and worked every day at every one of them with a fury for pre-eminence not equalled, perhaps, in ardour for superiority in personal accomplishments since the days of the chivalrous Lord Herbert of Cherbury." He travelled in a style that was even princely; not only from his equipages, out-riders, horses, and liveries, but from constantly having two of his attendants skilled in playing the French horn; and these were always stationed to recreate him with marches and warlike movements on the outside of the windows, when he took any repast.

This eccentric gentleman was the friend and patron of Dr. Burney; and a most interesting account of their first interview, at the ware-rooms of old Kirkman, the harpsichord-maker, may be found in Madame d'Arblay's *Memoirs of Dr. Burney*, vol. i, p. 26, *et seq.*

without a rival, and the wonder and delight of all who heard it; no virginal, spinet, or harpsichord, had yet been made capable of any modification of tone. The hammer harpsichord (for it was nothing more) obeyed the soul of the player, and, according to the pressure of the finger upon the key, passed through every gradation of *piano* and *forte*. This instrument became celebrated, and was known to all the dilettanti of London as "Mr. Greville's pianoforte." Plenius, the ingenious harpsichord-maker and inventor of the lyrichord (whom we have before mentioned), obtained permission of the proprietor to make a copy of it; but his efforts do not appear to have been attended with any great success.

At length, about the year 1760, many ingenious German mechanics left their country and came to England in search of employment as pianoforte-makers; this gave the instrument its first impetus. A party of twelve travelled hither in one company, and obtained, from this circumstance, the appellation of the "twelve apostles."

A German, named Viator, resident in London, had made several important improvements in the pianoforte. He was followed by Americus Backers, also a German *, who had been in the employ of Silbermann of Neuberg; but it does not appear that the instruments of these makers found much favour with the public.

An event happened about this time which gave a new impetus to the instrument, and awoke the ingenuity, as well as the ambition, of the chief performers and manufacturers in England. John Christian Bach, organist, pianist, and composer, arrived in this country, and established that series of concerts which first made familiar amongst us the grand classical music of the German schools †.

---

* "The name-board of a grand pianoforte is still in existence bearing the inscription

"AMERICUS BACKERS, FACTOR ET INVENTOR,

Jermyn Street, London, 1776."

(Pole's *Musical Instruments in the great Industrial Exhibition of* 1851).

† "Mr. J. C. Bach, having very early in life been deprived of the instructions of his father, the great Sebastian Bach, was for some time a scholar of his eldest brother, the celebrated Charles Phil. Emanuel Bach, under whom he became a fine performer on keyed-instruments; but on quitting him and going to Italy, where his chief study was the composition of vocal music, he assured me that during many years he made little use of a harpsichord or pianoforte but to compose for or accompany a voice. When he arrived in England, his style of playing was so much admired that he recovered many of the losses his hand had

The harpsichord-makers now all lent their efforts to improve and popularize the new instrument. The most successful amongst them was a German, named John Zumpé (who had been in the employ of Tschudi), who succeeded in the construction of some small pianofortes (similar in shape and size to their progenitors, the clavichord and virginal), whereof the tone was peculiarly sweet, the touch good, and the price sufficiently moderate to place them within the reach of all those who had hitherto been purchasers of the harpsichord and spinet. "These instruments suddenly rose into such favour," says a contemporary, "that there was scarcely a house in the kingdom, where a stringed instrument had admission, but was supplied with one of *Zumpé's pianofortes,* for which there was nearly as great a demand in France as in England; in short, he could not make them fast enough to gratify the public fondness for them.*" Zumpé entered into partnership with Meyer, and afterwards with Buntebart; † and after realising an ample fortune, retired to his native country. A

---

sustained by disuse, and by being constantly cramped and crippled with a pen; but he was never able to reinstate it with force and readiness sufficient for great difficulties; and, in general, his compositions for the pianoforte are such as ladies can execute with little trouble, and the allegros rather resemble bravura songs than instrumental pieces for the display of great execution. On which account, they lose much of their effect when played without the accompaniments, which are admirable, and so masterly and interesting to an audience, that want of hand, or complication on the harpsichord part, is never discovered." Burney, *Hist. of Music,* iv, 482. Bach arrived in England in 1763, and established his concerts, conjointly with Abel, in the year following. These concerts subsisted for full twenty years,

* Capel Loft, in the *Monthly Magazine* for 1809, p. 23, says, "I wish to ascertain the exact period, if possible, of the introduction of the *pianoforte* into England. That its origin is German seems agreed; but neither the era of its invention there, nor of its being introduced either in France, Italy, or here, seems to be ascertained. I have seen, and often had the pleasure of hearing, a good *pianoforte,* dated 1775; but I am not sure that this date might not belong to it in a harpsichord state, and the pianoforte improvement be made afterwards. I have seen another which, in its whole structure and appearance, indicates that when first made it had its present construction. This is at Bury, at Mr. Ramsay's. The superscription in front is:

'JOANNES ZUMPE, fecit, 1766,
'Princes Street, Hanover Square.'"

In a subsequent page of the same volume, a correspondent informs Capel Loft that he has a square pianoforte made by Zumpé in 1768; he adds, "it is upon the common construction with two wires to each note, with the mark XVIII upon it, which appears to have been the number he had then made."

† He was in partnership with Meyer in 1778, and in 1784 with Buntebart. My friend, Mr. Charles Salaman, has a charming little instrument made by John Zumpé et Meyer, 1778. Sir George Smart has one of Zumpé's pianofortes with *quarter* tones.

recent writer says, " the place of his retirement we well remember, and have heard good report of his cheerful glass and well-filled pipe, without which, in those days, a German did not acknowledge that he lived."

Contemporary with Zumpé was John Pohlman, who, although his pianofortes were of inferior tone, made a fortune by supplying those who could not obtain the instruments of his more skilful countryman *.

The pianoforte as yet was considered as merely a "household" instrument; its limits being confined to private circles. In the year 1767, it was introduced on the stage of Covent Garden Theatre, as *a new instrument*. We have much pleasure in giving the following copy of an old play-bill, now in the possession of Messrs. Broadwoods, which records its first *public* announcement:

"*By particular desire—For the Benefit of Miss Brickler.*

"THEATRE ROYAL IN COVENT GARDEN.

" On Saturday next, being the 16th of May, 1767, THE BEGGAR'S OPERA. *Captain Macheath*, by Mr. Beard; *Peacham*, by Mr. Shuter; *Lockit*, by Mr. Dunstall; *Filch*, by Mr. Holtom; *Player*, by Mr. Gardner; *Beggar*, by Mr. Bennet; *Mat o' the Mint*, by Mr. Baker; *Mrs. Peacham*, by Mrs. Stephens; *Diana Trapes*, by Mrs. Copin; *Mrs. Slammekin*, by Mrs. Green; *Polly*, by Miss Brickler; with a Hornpipe by Miss D. Twist; and a Country Dance by the Characters in the Opera.

" End of Act 1, Miss Brickler will sing a favourite Song from Judith, accompanied by Mr. Dibdin, ON A NEW INSTRUMENT CALLED PIANO-FORTE.

" To which will be added a FARCE called the UPHOLSTERER. *The Barber*, by Mrs. Woodward; *Feeble*, by Mr. Murden; *Bellmour*, by Mr. Perry; *Rovewell*, by Mr. Davis; *Watchman*, by Mr. Weller; *Quidnunc*, by Mr. Dunstall: *Pamphlet*, by Mr. Shuter; *Harriet*, by Miss Vincent; *Maid*, by Miss Cokayne; *Termagant*, by Mrs. Green.

" *Tickets to be had of Mr. Sarjant, at the Stage-door, where places for the Boxes may be taken.*"

Charles Dibdin, who has the merit of being the first person to perform *publicly* on the pianoforte in this country, was born near Southampton in 1745. His mother

---

* A pianoforte made by Pohlman in 1772, for the great composer Gluck, is thus described by Thalberg: " It was four feet and a half in length, and two feet in width, with a small square sounding-board at the end. The wires were little more than threads, and the hammers consisted of a few piles of leather over the head of a horizontal jack working on a hinge."—*Report of the Juries*, &c.

had attained her fiftieth year at his birth, and he was her eighteenth child. He was educated at Winchester for the clerical profession, but his love of music predominated, and he received his first instructions from Mr. Fussel, organist of Winchester Cathedral. At the age of fifteen, he went to London, and, at sixteen, produced an operetta in two acts, at Covent Garden Theatre, under the title of *The Shepherd's Artifice*. As an actor he first appeared as *Damætas*, in *Midas*, and was the original *Mungo* in *The Padlock*, as well as *Ralph* in the *Maid of the Mill*. In 1778, he became composer to Covent Garden Theatre, at a salary of ten pounds a week. About 1782, he built the Circus (now the Surrey) Theatre, which he managed four years. In 1788, he produced at Hutchin's Auction Rooms, in King Street, Covent Garden, the first of those entertainments which originated with him, under the title of *The Whim of the Moment*. In this was the ballad 'Poor Jack,' of which seventeen thousand copies were finally sold.

Dibdin, encouraged by his success, in 1791 fitted up a room in the Strand, opposite Beaufort Buildings, which he called *Sans Souci*, and opened it with an entertainment entitled *Private Theatricals*. In 1793, he built himself a small theatre in Leicester Place, under the same name. Park, in his *Musical Memoirs* (i, 175), says: "As a proof of the versatility of Dibdin's genius, it need only be stated that this pretty little theatre was planned, painted, and decorated by himself; and that he wrote the recitation and songs, composed the music to them, and sang, and accompanied them on an *organised pianoforte of his own invention*." Here he continued his own unaided exertions, with varied success, till he retired in 1805, when he disposed of his stock, copyright, &c. to Messrs. Bland and Weller, for the sum of £1,800.

This great genius died in 1814, and his remains were deposited in St. Martin's Burying-ground, Camden Town.

The English pianoforte is said to have received considerable improvements from the poet Mason. By some, indeed, he is considered its inventor. Before, however, noticing his particular claims, we shall give a slight sketch of his biography.

William Mason was born in the year 1725; his father, a clergyman of great respectability, held the vicarage of the Holy Trinity, in Kingston upon Hull, Yorkshire. Of the early part of his education little is known. Having been admitted of St. John's

College, Cambridge, he took his first degree in 1745; from thence he removed to Pembroke Hall, of which Society he was elected a Fellow in 1747. The degree of Master of Arts was conferred upon him two years afterwards, when he first distinguished himself as a poet, by an Ode on the Installation of the Duke of Newcastle as Chancellor of the University of Cambridge. One of his next poetical productions was *Isis*, an elegy, which occasioned an answer from Thomas Warton, in his noble poem entitled *The Triumph of Isis*, in which that celebrated writer endeavoured to rescue his favorite place of residence from the imputations cast upon it by his formidable rival. Mason's fame was, however, speedily secured by the publication of his drama of *Elfrida*, in the year 1752; this was followed, after a short interval, by *Caractacus*, which performance contains some of his finest writing, particularly the odes. In the year 1754, he took holy orders, and was fortunate enough to obtain the patronage of the Earl of Holdernesse, who procured for him the appointment of Chaplain to his Majesty, and presented him with the valuable rectory of Aston, in Yorkshire. Previous to his leaving college, Mason had attracted the attention of the poet Gray by his imitations of *L'Allegro* and *Il Pensieroso;* and from the congeniality of their pursuits and dispositions, a friendship was speedily contracted, which terminated only on the decease of the latter in 1771. This circumstance exhibits, in an eminent degree, that warmth and fervour of affection which characterized Mason through life; he regarded the genius of Gray with an enthusiasm "bordering upon idolatry." And upon the melancholy event of his decease, he took upon himself the office of his biographer, and the editor of such part of his works as were in a state fit for publication.*

Besides the church preferments which we have mentioned Mason to have attained in the early part of his life, he was appointed Canon Residentiary and Precentor of the Cathedral of York. For the latter office, which he discharged with unwearied attention and ability, he was peculiarly qualified, from his knowledge of the science of music, and the warm affection he felt towards it, of which he evinced a very sufficient proof in his interesting *Essays, Historical and Critical, on English Church Music,*

---

* Gray bequeathed to him the whole of his library and MSS.

printed at York, 12mo. 1795. Of the sister art of painting he was a professed admirer, which no doubt actuated him towards the translation of Fresnoy's exquisite latin poem; a work in which purity, elegance of style, and beauty of versification, are eminently conspicuous.

Mason married a most amiable woman, the daughter of William Sherman, Esq. of Kingston upon Hull, with whom he enjoyed the most perfect human happiness. She died at the early age of twenty-eight. The poet survived her near thirty years; his own death was occasioned by a hurt received in stepping from a carriage, which produced a mortification. He died in the month of April 1797, in the seventy-second year of his age, bequeathing a name to posterity not more distinguished for exemplary worth and philanthropy, than for brilliancy of genius and talents, correctness of taste, and the most consummate skill and excellence as a writer. A monument was, in the early part of the present century, erected to his memory in the Poet's Corner of Westminster Abbey, adjoining to that of Gray. The design is well executed by Bacon, and represents a figure of Poetry holding a medallion of the deceased, whose loss she is deploring. The inscription commemorates little more than his name and the day of his death.

Mason's love of music prompted him to turn his attention to the defects of the pianoforte; but the precise date at which he devoted his talent to the subject is not known. It was probably shortly after his German tour in 1755. Under the date of June 27, he thus writes to his friend from Hanover. "Oh, Mr. Gray! I bought at Hamburgh such a *pianoforte*, and so cheap! It is a harpsichord too of two unisons, and the jacks serve as mutes when the pianoforte stop is played, by the cleverest mechanism imaginable,—won't you buy my Kirkman?"*

The writer of the article Pianoforte, in the fourth edition of the *Encyclopædia Britannica*, 1810, vol. xvi, says: "The piano has been called a national instrument, because it is said to be an English contrivance, the invention of the celebrated poet, Mason. Mr. Mason had seen some attempts that were made by the Germans to make keyed dulcimers, which were in some measure susceptible of the *forte* and *piano*;

---

* *The Correspondence of Thomas Gray and William Mason, edited by the Rev. J. Mitford*, 8vo. 1853, p. 29.

but as they were all constructed on one principle, and required a particular touch of the finger, which was of difficult acquisition, and which spoiled it for harpsichord practice; as they were also deficient in delicacy and justness; and as the performer was by no means certain of producing the very strength of sound intended, Mr. Mason removed all those imperfections, by detaching the mallet entirely from the key, and giving them only a momentary connection. It is by this improvement that the English pianoforte is distinguished from all others. Mr. Mason's general principle may be fully understood by the following description."

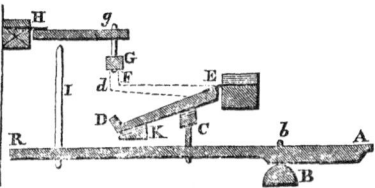

"The parts are represented in their state of inaction. The key A B K turns, as usual, on the round edge of the bar B; and a pin b, driven into the bar, keeps it in its place. The dot F represents a section of the spring. E D is the mallet, having a hinge of vellum, by which it is attached to the upper surface of the bar E. At the other end is the head D, of wood, covered with some folds of prepared leather. The mallet lies in the position represented in the figure, its lower end resting on a cushion-bar K, which lies horizontally under the whole row of mallets. The key A R has a pin C, tipt with a bit of the softest cork or buckskin. This reaches to within one-twentieth of an inch of the shank of the mallet, but must not touch it. The distance E e is about one-third or one-fourth of the length of the shank. When the end A of the key is pressed down on the stuffing (two or three thicknesses of the most elastic woollen list), it raises the mallet, by means of the pin C, to the horizontal position E d, within one-eighth or one-tenth of an inch of the wire F; but it cannot be so much pressed down as to make the mallet touch the wire. At the same time that the key raises the mallet by means of the pin C, it also lifts off the damper G (a bit of sponge) from the wire. This damper is fixed on the end of a little wooden pin G g connected with the lever g H, which has a vellum hinge at H. This motion of the damper is caused by the pin I, which is fixed into the key near to R. These pieces are so adjusted that the first touch of the key lifts the damper, and, immediately after, the pin C acts on the shank of the mallet. As it acts so near to its centre of motion, it causes the head D to move briskly through a considerable arch D d. Being made extremely moveable and very light, it is thus *tossed* beyond the horizontal position E d, and it strikes the wire F, which is now at liberty to vibrate up and down, by the previous removal of the damper G. Having made its stroke, the mallet falls down again, and rubs on the soft substance on the pin C. It is of essential importance that this mallet be extremely light. Were it heavy, it would have so much force, after rebounding from the wire, that it would rebound from the pin C, and again strike the wire. For it will be recollected that the key is, at this time, down, and the pin C raised as high as possible, so that there is very little room for this rebound. Lessening the momentum of the mallet, by making it very light, making the cushion on the top of the pin C very soft, and great precision in the shape and figure of all the parts, are the only securities against the disagreeable rattling which these rebounds would occasion. In respect to the solidity and precision of workmanship, the British instruments are unrivalled, and vast numbers of them have been sent to all parts of the Continent.

"As the blow of so light a mallet cannot bring much sound from a wire, it has always been found necessary to have two strings for each note. Another circumstance contributes to enfeeble the sound. The mechanism necessary for producing it makes it almost impossible to give any considerable extent to the belly or sound board of the instrument. There is seldom any more of it than what occupies the space between the turning pins and the bridge. This is the more to be regretted, because the basses are commonly covered strings, that they may be of moderate length. The bass notes are also of brass, which has a considerable lower tone than a steel wire of the same diameter and tension. Yet even this substitution for steel in the bass strings is not enough. The highest of them are much too slack, and the lowest ones must be loaded, to compensate for want of length. This greatly diminishes the fullness, and still more the mellowness and distinctness of the tone, and frequently makes the very lowest notes hardly appreciable. This inequality of tone about the middle of the instrument is somewhat diminished by constructing the instrument with two bridges; one for the steel, and the other for the brass wires. But still the bass notes are very much inferior to the treble."

The mechanism of the grand pianoforte received considerable improvement from the talents of Joseph Merlin, of whom we have given a particular account when speaking of the harpsichord (see *ante*, p. 92). Many stories of his ingenuity are still handed down in the traditions of the pianoforte manufactory. In the well-known portrait of Fischer, the oboe player, by Gainsborough, now in Hampton Court Palace, that celebrated performer is depicted leaning upon a grand pianoforte, upon the name board of which is inscribed "Josephus Merlin Fecit."

The progress of the pianoforte in this country is characteristically exhibited in the following extracts from the reminiscences of two well-known veterans in the art:

William Gardiner, of Leicester, who was born in 1743, speaking of his youthful days, in his pleasant book of gossip, entitled *Music and Friends*, says (vol. i, p. 12): "My mother bought me a *pianoforte* of German make, not much bigger than two writing desks put together. Upon this I began with the lessons of Caspar Heck, and the thorough-bass of Pasquali." Again (p. 33) he says: "About the year 1782, young Crotch was brought to Leicester, as a musical prodigy, being then not more than five years old. He was brought first to our house, and played upon the *pianoforte* as he sat upon his mother's knee. At that time there were not more than two or three pianofortes in the town or neighbourhood; mine was esteemed a good one, made by

John Pohlman, I suppose in Germany, and before any were made in England.* Upon this instrument Crotch first exhibited his extraordinary talent in Leicester."

Michael Kelly, in his *Reminiscences* (vol. i, p. 21), speaking of the preparations for his continental journey, in 1779, says: " As good *pianofortes* were in these times scarce everywhere—in Italy particularly, my father bought a grand one made by one of the first London makers." This instrument formed part of Kelly's baggage during his travels; and he remarks: " It turned out in every respect excellent."

The same author (vol. ii, p. 161), describing Sheridan dining with him, shortly before the production of *Pizarro* (to which Kelly wrote the music), adds: " I had pen, ink, music-paper, and a small *pianoforte*, which the Duke of Queensbery had given me, and which he had been accustomed to take with him in his carriage when he travelled."

The pianoforte was common in the orchestras of our theatres during the last twenty years of the eighteenth century. In 1770, Mr. Burney, the nephew of Dr. Burney, was appointed *pianist* to Drury Lane Theatre; and a few years afterwads, Mr. Griffith Jones was nominated to the same office at the rival house of Covent Garden. Kelly, describing the performance of *Lionel and Clarissa*, at Dublin, in 1779, says: " Michael Arne presided at the *pianoforte* in the orchestra."

We have now arrived at the period of the foundation of the two large firms whose names are " household words" at the present day—Messrs. Broadwood and Stodart.

John Broadwood (the founder of the firm of Broadwood and Sons) was born in Scotland, in the year 1731; and, when about twenty years of age, travelled up from that country in search of employment in London. He was a carpenter or joiner by trade, and entered the firm of Tschudi, the eminent harpsichord maker, of whom we have before given some account (see p. 88 *ante*). Here he ingratiated himself so completely with his master that he became his son-in-law, partner, and successor. The earliest notice of a pianoforte of the *square* form in Messrs. Broadwood's books is

---

* The writer is here mistaken; John Pohlman was a German maker, resident in this country. (See p. 133 *ante*.)

dated 1771; the earliest of the *grand* form, in 1781.* In 1783, the books of the Great Seal Patent Office contain an entry of a grant (July 18th) " To John Broadwood, of Great Pulteney Street, Golden Square, '*pianoforte maker*,' for his new constructed pianoforte, which is far superior to any instrument of the kind hitherto made." This ingenious artist and worthy man died in 1812, at the advanced age of eighty-one, being succeeded by his son James Shudi Broadwood. There is an excellent folio mezzotint engraving of him by Messrs. Harrison and Say.

Robert Stodart, the fellow workman of John Broadwood, succeeded Americus Backers, before mentioned, and founded the firm so well known as John, William, and Matthew Stodart. The Patent Office Books, under the date Nov. 21, 1777, contain the entry of a grant to " Robert Stodart, of Wardour Street, Soho, musical instrument maker, for his new invented sort of instrument, or of *grand forte piano*, with an octave swell, and to produce various fine tones, together or separate, at the option of the performer." This seems to be a combination of the harpsichord and grand pianoforte, similar to that of Merlin's, before mentioned. It is stated that the grand pianoforte action, known as " the old English direct or *common* action," was the joint contrivance of John Broadwood, Robert Stodart, and Becker, a German mechanic, in the employ of Tschudi. James Broadwood, in a letter in the *Gentleman's Magazine*, 1812, attributed the invention to H. Baccers, a Dutchman, in 1772. We suspect that Americus Backers, Becker, and H. Baccers, were one and the same person.

Jacob Kirkman, the founder of the eminent firm of Joseph Kirkman and Son, was succeeded by his nephew Abraham, who was among the early improvers of the pianoforte. Harpsichords, nevertheless, were made by this house as late as 1800.

In 1786, John Gieb, an ingenious mechanic, effected a great improvement in the pianoforte, by the invention of what is called the *grasshopper action*. It consisted in the placing of an additional lever under that of the hopper hammer, the object of which was to apply the moving power as near as possible to the pivot of the hammer, which, it is evident, increased the rapidity of the blow. The end of the under lever

---

* It should be noticed that the first account book of the firm is, unfortunately, lost. Between 1771 and 1851, this eminent establishment made no fewer than 103,750 pianos!

rested on a little piece of mechanism, fixed in the finger key, and called a *grasshopper*, not unlike, in its object and contrivance, to that of the jack of the harpsichord. When the key was struck, the upper end of the grasshopper, which was about the eighth of an inch in thickness only, was carried past the end of the under lever, which rested on it, but communicated its impulse in passing, and received the end of the lever on a little block of wood glued on about a quarter of an inch below. In returning, the grasshopper, which was kept in its upright position by a slight spring of brass wire, yielded and passed the end of the lever again to its original position. Improvements in this action were patented, in 1794 and 1798, by William Southwell.

"The merit of the pianoforte," says the writer of an excellent article in Brewster's *Cyclopediæ*, vol. xvi, p. ii, p. 601, " was not immediately acknowledged in any of the three countries, Italy, France, or Germany; nor was it in its own country that it came first into vogue. In England it was little better. The elder Broadwood, by executing the mechanism in a superior style, first put the superiority of the instrument over the harpsichord beyond question; and, although some maintained the orthodoxy of the latter, the innovation gradually forced its way; and it had, in a great measure, taken possession of the public taste here, while the musicians of the Continent still clung to the harpsichord.

" Ever since the pianoforte came into general use, the ingenuity of rival makers has been exerted to improve the instrument in power and quality of tone, and in the delicacy and effectiveness of the touch. These improvements have been effected chiefly by enlarging the instrument in general, by extending the scale and increasing the weight of the strings, by correspondently strengthening the frame-work, and by improving the mechanism of the action.

" The original scale of the pianoforte was from FF (octave below that immediately under the bass staff) up to f in alt, comprising five octaves; and this has been gradually extended. The first addition was of half an octave upwards to C in altissimo. Then the scale was carried down to CCC; that is, half an octave lower than FF."

Francis Panormo, who was born in 1764, and died at the age of eighty, December 29, 1844, was the person who first suggested the *additional* keys to the pianoforte; viz. those from f to C; and found great difficulty in persuading the makers to listen to the proposition. The first pianoforte with these *additional* keys, made by Messrs. Broadwood, was used at the Rotunda, Dublin, in a concert given by Ferdinand Panormo, who was considered a fine performer in his time.

We have already shown that the pianoforte was first used on the public stage in 1767, and it is not a little singular that the same year was also productive of another event equally important in the history of its progress—viz. the arrival of J. S. Schroeter in England.* Dr. Burney (Rees' *Cyclopedia*, in v. Schroeter) says: " The pianoforte was a new instrument in this country : when he (Schroeter) first arrived, the hammer instruments of a large size were bad, and harpsichord players produced no great effects upon them; but Schroeter may be said to have been the first who brought into England the true art of treating that instrument. We were unwilling to give up the harpsichord, and thought the tone of the pianoforte spiritless and insipid, till expression and better instruments vanished our prejudices ; and the expression and the *chiar' oscuro*, in performing music expressly composed for that instrument, made us amends for the want of brilliancy in the tone so much that we soon found the scratching of the quill in the harpsichord intolerable, compared with the tone produced by the hammer."

The compositions and public performances of Clementi tended fully to establish the new instrument in the confidence of the musical world. He is called, by Dr. Crotch, and justly, " the father of pianoforte music." He occupies a very distinguished position in the annals of music, whether we regard him as composer, performer, inventor, or as an improver of the mechanism of the pianoforte.

---

* The *Belle Assemblée* for August, 1807, having named C. G. Schroter, organist of Nordhausen, Germany, as the inventor of the pianoforte, produced the following reply, in the *Gentleman's Magazine* of 1812, from James Broadwood : " If by the celebrated Schroter mentioned in the *Belle Assemblée* as having invented the pianoforte in 1717, the late composer for the pianoforte and first elegant performer on that instrument is meant, the article must be incorrect, as he only died about twenty years ago, aged about 58. The first maker of the grand pianoforte was H. Baccers, a Dutchman, who, in 1772, invented nearly the mechanism by which it is distinguished from the instrument with that name made in Germany. From the improvement by the English makers, particularly by my father, John Broadwood, who was the first *native of this Island* that attempted the business (before exclusively carried on by Germans and Flemings), it may be claimed as a British instrument, from its capacity of tone, extent of compass, superior in effect to every instrument of the same kind made on the continent." It is hardly necessary to say, that the writer of the above letter confounded the two Schroeters. We have quoted it for the information which it contains.

Muzio Clementi was born in the year 1752, at Rome, where his father followed the occupation of a chaser and embosser of silver vases and figures for the church service. He was related also to Buroni, afterwards principal composer at St. Peter's, from whom he received his earliest lessons in music. At six years of age, he commenced sol-fa-ing; at seven, he was placed under an organist of the name of Cordicelli, for instruction in harmony, and proceeded with such rapidity, that, at nine years old, he passed his examination and was admitted to an organist's place in his native city. His next masters were Santarelli, who is considered by the Italians the last great master of the vocal school, and Carpini, the deepest contrapuntist of his age in Rome. While studying under the latter, and as yet little more than twelve years old, young Clementi wrote, without the knowledge of his master, a mass for four voices, which was so much admired by his friends that at length Carpini desired to hear it; although not much addicted to bestowing praise, even Carpini could not refuse his tribute of applause, adding, however, what was probably very true, that if the youthful composer had consulted his master, "it might have been much better."

About this time, young Clementi's proficiency on the harpsichord, which, notwithstanding his other studies, he had assiduously practised, attracted the notice of the celebrated Peter Beckford, then on his travels in Italy. Mr. Beckford prevailed on the parents to consign their son's future education to his care, and brought him to England, to his seat in Dorsetshire, where the society and conversation of a family distinguished by literary habits and taste, as much as by wealth and rank, must have contributed in no small degree to inspire that relish for the whole circle of the belles lettres which led Clementi, independent of the study of his own art, to acquire an uncommon proficiency in both the living and dead languages, and an extensive acquaintance with literature and science in general. The works of Corelli, Alessandro Scarlatti, Paradies, and Handel, were the sources from which he derived musical instruction, and the examples on which he formed his taste; while at the same time he was indefatigable in the practice of the instrument to which he had devoted himself. His success was equal to his zeal and assiduity. At eighteen, he not only surpassed all his contemporaries in execution, taste, and expression, but had already composed (though it was not published till three years after) his celebrated Opera 2, a work which, by the common consent of all musicians, is entitled to the credit of being the basis on which the whole fabric of modern pianoforte sonatas has been founded, and which—though it is now, from the immense progress which manual dexterity has made in the last eighty years, within the powers of even fourth-rate performers—was, at the period of its production, the despair of such pianists as J. C. Bach and Schroeter, who were content to admire it, but declined the attempt to play what the latter professor declared could only be executed by its own composer, or by that great performer of all wonders and conqueror of all difficulties, the Devil.

While thus assiduous in the prosecution of his studies, Clementi was not, as many men of studious habits are, inattentive to his personal health. Aware of the injurious effects of constant sedentary application, he used every means that abstemiousness in diet and a regular and judicious plan of exercise afforded to counteract them; and, by this plan, he found his spirits unfailingly elastic, and his powers of application to study seldom wearied.

The time arranged by his father for his study with Mr. Beckford was no sooner completed, than his love of independence determined Clementi immediately to quit that gentleman's house and commence his career in the arena of the metropolis, where he was speedily engaged to preside at the harpsichord in the orchestra of the King's Theatre; and his reputation increased so rapidly, that he soon received as high remuneration for his lessons or performances as Bach or any of his most celebrated contemporaries. In 1780, at the suggestion of Pacchierotti, he determined to make a tour on the Continent, whither his compositions and the fame of his executive talent had long preceded him. In Paris, which was the first capital he visited, he remained till the summer of 1781; when he proceeded, by the way of Strasbourg and Munich, to Vienna, enjoying everywhere the patronage of sovereigns, the esteem and admiration of his brother musicians, and the enthusiastic applauses of the public. Accustomed to the measured and somewhat cold plaudits of an English audience, the first burst of Parisian enthusiasm so astonished him, that he frequently afterwards jocosely remarked, he could hardly believe himself the same Clementi in Paris as in London. In Vienna, he became acquainted with Haydn, Mozart, Saliéri, and many other celebrated musicians then resident in that city; and played alternately with Mozart before the

Emperor Joseph II, and the Grand Duke Paul (afterwards Emperor) of Russia, and his Consort. On one occasion, when the Imperial trio alone were present, Clementi and Mozart were desired to play. Some question of etiquette, as to which should begin, arising, the Emperor decided it by calling on Clementi, who, after preluding for some time, performed a sonata; and was followed by Mozart, who, without any other exordium than striking the chord of the key, also played a sonata. The Grand Duchess then said that one of her masters had written some pieces for her which were beyond her powers, but that she should much like to hear their effect; and producing two, Clementi played one, and Mozart the other, at first sight. She next proposed a theme, on which, at her request, the two great masters extemporized, alternately, to the astonishment and delight of their Imperial audience. The plan was evidently premeditated, and hardly fair towards the eminent professors who were thus surprised into immediate competition. The result, however, was equally honorable to both, between whom existed no unworthy feeling of jealousy, and creditable to them as artistes, on whose talents the demand, however unexpected or unusual, could not be too great.

In the course of his tour on the Continent, Clementi had written, in Paris, his operas 5 and 6; and in Vienna, his operas 7, 8, 9, and 10. On his return to England, he published his operas 11 and 12. In the Autumn of 1783, he performed publicly on the *pianoforte* at a series of concerts given at the Pantheon in Oxford Street. In the same year, J. B. Cramer, then about fourteen or fifteen years old, and who had previously received some lessons from Schroeter, and was studying counterpoint under Abel, became his pupil, and attended him almost daily, until Clementi went again for a short time to Paris, whence, however, he returned the following year; and from 1784 to 1802, continued in London, pursuing his professional career with increasing reputation as an instructor, composer, and performer.

About the year 1798, upon the failure of the house of Longman and Broderip, by which Clementi lost considerably, he was induced, by the representations of some eminent mercantile men, to engage in the music publishing and pianoforte manufacturing business. A new firm was quickly formed, at the head of which was Clementi's name; and from that period he declined taking pupils, but dedicated the time which was not demanded by his professional studies or mercantile engagements to improving the mechanism and construction of the instrument of which he may be said to have first established the popularity. He was associated in the manufacture of pianofortes with Mr. Frederick W. Collard. Thus arose the great firm of Collard and Collard.

In 1802, Clementi visited the Continent for the third time, remaining abroad about eight years. While in Berlin, he married his first wife; but he had soon to regret her loss. The widower, having recourse to travel to dissipate his grief, set out for St. Petersburgh; but very speedily left Russia and proceeded to Vienna, whence he was soon called by the death of his brother, which rendered his presence in Rome necessary. In 1810, he returned to England, and, in the year succeeding, entered again into the matrimonial state. He now published other works, and among them his *Practical Harmony*, in four volumes, and his *Gradus ad Parnassum*, in three.

Clementi was one of the founders and directors of the Philharmonic Society, to which he presented two symphonies, and every season conducted one of the concerts of that Institution. In 1827, the musical profession, as a testimony of affection and respect, invited him to a dinner at the Albion Tavern; and during the evening he was prevailed on to sit down to the pianoforte, when, choosing a subject from Handel's First Organ Concerto, he extemporized on it in a manner that proved how little his powers of imagination were affected by time, and excited the wonder of a very numerous company of judges assembled on the memorable occasion.

Clementi died on the 10th of March, 1832, after an illness of short duration, though his mind had for some time previous been gradually yielding to the attacks of age. His remains were deposited in the cloisters of Westminster Abbey, the three choirs of London and a great number of his brother-professors attending to pay the last tribute of respect to so valuable a man, and so eminent a composer.

The pianoforte was now firmly established in the public favour, and the date of Clementi's commencing manufacturer, i. e. 1800, gave the death blow to the old harpsichord. " Clementi's successors," says a recent writer, " worthily followed in his steps; finding new wants arise, from time to time, they demanded new improvements to satisfy them; and thus the player and manufacturer vied with each other in the general advance."

Before closing this chapter, it will be interesting here to chronicle a list of harpsichord and pianoforte makers resident in London at the end of the eighteenth century, which we are enabled to do from a rare and perhaps unique *Musical Directory for the Year* 1794.*

"BECK, Pia Forte Maker, 10, Broad St. Carnaby Market.

"BUNTLEBART and SIEVERS, Instrument Makers, 7, Princes St. Hanover Square.

"CORRIE, Pia Forte Maker, 41, Broad St. Carnaby Market.

"DONE (Joshua), Pia Forte Maker, 30, Chancery Lane.

"ELWICK, Harpsichord Maker, Long Acre.

"GANER, Pia Maker, 48, Broad St. Carnaby Market.

"HANCOCK, Organized Pia Maker, Parliament St. Westminster.

"HOUSTON and Co. Pia Makers, 54, Great Marlborough St.

"KIRKMAN and SON, Harpsichord Makers, 19, Broad St. Carnaby Market.

"LONGMAN and BRODERIP, Pia Makers, 26, Cheapside; 13, Haymarket; and Tottenham Court Road.

"PETHER (George), Instrument Maker, Oxford St.

"SHUDI and BROADWOOD, Instrument Makers, Great Pulteney St. Golden Square.

"STODDART, Pia Forte Maker, Wardour St."

---

* This volume consists of 84 pages, besides 6 of introductory matter. It was compiled, according to the signature at the end of the preface, by J. Doane. The copy to which we refer is in the valuable library of the Sacred Harmonic Society.

CHAPTER X.

THE PROGRESS OF THE PIANOFORTE IN THE NINETEENTH CENTURY.

AT the beginning of the nineteenth century, pianoforte making rapidly increased in every part of Europe, especially in Germany, France, and England; showing, as M. Thalberg expresses it, "how broad spread became the estimation of the instrument." From the year 1800 to the present time, scarce a year has passed without the appearance in England alone of patents for real or imaginary improvements, "countless experiments being made, most of them totally empirical and unimportant, but some, especially in the last thirty years, truly scientific, resulting in the enlargement and improvement which we now find."

It is not possible to enter into minute details respecting all the various experiments that have gradually brought the pianoforte to its present state of perfection, nor to do full justice to those scientific men who have directed their talents and energies to the subject; but we have thought that a list of patents, chronologically arranged, from the year 1694 to the year 1851, and carefully extracted from the valuable Indices prepared by Mr. Woodcroft, would be an acceptable record to those interested in the subject of the present work. We have the more pleasure in presenting this list to our readers, because it corrects many errors prevalent in the "trade" respecting the precise period that gave birth to certain important improvements now in daily use.*

---

* The Indices prepared by Mr. Woodcroft out of the materials accumulated during two centuries in the Great Seal Patent Office are valuable memorials of patient industry and extensive practical knowledge. They are four in number. The first gives at length the titles of the patents with a progressive number prefixed. From this

1694. (Oct. 20.)	GEORGE JOYCE and PETER EAST—"a speciall lycence for the sole use and exercise of their new invention of an instrument, which being applyd to organs, clockys, or any other key instrument, as harpsicord, virginalls, or the like, will cause the same too chyme or playe any mannere of tune, air, or notes plain, or perform a consort, and alterable to any tune or air in halfe an hour by any person, tho' noe master of musick, without changing the instrument."
1730. (Oct. 22.)	JOHN HARRIS, "harpsichord and spinnett maker"—a patent for his "new invention of an harpsichord, on which (having only two sets of strings) may be performed either one or two unisons, or two unisons and one octave, either in the *forts* or *pianos*, or loud or soft, and the contrary, may be executed as quick as thought, and also double basses, by touching only single keys, whereby hard divisions to the basse part may be well played in a double manner without the thumb and finger together."
1730. (Dec. 17.)	WILLIAM BARTON, for his "new invencion of pens of silver, brass, steel, and all other sorts of metals, to improve the use of harpsichords and spinnets, which will improve the tone of the said instruments, and last many years without amendment; crow and raven's quills, of which they are now made, requiring frequent change and trouble in repairing."
1741. (Dec. 30.)	ROGER PLENIUS, of the parish of St. George, Hanover Square, harpsichord maker, for "his new invencion of meliorating the musical instruments called harpsichords, lyrichords (which are harpsichords strung with cat gut), and spinnets."
1745. (July 10.)	ROGER PLENIUS, of St. George, Hanover Square, harpsichord maker, for the "sole use and exercise of his new invencion for the great improvement of musical instruments called harpsicords and spinnets."
1769. (Dec. 18.)	BURKAT SHUDI, harpsichord maker, for "his invention of a piece of mechanism or machinery by which the harpsichord is very much improved."
1770. (Dec. 28.)	THOMAS HAXBY, of York, musical instrument maker, for "his new invented single harpsichord, to answer all the purposes of a double one, and sell for the common price of a single one."
1772. (July 29.)	ADAM WALKER, of Manchester, "teacher of natural philosophy," for "his new invented method of producing continued tones from the wire strings of an harpsichord, and thereby remedying the acknowledged defect of these kinds of instruments, giving them all the powers of musical expression which the organ, violin, lyrichord, or harmonica, are capable of; and that he can adapt this improvement, which he calls a *cœlestina*, to any harpsichord without altering either the form of the instrument or any of its stops, by adding a new piece of mechanism to it, of which he hath been the sole inventor."

---

catalogue is formed: 1st, an index of subjects, classified and alphabetically arranged; and 2nd, an alphabetical index of names, &c. The series is rendered complete by a "Reference Index," giving under each progressive number the title and vol. of every work in which any notice or description of the invention represented by that number has appeared. Not, at first, being aware of this valuable record, we took the trouble to compile a similar list of "Inventions and Improvements in the Pianoforte" from such works as were accessible: i. e. *The Repertory of Arts and Manufactures; Newton's London Journal of Arts;* the *Official Catalogues* and *Jury Reports* of the Exhibition of 1851, &c. It is hardly necessary to say that the present list is much more extensive, and to be relied on for its accuracy. We have added a few remarks between brackets: those in italics are Mr. Woodcroft's.

1774. (Sept. 12.)	JOSEPH MERLIN, of Little Queen Ann Street, Mary-le-Bone, mathematical instrument maker, for "his new invented kind of compound harpsichord, in which, besides the jacks with quills, a set of hammers, of the nature of those used in the kind of harpsichords called *piano forte*, are introduced in such manner that either may be played separately or both together, at the pleasure of the performer; and for adding the aforesaid hammers to an harpsichord of the common kind already made, so as to render it such compound harpsichord."
1774. (Dec. 28.)	SAMUEL GILLESPY, of Brownlow Street, St. Giles-in-the-Fields, harpsichord maker, for "his new constructed principle of putting on the quills to strike the strings of a harpsichord with a peddle and swell, which raises the top, brings on the tone, and swells a new celestial stop, at the same time preserving the instrument compleat."
1777. (Nov. 21.)	ROBERT STODART, of Wardour Street, Soho, musical instrument maker, for "his new invented sort of instrument, or of *grand forte piano* with an octave swell, and to produce various fine tones, together or separate, at the option of the performer." (A combination of the harpsichord and grand pianoforte.)
1783. (July 18.)	JOHN BROADWOOD, of Great Pulteney Street, Golden Square, *piano forte maker*, for "his new constructed piano forte which is far superior to any instrument of the kind heretofore made."
1786. (Nov. 9.)	JOHN GIEB, of the Old Baily, musical instrument maker, for "his new improvement upon the musical instruments called the *piano forte* and harpsichord, by which the same will become perfect and compleat instruments of their kind, which hath never before been discovered, and by which the same can be more easily tuned and played upon; and that such improvement extends to each of such instruments equally alike." (The grasshopper action, which is still in use for square instruments, is included in this patent.)
1787. (March 31.)	JOHN LANDRETH, of Tabernacle Walk, near Old Street, musical instrument maker, for "his new improvement upon the several musical instruments called *piano forte*, harpsichord, organ and guitar, and upon various other musical instruments, by which the same can be more easily kept in order and played upon, and by which the same will become perfect and compleat instruments of their kind, which hath never before been discovered."
1787. (May 25.)	HUMPHREY WALTON, of the parish of St. Pancras, musical instrument maker, for "his new improvements on the musical instrument called the *piano forte*, and other instruments, which he believes will render them more compleat and perfect than any now in use."
1790. (April 13.)	JOHN CRANG HANCOCK, of Wych Street, St. Clement Danes, organ builder, for "his new invented *grand pianoforte* with a spring key touch, German flute, and harp, which is preferable to any hitherto discovered."
1792. (Feb. 4.)	GEORGE GARCKA, of Wardour Street, Soho, musical instrument maker, for his "new improvements on the *piano forte*, which will render that instrument more perfect than any now in use."
1792. (June 6.)	JAMES DAVIS, of Tottenham Court Road, organ builder, for "his new invented improvements upon the several musical instruments called *piano fortes* and harpsichords."
1790. (Nov. 16.)	JAMES BALL, of Duke Street, Grosvenor Square, piano forte maker, for "his new invented improvements upon the *square* and other piano fortes, which will render these instruments more perfect than any hitherto made."

1792. (Jan. 26.)	GEORGE BUTTERY, of the parish of St. Martin-in-the-Fields, musical instrument maker, for "his new improvement in the construction of *piano fortes* and all other musical instruments in which hammers are or can be made use of."
1794. (Oct. 17.)	SEBASTIAN ERARD, of Great Marlborough Street, musical instrument maker, for "his new invented improvements in the construction of harps and *pianofortes*, both large and small, and which improvements may also be applied to all kinds of instruments where keys are used."
1794. (Oct. 18.)	WILLIAM SOUTHWELL, late of Dublin, but now of Lad Lane, London, musical instrument maker, for "his new invented improvements in the construction of the musical instrument called a *piano forte*, by which improvements the tones of such instruments are rendered more distinct and perfect, and the players playing on such instruments have a power to produce the gradations of tones from piano to forte with greater effect than they are able at present to produce the same; and an additional number of keys may be put to such instruments in a new manner, upon a better construction than such keys can be put to piano fortes at present." (Improvements in the dampers form the basis of this patent.)
1795. (Jan. 12.)	WILLIAM STODART, of Golden Square, piano forte maker, for "his new invented *upright grand piano forte*, of the form of a book case, the mechanism of which is upon an entire new construction."
1797. (Jan. 31.)	WILLIAM ROLFE and SAMUEL DAVIS, of Cheapside, musical instrument maker, for "new invented improvements upon the musical instruments called the harpsichord, *grand piano forte*, and *square piano forte*. (See *The Repertory of Arts and Manufactures*, vol. vii, p. 431.)
1798. (Nov. 8.)	WILLIAM SOUTHWELL, of Broad Court, St. Martin-in-the-Fields, musical instrument maker, for "his new invented improvements on the *action* and construction of *piano fortes* and other musical instruments." (Further improvements in the dampers.)
1799. (Oct. 3.)	JOSEPH SMITH, of the parish of St. Martin-in-the-Fields, gentleman, for "his new invented improvements in the internal bracings of *piano fortes*, so as to admit the introduction into the internal part of the instrument of a drum, tabour, or tambourine, with sticks or beaters thereunto belonging, together with other improvements thereon." (See *The Repertory of Arts and Manufactures*, vol. x, 215; xii, 71; xv, 215.)
1801. (May 16.)	SEBASTIAN ERARD, for "his new invented improvements in the construction of harps and *piano fortes*.
1801. (Nov. 7.)	JOHN CONRAD BECKER, of Princes Street, Soho, musical instrument maker, for "his new invented improvements in musical instruments, chiefly applicable to harps and *piano fortes*." (See *The Repertory of Arts and Manufactures*, vol. xvi, p. 146.)
1801. (Nov. 10.)	ANTONIUS BEMETZRIEDER, of Chelsea, master of arts, and ROBERT SCOTT, JOHN SCOTT, and ALEXANDER SCOTT, of Margaret Street, Cavendish Square, musical instrument makers, for "their new invented method of making piano fortes, entirely new, both in principle, construction, and shape." (See *The Repertory of Arts and Manufactures*, vol. xvi, p. 143.)
1801. (Nov. 28.)	EDWARD RYLEY, of Kingston-upon-Hull, organ builder, and piano forte maker, for "his new invented moveable keys for pianofortes, organs, and other instruments." (See *The Repertory of Arts and Manufactures*, vol. xvi, p. 144.)

1802. (Mar. 9.)	THOMAS LOUD, of Hoxton, musical instrument maker, for "his new invented improvements in the action and construction of upright piano fortes."
1803. (June 28.)	GEORGE WOODS, of Barbican, gentleman, for "his new invented method of constructing harps, harpsichords, piano fortes, violins, guitars, and other stringed musical instruments."
1807. (April 8.)	WILLIAM SOUTHWELL, of the city of Dublin, musical instrument maker, for "his invented certain improvements upon a piano forte, which is so constructed as to prevent the possibility of its being so frequently out of tune as piano fortes now generally are, which he denominates '*a cabinet piano forte.*'"
1808. (Sept. 24.)	SEBASTIAN ERARD, of Great Marlborough Street, for "his invented certain improvements upon piano fortes large and small, and upon harps, for which he has already obtained a patent." (The *up*-bearing is included in this patent. By this the stroke of the hammer forced the string against the nut, instead of away from it, which was the case with the *down*-bearing. A firmer and increased tone is the result.)
1809. (July 26.)	DAVID LOESCHMAN, of Newman Street, piano forte maker, for "his invented certain improvements in the musical scale of keyed instruments with fixed tones, such as pianos, organs, &c." (The *Enharmonic* piano, an account of which may be seen in the *Monthly Magazine*, 1812, pp. 9, 213, 409.)
1810. (May 2.)	SEBASTIAN ERARD, of Great Marlborough Street, for "his invented certain improvements on piano fortes and harps."
1811. (March 4.)	WILLIAM SOUTHWELL, of Gresse Street, Rathbone Place, piano forte maker, for "his invented certain improvements in the construction of a pianoforte."
1811. (March 26.)	ROBERT WORNUM, the younger, of Princes Street, Hanover Square, piano forte maker, for "his invented improved upright piano forte."
1811. (Sept. 9.)	WILLIAM FREDERICK COLLARD, of Tottenham Court Road, musical instrument maker, for "his invented certain improvements upon an upright piano forte."
1816. (May 14.)	WILLIAM SIMMONS, of Wigan, Lancashire, writing master and teacher of accounts, for "his invented certain improvements applicable to keyed instruments, as the organ, piano forte, harpsichord, or to any instrument or set of instruments to which keys are, or may, or can be affixed."
1816. (Oct. 14.)	JOSEPH KIRKMAN, of Broad Street, St. James's, piano forte maker, for "his invented improved method of applying an octave stop to piano fortes."
1816. (Nov. 14.)	JOHN DAY, of Brompton, lieutenant on half-pay, of our 11th regiment of foot, for "his invented 'certain improvements and additions in the construction of piano fortes and other keyed musical instruments.'"
1817. (Feb. 1.)	ISAAC HENRY ROBERT MOTT, of Brighton, composer and teacher of music, for "his invented 'Method of producing from vibrating substances a tone or musical sound, the peculiar powers in the management whereof are entirely new, and which musical instrument he denominates the *sostinente* piano forte.'"
1820. (Jan. 15.)	JAMES THOM, of Wells Street, Mary-le-bone, piano forte maker, and WILLIAM ALLEN, of Castle Street, ditto, piano forte maker, "for their invented or found out 'a certain improvement in piano fortes.'" (This patent was brought out by Stodart; it was for the metal tube bracing. Before this, however, Hawkins and Braithwaite had both made use of metal bars for upright instruments. This bracing was also *compensating*, as the metallic tubes possessing the same properties as the strings, extended or relaxed simultaneously with them.)

1820. (May 13.)	ROBERT WORNUM, of Wigmore Street, Cavendish Square, piano forte maker, for "his invented improvement on piano fortes and certain other stringed instruments." (Equal tension stringing: this plan has not been generally adopted.)
1821. (March 8.)	WILLIAM FREDERICK COLLARD, of No. 195, Tottenham Court Road, &c. for "his invented certain improvements on musical instruments called piano fortes" (*an additional bridge and a moveable damper*).
1821. (April 5.)	WILLIAM SOUTHWELL, of Gresse Street, Rathbone Place, piano forte manufacturer, for "certain improvements on cabinet pianofortes" (*the action parts*).
1821. (Dec. 22.)	PIERRE ERARD, of Great Marlborough Street, musical instrument maker, "in consequence of communications made to him by a certain foreigner residing abroad, he is in possession of 'an invention of certain improvements on piano fortes and other keyed instruments.'" (The repetition action This is a beautiful piece of mechanism, which, while it gives a blow of great force, can also be modified to the most delicate touch, the action being always under the hand ready for the repetition of the stroke.)
1823. (Feb. 18.)	FRANCIS DEAKIN, of Birmingham, sword maker, for "his improvements to piano fortes and other stringed instruments."
1823. (July 24.)	HENRY SMART, of Berners Street, piano manufacturer, for "certain improvements in the construction of pianofortes."
1823. (Dec. 4.)	THOMAS TODD, of Swansea, South Wales, organ builder, for his "improvement in producing tone upon musical instruments of various descriptions" (*obtaining violin notes from pianofortes*).
1824. (July 29.)	WILLIAM WHEATSTONE, of No. 118, Jermyn Street, St. James's, music seller, for "a new method of improving and augmenting the tones of piano fortes, organs, and euphonions" (*by introducing drums*).
1825. (Jan. 5.)	PIERRE ERARD, &c. "in consequence of communications made to him by a certain foreigner residing abroad, of 'certain improvements on pianofortes.'" (The system of fixed metal-bracing, which is now generally adopted.)
1825. (Jan. 18.)	FRANCIS MELVILLE, of Argyll Street, in the city of Glasgow, piano forte maker, for an "improved method of securing that description of small piano fortes commonly called square piano fortes from the injuries to which they are liable from the tension of the strings."
1825. (Feb. 26.)	GEORGE AUGUSTUS KOLLMAN, of the Friary, St. James's Palace, professor of music, for "certain improvements in the mechanism and general construction of piano fortes."
1825. (Oct. 6.)	JAMES SHUDI BROADWOOD, of Great Pulteney Street, Golden Square, for "certain improvements in small, or what are commonly called square pianofortes" (*preventing the recoil of the hammer*).
1826. (July 4.)	ROBERT WORNUM, &c. for "certain improvements on piano fortes (*the action part*).
1827. (Feb. 20.)	PIERRE ERARD, &c. "in consequence of communications made to him by a certain foreigner residing abroad," of "certain improvements in the construction of piano fortes."
1827. (March 22.)	JAMES STEWART, of Store Street, Bedford Square, piano forte maker, for his "certain improvements in piano fortes, and in the mode of stringing the same." (A new damper arrangement forms part of this patent, in which the vertical wire was made to rise at some distance behind the strings actually struck, the head being elongated this distance forwards. In the old system, the damper wire, rising close by the side of the

vibrating strings, was apt to jar against them—an evil which this improvement removed. This patent was brought forward by Messrs. Collard.)

1827. (April 9.) JAMES SHUDI BROADWOOD, &c. for "certain improvements in the grand piano fortes."

1827. (July 25.) EDWARD DODD, of 62, Berwick Street, Oxford Street, instrument maker, for "certain improvements on piano fortes."

1827. (Aug. 30.) WILLIAM DETTMAR, of Upper Mary-le-bone, piano forte maker, for "certain improvements on piano fortes" (*altering the pitch*).

1828. (July 10.) JOHN HENRY ANTHONY GUNTER, of Camden Town, piano forte manufacturer, for "certain improvements on piano fortes" (*an additional sounding board*).

1828. (July 24.) ROBERT WORNUM, &c. for "certain improvements on upright piano fortes." (The *piccolo* action, which has been extensively followed by the foreign makers.)

1829. (June 19.) FRANCIS DAY, of the Poultry, optician, and AUGUST MÜNCK, mechanic, of the same place, "in consequence of a communication made to them by a certain foreigner residing abroad, and inventions by themselves," for "certain improvements on musical instruments" (*adapting sonorous metallic springs to a piano forte*).

1829. (Aug. 11.) THOMAS HALL ROLFE, of Cheapside, musical instrument maker, for "an improvement or improvements upon the self-acting piano forte."

1829. (Nov. 2.) JAMES STEWART, of George Street, Euston Square, piano forte maker, for "certain improvements on piano fortes." (A check to the under hammer, to prevent the rebound of the hammer against the string. This patent was brought out by Messrs. Collard.)

1830. Feb. 27.) SIMON THOMPSON, of Great Yarmouth, mariner's compass maker, for "certain improvements in piano fortes" (*keys and action part*).

1831. (Feb. 2.) JOHN CHARLES SCHWIESO, of Regent Street, musical instrument maker, for "certain improvements on piano fortes and other stringed instruments."

1831. (July 20.) WILLIAM ALLEN, of Catherine Street, Strand, piano forte maker, for "certain improvements upon piano fortes."

1832. (Sept. 8.) PIERRE FREDERIC FISCHER, of Chester Place, Regent's Park, gentleman, for an invention communicated to him by a certain foreigner residing abroad, of "certain improvements in piano fortes."

1833. (Nov. 1.) JACOB FREDERICK ZEITTER, of New Cavendish Street, Portland Street, piano forte maker, for his invention of "certain improvements on piano-fortes and other stringed musical instruments."

1835. (Jan. 15.) JAMES STEWART, of George Street, Euston Square, piano forte maker, for his invention of "improvements in the mechanism of horizontal grand and square piano fortes." (A new construction of the action, the escapement being placed upon the key, and, coming into contact with a lever or crank, thus regulating the rise and fall of the hammer.)

1835. (March 2.) FREDERICK LUDWIG HAHN DANCHELL, of Great Marlborough Street, musical instrument maker, for "certain improvements in piano fortes; being a communication partly from his partner, FREDERICK GEORGE GREINER, a foreigner residing abroad."

1835. (March 2.)	ROBERT WOLF, of Cornhill, musical instrument maker, for "an improvement in pianofortes, consisting in the new construction, on the principle of acoustics, of a sounding body applicable to every description of piano fortes."
1835. (May 13.)	PIERRE FREDERICK FISCHER, of Great Marlborough Street, merchant, for "certain improvements in piano fortes."
1835. (Dec. 31.)	PIERRE ERARD, of Great Marlborough Street, musical instrument maker, for "certain improvements in piano fortes," being an extension of former Letters Patent granted by His late Majesty George IV.
1836. (Feb. 17.)	JOSEPH LIDEL, of Arundel Street, Panton Square, professor of music, for "certain improvements in piano fortes, being a communication from a foreigner residing abroad."
1836. (March 8.)	JOHN GODWIN, of Cumberland Street, Hackney Road, piano forte maker, for "an improvement in the making or construction of piano fortes."
1836. (March 8.)	CHARLES GUYNEMER, of Manchester Street, Manchester Square, professor of singing, for "certain improvements in piano fortes, being a communication from a foreigner residing abroad."
1836. (May 14.)	WHEATLEY KIRK, of Commercial Street, Leeds, musicseller, and manufacturer of piano fortes, for "certain improvements in piano fortes."
1837. (Aug. 24.)	WILLIAM SOUTHWELL, of No. 5, Winchester Row, New Road, piano forte maker, for "a certain improvement in piano fortes."
1839. (Feb. 21.)	JOHANN ANDREAS STUMPFF, of Great Portland Street, musical instrument maker, for "improvements in grand and other piano fortes."
1839. (Feb. 23.)	GEORGE AUGUSTUS KOLLMAN, of the Friary, St. James's Palace, professor of music—an extension of former Letters Patent for "certain improvements in the mechanism and general construction of piano fortes."
1840. (Feb. 14.)	JOSEPH CLARK, of Boston, in the county of Lincoln, printer, for his invention of "improvements in piano fortes."
1840. (June 1.)	JOHN HAWLEY, of Frith Street, Soho, watch maker, for "improvements in pianos and harps."
1840. (Sept. 24.)	PIERRE ERARD, for his invention of improvements in piano fortes." (An action for the oblique pianoforte.)
1840. (Nov. 7.)	EDWARD DODD, of Kentish Town, musical instrument maker, for his invention of "improvements in piano fortes."
1840. (Dec. 16.)	JOHN STEWARD, of Wolverhampton, in the county of Stafford, esquire, for his invention of "an improvement in the construction of pianofortes, harpsichords, and other similar stringed musical instruments."
1841. (June 23.)	JOHN GODWIN, of Cumberland Street, Hackney Road, pianoforte maker, for his invention of "an improved construction of pianofortes of certain descriptions."
1841. (July 7.)	JAMES STEWARD, of Wolverhampton, in the county of Stafford, esquire, for his invention of "certain improvements in the construction of pianofortes. (The Euphonicon; an upright pianoforte, the framework entirely of iron, with the bass strings exposed in the form of a harp. It had three sound-boards.)
1841. (Nov. 11.)	JAMES STEWART, of 21, Osnaburgh Street, pianoforte maker, for "certain improvements in the action of horizontal pianofortes." (The introduction of the traversing escapement fixed upon the hammer-rail,

thereby admitting of a firmer blow, and greater resistance; as also a new repetition movement.

1842. (Jan. 15.) THOMAS LAMBERT, of Regent's Park, musical instrument maker, for "improvements in the action of cabinet pianofortes."

1842. (Feb. 8.) HENRY FOWLER BROADWOOD, of 33, Great Pulteney Street, Golden Square, for "an improvement in that part of a pianoforte or harpsichord, or other like instrument, commonly called the name board."

1842. (Feb. 15.) ROBERT WORNUM, of Store Street, Bedford Square, for "improvements in the action of pianofortes."

1843. (Jan. 19.) JOSEPH KIRKMAN, jun. of Soho Square, pianoforte manufacturer, for "improvements in the action of pianofortes."

1843. (Feb. 11.) HENRY DU BOCHET, of 46, South Mall, in the city of Cork, Ireland, pianoforte tuner, for "a new method of making pianofortes."

1843. (April 29.) JAMES STEWART, of No. 3, Gloucester Crescent, Regent's Park, pianoforte maker, and THOMAS LAMBERT, of 91, Albany Street, pianoforte maker, for "improvements in the action of pianofortes."

1844. (July 3.) CHARLES MAURICE ELIZEE SAUTTER, of Austin Friars, gentleman, for "improvements in pianofortes."

1844. (Oct. 10.) OBED MITCHELL COLEMAN, of Fitzroy Square, gentleman, for "improvements in pianofortes."

1844. (Dec. 12.) SEBASTIEN MERCIER, of Paris, manufacturer of pianofortes, for "improvements in pianofortes."

1845. (April 7.) WILLIAM HATTERSLEY, of Regent Street, Westminster, pianoforte maker, for "certain improvements in the construction of pianofortes."

1845. (Oct. 10.) EDWARD LESLEY WALKER, of Foley Place, professor of music, for "improvements in pianofortes."

1845. (Oct. 27.) BENJAMIN NICKELS, of York Street, Lambeth, machinist, for "improvements in pianofortes."

1845. (Nov. 11.) SAMUEL THOMAL CROMWELL, of Romsey, Hants, teacher of music, for "improvements in apparatus to be applied to pianofortes."

1846. (April 28.) ISAAC HENRY ROBERT MOTT, of No. 76, Strand, pianoforte maker, for "certain improvements in musical instruments, whereby they are rendered much more durable, much more capable of resisting the injurious and destructive effects of the atmosphere (especially of extreme climates), and whereby the quality of their tone is greatly improved and remains good for a much longer period."

1846. (June 16.) FREDERIC HANDELL BURKINYOUNG, of Baker Street, gentleman, for "improvements in pianofortes."

1846. (July 8.) THOMAS WOOLLEY, of Nottingham, pianoforte manufacturer, for "improvements in pianofortes."

1846. (July 31.) THEOPHILE AUGUSTE DRESCHKE, of Rue Thérése, Paris, late an officer of artillery in the service of Prussia, and late professor of sacred music at the University of Berlin, for "improvements in the keys of pianofortes and other keyed musical instruments."

1846. (Aug. 29.)	ALEXANDRE DEBAIN, manufacturer, of Paris, for "certain improvements applicable to keyed musical instruments."
1847. (April 29.)	JOHN SPEAR, of Gloucester Road, Hyde Park Gardens, gentleman, for "improvements in pianofortes and in the musical scale of notes in use for such instruments; and also in apparatus to facilitate the action of the fingers on the keys of pianofortes."
1848. (Jan. 11.)	JAMES MONTGOMERY, of Salisbury Street, engineer, for "certain improvements in pianofortes and other similar finger keyed instruments."
1849. (May 15.)	WILLIAM PHILLIP PARKER, of Lime Street, City, gentleman, for "improvements in the construction of pianofortes."
1850. (Sept. 12.)	PIERRE ERARD, of Paris, for "improvements in the construction of pianofortes." (The addition of pedal keys. The patent also includes the metal wrest-plank.)
1851. (June 3.)	JOHN HOPKINSON, of Oxford Street, pianoforte manufacturer, for "improvements in pianofortes." (The repetition and tremolo action.)

To take a retrospective glance at the interesting information furnished by this list,—

We find, as early as 1774, mention of the "pianoforte" in the patent granted to Joseph Merlin. This is followed up, in 1777, by Robert Stodart's "newly invented grand pianoforte." Then, in 1783, we have "John Broadwood, of Great Pulteney Street, Golden Square" (the locale of the firm at the present day), "pianoforte maker." In succeeding years, we find Gieb, Landreth, Walton, Hancock, Garcka, Davis, Bull, and Buttery—all unknown men to the present generation—each contributing his quota towards the perfection of the pianoforte.

In 1794, we first notice the great name of Sebastian Erard; followed, in the same year, by William Southwell, an artist of considerable skill, and to whom the instrument is indebted for many of its greatest improvements. Then comes Stodart, with his invention of the "upright grand" pianoforte; and William Rolfe, the founder of a most respectable house, in being at the present day. The century is well closed by Southwell's perfection of his damper action.

The nineteenth century is commenced by the name of Erard; and followed, shortly afterwards (in 1807), by Southwell's invention of the "cabinet" pianoforte. In 1811, the name of Robert Wornum first appears, as an improver of the "upright" pianoforte—an instrument which he afterwards, in the name of the "Cottage" and the "Piccolo," made his own. Wornum was an artist of extensive practical knowledge, and profound mechanical skill. Many of his inventions are now spread over the Continent as well as England.

The well-known name of Collard makes its first appearance in the Patent books of 1811; but the factory, as we have shown, under the names of Longman and Broderip, and afterwards under that of Clementi, was established in the previous century. Joseph Kirkman follows, in 1816, with the curious invention (derived from the harpsichord) of an "octave stop" to the pianoforte. This is the first appearance of another great name in the books of the Patent Office. The year 1817 introduces us to Isaac Mott's "Sostinente pianoforte," an improvement of the "celestina," as patented by the philosopher, Adam Walker, in 1772.

The year 1820 exhibits a new era in the construction of pianofortes—the invention of "metallic tubes" by Messrs. Thom and Allen. This paved the way for various patents introduced by the great makers at different periods: i. e. for the introduction of steel tension bars, metal bracings of various kinds, and steel string plates; all having for their object the strengthening of the instrument, so as to enable it to resist the enormous strain from the increased and increasing weight or tension of the strings.

A more perfect mechanism of touch was the next great desideratum; and in the next year (1821), Erard took out the patent for his beautiful piece of mechanism known as the "repetition action." The touch has been brought to still greater perfection by the ingenious Mr. John Hopkinson, whose first patent for his "repetition and tremolo action," taken out in 1851, closes our list.

It would have been desirable to have recorded a similar list of patents taken out in foreign countries; but the task was impossible, from the imperfect manner in which such records are kept in most continental cities. It would have been impossible on another account, which will be readily understood when we inform our readers that one maker—the ingenious M. Pape, of Paris—enumerates no fewer than 120 patents (more than all the English patents put together, from 1694 to 1851) taken out by himself alone! "Trifles light as air." All the really important inventions of recent date, relative to the pianoforte, are due to the talents of the English, who, in this particular at least, far excell all other countries.

A number of ingenious inventions may be claimed for the natives of Germany, France, Belgium, Austria, the United States, &c. some of the most important of which will receive attention in the Second Part of our work.

We may here remark that the "Vienna action" is more simple and less expensive than our own; and its results are totally different, both in touch and tone; the former being extremely light, the latter very thin. It was formerly in use throughout Germany; but, of late years, the English mechanism, "*die englische Mechanik*," has been more generally adopted in Germany and elsewhere; and hence the remarkable improvement of pianofortes on the Continent.

In pointing out a few of the most eminent Continental pianoforte makers of the nineteenth century, we may instance Bessalié, of Breslau; Dörner, of Stuttgart; Heitemeyer, of Münsten; Rühms, of Altona; and Hoxa and Seuffert, of Vienna. In France, we have Pfeiffer, Petzold, Herz, Pape, Pleyel, &c. Russia has an excellent artist in Lichtenthal; and Denmark, in Hornung. Both these latter makers use the English action.

In the United States, we have Messrs. Nunns and Clark, Driggs, and Pirsson, of New York; and in Boston, the eminent firm of the Chickerings. The latter may truly be termed the Broadwoods of America.

"The manufacture of the piano as a branch of trade," says M. Thalberg, in his excellent remarks drawn up for the Jury of the Exhibition of 1851, "is of very great importance, from the superior character of the principal workmen, and the vast numbers employed, directly and indirectly, in connection with it. In all the cities of the civilized world, there are numerous makers of this instrument, with immense numbers of workmen; and in most secondary towns throughout Europe, there are small makers; while the increase of the number of pianos, compared with the population, is every year more rapid—a circumstance which is not observed in regard to other musical instruments. This is corroborated by the fact, that, some years ago, pianoforte-music constituted only a very modest portion of a music-seller's stock; whereas now it fills more than three-quarters of his shelves, and makes his chief business. The number of teachers is something wonderful. Many are reduced ladies, who find in this exercise of their acquirements the most available means of support.

Every professional pianist has often had occasion to exercise his kindly and generous feelings in recommending and assisting accomplished women, whose helpless families would otherwise have been utterly destitute.

"The social importance of the piano is, beyond all question, far greater than that of any other instrument of music. One of the most marked changes in the habits of society, as civilization advances, is with respect to the character of its amusements. Formerly, nearly all such amusements were away from home, and in public; now, with the more educated portion of society, the greatest part is at home, and within the family circle—music on the piano contributing the greatest portion of it. In the more fashionable circles of cities, private concerts increase year by year, and in them the piano is the principal feature. Many a man, engaged in commercial and other active pursuits, finds the chief charm of his drawing-room in the intellectual enjoyment afforded by the piano.

"In many parts of Europe, this instrument is the greatest solace of the studious and the solitary. Even steam and sailing vessels for passengers on long voyages are now obliged, by the fixed habits of society, to be furnished with pianofortes; thus transferring to the ocean itself something of the character of home enjoyments.

"By the use of the piano, many who never visit the opera or the concerts become thoroughly acquainted with the choicest dramatic and orchestral compositions. This influence of the piano is not confined to them, but extends to all classes; and while considerable towns have often no orchestra, families possess the best possible substitute, making them familiar with the finest compositions. The study of such compositions, and the application necessary for their proper execution, may be, and ought to be, made the means of greatly improving the general education, habits, and tastes of piano students; and thus exerting an elevating influence, in addition to that refined and elegant pleasure which it directly dispenses."

Heartily do we concur in the opinions expressed by the great artist. The pianoforte cannot become too general—" transposing pianos—repetition pianos—patented pianos with hard names of unknown derivation—pianos of seven octaves in compass—pianos adorned in richest carvings, built of costliest woods, and illustrative of all the wealth, ingenuity, and tastefulness of the age—better still, little Quaker-like pianos of white wood, fine tone, and most moderate price, built by a maker who stands at the head and front of his trade, and by him offered to the public of small means—the needy clerk, the poor teacher, the upper-class mechanic. This last," says the eloquent writer in *Chambers's Journal*, from whom we have quoted, " is the very test and triumph of the pianoforte—as glorious a transition in its degree, from the time of the rare and royal virginals, as is the daily press and cheap literature of the nineteenth century from the darkness of that time when a scholar transcribed the classics with his own hand, and the parish Bible was chained to the reading desk in the middle of the church."

The pianoforte monopoly is now at an end. The " high-priced" makers have had their day; " small makers" are now rapidly advancing in public favour, and good and cheap instruments, of all classes, are now things of every-day occurrence. Men of intellect are beginning to turn their attention to " cheap" pianos; new and more simple actions are being invented; and the dawn of that day is visible when the " box of stretched strings," giving forth sweet sounds, shall be in every man's house, his comfort, his solace, his companion—aye, his *friend!* Let us then look forward to that day. Shall we not be a happier, if not a better people?

PART II.

THE CONSTRUCTION OF THE PIANOFORTE.

CHAPTER I.

The pianoforte appears usually in one of three forms; called respectively the grand, the square, and the upright. In the two former, the strings lie horizontally; in the latter, they are placed vertically. In entering on the construction of the instrument, it must be borne in mind that the pianoforte, whatever its shape, consists of four distinct parts; viz. the framing and sound-board, the stringing, the keys and machinery attached for striking the strings (technically called the action), and the ornamented case enclosing the whole. The latter of these belongs to cabinet manufacture and decorative art, with which we have nothing to do. The other three offer subjects for our consideration; and first, of

THE FRAMING.

When we open a pianoforte, especially a " grand," we are struck by the appearance of bars, and rods, and strengtheners of various kinds, placed in different directions, not merely with a view to give form and stability to the instrument, but to resist the powerful strain to which it is exposed by the tension of the strings. This tension is something extraordinary, and requires, for its due appreciation, a little consideration of the phenomena of a stretched string or wire. Let us suppose that a wire is wound round two pegs or pins placed a yard apart, and that it is merely brought into a straight line, without any attempt at stretching it. If struck with a soft hammer, it will yield a low sound, due to a small number of vibrations per second;

but if we wish to elevate the pitch of the tone, we can do so by increasing the tension or stiffness of the wire. A tuning key being placed on one of the pegs to which the wire is attached, the peg can be turned round, and a portion of the wire wound on it: this necessarily increases the tension of the portion of wire extending between the pegs; the increase of tension increases the rapidity of the vibrations when the wire is struck, and this increased rapidity gives a more elevated pitch to the tone elicited. Now, in conformity with one of the laws of force, the wire pulls with a power equal to that by which it has been stretched; it tends to regain the state which it originally had, and by this tendency exerts a powerful dragging or pulling force on the pins to which its two ends are attached, and on the frame-work wherein the pins are inserted. This force is exerted by every wire, according to the tension given to it; and the aggregate force is surprisingly great. It is calculated that the tension of the strings in a full-sized grand pianoforte amounts to eleven or twelve tons, or about twenty-five thousand pounds! This is, in fact, the force tending to draw together the two ends of the frame-work to which the wires are attached. It may easily be conceived that the strength of the framing necessary to resist this force must be very considerable. The various pieces of wood are in many places " glued up" so that the grain of one component part shall extend in one direction, and that of the other at right angles to it.

" Formerly," says a writer* whom we shall frequently quote in the ensuing pages, " this framing was constructed of timber only. The strings were looped at one end upon studs driven into a solid block of wood, which we may call the string-block; while the other ends were wrapped round a series of iron pins, called wrest-pins†, and inserted into another bed of timber, called the wrest-plank. The string-block and the wrest-plank, thus carrying the two ends of the strings, were kept apart by a framing of carpentry, trussed in such a manner as to offer the best conditions for resisting the tension. But, however ingenious this trussing might be contrived, or

---

* William Pole, Esq. F.R.A.S.—*Musical Instruments in the Great Industrial Exhibition of* 1851. Printed for private circulation.

† These are often erroneously called *rest*-pins; but, Mr. Pole says, the orthography in the text is the true one; the word *wrest*—" to twist by violence"—referring to the action of drawing up the strings in tuning.

however carefully seasoned the timber of which it was composed, it was found insufficient in strength, and subject, in course of time, to give way and become distorted in shape under the immense strain,—causing the pianoforte to lose its permanence of pitch, and to get out of tune. Moreover, the want of reliance on this part of the instrument prevented the introduction of heavier strings, which the makers, urged by the general call for improvement, were desirous of adopting, in order to increase the power, and augment the tone. At length, the idea arose of strengthening the framing with the more permanent and stronger material—metal; and a series of improvements were made, which have resulted in the compound wood and metal framing, now used, with slight modifications, by all makers; and which, in its general features, as applied to the grand pianoforte, may be described as follows. The studs, upon which the back ends of the strings are secured, instead of being driven into a wood block, as formerly, are now attached to an iron plate, curved to the form of the hollow side of the instrument, and called the *string-plate*. From this plate, metallic bars are extended longitudinally above the strings, and parallel with them, to the wrest-plank; their ends being so firmly connected with the string-plate and wrest-plank respectively, as to take upon themselves, in a great measure, the force of tension of the strings. At the same time, the string-plate, being screwed firmly down to the timber-framing below, and the metallic bars also secured thereto at intervals in their length, the whole forms one strong combined trussing, in which both wood and iron contribute to the strength. The bars and string-plate are usually of wrought-iron or steel. The principal parts of the wood-framing are composed of the best and soundest oak, thoroughly seasoned and dried, and " glued up" in several thicknesses, by which greater permanence of form is secured."

" It will be noticed, on inspecting a grand pianoforte," continues Mr. Pole, " that the wood-framing under the strings is, of necessity, severed completely across by the opening through which the hammers rise to strike the under side of the wires. To convey the thrust across this chasm, small thin arches of metal are interposed, abutting on one side against the wrest-plank, and on the other against a transverse rail, forming a portion of the main body of the framing, and called the belly-rail. This interruption to the continuity of the under framing is a great, but unavoidable inconvenience, and did it not exist, probably the aid of the metal bars might be dispensed with altogether."

The introduction of metallic bracing was suggested by the important part which iron, under the auspices of the engineering profession, began to take in the constructive arts at the commencement of the present century. As early as 1808, Messrs. Broadwood applied metal tension bars to the treble. In 1820, Mr. Stodart patented the first perfect system of metallic bracing for grand pianos*, consisting of the string-plate and bars united. And between this date and 1827, other makers applied various modifications of this system, which has resulted in the general plan now in use.

Stodart's patent, besides being entitled to especial notice as the first of its kind, professed other important considerations than that of merely strengthening the framing of the instrument; it was intended to prevent those fluctuations in the pitch of the strings which arise from change of atmospheric temperature. The idea is simple and philosophical, and has been long since applied to chronometers, though its operation in those delicate instruments is the reverse of that to which it has now been turned. The principle is to compensate the natural expansion of strings through heat, or their contraction through cold, by providing an apparatus possessing the same properties as the strings themselves, upon which they are stretched. To this intent, a plate of brass is laid over the belly of the instrument, of about two inches wide, and corresponding in shape with, and placed close to, the curved side of the instrument: to this the strings are fastened in the usual way. The bar which constitutes the front is fixed in its place, about nine inches from the front, by iron clamps, which preclude its moving, and under this bar the strings pass to the pegs, as is customary in other pianofortes. Within this frame, and parallel to the strings, but above them, are placed tubes, about three quarters of an inch in diameter, of a similar metal to the string beneath—i. e. brass above the brass, and steel above the steel. One end of these tubes is placed against the curved side of the frame, the other against the straight bar. They are prevented from rising or curving upwards, through the stress of the tension upon the string, by stout bars of wood laid across. The effect contemplated

---

* Purchased of Messrs. Thom and Allen, two ingenious workmen in his establishment.

in this construction is, that as the temperature affects the strings either by expansion or contraction, it will also affect the tubes, which extending or relaxing consentaneously, as it were, with the strings*, will compensate the difference by allowing the whole frame to coincide with their action. The only conjecture unfavourable to this project which reason suggests, appears to lie in the size of the different masses of metal to be acted upon by heat and cold; but, according to an authority, " experiment has determined that the expansion and contraction of the larger and the smaller body are so nearly alike as entirely to answer the purpose." A grand pianoforte, it is said, has been removed from a low to a high temperature, and back again, without undergoing any perceptible difference in the pitch, or going out of tune in the smallest degree.

An instrument of the grand form, by Messrs. Stodart, upon this plan, was exhibited in 1851, upon which Mr. Pole makes the following sensible remarks: " This is the original of all the varieties of metallic bracing now in use, and its leading features—viz. a metallic string-plate kept apart from the wrest-plank by a system of longitudinal metallic bars—are essentially the same as have ever since been followed. The only variations from the more modern systems in matters of detail are, that the longitudinal stretchers are hollow tubes instead of flat bars, and that the string-plate is detached from the wood framing below. With regard to the form of the stretcher, there is no doubt the hollow tube is the more correct form, on mechanical principles, as being better calculated to offer the greatest resistance to a compressive force, with the least quantity of material. Every one acquainted with constructive science knows that a hollow tube is the most advantageous form for a column; and the function of the metallic stretchers in a pianoforte is precisely analogous. The object of leaving the string-plate detached from the wood-work below, was to allow the whole metallic frame, with the strings it carried, to contract and expand together, under atmospheric changes, without straining the wood-work, since wood and metal are, as is well known, differently influenced in this respect. The experience of other makers has not shown

---

* Some authorities tell us that strings will stretch almost indefinitely if the tension be conducted slowly and gradually; but this theory is not supported by facts.

this to be of much importance in practice; and therefore the separation of the wood and metal framing is but seldom adhered to; but the idea is ingenious, and the principle correct. Altogether, Mr. Stodart's system of metallic framing, adopted at such an early date, is a good example of the application of scientific knowledge to the construction of the pianoforte; and the very general way in which it has been since followed, corroborates the universal rule, that improvements based on correct principles are those which will be ultimately found of the greatest practical value. A peculiarity in the framing of this pianoforte, although not a part of the original system, is, that the wrest-plank is turned upside down, being placed above the strings, instead of below them. By this arrangement the strings are struck against their rests without the necessity for an upward bearing stud; while the metallic stretcher-bars bear directly against the plank, instead of being cranked down to it, as in the common plan. The wrest-pins pass completely through the plank, and their squared ends appear above it, so as to offer facilities for tuning. The inverted wrest-plank is a remnant of a system introduced by Mr. Wornum, in which the entire wood-framing was placed above the strings; but which, from its inconvenience, has not continued in use."

Messrs. Broadwood adopt, in some cases, a metal bar, running transversely over the wrest-plank, in a direction nearly at right angles to the longitudinal bars, and secured firmly thereto. From this transverse bar, a set of screws descend into the wrest-plank; the object being to hold this part of the frame more firmly in its place, and thereby to insure the stability of the instrument, and the steadiness of the tone. When this bar is added, the number of longitudinal bars may be reduced from four or five to two. The same firm have also lately adopted another system of metallic bracing, the peculiarity of which is, that some of the tension bars, instead of running parallel with the strings, are placed diagonally*.

---

* Messrs. Broadwood introduced the following improvements in 1847:—

1. A newly revised harmonic scale of strings.
2. A peculiar method of fixing the sounding-board.
3. The transverse metal suspension bar, by which several tension-bars were dispensed with.
4. The construction of the tension-bars, so as to combine the maximum of *strength*, with the minimum of weight.

Messrs. Erard exhibited, in 1851, a full-sized grand instrument, the peculiarity of which was, that, in addition to the metallic string-plate and longitudinal tension bars, the wrest-block was also of metal, being formed of a frame-work of brass, in which was fixed a strip of beech-wood to receive the wrest-pins. This, in conjunction with the longitudinal bars and the string-plate, formed an entire metallic framing, extending from one end of the instrument to the other. Frames partially of metal had previously been used for upright instruments in this country.*

Entire frames of metal have lately been adopted in America and Denmark, for grand and square instruments. Messrs. Chickering, of Boston, exhibited, in 1851, a grand in which the whole framing, consisting of string-plate, longitudinal bars, wrest-block and drilled bridge (for upward bearing), was of cast iron, cast in one piece. This plan has since been followed by several American makers. Hornung, of Copenhagen, exhibited two instruments, a grand and a square, in which the various parts were cast in one piece of iron, on the American plan.

We agree with Mr. Pole that the growing tendency to the use of too much metal in the construction of pianofortes, is injurious to the quality of the tone. It also adds greatly to the weight of the instrument, and consequently diminishes its portability and general usefulness. Nevertheless, the use of metal up to a certain point has its advantages; in fact, owing to the increased weight of the strings, it cannot now be dispensed with.

The square pianoforte presents considerable difficulties, as regards the strengthening of its frame, by reason of the separation of the wrest-plank from the string-plate, by the wide and deep space required for the keys and action. The strengthening is principally effected by bolting the wrest-plank and string-plate firmly down to a strong bed of timber, extending underneath the keys over the whole surface of the instrument, and forming thereto a thick, solid bottom. In addition to this, one or two

---

5. The fixing these tension-bars in the string-plate by means of wedges, thus ensuring equal tension.

6. The diagonal tension-bars. These abut against the strongest angle of the wrest-plank and *bass* scale. They meet effectually what is termed the "side-swag" of the string-plate, and they enable the maker to do with a single direct tension bar.

* By John Isaac Hawkins. See the *Repertory of Arts*, vol. xiv, p, 143.

metallic bars are, in the best instruments, stretched across from the string-plate to the wrest-plank, over the strings and parallel to them.

A simple and philosophical alteration has lately been made in the construction of the square pianoforte by an American maker, Mr. Spencer Driggs, of New York. By this invention, the thick plank bottom and the interior blocking of wood are dispensed with, and a greater strength and compactness gained by means of an entire iron frame, independent of the case*.

The framing of the upright pianoforte is perhaps the most simple of any description of pianoforte, in consequence of its continuity being unbroken by any openings. This may easily be seen by the following diagrams:

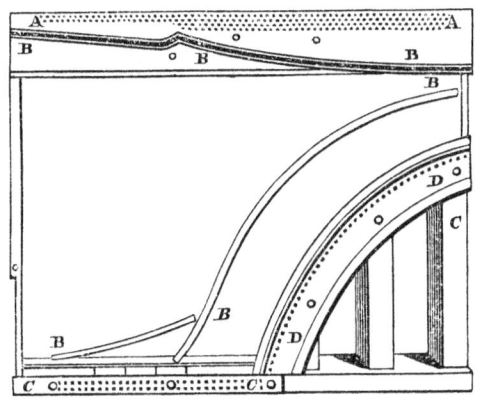

Front View without the Strings.

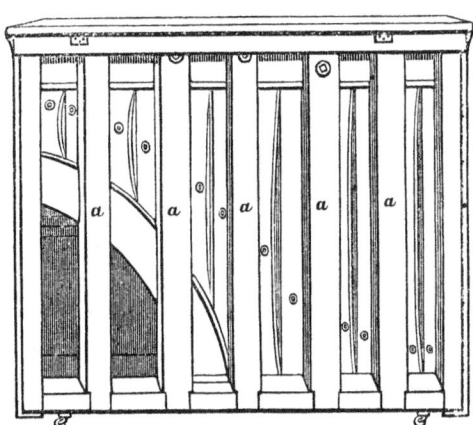

Back View, showing the Bracings a a a a.

The letters (A A), in the first diagram, show the round pegs of iron, the ends of which screw into the wooden substance of the sounding-board, and may be turned at pleasure by a tuning key, so as to increase or diminish the tension of a string. The thickness of wire used for each note is determined by pieces of wood called bridges, fixed firmly on the sounding-board (B B). The curve and position of the top and lower bridges are regulated by a guage, as is also the arrangement of the pins inserted in it. These pins are so placed that the strings rest against them, being thereby bent out of their rectilinear course, and their vibration thus limited to the space between the bridges (B B). The metallic plate (C C) is used to check the violent pull of the bass strings upon the sounding-board, and is an improvement now in general use. The belt (D D) serves to give additional strength.

---

* This remarkable pianoforte is highly spoken of by some of the most eminent pianoforte players, including Thalberg. A company has been formed in New York for its manufacture, under the title of "The Wallace Pianoforte Company," and from the prospectus now before us we extract the following particulars:—"The strength

The tension is sustained by strong struts or bars of timber placed vertically at the back of the instrument (*see the second diagram*), to which the wrest-plank and string-plate are firmly secured; so that the force of the tension is resisted by the bars in the direction of their length. As Mr. Pole remarks, "they are, in fact, simple columns, and receive their load in nearly the same manner as pillars supporting a building." Iron bracing is sometimes used at the back of the framing to counteract the pull of the strings on the opposite side; but perhaps the most satisfactory and philosophical mode of strengthening the upright pianoforte is the tubes of metal, in place of the bars of timber, as invented by Mr. Rüst. The metallic tubes not only strengthen the instrument in the most satisfactory manner, but also materially improve the tone of the pianoforte.

The surface of wood lying extended immediately under the strings, in a grand

---

of these instruments, by which is meant their power to hold or resist the tension of the strings, is derived wholly from an iron frame, so constructed as to unite the greatest strength with the least weight. This iron frame, and a light wooden frame, having the general form of the piano, and to which the iron frame is let in and bolted, constitute the interior of the instrument. The wrest-plank is fastened to the top of the iron frame or plate, and rests firmly against a flange, elevated from its inner margin. The sounding-board, which is made thin and arching, and *without ribbing*, preserves its shape and stiffness by means of a small iron frame into which its edge is fastened, thus retaining all its delicate sensitiveness and vibratory power. The bridge, which is made in a peculiar manner, is glued along the most crowning part of the sounding-board, and secures the equal and continuous bearing of the strings. At this point in their manufacture, the strings are put on and drawn up, and the action is put in and fitted. It will be observed that all this is done *independent of the case*. This is a mere shell, only three quarters of an inch thick, and which in the mean time has been making in another part of the factory. It is now slipped on over the instrument, and glued to it. The bottom sounding-board, which is a single veneer, about the eighth of an inch thick, made arching, and slightly ribbed, with its convex surface downward, is then glued on to the under side of the wooden frame, with its edges resting against a projection of the case which comes slightly below it. This lower sounding-board, covering the whole expanse of the instrument, and connected to the upper one by a sound-post, through which the least vibration of the one is instantly conveyed to the other, is an exceedingly valuable feature in the invention, and one which it is impossible to use in any other Pianoforte. To any one acquainted with the method of making the ordinary Piano, and with the laws of sound, it must be apparent that the process here described differs in all respects from that method; and that this new and perfected instrument, preserving in its construction the principal characteristics of the violin, with its immense sounding surfaces, its vast and unobstructed chamber, and its exquisite sensitiveness to the slightest vibration of the strings, must, in all philosophy and reason, be much better adapted to the production of musical sounds than the common Piano. That has a thick case, with ponderous inside blocking; a bottom from four to six inches in thickness; a small, flat, and heavily-ribbed sound-board; its strength, durability, and tone, all depending on the uncertain seasoning of its wood, and forming together a solid, dull mass, with barely sufficient room inside for the working of the action."

or square pianoforte, or behind them in an upright instrument, is called the *sounding-board* (sometimes *sound-board*), or belly. In a grand pianoforte, it occupies the entire area of the instrument: in the square, about two fifths of its length. It is analogous to the belly of the violin, and is composed of a thin boarding of the best Swiss pine, or of fir-wood, perfectly free from knots or imperfections, cut in a particular direction of the grain, and thoroughly seasoned. It is about one fifth of an inch in thickness, strengthened on the under side with small ribs, and put together with the utmost possible care. The edges of the sounding-board are attached to the framing of the instrument, the whole of the middle part being left perfectly free, to vibrate under the impulse received from the percussion of the strings*.

It will be observed, from what we have said, that the only support of the sounding-board consists in the bars glued on at the back. If these are sufficiently strong to resist the pressure of the strings, they are found too stiff to allow of the requisite vibration. If, on the contrary, the bars are made sufficiently weak to admit of a free vibration, they are found unequal to resist the pressure of the strings, and the sounding-board is deflected, or forced out of its true position—that of a perfectly flat surface,—its relation to the strings deranged, and the tone of the instrument constantly impaired by degrees, as has been found frequently in pianofortes after they have been in use for some years.

These considerations have led to the invention of the " Harmonic Chambers," which are hollow generators of sound, made on the principle of a violin, applied to the sounding-board, and adjusted by screws to any pressure, thus giving the exact amount of support that may be required. This invention has been patented by Mr. Dreaper, of Liverpool; but we have had no means of testing its merits.

---

* Dr. Brewer says—" The *sound-board* should be made of some light pale wood. The slit cut along it in the shape of a fanciful curve (!), as well as the two carved openings covered with silk in the front board, are designed to allow the air in the case to play more freely on the external air; so that the wooden lining called the belly, the sounding-board, and the vast body of air enclosed, all vibrate in unison with the strings, and contribute to augment the force of the sound." (! !)—*Sound and its Phenomena*, p. 163. The author has committed a two-fold blunder. He supposes the sounding-board and the belly to be two distinct parts of the instrument; whereas they are one and the same thing. What he dignifies by the name of the sounding-board is merely the " shade" of the old square pianoforte, invented to keep out the dust!

There is little doubt that the derangement of the sounding-board, by the constant tension of the strings, is the principal reason why pianofortes have generally lost their tone as they have become older; for we know, by the analogy of the violin, that, supposing all the parts to remain undisturbed, the effect of age ought rather to improve than to deteriorate instruments depending on wood for their sonority.

M. Pape, an ingenious Frenchman, gets rid of this evil by placing the sounding-board on the opposite side of the framing to that occupied by the strings. A strong open frame of cast-iron, or wood strengthened with iron, extends over the whole size of the instrument, forming the bottom of the piano. On the upper side of this, the strings are stretched; and on the lower side is fixed the sounding-board; by which arrangement the pull of the strings can have no tendency to compress the sounding-board; but if any action at all is produced upon it, it must be that of extension, which is rather beneficial than otherwise. The bridge over which the strings pass (and which, in the ordinary construction, is glued upon the sounding-board) is, in the new arrangement, a loose piece, communicating with the sounding-board by sound-posts, similar to that of a violin, which transmit the vibrations to the sounding-board exactly in an analogous manner. Another advantage is obtained by this arrangement; viz. that the sound-board may be considerably enlarged. In the ordinary construction, its size is bounded by the blocks and points of attachment of the strings to the framing; whereas, in this plan, no such limitation being necessary, the sounding-board may extend over the whole surface of the instrument, by which increase of dimensions a proportionately greater resonance is obtained. This is of especial value in the small upright forms. Another alteration in the sounding-board is in the position of the strengthening ribs. These are usually fixed on the side opposite to the strings. M. Pape places them towards the strings; which position he considers much more favourable, inasmuch as the strain tends to fix them more firmly, instead of to loosen their ends, as in the ordinary plan. The sounding-board is also made thicker and more solid than usual. M. Pape occasionally makes grands of the compass of eight octaves, F to F. For these, the new arrangement of the sounding-board gives the means of obtaining the requisite length for the tenor notes, without increasing the size of the case beyond that of an ordinary grand.

Mr. Cadby considers the ordinary mode of glueing the edges of the sounding-board firmly to the framing of the instrument, very detrimental to the brilliancy of the tone, owing to the fact that it is not strained tight. He has adopted the plan of securing the sounding-board to the frame-work of the instrument solely by metal clamps, in such a manner as to admit of its being strained and tightened when desired, like the parchment head of a drum. The principle is undoubtedly good, and, probably, at some future time will be generally adopted.

CHAPTER II.

THE STRINGING.

PREPARATORY to noticing this important part of the pianoforte, we must offer a few words on the *vibrations of strings*, which we are enabled to do, satisfactorily, from Dr. Brewer's recently published work on *Sound and its Phenomena*.

Sounds differ from each other in three essential particulars: 1, In pitch, that is, in gravity or acuteness; 2, In loudness, or intensity; 3, In *timbre*, or quality of tone.

The pitch of a sound always depends on the number of vibrations communicated to the air in a given time. Rapid vibrations produce sharp, shrill sounds; slower vibrations, those which are more grave.

The low C of a pianoforte gives a deep bass note; the highest C, an acute treble one. Not that one of these notes is touched more energetically than the other, but that the string of the former *vibrates more slowly* than that of the latter. Thus the lowest C of a six-octave piano makes only 64 vibrations, while the highest C makes 2048.

A string is made to vibrate more slowly: 1, By augmenting its length; 2, By augmenting its weight; 3, By decreasing its tension.

The canons of vibrating strings, which had engaged the attention of philosophers for about half a century, were first established by Dr. Brook Taylor, of Edmonton, who published his valuable treatise, called *Methodus Incrementum*, in the year 1716.

These canons were established by means of the monochord, or sonometer, which consists of a single string of wire or catgut, fixed at one end, and stretched by a weight at the other over a frame. The *tension* of the string is increased or diminished by increasing or diminishing the weight attached to it; and the *length* of the vibrating part is varied by means of a moveable bridge on which the string rests.

Suppose the string of a monochord adjusted for any given note, and you require to produce its octave: this may be accomplished in three different ways: (1) By shortening the string; (2) By stretching it with a greater weight; and (3) By employing another string less heavy. If the *first* of these plans be adopted, you must shorten the string *one half*. If the *last*, you must use a string of *half* the weight. If the middle plan be preferred, the weight employed to stretch the string must be *four times* as heavy as the former.

First Canon of the Stretched String.

The vibrations of stretched strings are in inverse proportion to their lengths; or, in other words, as a string is *lengthened*, it vibrates more slowly, and produces a graver note; as it is *shortened*, it vibrates more quickly, and gives a higher note.

The diminution of length needful in order to obtain the successive notes of an octave, is not the same for any two intervals. If a string 180 lines (15 inches) long give the C of any octave, it must be shortened 20 lines in order to obtain D, 16 more to produce E, only 9 more for the next note, F, 15 more for G, 8 for A, and 12 for B. Supposing the length of the string in the first instance to be one yard, or one foot, it will be found by the monochord that the relative lengths of string for the seven successive notes will be as follows:

Relative Length of each String.

C	D	E	F	G	A	B	C octave.
1	$\frac{8}{9}$	$\frac{4}{5}$	$\frac{3}{4}$	$\frac{2}{3}$	$\frac{3}{5}$	$\frac{8}{15}$	$\frac{1}{2}$

That is—if a string 1 yard or 36 inches long give C, in order to produce D it must be eight-ninths of a yard, or 32 inches; in order to produce E, it must be four-fifths of a yard, or $28\frac{4}{5}$ inches; in order to produce F, it must be three-fourths of a yard, or 27 inches; &c.—and in order to produce the octave, it must be exactly half its original length.

As the number of vibrations from different strings is always in *inverse proportion*

THE STRINGING.

to their length, the relative number of vibrations of any given octave may be obtained by inverting the fractions of the foregoing table. Thus:

For	C	D	E	F	G	A	B	C
	1	$\frac{9}{8}$	$\frac{5}{4}$	$\frac{4}{3}$	$\frac{3}{2}$	$\frac{5}{3}$	$\frac{15}{8}$	2

Or, in whole numbers:

C	D	E	F	G	A	B	C
24	27	30	32	36	40	45	48

That is, in the time that C is making 8 vibrations, D makes 9; in the time that C is making 4 vibrations, E makes 5; in the time that C is making 3 vibrations, F makes 4; &c.—and in the time the fundamental note makes 1 vibration, its octave makes 2.

It will now be readily understood why the strings of a harp, or of a pianoforte, differ in length; and why their difference of length is not *uniform*.

Second Canon of the Stretched String.

The vibrations of stretched strings are in proportion to the square root of their tension. If the string of a monochord stretched by the weight of 1 lb. gives a certain number of vibrations in a second, and you wish, without altering its length, to obtain from the same string the octave, a note which gives *twice* the number of vibrations in the same time, you must change the weight for one of 4 lbs. If, again, you would obtain from the same string the 12th (or *octave* of the *fifth*), which makes *three* vibrations for one of the fundamental, you must apply a weight equal to 9 lbs. If you wish to procure from the same string, without altering its length, the *double* octave, a note which vibrates *four times* as fast as the fundamental, you must attach to the end a weight of 16 lbs.; and so on.

Hence it may be perceived that the *tighter* a string is drawn, the *faster* it vibrates, and the sharper or higher its pitch. On the other hand, the *looser* a string, the *slower* its vibrations, and the flatter or graver the note which it produces.

Third Canon of the Stretched String.

When strings have the same length and tension, but differ in *weight* or thickness, their vibrations are in inverse proportion to their weight. If a given string makes a certain number of vibrations in a second, another *twice as heavy* will, under similar circumstances, give only *half* the former number of vibrations in the same time; one *thrice as thick* will make *one third* as many; and one *four times as heavy* will produce only *one-fourth* the number of the first string.

This law finds an illustration in the common practice of making bass strings of musical instruments *thicker*, or of a heavier material, than the treble ones. Sometimes a metal wire is coiled round the lower strings of a harp or pianoforte, to increase their weight. Sometimes different metals are employed, as copper, brass, and steel; the heaviest metal being always made to represent the lowest notes.

Thus, the manufacturer does not adopt any one of these methods of adjusting tones of which we have spoken, to the exclusion of the others: he avails himself of all. " Twelve strings of the same length and thickness," writes Mr. Dodd, in a clever article on the pianoforte in *British Manufactures*[*], " might be so different in tension as to yield the twelve semitones of an octave; twelve strings of the same thickness and tension might be of such different lengths as to yield the twelve semitones; or, lastly, twelve strings of the same length and tension might be made to produce these effects by having the thicknesses different. But, in practice, the tones produced by either of these methods would be very defective in character. Each degree of thickness, of length, and of tension, produces its own peculiar effects on the *timbre*, or quality of tone. If two strings of the same length and thickness were so stretched as to produce tones differing by an octave in pitch, one would be strained nearly to breaking, and the other would produce a dull, weak, and smothered sound. If, while producing these two notes, the strings differed only in length or in thickness, the qualities of tone would not be so much at variance as in the case just supposed; but still the required equable character of tone would not be produced. The plan adopted, therefore, is to let the length, the thickness, and the tension, all vary together.

---

[*] 2 vols. 12mo. 1847.

"This explanation will enable us to understand the reason for the observed difference in the strings of the pianoforte. We perceive that the strings for the upper notes are not only shorter, but also thinner, than those for the lower; and we should find, though it is not perceptible to the eye, that the tension is likewise different. The thickness, the length, and the tension, all diminish (but not uniformly) from the lower to the upper notes; *tension* being here used to express the force employed in stretching the string to the required degree. In a grand pianoforte there are fourteen different thicknesses of wire; the smaller, for the upper notes, being plain polished steel wire, and the thicker, for the lower notes, being coated with a very fine coil of copper wire."

The strings of the pianoforte were originally of very thin wire. The difference indeed between them and those now in use is very striking. As an illustration, we may remark that the smallest wire formerly used for the C in the third space of the treble staff was No. 7; that now used for the same note is No. 16. The weight of the striking length of the first is five and a half grains; of that of the second, twenty-one grains. This is sufficient to account for the increased bracing required in the modern pianoforte.

Grand pianofortes have three strings to each note; upright instruments, generally two. Of late, however, three strings are often used in grands for the treble notes, two for the middle of the instrument, and one for the bass. The strings for upright pianofortes, instead of being placed vertically, sometimes (in more modern instruments) run obliquely across the frame, by which a greater length is gained, without increasing the height of the case.

Formerly each string was formed of a separate wire, one end of which was twisted into a loop, and passed over the stud in the string-block; the other end being wrapped round the wrest-pin. A great improvement in the mode of applying the string, so as to avoid the noose by which they are ordinarily attached, was patented by Messrs. Collard in 1827. This is effected by using only one hitch-pin (of double the usual size), instead of two, and passing the string from one tuning-pin to the other round this single hitch-pin, in one continuous piece of wire. The object of this is to prevent the distortion of the fibres of the wire by twisting, which often makes them false, to obviate the giving of the wire at the noose, and to avoid the frequent snapping of the string at the twist. Notwithstanding that both unisons are made by one continuous wire, yet such is the tenacity caused by the friction on the single hitch-pin, that one of the unisons may be lowered several semitones without in the least affecting the pitch of the other. So great is the advantage gained by this mode of applying the strings, that a string is seldom or never known to break; it is brought up to its pitch almost instantaneously; and a person who has never before put a string on a pianoforte, may do it without the smallest difficulty. Since the expiration of the patent, this method of stringing has been almost universally adopted.

Another important improvement, applied to the stringing of grand pianofortes, is that of the upward bearing of the string at the striking end. In describing this, we shall use Mr. Pole's words. "The length of the vibrating part of the string is determined by two bridges, over which each wire passes; one fixed to the soundboard, the other to the wrest-plank, a little in front of the striking point of the string. Now the original plan was, so to arrange the levels of these two bridges, with reference to the ends of the wire, that the string might, when stretched, have a downward pressure upon both. But since the hammer strikes upwards, it is evident that a heavy blow must exert a tendency, more or less, to lift the string off its bearing; the effect of which is considered detrimental to the tone. On this account, the direction of the bearing on the front bridge was reversed, or rather the bridge itself was changed for a plate pierced with a series of holes, through which the strings passed, turning immediately upwards towards the wrest-pins. This gave each string an upward, instead of a downward bearing at the front end; the effect of the blow being, under these altered circumstances, to force the string against its rest, instead of lifting it from it, as before. The upward bearing is claimed by Messrs. Erard, as having been described by them in a patent of 1808, and modified and improved in 1821."

The plan of employing one large string to each note of the pianoforte, upon which the French dilate largely, is an invention, if it may be so called, derived from this country. Lord Stanhope, in 1815, was amongst the first who made this attempt; but the false and crazy tone rendered by the treble strings, particularly when so enlarged as to produce the quantity of tone required, was an insurmountable obstacle to its success. A contemporary journal speaks of this instrument in the following manner:

"Mr. D. Loeschmann, Newman Street, has lately constructed a new pianoforte, under the direction of Earl Stanhope, with *single* steel wires to each finger key, of his lordship's invention. The lower wires are about the tenth of an inch in diameter, and more resemble musical bars than wires, in their tone and effect." *

The "unachord" instruments have been greatly improved since the time of the noble Earl; and when we consider the diminution of outlay in their construction, it will be at once seen that the plan possessed some advantages.

In 1819, the ingenious Mr. Wornum turned his attention to the reduction of all the strings to one size and tension. The origin, progress, and effects of his enquiries, are thus explained in the *Quarterly Musical Review* for 1820:† "All pianofortes are subject to a falling of the middle and upper octaves; and so much are most manufacturers accustomed to this circumstance, that it is now scarcely considered in any other light than that of a failing in the tuning. But it seems that Mr. Wornum did not so regard it, but in the light of a distinct evil, and as one of a most disagreeable character, especially when two performers are engaged at one instrument. In the course of last year, he was led to make particular enquiry into the subject; and his first effort in the cause was to examine minutely the construction and parts of a cabinet pianoforte. The materials were evidently well selected, the workmanship was good, the construction of the case perfectly mechanical, and the action neat, simple, and efficient. To these parts, therefore, it did not appear that any portion of the defect could possibly attach. He then directed his attention to the stringing, where he scarcely expected to make any progress in his pursuit, the scale having been laid down on the most approved principle, and the strings being all of Berlin steel. However, for enquiry's sake, he proceeded, laid aside the approved character of the scale, and argued that, as the effect was imperfect, it was probable that the cause was incorrect. Thus presuming, he tried the octaves, and found them, as usual, all flat —less so in the bass than in the treble; the unisons, generally speaking, were in

---

* Gentleman's Magazine, September, 1815. † Vol. ii, p. 305.

tune. His next proceeding was to examine the octaves and unisons in their relative construction and circumstances. The construction of the octave he found to be of *unequal tension*, and, at certain distances, of *unequal size*; but the construction of the unisons were of *equal tension invariably*, and the *same* in *size*. And here at once was discovered the seat and cause of the defect under enquiry; for it was evident that the superior accordancy of the unisons arose from their being of equal size and tension, and that the defective state of the octaves arose from their want of *similar uniformity*. Mr. Wornum now transferred his enquiry to the monochord, where, by taking the length of the longest plain string, and subdividing that length, according to a given temperament, into all the ascending degrees of the scale, he graduated an entirely new scale for the pianoforte; in which all the plain strings were reduced to one size and tension, and such as required covering were severally weighted with covering wire until they arrived at the same force. The instruments constructed from this scale answered most satisfactorily, and were an ample reward for the labours of the experiment. Their tones were firm, sonorous, and brilliant; and their standing warranted the highest opinion of the principle. On comparing the best common method of laying down scales for the strings of pianofortes, with the one above described, a very great difference will be observable. By the equal tension, the octaves are all doubled, and the other intervals are severally taken as given by the length and tension of the octaves. In the common method, the octaves are not doubled, but are successively reduced, and larger-sized wire employed, at certain distances, to correct the bad effects of that reduction; and the other intervals receive the lengths that *may fall* to them by the *accidental* circumstance of an *easy sweep* from one octave to another in the formation of the patterns. Now, in the new method, we have perfect equality; in the old, systematic inequality. The former is the dictate of nature—consequently of pure science; but for the latter we are indebted entirely to mechanical *convenience*, which, in the present enlightened state of society, is rather a compromise than an attainment of the object."

Notwithstanding the philosophy and excellence of the late Mr. Wornum's discovery, a patent for which was taken out in 1820, the system of *equal tension* never came into general use.

The curved piece of wood fixed on the sound-board which regulates the sounding length of the strings, is called the bridge. Messrs. Clementi and Collard invented, in 1821, an additional bridge, not for the purpose of regulating musical intervals, but of augmenting the duration of the vibration, and consequently increasing and beautifying the tone. This new bridge, called "the bridge of reverberation," was placed at a regulated distance on the sound-board, and the important advantage resulting from it was, that the motion given to the principal part of the string by the impulse of the hammer was kept up by the bridge of reverberation, instead of being suddenly checked by an attachment to an unyielding substance. The prolonged vibration produced an extraordinary purity, power, and continuity of sound somewhat resembling the richness of an octave below.

On the old plan of passing the strings directly from the side of the case to the original bridge on the sound-board, it became necessary, in order to prevent the jarring noise of those portions of the wire which lie between them, not only to place some soft substance on the top of the moulding, but also to weave a piece of cloth between the strings. In the invention under notice, a novel action was substituted for those portions of the string situated between the two bridges, yielding most sweet and melodious tones. The performer, by lifting a valve, was enabled to elicit those harmonious sounds, through a well-known sympathetic relation between accordant strings, without touching those portions of the strings which produce them. The augmentation of sound caused by this means resembled in some measure the effect of lifting the dampers, but without producing the same confusion, since every note on the body of the instrument was regularly damped as the performer lifted his finger. By this apparatus a threefold power of augmenting the sound was acquired; whereas, instruments of the common construction have but the one caused by lifting the dampers. The first augmentation of power was by lifting the harmonic swell. The second—by dropping the harmonic swell and raising the dampers. The third—by raising the harmonic swell and the dampers together. By the last means, the performer added all the tones which were sympathetically elicited from the strings between the original bridge and bridge of reverberation, over and above all that could be produced on instruments of the common construction, and the effect was accordingly of extraordinary richness and power. These inventions were applied to upright and square pianofortes, but, like many other excellent improvements, are now only numbered among the " things that were."

A great improvement in the stringing of grand horizontal pianofortes has of late years been introduced by Erard. Formerly, each note of the lowest octave of the bass has been produced by the action of the hammer upon two strings. It was found that in strings of such length, there was a constant liability of their striking each other, and jarring during their vibration; and this injured the effect of their tone. This defect is removed, in the improved instrument, by making each hammer of the lowest octave act upon a single string, whose thickness is increased as well as its length. By this expedient, the jar which prevailed previously is effectually prevented, and force and fulness of tone are obtained, which exceed in a striking degree the effect of the instruments of the old construction.

The strings of the early pianofortes were partly of steel and partly of brass, the treble notes of steel, and the lower notes of brass, a few of which in the bass were over-lapped or covered, rather open, with plated copper wire. The covering was to give them more gravity according to the length attainable in the instrument. But modern pianofortes have steel wire throughout, with about one octave in the bass closely lapped. The wrapping wire is of soft iron for the upper part of the octave, and of copper for the lower. The wrapping too is close, like that of the fourth string of a violin; whereas, formerly, it was open like the worm of a corkscrew. In the lowest bass notes of grand instruments, the copper-lapped strings are of considerable diameter.

The steel wire now in general use is the manufacture of Mr. Webster, of Penn's Mills, near Birmingham, and is greatly superior to the once-famed Berlin wire, now no more in esteem with English manufacturers, from the bad quality of the metal, and the very imperfect manner in which it was drawn; when perfectly round, which it ought always to be, it was generally too soft; and when sufficiently hard, it was scarcely ever well manufactured, from which circumstance it was constantly false in vibration.

CHAPTER III.

THE ACTION.

By the action is understood the machinery through which the impulse given by the finger of the performer is transmitted to the string of the instrument. The parts we have hitherto considered may be said to be parts at rest, whose peculiarities consist in their statical qualities. The action is the *moving* part, and upon its capability to speak the will or mind of the player depends its excellence.

The earliest actions, as we have seen, were very rude. The hammer was lifted by an upright wire, attached to the back end of the key, and capped with a leather button, which came in contact with the under side of the hammer. The height of this button was so adjusted, that when the key was pressed down as far as it would go, the hammer was a short distance from the string; the effect of this adjustment being, that, after the impulse given to the hammer had caused it to strike the blow, it fell back upon the button, and so left the string free to vibrate. This was called the " single action." " It was," says Mr. Pole, " the simplest form of mechanism, and probably the earliest that obtained for the pianoforte any share of public favour. Square instruments were made with this action as late as the commencement of the present century, and probably many of them are in existence still."

The invention of the " hopper " was the next great improvement. " The evil of the single action," says the authority we have quoted, " was, that owing to the adjustment already mentioned, the hammer would not reach the string, unless the key were thrust down with sufficient force to give it considerable impetus; — so that it was impossible to play very *piano ;* while if, to remedy this evil, the adjustment of the button was altered to bring the hammer nearer to the string, there was a danger of its not leaving it after the blow—a defect technically called 'blocking.' The hopper remedied this evil. It was a jointed upright piece, attached to the back end of the key, and used to lift the hammer, in place of the stiff wire and button of the former mechanism. When the key was pressed down, the hopper, engaging in a notch on the under side of the hammer, lifted it to within a very short distance of the string; so near, in fact, that almost the slightest pressure would cause it to strike; but at this moment, while the key was still pressed down, the jointed part of the hopper coming in contact with a fixed button as it rose, escaped from, or 'hopped' out of the notch, and let the hammer fall clear away from the string. This mechanism, as applied, with trifling variation, to the square pianoforte, was called the 'double action,' and is extensively in use for this and the upright form at the present day."

The invention of the "check" remedied a defect which we shall next explain. "The hammer, when liberated from the hopper, fell upon a rail covered with cloth, or some other soft bed prepared to receive it. Now, when a forcible blow was struck, there was always a danger of the hammer rebounding; or, in other words, the elasticity of the struck wire would send it down with such force that it rebounded from its bed, touched the string a second time, and so damped the vibration and injured the tone. The remedy for this was found in fixing to the back end of the key a projection called a 'check,' which caught the edge of the hammer as it fell, and held it down so firmly that it could not again rise. The check was one of the most important additions ever made to the action; and no pianoforte, of any pretensions, is considered complete without it."

The next invention applied to the action of the pianoforte is called the "repetition" mechanism, and its object is thus explained: "In the ordinary action, after the hammer has fallen, the key must rise to its position of rest before the hopper will engage again in the notch of the hammer, so as to be ready for another stroke; and hence a note cannot be repeated without not only requiring the finger to be lifted through the entire height of the key's motion, but also demanding a length of time between the repetitions sufficient to allow of its full rise. The contrivances by which this inconvenience has been overcome, are of various kinds, according to the fancy or ingenuity of the makers; but they all act on the same principle; namely, by holding up the hammer at a certain height while the key returns; by which means the hopper is allowed to engage itself under the hammer earlier, and to reproduce the note in less time, and with less labour to the finger, than before."*

The last invention, which seems to have brought the mechanism of the pianoforte to perfection, is the repetition and "tremolo" action of the Messrs. Hopkinson. This is accomplished by means of a pin-jointed sticker, attached to the key and hammer-stick; which sticker, being in connection with the relieving action, brings the action of the hammer upon the strings completely under the control of the performer. A check is provided to prevent the hammer from vibrating after a powerful stroke; but for a gentle touch the check is not required, and the hammer remains near the string, ready to be acted upon by the slightest movement of the finger. By means of this mechanism, the utmost possible delicacy of touch is combined with a far greater power than has hitherto been obtained in any pianoforte we have seen. So sensitive is this action, and so accurately may the amount of tone desired be regulated, that the "tremolo" (similar in effect to that produced by the violinist, or the voice of a finished singer) may be produced by the mere trembling of the finger when pressed upon the key; at the same time, a performer of only moderate power of finger can by it fully develop the most powerful effects of the modern style of pianoforte playing.

We shall now give a brief explanation of the action of a pianoforte, and shall take for our example the mechanism of the ordinary upright instrument, termed the "Cottage."

---

* "When it is considered that all the delicacies of expression and articulation, and all the lights and shades of the performance depend upon the precision, certainty, and promptitude with which the hammer responds to the touch of the finger, the immense importance of the mechanism of the key will be duly appreciated. Yet it is a curious fact in the records of the progress of this instrument, that the mechanism of the key has been the last part of it to which attention has imparted perfection; and that, even at the present time, notwithstanding the advanced state of the musical art, and the all but universal cultivation of the pianoforte, the key mechanism is constructed on imperfect principles, and is, consequently, productive of unsatisfactory effects."—Dr. Lardner's *Popular Essays on Scientific Subjects*, 1852, 12mo.

THE ACTION.

The Action while the Key is at Rest. *The same with the Key pressed down.*

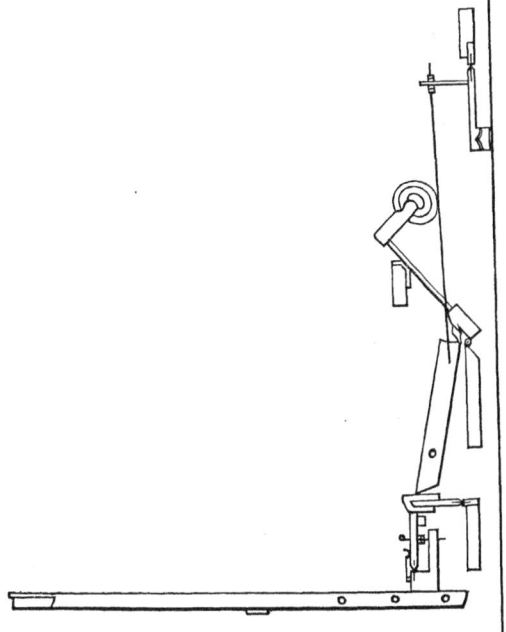
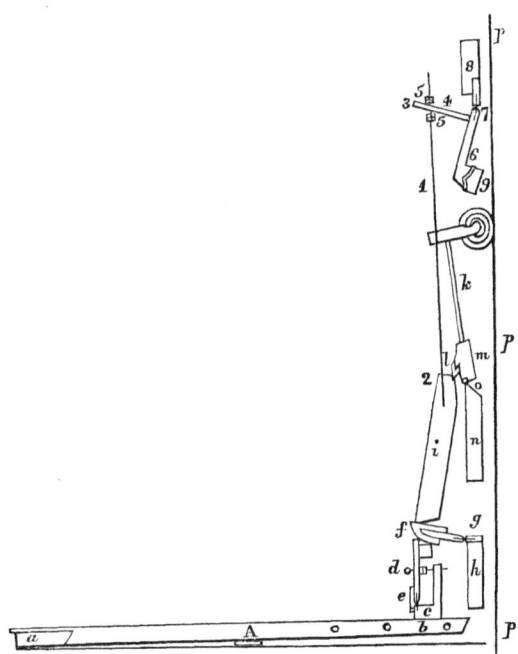

The key (A) forms a lever, one end of which (*a*), being pressed down, raises the other end (*b*), which in turn pushes up the hopper (*c*). (The regulating pin (*d*) and spring (*e*) determine the touch). The hopper is met by the lever or under hammer (*f*), which by a hinge (*g*) is fastened to the lever rail (*h*). Above this is the sticker (*i*), to which the hammer (*k*) is hinged at (*l*) by a fastening of wash-leather. The butt (*m*) of the hammer being hinged to the hammer rail (*n*), in the point (*o*), it is obvious that the pressing down of the key (A) must drive up the sticker (*i*), and consequently cause the hammer (*k*) to strike against the string (*p p p*).

Thus far, then, we have the means of producing the sound from the string. But a little consideration will show us that we also require the means of limiting the *duration* of each particular sound. For this purpose the damper is employed, the form and parts of which, viewed sideways, are shown in the above diagrams.

The damper wire (1) is fastened sideways into the sticker at (2), so as to pass upright between the butts (*m*). The top of the wire forms the screw (3), passing through the arm of the damper (4), which is secured to it by buttons (5 5). The damper (6), which is fixed by a hinge (7) to the damper rail (8), being thus elevated with the sticker (*i*), raises its felt surface (9) off the string (*p p p*), and leaves the sound clear and open. Immediately upon the hand being taken off the key, the weight of the sticker (*i*) causes the wire to fall, and consequently presses it against the string, muffling and stopping the vibration. Thus, as long as the hand is held on the key, the vibration will continue, and no longer.

Some pianos have two *pedals*; one to soften the sound, and the other to augment it. When a piano has but one, it is always the "*forte*" pedal. The usual action of the "*soft*" pedal is to shift the hammers sideways, so that they strike only *one* string instead of two, or two strings instead of three, for each note.

The action of the "*forte*" pedal is to lift the dampers off the strings, so that each set of strings may have a larger field of vibration, and that all the strings together may contribute to swell the force of the note struck, by sympathetic vibrations. Immediately the foot is removed, the hammers and dampers return to their original position, and the effect of the pedal ceases.

The action of the pianoforte has afforded unlimited scope for the ingenuity of the manufacturers; and almost every maker of note has his own particular mechanism. The same essential parts, however, are found in all the best instruments, more or less modified in their shape and arrangement. Thus we have the hammer, the hopper, the check, and the contrivance for repetition. To particularize all the various actions of the 200 pianoforte makers whose names are found in the London Directory, would be an unprofitable labour; or even all the good actions: we must be content with a few of those in common use.

ACTIONS OF VARIOUS MAKERS.

The Action of the modern Square Pianoforte, exhibiting all its Varieties.

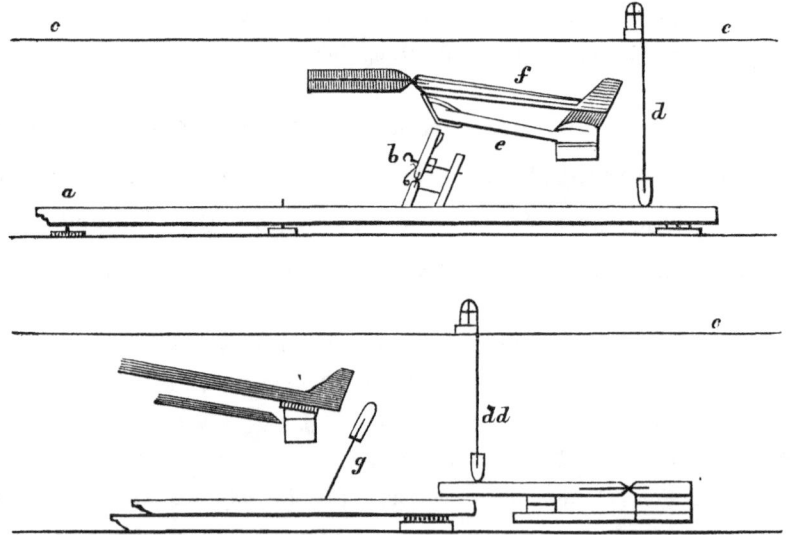

a, key. *b*, hopper by which the escape of the hammer is effected. *c*, string. *d*, Irish damper. *d d*, crank damper. *e*, under hammer. *f*, hammer. *g*, check.

THE ACTION.

The common Grand Pianoforte Action.

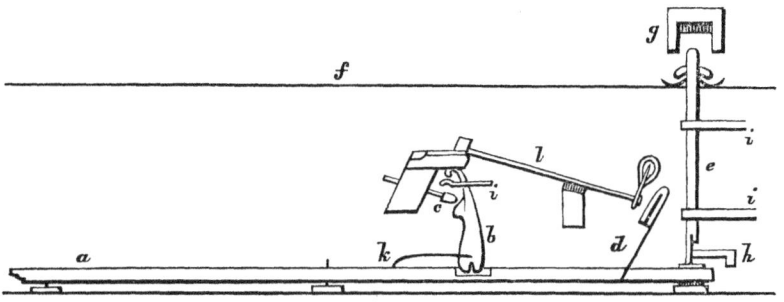

a, key. *b*, lever. *c*, button. *d*, check. *e*, damper. *f*, string. *g*, ruler. *h*, damper pedal lifter. *i i i*, rails and sockets. *k*, spring. *l*, hammer.

Messrs. Broadwood's former and new Patent Grand Actions.

[*The improvements by Mr. Southwell.*]

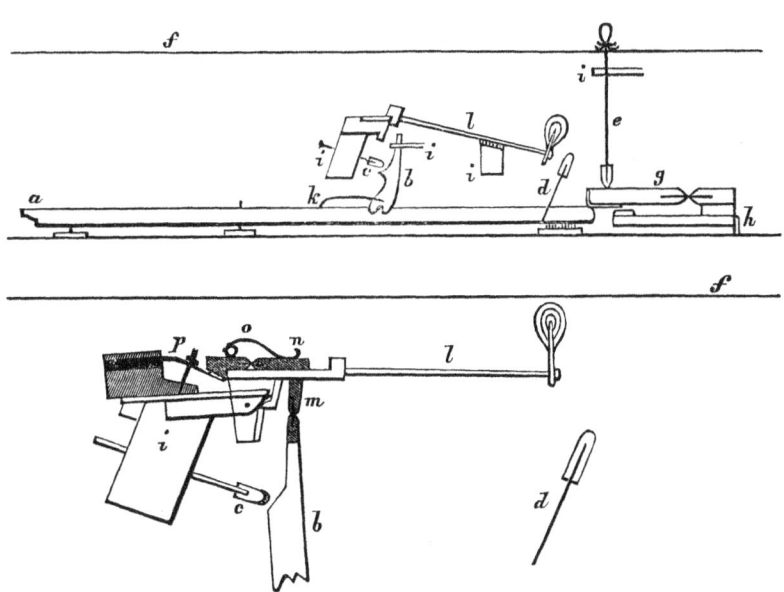

The shaded parts show the new additions; the improvement being the keeping the hammer at a certain distance from the string when the finger is on the key.

a, key. *b*, lever. *c*, button. *d*, check. *e.* damper. *f*, string. *g*, crank for damper. *h*, damper pedal lifter. *i i i i*, rails and socket. *k*, spring. *l*, hammer. *m, n*, block passed through the hammer butt. *o*, spring fixed at the back of *n*, and pressing upon the front of it; by which arrangement, when the lever passes the notch, it is caught by *m*, and the hammer is sustained at the given height. *p*, another spring, which regulates the action of *a*, and determines the height it shall rise.

190 THE ACTION.

Messrs. Collard's Patent Grand Action.   (*Invented by Mr. George Stewart.*)

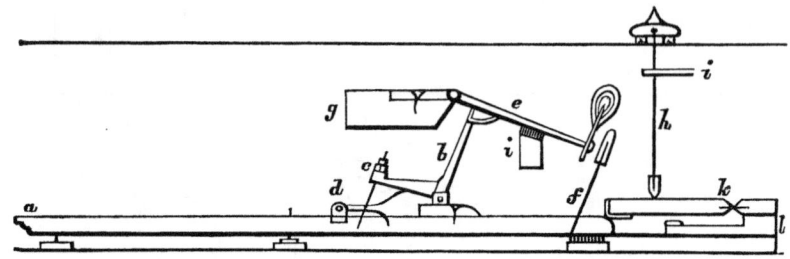

a, key. *b*, hopper. *c*, button. *d*, hopper spring. *e*, hammer. *f*, check. *g*, hammer rail. *h*, damper. *i i*, rail and socket. *k*, crank for damper. *l*, damper pedal lifter.

Erard's Patent Grand Action.   (*Invented by Sebastian Erard.*)

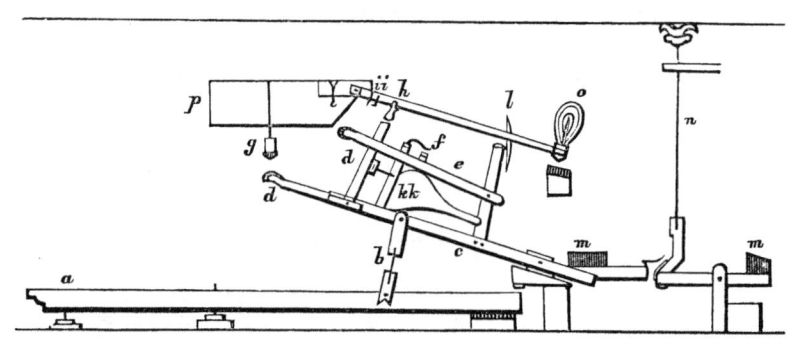

a, key. *b*, lifter centered in the key and the hopper lever. *c*. hopper lever. *d d*, hopper. *e*, hammer sustaining lever. *f*, stop for *e*. *g*, hopper button. *h*, butt for the hopper to strike against. *i i*, two small wire stops acting upon *e*. *k k*, springs acting upon hopper lever and hammer lever. *l*, check. *m m*, balance weights of lead. *n*, damper. *o*, hammer. *p*, hammer rail.

Wornum's Grand Action.   (*This action is based on the Piccolo Action.*)

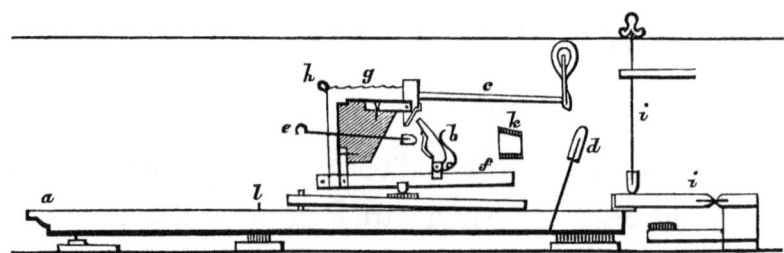

a, key. *b*, hopper and spring. *c*, hammer. *d*, check. *e*, button to set off the hopper. *f*, hopper lever. *g*, tie attached to the butt of the hammer. *h*, sustaining spring linked at the end of the tie, and fixed in the front end of the hopper lever, the rising of which puts the sustaining spring in action. This spring gives the *piano* blow and assists in the *forte* and repetition.   damper and fixings. *k*, hammer ruler and back touch. *l*, wood spring to set up the hoppers.

Zeitter's Grand Action.

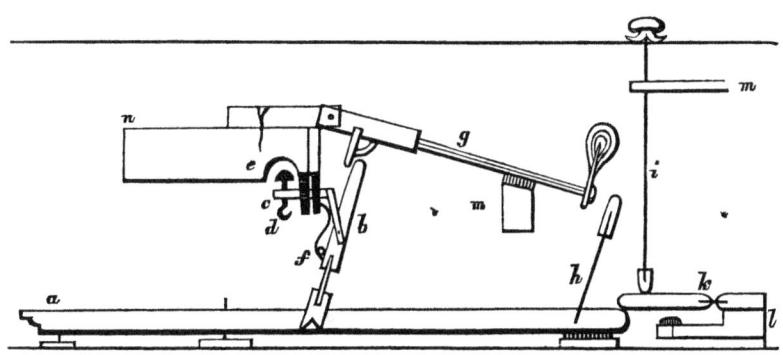

a, key. *b*, hopper, which works in the key with what is called a *bird's mouth*. *c*, escapement part of the hopper, and the setting off which is effected by the button working in the arched part above it, *d, e*. *d*, button and wire. *e*, arch in which the button acts. *f*, hopper spring. *g*, hammer. *h*, check. *i*, damper. *k*, damper crank. *l*, damper pedal action. *m m*, rail and socket. *n*, hammer rail.

Wornum's Unique Action.   Wornum's Double or Piccolo Action.

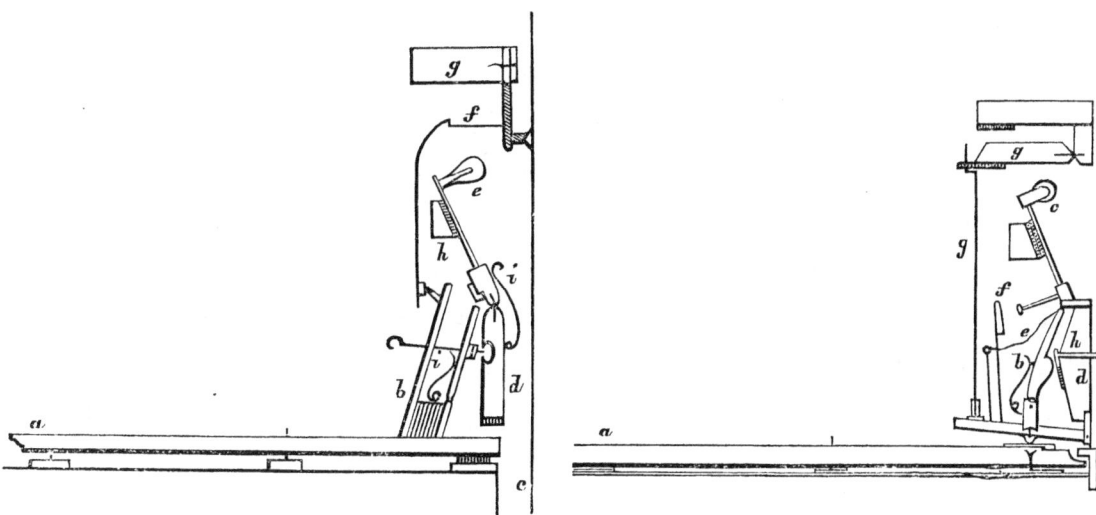

a, key. *b*, hopper. *c*, string. *d*, hammer rail. *e*, hammer. *f*, damper and wire. *g*, damper rail. *h*, ruler. *i i*, springs.

a, key. *b*, hopper and spring. *c*, hammer. *d*, hammer rail. *e*, tie and wire. *f*, check. *g g*, damper and wire. *h*, setting off screw.

While the improvements in the mechanism of the action have been in progress, others have been effected, individually less important, and demanding less refined efforts of invention, but which collectively have augmented the power, improved the tone, and increased the durability of the pianoforte, rendering it at the same time more retentive of pitch and tone, and more capable of withstanding the deteriorating influences of climate and vicissitudes of temperature.

In treating of the action of the pianoforte, our work would be incomplete without some notice of the German mechanism known as the "Vienna action." This we shall briefly record in the words of the eminent pianist, M. Thalberg.

" During the first years of this century, two systems chiefly prevailed with regard to the grand piano: the older one followed by the London makers, known as the English system, and the newer one in Germany, called the Vienna system. The difference was principally in the action; that of the English being the common grand action, the origin of which is unfortunately unknown; and that of Vienna, a new action, invented, it is said, at Augsburg, by an organ-builder. The old grand action gave a more powerful blow, and produced a fuller and finer tone, while the lightness of touch of the Vienna action afforded far greater facilities of expression, and caused it, therefore, to be adopted by most of the eminent pianists of the time. This is not at all to be wondered at, when we consider the immense importance of the action of the piano in bringing out the elements of expression which are peculiar to the instrument. Between the mind of the player that conceives, and the string that expresses by its sound the conception, there is a double mechanical action: one belonging to the player, in his fingers and wrists; the other to the piano, in the parts which put the strings in motion. No two piano players touch the instrument alike; that is, no two players have the same mechanical action in their fingers, or produce the same tones; and the difference in the style and degrees of excellence of pianists is more owing to this than to any other cause. It is, therefore, self-evident that that part of the piano which continues the action of the fingers, and completes the connection between the mind of the player and the strings of the instrument, should have a delicacy and a power answering as near as possible to those of the hand of the player. Every difference in the action of the piano will give a corresponding difference in tone and expression; and hence this part of the instrument has at all times been justly considered of paramount importance, not only by the great professional pianists, but by the highly cultivated amateur player. Now, however, we have an action, the invention of the late Sebastian Erard, which gives a more powerful blow than the old grand action, and a far more rapid and delicate effect than the old Vienna action—thus combining the advantages of both systems.

"To give an idea of the degrees of perfection attained at the present day in the construction of the piano, we will describe one of the grand pianos in the Exhibition*. This instrument is 8¼ feet in length, and 4½ feet in its greatest width; its frame is of an enormous strength, compared with the instruments of former times, being heavily braced with wood below the strings, having a complete system of metallic bracing above the strings, firmly abutted, and consisting of longitudinal bars let into metal at each end, and having the curved side formed of a number of separate pieces glued together in a mould, to ensure durability and fixedness of form. Its sounding-board extends to the frame on all sides, except the space left for the action. The strings are made entirely of steel, and of wire so thick that the tension necessary to bring them to the proper pitch, produces an aggregate strain equal to at least twelve tons weight, while they are passed through studs drilled into the metal wrest-plank, thus giving the strings an upbearing position, which prevents the slightest displacement of the point of contact by any force of the hammers; and the system of placing the strings on the instrument, determined by accurate acoustic experiments, causes them to be struck by the hammer at the precise nodical point which produces the freest and clearest tone. The compass is extended to seven octaves, from A to A. The action of this piano is described by Dr. Lardner, in a work just published on Mechanics†, as ' a beautiful example of complex leverage in the mechanism which connects the key and hammer. In this instrument, the object is to convey, from the point where the finger acts upon the key to that at which the hammer acts upon the string, all the delicacy of action of the finger; so that the piano may participate, to a certain extent, in that sensibility of touch which is observable in the harp, and which is the conse-

---

* The magnificent instrument by Erard in the British department of the Exhibition of 1851.

† See Dr. Lardner's *Popular Essays on Scientific Subjects*, 12mo. Longman, 1852.

quence of the finger acting immediately on the string in that instrument, without the intervention of any other mechanism.' The power of this instrument depending on the quantity of matter brought into vibration, the resonance, or the perfection of that vibration, depending on the correct proportions of its parts, and the accuracy of intonation depending on the nature of the bridging, the proportions of the strings, and their arrangement with regard to the blow of the hammer, are all most admirable; while the action depending on the peculiar mechanism employed far surpasses every thing else of the kind; for it enables the player to communicate to the strings all that the finest-formed and most skilful hand can express, and becomes, as it were, a part of himself, reflecting every shade of his feelings, from the most powerful to the softest and most delicate sounds. This action is indeed so perfect, particularly in its power of delicate repetition, that if any note is missed in execution upon it, it is the fault of the player, and not of the instrument. Many persons have a very meagre notion of the power of expression possessed by the pianoforte. The fact is, however, that it really possesses almost all those elements of expression which belong to any other instrument, and several which are peculiar to itself, from the circumstance of the various parts of music adapted to the instrument being brought out by the same hand and the same feeling. An immense difference of volume of tone, and of effect, is produced by the manner of touching the keys, and by the use of the pedals, especially upon an instrument of great power, fine quality of tone, and delicate mechanism in the action." *

From the earliest period in the history of the pianoforte, as we have shown in the first part of our volume, makers have bestowed their time and attention in contriving a system of action for striking the strings *downwards*, instead of upwards. In addition to the early makers whom we have named, we may instance Messrs. Stodart, Wornum, Kollman, and Pape. Many advantages undoubtedly attend this plan, some of which are enumerated in the following extract from a report on M. Pape's instruments, signed by Cherubini, Lesueur, Boieldieu, Auber, Paer, and Berton:

" The advantages which these newly invented pianos offer are the following :—

---

* M. Thalberg's remarks in the Jury Report of the Exhibition of 1851.

THE ACTION. 195

they unite more richness, as well as sweetness of tone and power, to a greater solidity and less external size. One of the greatest defects in the old system, against which the manufacturers have struggled in vain for the last twenty years, arose from the mechanism being placed beneath the sounding-board; whence it became necessary, in order that the hammers might strike the string, to form an opening in the sounding-board, by which the solidity of the instrument was more or less compromised. Endeavours had been made to remedy this defect by double bracing, so as to prevent the resistance of the strings; but complete success had never attended these attempts: and as to the opening on the sounding-board, and the injurious influence it had in diminishing the tone of the instrument, it was impossible, under such a system, to obviate it. With such difficulties, therefore, it became necessary to change the whole plan.

"In the new invention of M. Pape, the mechanism of the instrument being placed above the sounding-board, the two blocks now form but one; since they are, as well as the sounding-board, directly united and without any opening whatever; by which arrangement such a solidity is obtained, that it is next to impossible for the sounding-board or block to give way—a circumstance of very frequent occurrence in pianos constructed upon the old system. Besides, the keys communicating more immediately with the mechanism of the instrument; and the hammers striking the strings from above, against the bridge and the sounding-board, there results a much greater power and clearness of sound, as well as a greater facility in execution. The strings likewise being pressed by every stroke of the hammer upon the bridge, retain the instruments in tune a greater length of time than in the old pianos, in which the strings were continually being lifted up. A fortunate circumstance in the present invention is, that it requires much less solid wood; and the iron bars which they were compelled to make use of under the old plan, have been entirely laid aside."

The arrangement of the mechanism in M. Pape's instruments has likewise another peculiarity. In the generality of down-striking actions, the hammers are situated at the back end of the key frame, and are moved by the back ends of the keys; in the present action, on the contrary, the hammers are placed under the keys, and are worked from their *front* ends, directly under the part struck by the fingers; so that the thrust passes immediately downwards, in a direction nearly vertical, from the finger to the hammer, and thence to the string below. The firmness which this direct action gives to the blow may be easily understood. Moreover, there is another great advantage attending this disposition of action, namely, that from the hammers being brought so far forward, a much greater length of string is obtained than on the ordinary plan, with the same length of case. In up-striking instruments (as well as in down-striking ones having the hammer at the back), the front end of the string must, of necessity, lie at some distance from the front end of the instrument; while in M. Pape's arrangement the string is brought completely up to the front, and thus an increase of about a foot in length is obtained, or, which is the same thing, an equal diminution in the length of the instrument for the same length of string.

"There are some peculiarities," says Mr. Pole, " common to all the varieties of action, as made by M. Pape, well worthy of imitation, but which have been little attended to by the majority of makers. All the parts are perfectly accessible, and every point liable to wear is provided with a mode of adjustment. For example, the grand action, although apparently buried in the case, can in a moment be turned round, and every part exposed to view; while the escapement, the effective length of hopper, the key-centre, and the front pinhole, the dampers, the height of the key, &c. have all adjusting screws, by which they can be regulated with the greatest facility when worn, or otherwise out of adjustment. By these means, all rattling of the keys and action, unevenness in the touch, imperfect damping, &c. which so often occur almost irremediably in old instruments, may be at once removed, and the mechanism restored to its original good condition. The key-centres, instead of working on a vertical pin, as commonly made, turn on a horizontal wire—a plan more in accordance with mechanical rules, and less liable to derangement."

CHAPTER IV.

VARIOUS MECHANICAL CONTRIVANCES APPLIED TO THE PIANOFORTE IN ORDER TO OBTAIN SUSTAINED SOUNDS.

The absence of the means of sustaining sounds in the pianoforte has suggested to ingenious men, at various periods, the possibility of devising some intermediate agent, to act between the keys and the strings, that would accomplish this desired object. But, as it has been remarked, it is much more easy to draw true harmony from square or cylindrical pipes by artificial means, than to intone elastic strings, which borrow a part of their sound from the body upon which they are mounted. The bow, in the hand of an able performer, has power to act upon the mass of air contained in the sonorous body of the violin, tenor, or bass, and to bring it in contact with the external air; but it is different to produce the same effect by means of a mechanical bow. If it is sought to give it sufficient power for this purpose, the motion of the machine becomes hard, restive, and almost impossible. On the contrary, if that degree of suppleness be left to the bow which is often necessary, the only sound obtained is meagre and devoid of intensity. All the researches and trials hitherto made have failed in removing these obstacles, and perhaps the latest invention is as imperfect as the first.

The earliest attempt to produce sustained sounds in a keyed-stringed instrument was made by John Heyden, about the year 1600. The instrument was called the "*Clavecin viole*," or "*Geigen clavicymbal.*" The mechanism consisted of a series of cylindrical bows, made to act, by means of a pedal, upon an ordinary harpsichord with metallic strings. Heyden was a distinguished musician of Nuremberg, and the organist of the church of St. Sebald in that city*. He visited Prague early in the seventeenth century, and exhibited his instrument to Rudolph the Second, from which prince he obtained for himself and his heirs the sole right of constructing the instrument. In 1605 and 1610, he published descriptions of his invention, in German and Latin; and it is honourably mentioned by Prætorius and Mersennus, in their respective works†. Heyden died at Nuremberg in 1613.

More than a quarter of a century afterwards, Father Kircher, the visionary author of *Musurgia Universelle*, mentions the possibility of constructing an instrument upon a similar plan; but his description is too vague to be of any interest at the present day.

In 1664, John Evelyn records, in his valuable Diary—" October 5th—To our Society [i. e. the Royal] there was brought a new-invented instrument of music, being a harpsichord with gut-strings, sounding like a concert of viols with an organ, made vocal by a wheel and zone of parchment that rubbed horizontally against the strings." ‡

In 1717, Marius, the harpsichord maker of Paris (before noticed as a claimant to the invention of the pianoforte), contributed an instrument of a similar description, to which he gave the name of *Clavecin vielle*. It met with the approval of the *Académie des Sciences*, and the model is, we believe, still to be seen among the collection of " machines" preserved by that institution.

In 1754, Hohlfeld, an ingenious mechanic of Berlin, who had rendered himself worthy of notice by several important inventions, conceived the idea of his *Bowed* harpsichord, a model of which he presented to the King of Prussia in that year. This instrument was mounted with cat-gut strings, under which was placed a hair bow, put in motion by a little wheel. Small hooks attached to the keys pressed the strings upon the bow, which, by its action on the strings, drew forth the sounds. It differed very little, we believe, from Marius's *Clavecin vielle*.

---

* He was the son of Sebastian Heyden, and born in 1540. See Fétis's *Biographie des Musiciens*.

† Prætorius gives a drawing of the mechanism of Heyden's " Geigen clavicymbal" (*Syntagma Musicum*, tom. ii, p. 67). An engraving of the exterior may also be seen in Doppelmayr's *Nachricht von dem Nürnbergischen Mathematicis und Kunstlern*, folio, Nuremberg, 1730.

‡ *Diary*, vol. i, p. 381, edit. 1850.

This was followed by the Lyrichord, an instrument exhibited in London in 1755; and afterwards by the Celestina, an invention of Adam Walker, the philosopher, and friend of Dr. Priestly.* Walker introduced it with considerable effect in his *Eidouranion*, or transparent orrery, exhibited at the Haymarket Theatre in 1778.

About the same time, the Rev. William Mason, whom we have before had occasion to mention, in connection with the pianoforte, turned his attention to the subject under consideration. Horace Walpole, in a letter to the poet, dated Feb. 29, 1776, says, speaking of Dr. Burney, " I perceive he did not know that you are an *inventor* in the science, and have begotten a new instrument by the marriage of two others." This instrument was called the *Cœlestinettes*. The Rev. J. Mitford, in his *Correspondence of Horace Walpole and the Rev. William Mason*, published in 1851, adds, in a note (vol. i, p. 431): " It [the Cœlestinettes] is not, however, to be found among the other works of art still remaining at Aston; all his music [and instruments] having, I believe, been bequeathed to a friend. However, by the favour of Miss Alderson, a MS. description of it, in Mason's writing, dated Aston, March 30, 1761, is now before me. It consists of ten pages, and enters into all the minute particulars of its formation. The beginning is as follows: ' For the proper preparation of the horse-hair of the bow used in performing on the Cœlestinettes, the clearness of the tone of the instrument, the facility of its touch, and, in short, every thing that makes any degree of execution practicable upon it, all depends principally on that part of it which is employed in making it sound; namely, the single horse-hair attached to the moveable ruler or bow, which is drawn backwards and forwards over the strings by the left hand of the performer, while his right is employed in pushing down the keys. To perform this properly, four circumstances must be particularly attended to: 1, the size of the hair; 2, its length; 3, its texture; 4, and principal, its due degree of resin;' &c. The instrument is still remembered at Aston, as resembling in shape the old spinette or harpsichord."

---

* This invention is included in the patent granted to Adam Walker, of Manchester, "teacher of natural philosophy," July 29, 1772. See page 149, *ante*.

Towards the close of the eighteenth century, Gerli, a mechanist of Milan, produced an instrument mounted with cat-gut strings, and acted upon by means of finger-keys and horse-hair bows, in the manner of the clavecins we have described, but with a greater degree of perfection. According to the Italian journals, it was used at several concerts, and introduced into the churches; but it seems probable that the instrument was found to have insurmountable defects, for it soon fell into oblivion.

The next attempt of the kind was by Schmidt, a pianoforte manufacturer at Paris[*], who produced an instrument in the form of a long square chest, which was shown in the exhibition of the products of industry at the *Invalides* in 1806. At one of the extremities of his instrument was a key-board, with the mechanism of a common pianoforte; at the other was another key-board, intended to put in motion a number of small cylindrical bows, by means of which the cat-gut strings were intoned. The sounds obtained by this mechanism resembled those of the cymbal; not corresponding to the intention of the maker, who sought to imitate bowed instruments. However, M. Schmidt obtained an honourable mention of his endeavours.

In 1810, M. de St. Perne, an amateur, invented, under the name of *Organon-Lyricon*, an instrument which, besides the common pianoforte, comprised a dozen wind instruments, all of which could act in concert with it. By an ingenious, but somewhat complicated piece of mechanism, the performer could, by the assistance of a double key-board, produce the tones, either separately or together, of the pianoforte, flute, oboe, clarionet, &c.

About the same time, Pouleau invented his *Orchestrina*, which bore a considerable degree of analogy to the instrument of Schmidt, just mentioned. What particularly distinguished M. Pouleau's Orchestrina from all other inventions of the same kind, was a horse-hair bow, made without any visible suture, the secret of which he never revealed.

The next invention worthy of notice is that of our own countryman, Mr. Isaac Mott. The *Sostinente* is said to have resembled, in its tone, the *celestina* stop of the

---

[*] This artist, a distinguished mechanist, was born in the duchy of Nassau in 1768, and settled at Paris in 1795. He died in 1821.

harpsichord. But the effect was produced, not by drawing a skein of silk over the strings, as in that invention, but by a different and novel principle. A strong silk thread was stretched across the strings of the pianoforte, and to each finger-key there was also a silk thread, to which was attached a skein of silk, which skein passed over a cylinder of about two inches diameter, and was ultimately attached by three threads to the cross thread above mentioned. When the finger-key was pressed, it stretched the skein over the cylinder, and caused the cross thread to press on the string. At the same time the cylinder was turning on its axis, and, being touched with the dust of fiddle rosin, communicated vibration to the string*. This instrument was made in the grand upright form.

In 1822, the Abbe Gregorio Trentia invented an instrument to which he gave the name of *Violicembalo*. The *Gazetta di Milano* gives the following account of it: "The strings are of cat-gut, of various dimensions, of which the lowest are covered with metal wire, and each string is appropriated to a single tone. At the extremity of each key is a horizontal lever, by means of which the string is raised upwards to meet the action of the bow. This bow consists of a piece of woollen stuff, inwrought with silk threads instead of hair, which is drawn backwards and forwards by means of two cylinders, affixed to the sides, and set in motion by means of a fly wheel, worked by the right foot." The *Breton*, a journal of literature, &c. published at Nantes, says: "It is, perhaps, the most perfect instrument of the kind produced; yet it fails with respect to the bow, which, being made of *hairs* [sic], produces tones of a wiry and shrill kind. It seems to want the bow composed by M. Poulleau, the secret of which unfortunately died with him." A long article upon this invention, by the Conte Leopoldo Cigonare, may be seen in the *Effemeridi Litterarie di Roma*, vol. v, p. 29.

M. Lange, of Munich, next invented an instrument called the *Æolodikon*. It is said to have resembled the *Celestina* of Adam Walker; but we have not been able to meet with any account of it.

M. Gama, a pianoforte-maker of Nantes, invented, in 1827, an instrument to

---

* The patent for this ingenious invention is dated Feb. 1, 1817. See p. 152, *ante*.

which he gave the name of *Plectroeuphon* (i. e. harmonious bow). " While in its mode of performance," according to the journal of the time, " it comprises all the facilities of the piano, it possesses all the additional advantage of diminishing or reinforcing the sounds at pleasure, and producing with ease the finest gradations of tone. It can, as occasion requires, supply the place of four stringed instruments; and offers, in other respects, resources not possessed by the piano." Notwithstanding this recommendation, the attempt to introduce it at Paris was altogether unsuccessful.

The imperfections of the previous instruments suggested to M. Dietz, of Paris, in 1827, his *Polyplectron*. The principles upon which it was constructed are more conformable to what observation teaches with respect to the resonance of instruments of the bow kind, than those adopted by his predecessors. Whether the bow acts longitudinally, or whether it be cylindrical, its horizontal movements can necessarily produce only a feeble sound, because, in acting upon the string, it can make it vibrate only in an opposite direction to the vibrations of the sounding-board. This was the predominant defect in all the instruments which have been described; and the observation of this led M. Dietz to form the idea of making his bow act perpendicularly on the strings, after the manner that the violin, bass, and every other bowed instrument is played. In order to effect this he had need of as many bows as notes; and this has been effected by means of a piece of mechanism of the most ingenious kind. Numerous bows, composed of thin slips of leather, were made to circulate upon a cylinder placed upon the upper part of the instrument, and over pulleys ranged on the lower. The motion of the key brought the bow in contact with the string, by means of a small thin piece of copper, and the sound was instantaneously produced. This sound was capable of assuming different characters, according to the degree of pressure applied to the key. Thus, when the artist played with a firm touch and *legato*, he obtained the effect of an excellent organ, and of a voluminous tone. If he played with lightness, whether *legato* or *staccato*, he produced the effect of bowed instruments. In the deeper part of the scale, and in the medium, the analogy was almost perfect with the double bass, violoncello, and tenor. In the higher range of notes, the sound assumed the character of different kinds of violas, rather than of the violin. The inventor did not succeed in producing the long-sought imitation of this admirable instrument.

The Polyplectron was also distinguished from the other instruments of its kind by the rapidity of its articulations, which allowed of its being played with all the facility of the pianoforte, in executing the most rapid and complicated passages.

Notwithstanding all these presumed advantages, M. Dietz's invention has shared the fate of its predecessors, and long since passed away.

This brings us down to the Great Industrial Exhibition of 1851. " We all remember," says a pleasant writer in *Chambers's Edinburgh Journal* (Oct. 27, 1855), " that ear-rending and infinitely distressing anomaly, the fiddle-piano, in the American department of the Industrial Building of 1851, wherein a violin, connected by mechanism with a second row of keys, played a dismal unison with the right hand of the performer, and put every listener out of spirits for the rest of the day."

Other attempts, similar to those we have briefly narrated, have been tried at various times, by Garbrecht, Grainer, Meyer, Müller, Hackel, Hawkins, Fiebig, &c.; but we are unable to describe them particularly; and as the results have not, in one single instance, been crowned with success, this is the less to be regretted.

The object so long sought after, of obtaining a sustaining power in the pianoforte, has been attempted in another way. The principle, which has been perfected by M. Isoard, an ingenious engineer and mechanician, consists in causing a current of air to act on the string, which prolongs its vibration somewhat on the principle of the Æolian harp. For this purpose there is an opening opposite to each string, through which a stream of air passes from a bellows, when a valve, corresponding to the given note, is opened by the key. The bellows are moved by pedals, in the same manner as those of the seraphine or harmonium*.

According to the following statement, which has lately gone the round of the press, this principle is about to be carried out in our own country; but we have little faith in its success.

---

* The application of wind to cause the vibration of strings was first tried at Paris about seventy years ago by a German pianoforte maker named Schnell (born in 1740). The idea was suggested to him by a harp hanging in the air. Many instruments of various kinds were constructed, such as the *Anemochorde*, the *Violine-eolie*, &c. before any perfection was attained.

"IMPORTANT MUSICAL INVENTION.—Mr. F. J. Julyan, of Gerrard-street, Soho-square, has invented and patented a new method of producing musical sounds, that will be the means of effecting great improvements in the construction of wind and stringed instruments. After making a great variety of experiments relating to the effect of wind upon musical strings; he has discovered a very simple and practicable means of causing strings and wires in a state of tension to vibrate without the agency of either percussion or friction, in fact without touching them. The motive power employed is a small current of air, either from the human mouth or a wind chest, being made to impinge upon the string at one end of it, passing over the string and into a narrow slit or groove immediately under it, the groove being quite parallel to the string and extending one-tenth along the length of it, leaving nine-tenths of the string available for fingering or attaching to a sound-board. The rapid alternate rarefaction and condensation of the air at the slit or mouthpiece performing a part equivalent to the bow of a violin, and sustaining the sound as long as the wind continues to act upon it. We have seen it applied to a sound-board and organ-pipes; and we have seen and heard an instrument made upon this principle, called the 'Eolian Monochord,' which has one bass string fifteen inches long, one end of which is fixed over a mouthpiece one and a half inch long, in the manner described above. It is held in the same position as a flute and blown with the breath. Three chromatic octaves can be produced on this very simple instrument. The tones are of a peculiar kind and of excellent quality."

CHAPTER V.

MELOGRAPHIC, MECHANICAL, AND TRANSPOSING PIANOS.

The idea of constructing a harpsichord or pianoforte by means of which the improvisations of a composer might be preserved, has considerably occupied the attention of several ingenious mechanists. The Rev. Mr. Creed, a clergyman of London, first conceived the idea of a musical instrument that, while performed upon, should trace on paper the music executed; and, in 1747, he submitted his project to the consideration of the Society for the Encouragement of Arts and Manufactures, in a memorial entitled *A Demonstration of the Possibility of making a Machine that shall write extempore Voluntaries, or other Pieces of Music, &c.*[*] It is asserted also, that a monk, of the name of Engramelle, about the year 1770, made an instrument of this kind, the success of which was complete; but the explanations which are given of it are very obscure, and of a kind to give rise to doubts concerning the truth of the facts. On the other hand, John Frederick Unger, counsellor of justice at Brunswick, in a German work printed in 1774, has claimed the invention of the instrument attributed to Creed, and proved that he had previously made a similar one[†].

---

[*] *A Letter to the President of the Royal Society, inclosing a Paper of the late Rev. Mr. Creed, concerning a Machine, &c.* is contained in the *Philosophical Transactions*, vol. xliv, p. 445. The author of the letter advocating Mr. Creed's notions was John Freke, the celebrated surgeon.

[†] *Entwurf einer Maschine, wodurch Alles, was auf dem Clavier gespielt wird, sie von selber in Noten setzt, im Jahr* 1752, *an die Königliche Akademie der Wissenshaften zu Berlin eingesandt, nebst dem mit dem Herrn Doctor Euler, darüber geführten Briefwechsel, und einigen an dem diesen Entwurf betreffenden Nachrichten.* Brunswick, 1774. 4to.

Hohlfeld, however, the ingenious mechanic of Berlin before mentioned, has the best claim to the invention. Availing himself of the suggestions of Euler, he, in 1752, made an instrument similar to that proposed by Creed and Unger, and presented it to the *Académie*. The invention consisted of two cylinders, so applied to a pianoforte, that, as they revolved during the performance, one received the paper unrolled from the other. By this means the notes were marked by a crayon upon the paper, which a spring kept in motion. But the operation was so fatiguing, that the *Académie* contented itself with admitting the great ingenuity of the contrivance, and awarding the inventer a handsome gratuity in compensation for his talents and trouble. Hohlfeld received back his machine, and, some years afterwards, sent it to his country seat near Berlin; where, in 1757, it was consumed by an accidental conflagration.

In the month of August, 1827, M. Carreyre made trial, before the Committee of the Fine Arts of the Institute of France, of a *melographic* piano, which consisted of a clock movement, which unrolled from one cylinder to another a thin plate of lead, on which were impressed, by the action of the keys of the instrument, certain peculiar signs, which might be translated into the ordinary notation by means of an explanatory table. After the experiment, the plate of lead was removed, to make the translation, and a commission was appointed to report; but as no report was ever made, it is probable that the translation was not found to be exact. At the same time, M. Baudouin read before the Institute a paper, accompanied with drawings, concerning another melographic piano; upon the merit of which we do not find that the Institute pronounced.

Self-acting virginals and harpsichords existed at an early period, as we have shown in our historical introduction. A self-acting pianoforte was invented by Messrs. Clementi and Collard early in the present century, which professes to be the first of its kind. According to the notices that appeared at the time, "This curious instrument, furnished with a horizontal cylinder, similar to that of a barrel-organ, and put in motion by a steel spring, performs, without external force or manual operation, the most intricate and difficult compositions; and, by comprising in its mechanism two complete instruments, each independent of the other, it admits, while the operation of the self-actuated instrument is proceeding within, of a distinct accompaniment on the keys without, which occupy the usual place in front, and may be played on at pleasure, with or without the self-acting part of the machine. This, the first instrument of its kind, when the spring is fully wound up, will act for more than half an hour, and may be again prepared for performance in half a minute; and, if required, stopped in an instant, while in full action. The time in which it executes any movement may be accelerated or retarded at pleasure: and while, by the delicacy and perfection of the mechanism, the *piano* and the *forte* passages are given with correctness and effect, the *fortzandi* and *diminuendi* are produced by the slightest motion of the hand applied to a sliding ball at the side of the instrument. When we consider the state of the pianoforte as originally constructed—its thin, wiry, jangling tone, ineffective weakness, and other numerous imperfections, and witness the complicated beauties and powers of this self-acting instrument, we must be both delighted and surprised,—and almost be persuaded, that to ingenuity, science, and industry, no excellence in musical mechanism is unattainable."

An ingenious contrivance of M. Debain, of Paris, intended to supersede the barrel hitherto employed, was shown in the London Exhibition of 1851. Instead of the music being pricked on a barrel, it is formed by a series of pins, fixed on the plane surface of a thin oblong tablet of wood, a few inches broad, giving to it the appearance of a currycomb. This is drawn, by a rack and pinion, through a frame, in which project wedge-shaped ends of levers, connected by rods with the hammers of the piano; so that, when any pin in the tune-tablet passes over one of these wedge-shaped lever ends, it depresses it, and thereby lifts the hammer, which, when the pin has passed over, is thrown back by a spring against the string. The mechanical apparatus is made to fit on the top of an ordinary cottage pianoforte, and may be detached at pleasure, leaving the instrument in its natural state for performance by the fingers.

Transposing instruments, the object being to suit voices of different compasses, are not of modern invention. Besides the instances noticed in the historical portion of our work, we may mention that Bauer, counsellor and chamberlain to the Prince of Prussia in 1786, constructed an instrument, the key-board of which was moveable, " transposing music one or two notes higher." Roller, of Paris, also manufactured pianos with a key-board capable of transposing 1, 2, 3, 4, or 5 *half-tones higher* or *lower*.

Transposing pianos are differently constructed. Sometimes the key-board and action, or the strings and framing, are shifted laterally, so as to make one hammer strike different strings, according to its position. The Royal Albert transposing piano differs from other instruments; as neither action nor strings are moveable. The keys may be described as divided at half their length, the front and back ends being capable of moving independently of each other, and the connection being made between them by means of a shifting lever underneath; so that by altering the position of this lever, the front end of the key C, for example, may be made to act at the back end of either of the keys C sharp, D, B, B flat, &c.

In the sketches which we have given of what relates to pianofortes and their manufacture, the reader may have been struck with the prodigious fruitfulness of imagination manifested in all these inventions. Will things remain stationary in this respect, or not? This is doubtful. The imagination of man will always be active; but it may be doubted whether there will be produced hereafter effects greatly superior to those which are now obtained. All the distinguished men, who have employed themselves in the construction of instruments, have sought to make improvements in them by a more severe application of theoretical principles; but, in practice, the results have not been such as they expected, either from unknown causes, or from their not having taken the necessary precautions. Theory is sometimes found in opposition to practice. For example, the principles of the sounding of vibrating surfaces demonstrate that violins, violas, and basses, are constructed on arbitrary rather than scientific rules; but, in the application of these principles, no one has yet been able to make instruments so good as those which were made by rules the foundation of which is unknown. The same thing may be remarked of pianofortes. Time alone will shed light on these mysterious circumstances*.

---

* These remarks are translated from M. Fétis's admirable little volme, *La Musique misè à la Partée de tout le Monde*. 2nd edit. Brussels, 1839.

CHAPTER VI.

STATISTICS OF PIANOFORTES AND PIANOFORTE MANUFACTURING AS AN ARTICLE OF TRADE; MATERIALS USED IN THE CONSTRUCTION OF PIANOFORTES, &c.

THE manufacture of pianofortes has become a branch of national industry of considerable importance, whether it be regarded with reference to the scale upon which it is conducted, or the class of labour it employs. Dr. Lardner* took some pains to collect statistical information; but remarks—" we have not been able to obtain any certain or exact statistical data by which a calculation of its magnitude or value can be estimated. In the absence of such precise data, however, some approximation may be made by comparison with the ascertained extent of the same manufacture in a neighbouring country, where it is certainly fifty per cent. less in quantity and value than in England.

" At the Great Exhibition of the Products of French Industry, which was held in Paris in 1849, it was ascertained, by official documents placed at the command of the juries, that the annual value of the pianos fabricated in France was above eight millions of francs; and, inasmuch as the manufacture was then, and has since been, in rapid development and increase, we shall not probably over-estimate its present amount by stating it at ten millions of francs, or four hundred thousand pounds sterling.

" So great a consumption of this manufacture may be explained, partly by the

---

* *Popular Essays on Scientific Subjects*, by Dr. Dionysius Lardner. 8vo. London, 1852. A charming series of papers, which originally appeared in the " Times," during the progress of the Great Exhibition of 1851. (Essay xiv, p. 363.)

inevitable effects of time and climate even on the most solid and durable mechanism, partly by the wear and tear proceeding from use and abuse, especially in the extensive class of instruments used for teaching, and partly by the augmented population to whose enjoyment the instrument administers; but much also must be ascribed to the increased cultivation of music, and to the rapidly progressive improvement of the mechanism of the piano, which presents to the more affluent a constant inducement—nay, a social necessity—to reject the pianos they possess, not because they are impaired by time or use, but because the genius and invention of the makers have placed before them better and more powerful instruments.

"Considering that by far the largest number of instruments constructed are of a small size and low price, we may take the average cost, one with another, at about a thousand francs, which would give the number of pianofortes annually fabricated in France to be ten thousand, of which about thirty per cent., or three thousand, are exported.

"The industry occupied in this business is nearly all of the class of skilled and artistic labour, and is consequently highly remunerated. In the report of the jury on the French Exposition, the average wages were estimated at five francs per day. The number of pairs of hands occupied in the manufacture may therefore be estimated at nearly seven thousand.

"If, in the absence of better and more exact means of calculation, it be assumed that the manufacture in England is double this in quantity and value, we may infer that in the United Kingdom the fabrication of pianos produces a gross return of £800,000; that about 20,000 instruments are fabricated annually; and that about 14,000 pairs of skilled hands are occupied in the business.

"This approximate estimate, considerable in amount as it will appear, is below that which has been made by others who have investigated the statistics of this branch of industry. The following appeared in one of the reviews of the Great Exhibition, which appeared in the journals.

"*Estimate of Pianofortes annually made in London.*

1,500 grands, bicords, and small grands, at £110 each		£165,000
1,500 squares	60	90,000
20,000 uprights of various kinds	35	700,000
23,000		£955,000

" According to this approximate estimate, the produce of the London manufacture alone, not including that of the cities of Edinburgh and Dublin, besides towns of less magnitude, amounts to a million sterling. If this estimate be correct, the extent of this branch of industry, in England, is about three times its amount in France."

The population returns of 1841, according to the Rev. W. W. Cazalet[*], show that there were then in England and Wales 378 organ builders; but, singularly enough, the pianoforte makers are not separately specified in the returns. From information given to the writer in 1851, the Messrs. Collard sold annually 1,600 instruments; or a gross amount, during the last twenty years, of about 32,000. The Messrs. Broadwood, during the same period, have sold 45,863 instruments, or an annual average of 2,293 and a fraction. " Taking the annual business," says the same writer, " of these houses at a round number of 4,000 pianos, and at an average price of 60 guineas, which must be much below the mark, it gives, for these two firms alone, the enormous gross return of upwards of a quarter of a million." Mr. Cazalet's deductions arrive at the same conclusion we have already given. He says, " Now the number of pianoforte makers in London is about 180. (I have taken this from the Directory.) It is not unreasonable, therefore, to state the gross return of this branch at considerably more than a million; as, by a probable estimate that has been made, it would appear that the number of instruments made and sold in the year is about 23,000, of all sorts."

---

[*] *A Lecture on the Musical Department of the late Great Exhibition, read before the Society of Arts,* May 6th, 1852. 8vo. 1852. The historical part of this lecture is very meagre and incorrect.

The prices of instruments made by the best houses, in plain mahogany cases, are for grands, 125 to 135 guineas; for bicord and small grands, 80 to 105 guineas; for grand squares, 50 to 100 guineas; for plain squares, 35 to 50 guineas; for cabinets, 75 to 85 guineas; for cottage and other small uprights, 45 to 70 guineas. These prices are often, however, increased for more expensive cases, in rose, walnut, or other fancy woods, enriched with ornamental carving or inlaying. Beautiful specimens of such were seen in the Great Exhibition of 1851. Messrs. Collard's principal instrument was valued at 500 guineas; Messrs. Erard's at 1000 guineas; and Messrs. Broadwood's at, we believe, 1200. "The enormous money value of these," says Mr. Pole, "is solely on account of the external decoration; as musical instruments, they are in no wise superior to the ordinary grands, sold at the prices above named. On the other hand, a class of instruments has been lately introduced by Messrs. Collard, with the laudable object of bringing the price of the ornamental part down to the lowest possible sum; and so putting pianofortes of the best make within the reach of purchasers with limited means. With this view, the most useful variety of the small upright is made, in a neat, plain case of deal or other cheap wood, and sold for about 30 guineas." The appearance of these instruments is very neat, and, we think, far preferable to the profusion of ornament, in the vilest possible taste, with which some makers cover their pianos. Small uprights, by makers of little eminence, are sold at much less prices than those of the large houses.

The principle of division of labour is adopted to a considerable extent in pianoforte making, precision of detail being of the utmost possible consequence. As an illustration of this, we may state that a grand pianoforte, in the course of its progress to completion, passes under the hands of upwards of forty different workmen, each of whom, with his assistants, is exclusively engaged in a special branch of the manufacture. They are as follows:*

---

* The documents upon which our information is founded were prepared by Messrs. Broadwood, on the occasion of the Great Exhibition of 1851. They show in detail the various classes of operations, and the different qualities and sorts of materials used in the manufacture of pianofortes. They are inserted in Dr. Lardner's interesting work before referred to; also in Mr. Pole's privately printed brochure.

1. The *key-maker* forms the entire key-board from one piece of lime-tree wood; fixes on the pieces of ivory and ebony; bores the necessary holes; and, finally, cuts the whole up into separate keys with a fine saw.

2, 3, 4, 5. The *hammer-maker*, the *check-maker*, the *damper-maker*, and the *damper-lifter-maker*, construct the parts of the action to which these names refer.

6. The *notch-maker* covers, with doe-skin and cloth, the notches or ends of the hammer-shanks into which the hoppers work.

7. The *hammer-leatherer* covers the hammer-heads with their different coats of leather and felt, and cuts them to their proper size.

8. The *beam-maker* makes the mahogany beam or rail extending across the action and covered with brass, in which the hammers are centered.

9, 10, 11. The *brass-stud-maker* and *brass-bridge-maker* form the upward bearing-studs and bridge; and the *wrest-pin-maker*, the iron tuning pins.

12, 13, 14, 15. The *metallic-brace-maker*, the *metallic-plate-maker*, the *steel-arch-maker*, and the *transverse-bar-maker*, all construct part of the metallic bracing. (The makers of the iron and brass work, for pianofortes and other musical instruments, are called *music-smiths*.)

16. The *spun-string-maker* makes the lapped or spun wires.

These parts, and other minor preparations, being supposed ready, the body of the instrument is made as follows:

17, 18. The *sawyer* saws the timber roughly into shape; the *bent-side-maker* then cuts it more accurately to its size and thickness, and bends, by a steaming process, the pieces destined to form the curved side of the instrument.

19, 20. The *case-maker* fashions, puts together, and veneers the timber-framing forming the principal body of the instrument; he also forms and fixes the wrest-plank. The *bracer* inserts the timber cross-bracing in the frame: this is, however, sometimes done by the case-maker.

21. The *bottom-maker* makes and fixes the framed bed, at the lower part of the instrument, to receive the key-board.

22, 23. The *sounding-board-maker* selects the timber for, cuts out, and joints, the sound-board. The *belly-man* planes it to its proper thickness, shapes it, finishes it, and fixes it in the case. He also forms and fixes upon it the beech bridge, upon which the strings take their bearing.

24. The *marker-off* has more to do than his name implies. He marks out the scale for the strings, fixes the pins on the beech bridge, and finishes it to its proper shape; he inserts the upward bearing bridge and studs in the wrest-plank, and bores it ready to receive the tuning pins; he also fits and fixes the metallic string-plate, longitudinal stretcher-bars, and other parts of the metallic bracing, by which the pianoforte is made ready to receive the strings.

25. The *stringer* puts on the strings, and fixes the wrest-pins in their places.

26. The *finisher* receives the keys and the various parts of the action from their respective makers; he constructs

the action-framing, puts the action together, fixes it in its place, and brings the whole of the mechanism generally into playing order.

27, 28. The *rougher-up* then tunes the instrument for the first time, stretching the strings to their proper tension; after which, the *tuner* puts it thoroughly and permanently in tune.

29, 30. The *regulator of action* then examines and carefully adjusts every part of the action, and completes the regulation of the touch; and, finally, the *regulator of tones* examines the tones and corrects all irregularities, making the pianoforte sound and perfect throughout.

The following operations, which have reference to the external part of the instrument, are done at various times in the course of its construction.

31, 32. The *top-maker* constructs and veneers the cover, and puts on the hinges. The *plinther* fixes and veneers the plinth.

33. The *fronter* shapes, hinges, and centres the fall or cylinder front; shapes the cheeks, makes and fixes the mouldings, puts on the locks, and attaches the ornaments.

34. The *canvass-frame-maker* makes an open wood frame-work, covered with canvass, which is fixed in the bottom of the instrument.

35. The *lyre-maker* makes the lyre-shaped bracket fixed under the instrument to carry the pedals.

36, 37. The *leg-block-maker* makes and fixes the blocks into which the legs are screwed; and the *leg-maker* makes the legs themselves.

38, 39, 40. The *tuner*, the *carver*, and the *gilder*, do all work wanted in their respective departments.

41, 42. The *scraper* scrapes and cleans the surface of the case, and prepares it, by rubbing it with glass-paper, for the *polisher*, who gives it its coat of French polish.

It is almost superfluous to add, that all the hands employed in the manufacture must be well skilled in their respective departments; and that the whole of the operations (but most particularly those connected with the framing and action) must be done with the utmost care, or a good result cannot follow. It is moreover found necessary, in order to ensure the good quality of the instrument, that the work be not hurried; but that it should progress slowly and gradually to completion. A grand pianoforte usually remains in hand upwards of six months.

The following table gives a list of the different materials required in the construction of a pianoforte, specifying the parts of the instrument where they are used.

MATERIALS.		WHERE USED.
Woods	*from*	
Oak	Riga	Framing, various parts.
Deal	Norway	Wood-bracing, &c.
Fir	Switzerland	Sounding-board.
Pine	America	Parts of framing, key-bed or bottom.
Mahogany	Honduras	Solid wood of top, and various parts of the framing and the action.
Beech	England	Wrest-plank, bridge or sound-board, centre of legs.
Beef-wood	Brazils	Tongues in the beam, forming the divisions between the hammers.
Birch	Canada	Belly-rail, a part of the framing.
Cedar	South America	Round shanks of hammers.
Lime-tree	England	Keys.
Pear-tree	—	Heads of dampers.
Sycamore	—	Hopper or levers, veneers on wrest-plank.
Ebony	Ceylon	Black keys.
Spanish Mahogany	Cuba	⎫
Rosewood	Rio Janeiro	⎪
Satinwood	East Indies	⎬ For decoration.
White Holly	England	⎪
Zebra-wood	Brazils	⎪
Other fancy woods		⎭

Woollen Fabrics.

Baize; green, blue, and brown...... Upper surface of key-frame, cushions for hammers to fall on, to damp dead part of strings, &c.

Cloth, various qualities............... For various parts of the action and in other places, to prevent jarring; also for dampers.

Felt...................................... External covering for hammers.

Leather.

Buffalo	Under covering of hammers—bass.
Saddle	Ditto ditto tenor and treble.
Basil	⎫
Calf	⎪
Doeskin	⎬ Various parts of the action.
Seal	⎪
Sheepskin	⎪
Morocco	⎭
Sole	Rings for pedal wires.

Metal.

Iron............................	
Steel...........................	Metallic bracing, and in various small screws, springs, centres, pins, &c. &c. throughout the instrument.
Brass...........................	
Gun-metal....................	
Steel wire.....................	Strings.
Steel spun wire..............	Lapped strings.
Covered copper wire.......	Ditto—lowest notes.

Various.

Ivory............................	White keys.
Black lead.....................	To smooth the rubbing surfaces of cloth or leather in the action.
Glue (of a particular quality, made expressly for this trade).........	Woodwork throughout.
Bees'wax, emery paper, glass paper, French polish, oil, putty powder, spirits of wine, &c. &c. ...	Cleaning and finishing.

The materials must all be of the best possible kinds. The timber especially, being the most important, must be selected of the soundest quality; it requires to be thoroughly seasoned (a process often of several years), and must then be dried by artificial heat before it is worked for use. A similar degree of care must be taken in the selection and preparation of all the other materials, or the quality of the instrument will suffer.

In comparing the French pianofortes exhibited at the Paris Exhibition of 1849, with the British instruments presented for exhibition in 1851, we observe one curious fact, which we must presume is to be ascribed to the fact that in this country the manufacture is limited to a small number of great capitalists, while in France it is distributed among a much greater number of makers working on a smaller scale. With a manufacture upon less than half the scale, and without the stimulus offered by unlimited, or indeed any, foreign competition, there were in the Paris Exposition nearly ninety exhibitors; while, with all the extraordinary excitement presented by the World's Fair, the Crystal Palace produced only forty native exhibitors.

The following carefully prepared table shows the proportions of pianofortes supplied by the industry of different countries, and also the particular description of instrument exhibited by each maker.

	ENGLAND. 1.—LONDON.	No. in the Catalogue.	Grand.	Square.	Cottage.
1	Addison	487			1
2	Akerman, W. H.	490			1
3	Allison	478			1
4	Allison, Ralph	480			1
5	Broadwood and Sons	518	4		
6	Brinsmead, J.	474			1
7	Cadby, C.	471	1		2
8	Collard and Collard	168	2	1	3
9	Deacon				1
10	Ennever and Steedman	479			2
11	Erard, P. O.	496	4		3
12	Greiner, J. F.	468	1		
13	Harrison, J.	464			1
14	Harwar, J.	493a			1
15	Holderness, C.	482			1
16	Hopkinson, J. and J.	500	1		2
17	Hund, F. and Son	486			1
18	Hunt, F.	477a		1	
19	Jenkins, W. and Son	484			2
20	Jones, J. C. and Co.	481			1
21	Kirkman and Son	487	3		1
22	Lambert and Company	100			2
23	Luff and Son	477			1
24	Metzler, George	475			1
25	Moore and Co.	476			1
26	Mott, J. H. R.	498	1		1
27	Oetzman and Plumb	683			2
28	Peachy, George				2
29	Rolfe, W. and Son	472			3
30	Southwell, W.	469	1		
31	Stodart and Son	470	1		
32	Towns and Packer	494	1		1
33	Wheatstone and Company	526			1
34	Wornum, R.	499	1		2

	II.—PROVINCIAL TOWNS.		No. in the Catalogue.	Grand.	Square.	Cottage.
1	M'Culloch	Belfast.	483			1
2	Smith and Roberts	Birmingham.	491			1
3	Dimoline, A.	Bristol.	489			2
4	Aggio, G. H.	Colchester.	488			1
5	Mathews, W.	Nottingham.	550			1
6	Woolley, F.	,,	493			2
	III.—COLONIES.					
1	Herberth and Co.	Montreal	92			1
2	Phillips, J. B.	Halifax				1
		Total...		21	3	53
	UNITED STATES.					
1	Chickering, J.	Boston.	458	1	1	
2	Gilbert and Co	,,	435		1	
3	Hews, G.	,,	438		1	
4	Meyer, Conrad	Philadelphia.	59		2	
5	Nunns and Clark	New York.	374		2	
6	Pirsson, James	,,	90	1	1	
7	Wood, James S.	,,			1	
		Total...		2	9	
	AUSTRIA.					
1	Hoxa.	Vienna.		1		
2	Pottje, J.	,,	141a	1		
3	Schneider, J.	,,	140	1		
4	Seuffert, E.	,,	141b			1
5	Viasky, J.	Prague.	141	1		
		Total...		4		1
	BELGIUM.					
1	Aerts, F. G.	Entwerp	186			1
2	Berden, F. and C.	Brussels	174			3
3	Deffaux.	,,	188			3
4	Jastrzébski, F.	,,	176			3
5	Sternberg, L.	,,	180			2
6	Verhasselt d'Oultrepont	,,	179			1
7	Vogelsang, F. and J.	,,	181	1		1
		Total...		1		14

			No. in the Catalogue.	Grand.	Square.	Cottage.
	DENMARK.					
1	Hornung, C. C.	Copenhagen	30	1	1	
2	Rühms, H.	Altona	14			1
		Total...		1	1	1
	FRANCE.					
	I.—PARIS.					
1	Aucher and Son.		404			2
2	Bord.		1099	1		
3	Collin.					2
4	Debain, A. C.		1172			2
5	Détis and Co.		476			2
6	Domeny, L. F.		477			1
7	Erard, P.		497	3	1	1
8	Franche, C.		1234			2
9	Herz, H.		1268	2		1
10	Jaulin, J.		1274			1
11	Kleinjasper, J. F.		1633			1
12	Mercier, S.		633			2
13	Montal, C.		1665			4
14	Van Overberg.					1
15	Pape, J. H.		943	1	2	2
16	Roller and Blanchet.		1687			6
17	Scholtus.		1482			2
18	Soufleto.		1482			3
		Total...		7	3	35
	II.—PROVINCES.					
1	Herding.	Angers.	335	1		1
2	Zeiger.	Lyons.	747			1
3	Cropet.	Toulouse.	131			2
		Total...		1		4
	SWITZERLAND.					
1	Hüni and Hubert.	Zurich.	87	1		
2	Kützing.	Berne.	89	1		
3	Sprecher and Beer.	Zurich.	103	1		
		Total...		3		

STATISTICS OF PIANOFORTES AND PIANOFORTE MANUFACTURING.

	GERMANY (ZOLLVEREIN), AND HAMBURG.		No. in the Catalogue.	Grand.	Square.	Cottage.
1	Dieudonné and Blädel	Stuttgart	20	1		
2	Dörner, F.	,,	21	1		1
3	Lipp, R. R.	,,	22			2
4	Schiedmayer and Son	,,	23	1	1	1
5	Scheel, C.	Cassel	668			1
6	Breitkopf and Härtel	Leipzig	25	1		
7	Zeitter and Winkelmann	Brunswick	709	1	1	1
8	Kühmst, G.	Darmstadt		1		
9	Schott and Son	Mayence	25	1		
10	Westermann and Co	Berlin	80	1		
11	Bessalié, H. P.	Breslau	71	1		
12	Klems, J. B.	Dusseldorf	595	1		
13	Gebauhr	Konisberg	848	1		
14	Heitermayer, T.	Münster	486		1	
15	Adam, G.	Wesel	487	1		1
16	Gurike, B.	Zoffen	73	1		
17	Schröder, C. H.	Hamburg	13	1		
		Total		14	3	7
	HOLLAND.					
1	Cuijpers, J. F.	Hague	95			1
	RUSSIA.					
1	Lichtenthal, M.	St. Petersburg	172	2		

SUMMARY.

England and the Colonies	42 makers, exhibiting 21 *grands*,	3 *squares*,	53 *cottages*.
France	21	8	3	39
Germany and Hamburg	17	14	3	7
United States	7	2	9	
Belgium	7	1		14
Austria	5	4		1
Holland and Switzerland	4	3		1
Denmark and Russia	3	3	1	1
Total	106	56	19	116

Mr. Pole, to whose labours we have been so largely indebted in the second part of our volume, speaking of the pianofortes in the Exhibition, has some very sensible remarks, which, as they immediately bear upon the portion of the subject before us, we beg to transfer to our pages.

"Notwithstanding the great intelligence and care that are brought to bear on the manufacture of pianofortes, we doubt whether the aid of science has been called in to the extent that could be wished, to guide their construction. Arrangements are often seen which appear unwarranted by the principles of mechanics; and, generally speaking, the *engineering* of the construction is not so well studied as it ought to be. But, in the application of the acoustical science, pianoforte-making is yet more behind hand. The theory of the production of tone, at least as regards its quality, is at present wrapt in mystery. Few persons seem to have any definite idea what are the essential conditions under which a good tone, in general, or still less, any particular quality of tone, can be ensured. A series of tentative experiments leads to certain methods of construction which are considered good; and all possible care is then taken to avoid defects in the manufacture; but the result is, after all, frequently due to some fortuitous combination of circumstances, which cannot be foreseen. Hence arises the variety in the qualities of tone, not only of instruments by different makers of equally good repute, but also in those turned out from the same house, and made apparently in precisely the same manner. Nay, even in the same pianoforte, it frequently happens that the practised ear can detect considerable variations. Sometimes a certain portion of the scale may be far superior to the rest; sometimes a few notes here and there may be deficient in resonance; sometimes one note only in the whole instrument may be faulty: but the reason for these anomalies it is impossible to explain.

"The general excellence of a pianoforte depends, however, not only on the design of its various parts, but also, as we have already stated, on the quality of the materials, and the amount of care bestowed on the workmanship. It is due principally to the great attention paid to these latter points by the chief London houses, that English pianoforte-making has obtained, and still retains, its high reputation.

"If there is any point to which, in preference, future attention should more particularly be directed, we think it is the *cheapening* of the better classes of instruments. A hundred and twenty or thirty guineas for a grand is a price altogether beyond the reach of multitudes, who both need and know how to appreciate a good piano. And yet the tendency of late has been rather to increase than diminish the cost. We admit readily that a good pianoforte, made purposely to attain the highest possible grade of perfection, must always bear a high price; but, at the same time, it is but reasonable that means should be found to bring a class of instruments, equal to the ordinary grand, within the reach of persons by whom it is now quite unattainable. The expediency of combining cheapness with excellence in quality has long been acknowledged and acted upon in almost every branch of manufacturing art, and indeed seems to be the ruling principle of commerce in the present day. It is beginning, though tardily, to extend itself to the pianoforte manufacture; and we hope, for the sake of the art, that the time may soon come when its influence will be more general."

PART THE THIRD.

SPECIMENS OF MUSIC.

PART III.

THE EARLY COMPOSERS FOR INSTRUMENTS OF THE PIANOFORTE CLASS.

Music, poetry, painting, architecture, and sculpture, included by our æsthetic philosophers as one fine art, are united in the closest ties, and might be supposed to have always flourished in unison; but a knowledge of the histories of the several arts show us that this was not the case. Although music was that art in the cycle which first revived in the early period of the middle ages, and is therefore entitled to be considered the eldest of the sisterhood, it at no period ever made the same advance as the other arts. The dogmas of the Grecian schoolmen surrounded music, and ages passed away before men dared shake off the fetters with which it was encircled.

As regards the first music of the pianoforte class, and indeed all music *unconnected* with the church, we are indebted for it to that important body of men in the middle ages,—the troubadours and minstrels.

" In all countries and in all ages the first and principal application of music has been uniformly to the purposes of religious worship; and in order to provide a competent succession of persons capable of singing the different portions in the church service, and to guard it from corruptions, in consequence of the ignorance of those by whom it was sung, it was found necessary that music should form a part of the clerical education. It was therefore taught in the schools belonging to the monasteries, to such of the children of the neighbourhood as were sent thither for education; the system of instruction in which appears to have consisted of learning the psalms, probably by heart, and acquiring the principles of music, singing, arithmetic, and grammar. By this method, boys were, from time to time, procured for the service of the choir, and a succession of singers secured to fill up such vacancies as might be occasioned by deaths; for some of these boys, when their voices broke, perhaps betook themselves to the church as their profession, embraced the monastic habit and rule, and became ecclesiastical members of the foundation where they had been educated. Others, on the contrary, disliking the monastic restraint, and availing themselves of their musical education, applied to music as their profession, and were occasionally employed in the monasteries, to assist in the choir on saints' days and high festivals, when a more solemn service was performed, and a greater number of performers required.

" In the intermediate space, these laymen subsisted by travelling about the court or palace of one prince or nobleman to that of another, to entertain the lord and his guests in the character of a minstrel, by singing legends of the saints in verse, historical ballads, romances in verse, and other vocal compositions, written and set to music by themselves, and which they also sung, accompanying themselves at the same time on some musical instrument.

" Between the common 'violar' and the character of the minstrel there existed this wide difference, that, while the former might be justly ranked with the lowest order of the people, the latter had the benefit of such a regular education, as would have qualified him for a profession of comparative learning and elegance. In the schools of the monasteries, the minstrel had learnt something of the theoretical principles of music, the practical part of singing, and the elements of grammar; including also, perhaps as much knowledge of poetry as was sufficient for the composition of a song or ballad. Persons already acquainted with the principles of music, could find little difficulty in acquiring sufficient skill to play, on the viol, the clavichord, or some other 'minstrel' instrument, a simple melody; and the whole of this together formed a sufficient body of theoretical science and practical skill, to enable them to compose and play a variety of simple tunes. Like the ecclesiastics, these men must have been disgusted with the monotony of the *plain chant;* and that disposition to hilarity and merriment which they appear to have possessed, would naturally lead them to the composition of gay and lively melodies. These they no doubt produced by making variations on the church melodies; a method known to those skilled in church music, by the name of Descant. Extending their skill still further, they at length formed melodies of more originality, and became in time the sole authors of the music, as well as of the words, of the compositions which they sung and played.

" Thus qualified by their education to teach what, it must be confessed, none were likely better to understand, it is no matter of surprise, that the minstrels and monks should have been, for some centuries, the only teachers of music in Europe. Travelling from place to place, and from the court of one prince to that of another, as the minstrels particularly did, they had the opportunities of disseminating the principles of musical erudition ; and in proportion to the degree of elegance and politeness to which their auditors had arrived, would be the disposition of those who heard their performances, to cultivate and practise the arts of music and poetry.

" In point of politeness and elegance of external behaviour, in gallantry towards the female sex, and in poetical compliments on their perfections, which were often set to music, the French have always professed to lead the way to the other nations of Europe; and probably for this reason it was, that the first efforts towards raising these arts to the rank which they merited, and from which they had fallen during the ignorance and barbarity of the middle ages, appear to have been made in Provence and the kingdom of Navarre. When once the inclination had been excited, the means of accomplishment were not difficult, as itinerant minstrels might easily be procured to teach the principles ; and in this manner, no doubt, was that science obtained, which gave birth to the class of Provençal poets.

" The time of their first appearance in the world has been stated, and apparently on the authority of Crescentini, to have been in the tenth century; but this is believed to be much too early. The most authentic account of them, written by Le Monge des Isles d'Or, who lived about 1248, and Henry de Saint Cezari, who flourished about 1435, two members of their own body, carries it no farther back than the twelfth century ; the earliest writer whom it mentions being Geoffry Rudel, Sieur de Blieux in Provence, who, according to their own account, lived in 1161.

" That the Provençal poets, who are also sometimes called Troubadours, were indebted for their instruction to the monks and minstrels, is perfectly clear; because at that time when this class of men first arose, whether it were in the tenth, or with more probability the twelfth, century, the monks and the minstrels were the only teachers of music, and they alone understood the art."*

From the time of the revival of the sciences in the fourteenth century, music also, as one of the number, was much encouraged; and its influence was particularly manifest when, towards the end of the fifteenth century, the effects of printing (an invention assigned to the year 1440) began to make itself powerfully prominent. Choirs of music were instituted in Italy and other countries towards the close of the fifteenth century. Ferdinand I of Naples founded one about the year 1470; and three highly accomplished Belgians (Joannes Tinctor, Gulielmus Guarnerius, and Bernardus Hycaert) were contemporary teachers in that monarch's capital. Somewhat later, Duke Sforza opened one at Milan, at the head of which was the highly celebrated Franchinus Gafurius, whose works were the first musical ones that issued from the press after the invention of printing.

It was in the fourteenth century that particular attention was first paid to the clavichord, and foremost among the musicians who cultivated it was Francesco Landini, called also *Francesco Cieco*, from his blindness, and *Francesco degli Organi*, from his skill on the organ. He was descended from the illustrious Landini family, and his father was a celebrated painter. He excelled on many instruments, and was a poet of no mean eminence. He visited Venice in 1364, when several superb fêtes were given in honor of the King of Cypres; upon which occasion he was crowned with laurel. He died at Florence in 1390.

Contemporary with Landini was Nicolo del Proposto, Jacopo di Bologna, and some others, who were not only skilful performers, but also distinguished for their compositions. Specimens of their vocal works are preserved in the Imperial Library at Paris. None of their organ or clavichord music having descended to our times, it is impossible to form any idea of its excellence. The Italian authors of the fifteenth century speak in flattering terms of their talents in this respect; it was therefore, doubtless, highly creditable for the early stage of the art.

---

* These excellent remarks, by the late J. S. Hawkins, F.S.A. are from an unpublished MS. in the author's possession. They have been partly reprinted in the Introduction to Stafford Smith's *Musica Antiqua*, and in Dr. Rimbault's *Little Book of Songs and Ballads from Ancient Musick Books*.

The next great player on record was Conrad Paulmann, who was born blind at Nuremberg in the early part of the fifteenth century. He performed on the organ, clavichord, violin, guitar, flute, trumpet, and several other instruments. He was greatly honoured by the princes and nobles of his time, particularly by Albert III, Duke of Bavaria, and the Emperor Frederick III. The latter presented him, on one occasion, with a sword with a golden blade, and a chain of the same material. He died at Munich in 1473, and was buried in the church of Notre Dame in that city. On his tomb he is represented performing upon the organ.

Antonio Squarcialupi, surnamed *Antonio degli Organi*, was also eminent in the same century. He was organist in the Cathedral of Florence, and lived in the reign of Lorenzo il Magnifico, about the year 1450. His pieces have not been printed; but Doni informs us that he possessed more than ten volumes of tablatures for the organ, clavichord, and lute, composed by Antonio di Bologna (*Squarcialupi*), Julio di Modena, Francesco di Milano, and Giacomo da Busa. The reputation of Squarcialupi was such that, after his death, a bust to his honour was erected in the Cathedral of Florence, with an inscription, in which his merits were celebrated in very flattering terms.

Among the most able performers on the clavichord of the sixteenth century, we may class Fattorini, Francesco Corteccia, Alessandro Striggio, and Claudio Merulo. The latter held the important posts of organist to the Duke of Ferrara and the Cathedral of Venice. The works of these masters consist in *ricercari* on the themes of madrigals or motetts, in variations on French or Italian songs, and in dances more or less ornamental. Some collections of these compositions have reached us, and are preserved in MS. in libraries and private collections.

Andrea Gabrielli was one of the most celebrated composers of the sixteenth century, and renowned for his compositions and performance on the organ and harpsichord. He lived at Venice, and was one of the organists of the Cathedral of Saint Mark in that city.

The number of other organists and players on the clavichord, harpsichord, and organ, who distinguished themselves at this epoch is very considerable. Among the most eminent we may cite Paul Hoffhaimer, born at Radstat in Stiria, and who was knighted by the Emperor Maximilian; Johann Buchner of Constance; Johann Kotter of Berne; Conrad of Spire; Schachinger, organist at Padua; Johann von Cologne, in Saxony; Melchier Neysidler, Valentine Greff, Enrico Rodesca da Faggia, of Turin; Bindella of Treviso; Vittoria of Bologna; Giulio Cesare Barbetta of Padua; Claudio di Correggio, Andrea de Canareggio, Paulo de Castello, Alessandro Milleville, &c.

England was not behind its neighbours in the production of music for keyed-stringed-instruments; and the sixteenth century—viz. from 1530 to 1570—introduces us to the names of Hugh Aston, Alwood, Redford, Shelbye, Newman, Heath, Farrant, Shepperd, Edwardes, Mundy, Carleton, Taverner, Johnson, Dr. Tye, Blitheman, Tallis, &c.; specimens of whose "virginal" music have descended to our times.*

The improvements of the harpsichord, in the following century, could not fail to excite a corresponding degree of emulation in the performers and composers for this instrument, and to produce a beneficial effect upon their talent. The first book of instruction published on the art of performing on the harpsichord, &c., dates from the commencement of the seventeenth century; it was the production of Geronimo Diruta, a member of the order of Friars Minor, who was born at Perugia, about the year 1580, and filled the situiaon of organist in the principal church of Chioggia, a small town in the Venetian State. His work is entitled *Il Transilvano, dialogo sopra il vero modo di suonar organi e stromente da penna.* Parte prima, Venezia, 1615, folio. The work is dedicated to a prince of Transylvania, who had been a pupil of the author, and to this circumstance it owes its title of *Il Transilvano.* Besides the didactic part, which treats of the method of fingering keyed instruments, and contains

---

* The volume containing the virginal music of these writers is a small oblong MS. in the original binding, on the sides of which are impressed, in a tooled border, H. R. (Henricus Rex), the portcullis and other badges of Henry VIII. It consists of Airs, Galliards, Voluntaries, Fantasias, In Nomines, &c. written on a staff of 12, 8, 7, and 6 lines, by the composers whose names are given above. On the fly-leaf is the MS. note—"Sum Liber Thomæ Mullineri, Johanne Heywoode teste." It was from this valuable and interesting MS. that Sir John Hawkins derived the pieces for the Appendix to his History of Music. On one of the leaves is the memorandum—"J. S. Smith, Lent to Sir John Hawkins, 1774." Upon the dispersion of J. S. Smith's Library. it came into the Author's possession. The celebrated *Virginal Book* of Queen Elizabeth has already been described.

a series of exercises for that purpose, bearing considerable analogy to those which still find a place in the greater part of modern books of instruction, we find a variety of *toccate*, and other pieces by Diruta, Claudio Merulo, Andrea Gabrieli, Luzaschi, Paulo Quagliati, Giuseppe Guami, and other celebrated composers. The second part of *Il Transilvano* was published at Venice in 1622, in the same form as the first. It is divided into four books; the first treats of *tablatura*, or the art of writing music for the organ and other keyed instruments; for the imperfect state of printing and engraving at this period rendered it necessary to make use of particular signs for representing notes and their comparative value. The second book relates to the rules of composition; the third, to the church tones and their transposition; and the fourth, to the mixed use of organ stops. A work of this kind is highly important as regards the history of the art; for it may be viewed as a summary of the knowledge possessed by the artists of that remote period. It is to be regretted that copies of the work are of the greatest rarity.

A great impetus was given to organ and harpsichord music in the early part of the seventeenth century by Girolamo Frescobaldi, organist of St. Peter's at Rome, and who was born at Ferrara, in 1591. His name was famous throughout Europe, and his works, which are still admired, have survived a multitude of other productions of that period. He was the scholar of Milleville, of Ferrara, and may be considered as the founder of the harpsichord school; for, before his time, there was no difference between the music written for the clavichord, spinet, and harpsichord, and that composed for the organ. He was the first who wrote exclusively for the harpsichord, and his compositions were published under the title, *Toccate d'intavolatura di Cembalo.* Rome, 1615, 1628, 1637, &c., folio. It may be remarked that the term *toccata* was the common one employed in the earlier part of the seventeenth century to designate pieces of music for keyed instruments. We agree with M. Fétis, who says, in his remarks upon Frescobaldi, "that true test of genius, expression, is perceptible in many of the compositions of this celebrated man, particularly in a song with variations under the name of *La Romanesca*. The character of melancholy which predominates in this piece, is, perhaps, one of the earliest examples in the monuments of art of the expressive style applied to instruments. As for the rest, the music of Frescobaldi abounds with ornament, and with elaborate passages, which would not be without their difficulties even to the most skilful of modern pianistes."

Frescobaldi formed several pupils, who carried into different parts of Europe the results of his excellent method of performance on the harpsichord, and which powerfully contributed to the rapid progress of this instrument. One of the most distinguished among them was Froberger, a young German, who was sent to Rome by the Emperor Ferdinand III, to profit by the instructions of the great Italian organist. No distinction had hitherto been made in Germany between compositions for the organ, and those for other keyed instruments. Froberger, having completed his musical education under this celebrated master, travelled through the greater part of Europe, and excited admiration wherever he went. After encountering various romantic adventures, and running several risks of his life, he happily terminated his career in the court of the Emperor of Austria, where he held the post of imperial organist. His influence, with respect to the progress of the harpsichord in Germany, was equal to that of his countryman and contemporary, Johann von Kerl, in regard to the organ. Two of his works remain as monuments to attest the degree of perfection to which he had carried his art. The first is entitled *Diverse curiose e rarissime Partite di Toccate, Ricercate, Caprici e Fantasie, &c.; per gli amatori di cembali, organi, e istrumenti.* Munich, 1695, folio. The second has for title, *Diverse ingeniosissime, rarissime e non mai più viste curiose Partite di Toccate, Canzone, Ricercate, Allemande, Correnti, Sarabande, e Gigue, di cembali, organi e istrumenti.* Munich, 1714, folio. These works were printed some time after the author's death, and the pompous titles given them prove the high degree of estimation in which they were held.

The residence of Froberger, at Paris, had a very important influence on the progress of the harpsichord among the French, about the middle of the seventeenth century. The most celebrated among the performers on this instrument, at this period, was Jacques Champion, son of Antoine Champion, who had been organist to Henry IV, and was the father of André Champion of Chambonnières. So lively was the impression made upon the latter by the performance of Froberger, that he at once caught his manner and spirit. He changed his style, which before had been bad, and adopted the more large and noble manner of the Italians, of which his model was a perfect master. The six books of harpsichord pieces which Chambonnières published at Paris in the beginning of the reign of Louis XIV, are proofs of his ability. These, like all the collections of that period, consist of a series of allemandes, gigues, and other dances, the harmony of which is pure, and the airs elegant and flowing. The principal difficulties of the harpsichord music of this period consisted in the obligation of playing four distinct parts. A profusion of shakes, beats, and other ornaments, compose the brilliant part of Chambonnières' music.

It will be interesting to extract here a few of the graces and embellishments in use at this period, which we are enabled to do from a copy of *Les Pièces de Clavesin de Monsieur de Chambonnières*, Paris, 1670, now before us:

The elder Couperin (Louis) was introduced at Court by Froberger, about the year 1665. Hardelle, Richard, La Barre, and, at a later period, D'Anglebart, Gautier, Buret, and François Couperin, were formed in the school of Chambonnières, and enjoyed considerable reputation in their time. François Couperin, whose name we have just mentioned, was remarkable for his noble and brilliant style of performance, as well as for the facility with which he overcame difficulties hitherto unknown on his instrument.

In Italy, several great writers for keyed instruments succeeded Frescobaldi. We may particularly point out Ercole Pasquino, Bernard Pasquino (the master of

Gasparini), Zipoli, and Domenico Scarlatti of Naples. The latter was one of the most gifted of the early writers for keyed instruments, and his works are listened to with pleasure to this day.

The great John Sebastian Bach was, as we have seen, one of the first artists who played the pianoforte, and brought it into vogue*; but it was his son, Carl Philip Emanuel, who contributed the most to the success of the instrument, by his elegant and graceful style of touch, as well as by his delightful compositions. As M. Fétis remarks, " the sonatas, concertos, and fantasias, published by this excellent musician, do not abound in any very great difficulties. It is true that the greater part of modern pianists would consider the various ornamental and other passages of these compositions as mere child's play; but it is not less true that the essential object of the art is better felt than in that multitude of notes with which modern pianoforte music is overloaded. As for the rest, it can well be conceived that the first pianoforte school did not regard the surmounting of difficulties as the ultimate object of music, and that the gradual march of showy and elaborate execution is the result of the necessity felt by the artist of distinguishing himself in proportion as ability becomes greater." Or, rather, as it has been remarked, the performer is now obliged to make up in rapidity of execution for want of invention and taste in the composition.

The Bachs had their followers and imitators; but they have long since been forgotten. Nevertheless they paved the way for the great schools of Mozart and Beethoven, Clementi and Dussek; for the great names of Ries, Weber, Moscheles, Mendelssohn, and Bennett; and for the more marvellous schools of Thalberg, Henselt, Chopin, and Liszt.

---

* " Though the French taste for frippery, in place of solid science, and the Italian instinct for rhythmical and easy melody, so o'erswept the European schools of instrumental music for a time, that even some among the family of the grand old fuguist did not escape the infection, and his " Well-tempered Clavier" was forgotten for the flimsier works of Hullmandel, Schobert, and Paradies,—it was but for a time. The honest old organist was, after a period of usurpation and famine, sought for and found—like the champions of the Swiss superstition—with grave patience awaiting in his tomb the moment when he should come forth and assist in the recovery of his olden heritage; and to-day he stands before us, vigorous, gigantic, and as undamaged by time as the youngest enthusiast who hastens to do him honour." This excellent remark is taken from a charming article on the *Pianoforte Composers* by H. F. Chorley, Esq. which appeared some few years ago in one of the monthly or quarterly magazines. We have the article, but have unfortunately mislaid the reference.

THE EARLY COMPOSERS FOR INSTRUMENTS OF THE PIANOFORTE CLASS.

These few remarks are intended only as introductions to the following selection of ancient pieces for keyed-stringed-instruments. For believing in Sir Joshua Reynolds's remark, that " art is best taught by examples," we have been at some pains to select only such pieces as will show the progress of what may be termed " pianoforte" playing at different epochs of the art. Most of the pieces are of the utmost rarity, and we have been careful to give them in all their original integrity.

They comprise—

1. Gloria Tibi Trinitas.................................William Blitheman.
    (Gentleman and Organist of Queen Elizabeth's Chapel. His epitaph is given in Stow's *Survey of London*, edit. 1633, from which it appears that he died in 1591.)

    From Thomas Mulliner's Booke for y*e* Virginalls, collated with another copy in Lady Neville's Virginal Book; both MSS. in the possession of the author.

2. Sellenger's Round. ....William Byrd.
    (Gentleman and Organist of Edward the Sixth's Chapel; born about 1538, died July 4, 1623.)

    From Queen Elizabeth's Virginal Book in the Fitzwilliam Museum, Cambridge, collated with another copy in the Earl of Leicester's Virginal Book in the possession of the author.

3. The King's Hunting Jigg. ....Dr. John Bull.
    (Born about the year 1563. He succeeded Blitheman as Organist of the Chapel Royal in 1591, and died March 12 or 13, 1628, at Antwerp.)

    From a MS. volume of Virginal Music, transcribed by Sir John Hawkins, in the possession of the author.

4. Les Buffons. ....Dr. John Bull.
    From the same MS.

5. Courante Jewell ....Dr. John Bull.
    From a Dutch MS. of Dr. Bull's compositions, written between 1621 and 1628, formerly in the library of Queen Caroline, Consort of George II.

6. Capriccio del Soggetto sopra l'Aria di Roggiero........Girolamo Frescobaldi.
    (Organist of St. Peter's, at Rome. Born about 1591, died in 1640.)

    From *Toccate e partite d'intavolatura di Cembalo*. Rome, 1615. Folio.

H H

7. Suite de Pièces..H. Dumont.

(Born at Liege in 1610, died in 1684. He was Chapel Master to Louis XIV.)

From *Meslanges à 2, 3, 4, et 5 Parties, avec la basse-continuée, contenant plusieurs Chansons, Motets, Magnificats, Preludes, Allemandes, &c.* Paris, 1657. 4to.

8. Suite de Pièces...Chambonnières.

(André Champion of Chambonnières was born about 1610, and died in 1670.)

From *Les Pièces de Clavesin de Monsieur de Chambonnières.* Paris, 1670. Oblong 4to.

9. Suite de Pièces..Jean Baptiste Lully.

(Born at Florence in 1634; died at Paris on March 22nd, 1687.)

From *Lessons for the Harpsichord or Spinnet. Printed by Daniel Wright, next the Tun Tavern, corner of Brook Street, Holborn* (1698). Ob. folio.

10. Prelude and Airs...Henry Purcell.

(Born in 1658, died in 1695.)

From *A Choice Collection of Lessons for the Harpsichord or Spinnet. Printed on Copper Plates for Mrs. Frances Purcell, Executrix of the Author.* London, 1696. Small oblong.

11. Variationes super Cantilenam.....................F. X. A. Mürshhauser.

(Born at Alsace in 1670; died at Munich in 1733.)

From *Octi-tonium Novum Organicum, octo Tonis Ecclesiasticis, ad Psalmos, et Magnificat, adhiberi solitis, respondens.* Augsburg, 1696. Ob. folio.

12. Sonata...Johann Kuhnau.

(Born, at Geysing, on the frontiers of Bohemia, in 1667; and died at Leipzig in 1722.)

From a MS. entitled *Histoires tirées de la Bible, avec les explications, en six sonates.* 1700.

13. Suite de Pièces..John Mattheson.

(Born at Hamburg, September 28, 1681; died at the same place in 1764.)

From *Sonates pour le Clavecin.* Hamburg, 1713. Folio.

14. Sonata in A minor..Domenico Scarlatti.

(Born at Naples in 1683; died at Madrid in 1757.)

From a magnificently written MS. volume of pieces (mostly unpublished) in the possession of the author, entitled *Libro de XLIV Sonatas modernas, para*

Clavicordio. Compuestas per il Senor D. Domingo Scarlatti, Cabaliero del Orden de Santiago, y Maestro de los Reyes Catolicos, D. Fernando el VI, y Dona Maria Barbara.

15. Sonata in G..................................Domenico Scarlatti.

    From the same MS.

16. Suites de Pièces...............................François Couperin.

    (Born in 1668; died in 1733.)

    From *Pièces de Clavecin*. Paris, 1713-19. Folio.

17. Capriccio..J. Seb. Bach.

    (Born in 1685; died in 1750.)

    From C. F. Becker's *Hausmusik in Deutschland in dem 16, 17, und 18. Jahrhunderte*. Leipzig, 1840. 4to.

18. Capriccio in G.....................................Handel.

    (Born in 1685; died in 1759.)

    From a beautiful MS. volume in the hand-writing of Smith; said to have been written for the Princess Amelia. Many of the pieces (including the one now published for the *first* time) are unknown.

19. Fantaisie. ....Theofilo Muffat.

    (Clavecin Master to the Imperial Family at Vienna, at the end of the seventeenth century.)

    From *Componimenti musicali per il Cembalo*. Vienna, 1727. Oblong folio.

20. Air...Theofilo Muffat.

    From the same work.

21. Allemand...Theofilo Muffat.

    From a MS. in the author's library.

22. Introduction and Toccata...........................De Mondonville.

    (Born at Narbonne, December 24, 1715; died in 1773.)

    From a contemporary MS. presented to the author by the late J. B. Cramer.

23. Rondo in E flat.............................Carl Philip Emanuel Bach.

    (Born in 1714; died in 1788.)

    From *Clavier Sonaten und Freye Fantasien nebst einigen Rondos fürs Fortepiano, &c.* Leipzig, 1787. Oblong folio.

24. Fantasia. ....C. P. E. Bach.

    From the same work.

A COLLECTION OF SPECIMENS
Illustrating
The Progress of Music
FOR
KEYED-STRINGED INSTRUMENTS.

"GLORIA TIBI TRINITAS."

WILLIAM BLITHEMAN, 1555.

238

"SELLENGER'S ROUND."

WILLIAM BYRD, 1580.

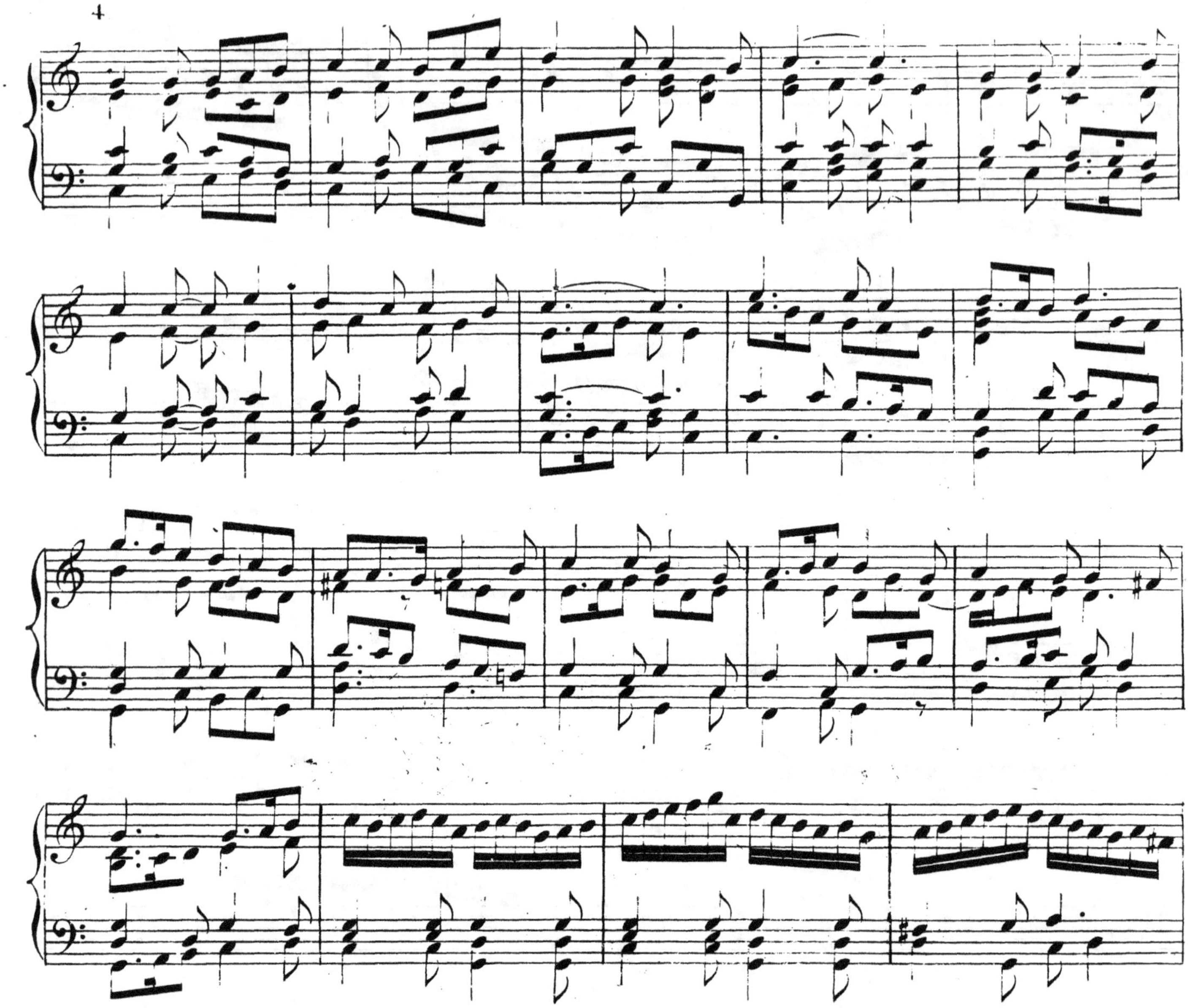
4
Close.
tr

"THE KING'S HUNTING JIGG."

Dr. JOHN BULL, 1604.

"LES BUFFONS."

Dr. JOHN BULL, 1628.

"COURANTE JEWEL"

Dr. JOHN BULL, 1628.

CAPRICCIO DEL SOGGETTO SOPRA L'ARIA DI ROGGIERO.

GIROLAMO FRESCOBALDI, 1616.

SUITE DE PIECES.

ALLEMANDE.

H. DU MONT, 1657.

ALLEMANDE GRAVE.

REPRISE.

SUITE DE PIECES.

SARABANDE.

CHAMBONNIÈRES, 1670.

ALLEMANDE LA DUNQUERQUE.

SUITE DE PIECES.

JEAN BAPTISTE LULLY, 1670.

SLOW AIRE.

273

SARABAND.

274

JIGG.

275

276

PRELUDE AND AIRS.

HENRY PURCELL, 1690.

PRELUDE.

No. 10.

ALMAND.

SARABAND.

CEBELL.

VARIATIONES SUPER CANTILENAM.

F. X. A. MURSHHAUSER, 1696.

ARIA PASTORALIS VARIATA.

VAR. 5.

SONATA.

JOHANN KUHNAU, 1700.

Allegro.

294

SUITE DE PIECES.

JOHN MATTHESON, 1703.

ALLEMAND.

302

COURANT.

SARABAND.

SONATA.

DOMENICO SCARLATTI, 1710.

Allegro.

Nº 14.

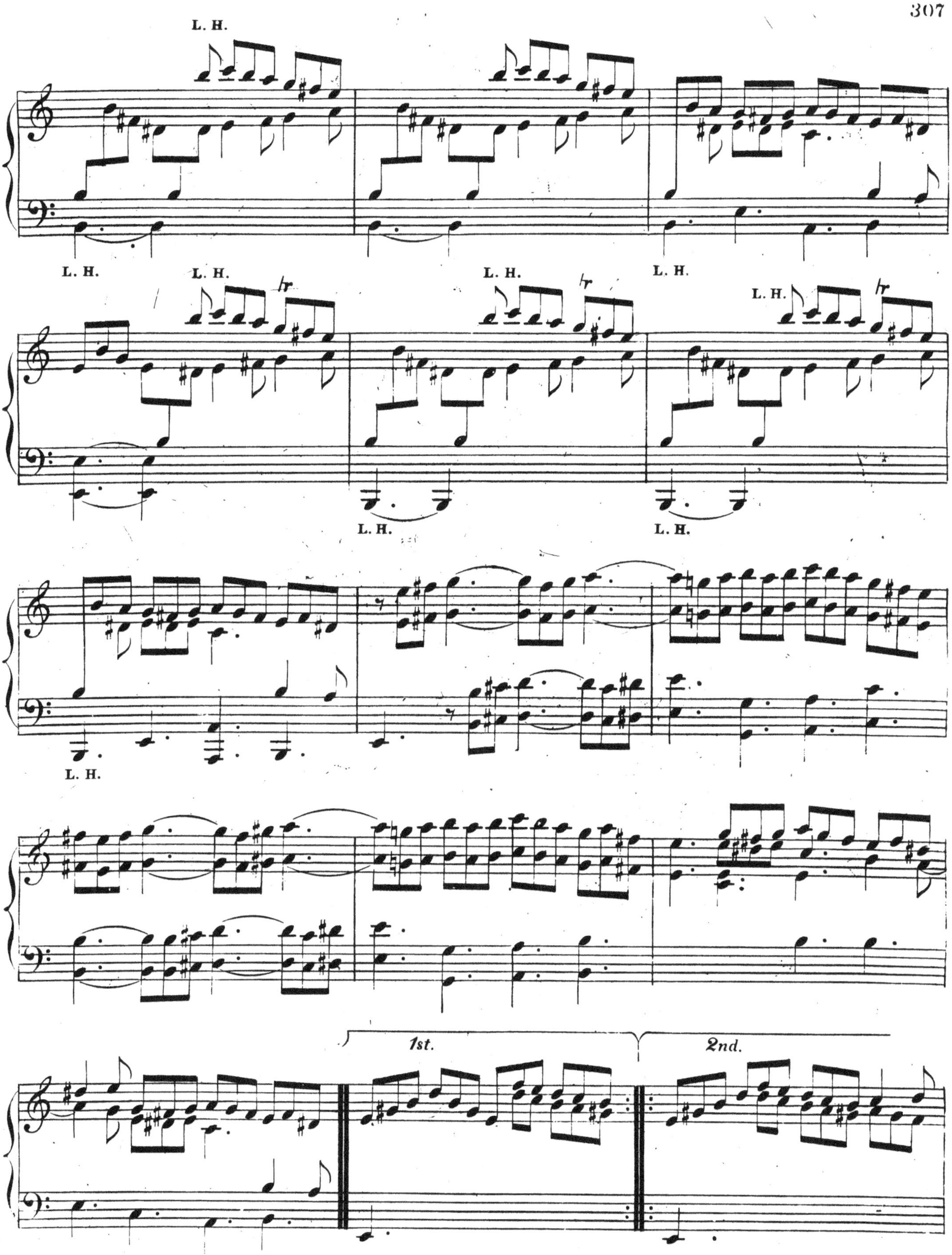

307

313

77

314

SUITE DE PIECES.

ALLEMANDE. FRANÇOIS COUPERIN, 1713.

Nº 16.

PREMIÈRE COURANTE.

319

SECONDE COURANTE.

SARABANDE.

323

MODERATO.

87

AFFETTUOSO.

CAPRICCIO.
Sopra la Lontananza del Fratre dilettissimo

JO. SEB. BACH, 1715.

ARIOSO. **Adagio.**

N.º 17.

Ist eine Schmeichelei der Freunde, um denselben von seiner Reise abzuhalten.

Andante con moto.

Ist eine Vorstellung unterschiedlicher casuum, die ihm in der Fremde könnten vorfallen.

Adagio.

Ist ein allgemeines Lamento der Freunde.

335

Andante.

336

ARIA DEL POSTIGLIONE.
Allegro poco.

FUGA AD IMITATIONE DI POSTA.

340

CAPRICCIO.

HANDEL, 1720.

Nº 18.

342

FANTAISIE.

THEOFILO MUFFAT, 1726.

345

Adagio.

346

FUGA.
Vivace.

AIR.

T. MUFFAT.

This Air is the original of Handel's March in Judas Maccabæus.

ALLEMAND.

T. MUFFAT.

INTRODUCTION AND TOCCATA.

I. J. DE MONDONVILLE, 1739.

356

RONDO.

CARL PHILIP EMANUEL BACH, 1760.

Andantino.

FANTASIA.

C. P. E. BACH.

Presto di molto.

No 24.

Andante.

Larghetto sostenuto.

APPENDICES.

APPENDIX I.

HINTS TO THOSE WHO HAVE THE CARE OF PIANOFORTES.

General Directions.

When we take into consideration the great variety of woods, metals, leathers, &c. used in the construction of the pianoforte, it will be obvious that the instrument should be zealously preserved from dampness and currents of air. All sonorous musical instruments are extremely susceptible on these points, and we cannot be too particular in our care of them.

1. A pianoforte should always stand in a place perfectly dry, and of mean temperature. It must never be placed on a damp ground floor; or between two windows; or between a door and a window. An instrument will never stand in tune, if exposed to draughts or currents of air.

2. A pianoforte should never be left open when it is not being used; and when the room is being cleaned, it would be well to cover the entire instrument with a baize, or skin case, fitted to its shape.

3. A pianoforte should never be placed too near a stove, chimney, or fire-place. Extreme heat is particularly injurious, and often causes the warping of some of the delicate machinery.

4. The instrument should always be kept clean and free from dust. No light substance, as a needle, pin, a bead, a crumb of bread, &c. should be suffered (in a square or grand pianoforte) to lie on the sounding-board or the strings of the instrument, as they will in all probability produce a disagreeable jingling or whizzing sound, the cause of which it is not always easy to detect.

5. It is also important to remark that the lid or top of the instrument should not be loaded with books, music, and other objects. All weights placed in this manner are calculated to injure the tone of the pianoforte, and to produce an unpleasant jarring during performance.

6. Keep the instrument always in tune, and fully drawn up to concert pitch. A pianoforte ought to be tuned once every six weeks, if much played on; and oftener, if new. Metal strings are generally a little too sharp in dry frosty weather, because the cold condenses their material and increases their tension. In hot summer weather, they are somewhat too flat. New strings require to be drawn up several times before they will stand well in tune. When a string breaks, it must be replaced by another of exactly similar thickness.

How to place a Pianoforte for Effect.

The walls, floor, and ceiling, echo every sound which is produced in a room, and increase by *resonance* its volume and length. It is of the utmost importance that buildings designed for audiences, particularly music rooms, should be so constructed that there may be no *perceptible* echo from the walls, but a sufficient resonance to give tone and volume to the sounds. The best form for the interior of such rooms is that their length be about two thirds greater than their breadth, in order that the sounds reflected from the side walls may mingle with the direct sounds and strengthen them. The height should somewhat exceed the breadth; and the ceiling is better when *coved*—that is, made in the shape of a coach roof. If a room has too great an echo, drapery should be hung upon the walls. Venetian shutters are excellent preventives of echo, especially when they are drawn forward. Carpets, matting, or any soft covering on the floor, absorbs reverberation; because the echo, which would otherwise combine with the direct sound and swell it, is smothered amidst the fibres.

The pianoforte, when possible, should be placed away from the wall, and as much *in the room* as convenient. The floor then, if hollow, acts as a large sounding board, and greatly enhances the effect. The reason of this is, that the sonorous vibrations created by the pianoforte puts the wood of the flooring upon which it is placed into a similar state of vibration, and its simultaneous shocks against the superincumbent air adds to the original tone and renders it more audible.

In Italy, orchestras are constructed with especial reference to the advantage to be derived from a reciprocating floor; but in this country, such things are paid but little attention to; the practical part of acoustics being sadly neglected.

How to prevent the Sounds of the Pianoforte from being heard in the adjoining Chambers.

We have many of us experienced, and are still experiencing, the intolerable nuisance of our next-door neighbours, on each side, right and left, practising the pianoforte at all hours, seasonable and unseasonable. Now all this might easily be remedied by constructing the walls of our dwelling-houses with *hollow* bricks, which are known to be non-conductors of sound. The reason of this is, that the hollow portion being filled with rarefied air, every sound which finds its way into such a mass is effectually buried there, and cannot penetrate to the outer surface. If the space between the two surfaces of the partition walls, and that between the ceiling of one room and the flooring of another, were filled with brown paper, gummed over with flock or sawdust, it would aid materially to deaden the sound. Or if the space were filled with shavings, tow, or cut straw, it would probably have the same effect. All these substances are bad conductors of sound; because they shut up a large quantity of air between their minute detached parts, so that they cannot readily transmit an impulse. The sound is thus *entangled*, as it were, and, being no longer able to preserve its regular outline, becomes deadened, if not altogether lost.

The Rev. Dr. Brown, from whose little volume on *Sound and its Phenomena* (Longmans, 1854) we gather much of our knowledge of these matters, says, "It is truly surprising that no ingenious mechanic has yet contrived a substance for partition-walls, where cheapness and lightness are especially considered. Nothing, for example, could be easier than to make panels with two sheets of common pasteboard or tarpauling, separated from each other by wooden blocks. Sawdust should be thickly strewed over the inner surfaces, and the intervening space be well filled with coarse tow or cut straw. A wooden "upright" of the thickness of the blocks would hold the panels in their place, especially if the edges were made to lie over the supporters. Such a partition wall would be a real boon in hotels, &c. where chambers are often separated by half-inch wood, or by simple canvass."

We have somewhere read, that if the walls of rooms were covered with a solution of *gutta percha* before papering, it would effectually deaden all sounds from the adjoining chambers. Or, we believe, a substitute for this is the *gutta percha* lining, extensively used of late years in covering damp walls.

APPENDIX II.

ON TUNING.

The system of tuning here explained is that of *Equal Temperament*, which is now universally adopted throughout Europe. Its inestimable advantage is, that it enables us to employ all the twelve major and minor scales with equal freedom, and without a fear of offending the ear in any of them more than in another; thus giving unlimited room of play to all the wonders of modern harmony.

The chief difficulty in tuning consists in making what is termed the *partition*; that is, so to tune the twelve semitones of an octave, that they may become a basis for tuning the rest of the instrument. By a peculiarity in the musical scale, if thirteen notes were tuned perfectly true, advancing by fifths (beginning, for instance, from C), the thirteenth note, a *sharp* forming the twelfth fifth, would not be a true octave to the first C, but would be found to be a little higher. It follows, therefore, that a pianoforte tuned in this manner would be false at the end of the operation. Hence the necessity of diminishing a little the elevation of each fifth—an operation to which has been given the name of Temperament.

The intervals of most use in tuning are the *unison*, the *octave*, the *fifth*, and the *major* and *minor* thirds.

The Unison.

The *unison*, or identical sound, is the easiest interval for the student to commence with. In instruments which have only two strings to each note, as in square, cabinet, and cottage pianofortes, one half the strings are always tuned by means of unisons; and in grand pianos, of three strings to each note, whether horizontal or upright, two thirds of the strings are so tuned. Hence, the unison, or identical sound, is the interval, if it may be so called, which most frequently occurs in tuning, and which it is of the highest importance should be tuned with perfect accuracy.

We will suppose that the student has provided himself with a *tuning hammer*, and that he has seated himself at the instrument. Let him then strike any note in the middle of the key-board;

APPENDIX II. 373

[♪ C] for example; and we shall at first suppose this note to be accurately in tune. If he listen attentively to the vibration of the strings, he will hear a steady, pure, continuous sound, such as is produced from a single string when struck alone. Then let him place his tuning hammer on one of the *pins* or *pegs* round which one of the strings belonging to the note C is coiled or twisted, and turn the hammer a very little towards the left: this, by relaxing the tension of the string, will sensibly flatten or depress its pitch; so that, instead of sounding [♪ C], the pitch of the string thus depressed will approach nearly to that of [♪ B], the note next below it. If he now strikes the C, he will hear nothing but a confused collision of harsh and jarring sounds, such as we are sensible of when we touch a note that is much out of tune. After striking the note thus purposely put out of tune several times, let him then turn the hammer to the right, gently and by almost imperceptible degrees, and, if he listens attentively as the pitch of the two strings approaches more and more nearly towards coincidence, he will at first hear several strong and quick *beats*, which, as he proceeds, will gradually become slower and slower, and fainter and fainter, till they subside into mere gentle *wavings*, or undulations of sound; and these, as he proceeds, will at length disappear, and give place to one steady, pure, and apparently single sound, which constitutes the real unison.

The student will at first experience considerable difficulty in tracing this progression from confusing and jarring sounds to *beats*, at first quick and strong, and then gradually slower and fainter, till they insensibly degenerate into mere *waves*, or gentle undulations of sound, and ultimately disappear, and give place to one pure and uninterrupted sound.*

Considerable practice is required to gain flexibility of wrist, so as to turn the hammer by extremely minute degrees. These gradations supply the only *mechanical* helps of which the tuner can avail himself; and without a distinct perception of them through their various degrees, it is impossible, even with the finest musical ear, to tune a pianoforte tolerably.

The Octave.

After the student is able to tune a perfect unison, he may proceed to the octave, which is the next interval to the unison in point of importance and facility. Here the sounds, though no longer identical, have so strong a resemblance to each other, that, when struck together and perfectly in tune, they seem

---

* The cause of this phenomenon is beautifully explained in *An Essay on the Theory and Practice of Tuning*, &c. published by Robert Cocks and Co. 1853, p. 34, *et seq.* See also Hamilton's *Art of Tuning*, to which valuable little work we have to acknowledge our obligations in drawing up the above rules.

to form but one single sound, the lower note, as it were, seeming to swallow up or absorb the upper one.

In tuning this interval, the student will discover the same progressive gradations of *beats*, *waves*, and final *coincidence* of tone, as in the unison.

For the purpose of tuning one note an octave to another, it becomes necessary to stop the vibrations of one of the strings belonging to the note to be tuned, in square, cottage, and cabinet pianos; and two of those strings in grand instruments. In square pianos, this is done by means of a little bit of leather, card, or even paper, which is called a *damper*, and which must be inserted between the string of which we wish to stop the vibration and the adjacent string, belonging to the next note to it. In cabinet and cottage pianos, the pedal, which is placed under the left side of the key-board, when pressed down by the foot, shifts the whole key-board a little to the right, so that the hammer strikes only one string belonging to each note throughout the instrument. In grand pianos of three strings, when the pedal is pressed down, the hammers will still strike two strings, unless the small vertical bolt which moves up and down in a groove on the right side of the key-board be first drawn up; and then, when the pedal is pressed down, the hammers will strike only one string belonging to each note.

When the student has tuned an octave, by striking the notes together, let him also try these in quick succession; thus:

at the same time holding the bottom note down: for the ear is apt to fancy them in tune, while they are in reality still too flat; and this striking them one after another will greatly assist him in detecting any mistake in this respect.

In tuning octaves in the bass, the student must be careful not to strike the notes too hard, particularly in the very low notes.

The Fifth.

When this concord is perfectly in tune, the ear cannot detect either *waves* or *beats*; but both notes unite in one pure, agreeable, uninterrupted *complex* sound. It will be desirable at first to tune the fifth perfect, though we shall presently show that it is not so tuned in practice.

Major and Minor Thirds.

The major and minor thirds are the most agreeable concords in music. In tuning, however, they are only employed as tests of the accuracy with which the other intervals have been tuned. When perfectly in tune, they have neither *beat* nor *wave*, but coalesce in one pure, agreeable, uninterrupted *complex* sound.

APPENDIX II.

On Laying the Bearings by Means of Fifths.

In studying the following diagram, or scheme for tuning the pianoforte, it must be borne in mind that the white note in each bar is already tuned, the black one remains to be adjusted.

Explanation of the Scheme.

In the above scheme it will be observed that the only intervals employed are the *octave* and the *fifth*. As it is more easy to tune the notes situated in the middle of the key-board with accuracy, than those which are placed towards the extreme ends of the instrument, the scheme is so devised as to include all the notes between [music] and [music].

The first note [music] is obtained by means of a C tuning fork*.

The octave, in our modern system of keyed-stringed-instruments, being divided into *twelve* semitones, and only one of these notes being given us by the tuning fork, the remaining eleven notes must be obtained by means of a circle or series of *eleven* fifths, as C, G, D, A, E, B, F♯, C♯, G♯ (tuned before); or A♭, E♭, B♭, F, C. The order in which the eleven fifths are tuned is indicated

---

* James Broadwood (the son of the first Broadwood) was the author of a *Practical Method of Tuning*, called "Broadwood's Temperament of the Musical Scale." He says, after mentioning that most tuners begin their operations with the note C, "I prefer tuning from A, the second space in the treble clef, as being less remote from the finishing fifths, than any other point of departure: the A being tuned to the fork, tune A below, an octave; then E above that octave, a fifth; then B above a fifth; then B below, an octave; the F♯ a fifth above; then its octave F♯ below; then C♯, its fifth above; then G♯, its fifth above; and then G♯, its octave below. We then take a fresh departure from A, tuning D, its fifth below; then G, its fifth below; then G, its octave above; then C, its fifth below; then C, its octave above; then F, its fifth below; then B♭, its fifth below; then B♭, its octave above; then E♭, its fifth below. The five fifths tuned from notes below are to be tuned flatter than the perfect fifth. and the six fifths tuned from tones above must be made sharper than the perfect fifth." This is similar to the equal temperament.

APPENDIX II.

by the figures 1, 2, 3, &c. *All octaves are to be tuned absolutely perfect. All the fifths are to be tuned a very little flatter than perfect.* This, as we have already explained, is called *tempering* them. When we arrive at the eighth fifth of the series, instead of proceeding onwards in the circle to D♯ or E♭, it will be better to return to C, and tune the remaining fifths backwards, as shown in the scheme. In adjusting these latter fifths, marked 9, 10, 11, the student must first tune the bottom note so as to form a perfect fifth with the upper note, and then *sharpen* it by exactly the same quantity as he depressed the upper notes of the fifths which were tuned *forwards*. By this means the interval of the fifth is still *diminished* or *flattened*, as the lower extremity is brought nearer to the upper one.

The operation we have thus explained is called laying the *bearings*; it forms the most delicate and important step in tuning, as all the other notes on the instrument are tuned to these notes by means of octaves above or below.

It is not, however, necessary to tune the whole circle of fifths before we have the means of trying the accuracy of what has already been done. As soon as we arrive at the fifth numbered **4** in the scheme, we may try the major third . If this third is properly in tune—that is, if it is somewhat sharper than perfect, but still very harmonious and agreeable—we may be sure that so far all is correctly adjusted. A similar test must be applied to all the subsequent fifths. These triads may be represented in notes, as follows:

When the *bearings* are laid with sufficient accuracy, it only remains to tune the remaining notes on the instrument in the relation of octaves to those already adjusted. This must be done in the following manner:

APPENDIX II.

After having tuned the bass notes, it is desirable to go over the octaves in the treble again, as they are apt to fall in pitch while the bass notes are being tuned. And, finally, before we consider the instrument as thoroughly in tune, each note should be compared with its octave and double octave below; thus:

In tuning a cottage, or semi-cottage, or piccolo piano, it will be desirable to adjust first the whole series of notes upon *one* string, and then to tune all the *second* strings in unison to those of the first series.

In a grand piano, after the second set of strings is tuned, we must tune the third set in unison to the first and second. In square pianos, the second string to each note must necessarily be tuned before we proceed to another note.

We do not intend to notice the various systems of *unequal temperament* that have been proposed, as they have long since been abandoned. The system of *equal temperament* is that which now prevails throughout Europe.

It is perhaps desirable to mention another method of laying the bearings, which has been adopted by some eminent tuners. The method is by fifths and fourths, omitting tuning the octaves until the groundwork is laid, as follows:

The fifths are tuned a little flat; and, by the same rule, the fourths a little sharp.

378 APPENDIX II.

In the above scheme, we shall have tuned the following notes within the circle of the octave; thus:

and have avoided the possibility, when tuning the octaves between the fifths, as in other methods, of not getting the octaves true. Besides which, the ground-work or bearings will be sooner laid down. The trials would be:

The great difficulty in tuning is the necessity of *tempering* the fifths. In this, professional tuners are guided by habit; but artists and amateurs who do not possess this practical skill are obliged to feel their way as they can, and by their repeated experiments, increasing and diminishing the tension of the strings, always injure their tone, and frequently end by breaking, without having the means of replacing them.

With a view to remove these objections, MM. Roller and Blanchet, of Paris, invented, in 1827, an instrument, to which they gave the name of *Chromamètre*, by the help of which a pianoforte can be tuned without the trouble of temperament. The instrument consists of a vertical monochord, which is sounded by means of a hammer placed internally, and which is put in motion by a key similar to that of a pianoforte. Its total length is thirty inches; its greatest breadth, four inches and a quarter; and its thickness, three quarters of an inch. The handle is furnished with a copper plate, divided into twelve degrees, which, like the heads of the jacks in a pianoforte, are inscribed with the initials C, C sharp, D, D sharp, E, F, F sharp, G, G sharp, A, A sharp, and B. The string is fastened to a pin at the upper end, and at the lower to a brass hook, mounted upon a screw, which works up or down with an easy action: by means of this, the pitch is gently raised or lowered at pleasure, steadily, and without effort. A bridge with a spring, which can be fixed at will upon either of the degrees, modifies the intonation, and according as it is placed on C, C sharp, or D, gives the C, C sharp, or D, and so on with the rest, continuing to B. After this, nothing remains but to tune each of these notes at the octave, to the two extremities of the piano.

The back of the *Chromamètre* is disposed in such a manner as to be adapted to all pianofortes at the height of the key-board; so that the note of this instrument, and that of the instrument intended to be tuned in unison, may be touched simultaneously.

The idea of such a regulator, however, was not entirely new. Francis Loulié, a French musician, had already proposed something of a similar kind, as far back as 1698, in a work entitled *Nouveau Système de Musique, avec la description du Sonomètre, instrument à cordes d'une nouvelle invention pour apprendre à accorder le clavecin.* But this *Sonomètre* being mounted with several strings, was obliged to be tuned beforehand, by which means it rendered all the expected results illusory.

Ambrose Warren, " a lover of musick," in the next century, invented an instrument which he called a *Tonometer*. A full description of it was printed in a now rare tract, entitled *The Tonometer ; Explaining and Demonstrating, by an easie Method, in Numbers and Proportion, all the 32 distinct and different Notes, Adjuncts or Supplements contained in each of Four Octaves inclusive, of the Gamut, or Common Scale of Musick. With their exact Difference and Distance. Whereby the Practitioner on any Key'd or Fretted Instrument, may easily know how to Tune the same, &c.* London, 1725.

Scheibler's apparatus for tuning pianofortes, consisting of a series of pulsatory tuning forks, answering exactly to the twelve semitones of the equalized scale, and the octave of the tonic, is the only satisfactory invention that has yet appeared. This ingenious artist has succeeded in providing for the musical world a measure of sound which, in regard to accuracy, surpasses the most rigorous demands that can be made upon it, whilst its application is as easy as it is free from the possibility of a mistake. We strongly recommend the perusal of *An Essay on the Theory and Practice of Tuning in General, and on Scheibler's Invention of Tuning Pianofortes and Organs by the Metronome*—a lucid and charmingly written little tract, published by Robert Cocks and Co. in 1853.

At the recent meeting of the British Association (Aberdeen, Sept. 1859), the Abbé Moigno made known a discovery which promises to be of the highest importance to musical science. He laid before the section of Physical Science a collection of sheets of paper in which were registered the sounds of the human voice, organ pipes, and the tuning fork, to the amount of 500 or 1,000 vibrations. So accurate a self-registration has never before been made, and was judged almost impossible by the great masters of science, and its success was greeted with enthusiastic admiration.

This continued enregistration forms an undulatory curve so perfectly and distinctly traced that the naked eye can easily reckon the innumerable vibrations, especially when it is divided in periods by the periodical intervention of a chronometer. It is very interesting to examine the variations which the curves undergo when the sounds are the results of the component parts of different harmony: for instance, a note with its octave, third, fourth, or fifth, or any other consonant relation, as the 17th or 19th. When the sounds are very nearly in harmony, but not in perfect accord, their simultaneous resonance produces beats, and these beats are perfectly indicated or made known to the naked eye.

APPENDIX III.

HOW TO REGULATE DEFECTS IN THE MECHANISM OF THE PIANOFORTE.

Most musical instruments are liable to defects, from various causes; but more especially the pianoforte, from the delicate and complicated nature of the machinery appertaining to the "action."

The following brief directions have been carefully gleaned from those whose experience entitles them to consideration. They are not put forth with a view to supersede the *professional* regulator. Far from it. They have been compiled solely for the purpose of aiding and assisting those who, from circumstance or situation, are unable to secure the services of the experienced in these matters; and as mere "hints," they may probably prove acceptable to many.

The Sticking of the Keys.

The causes of some of the accidents that take place in the key department of the pianoforte are as follows:—1. When either pin is too tight in the mortices. 2. When the hopper spring is too strong. 3. When the end of the hopper that touches the under hammer is rough. 4. When one key sticks against another. 5. When a key touches the front slip. 6. When a pin, needle, or any other detached substance, is between two keys. 7. When a key touches the cheeks of the key-frame. 8. When a key touches the pillar of the hammer-rail. 9. When any glutinous substance is under a key, or betwixt two keys. 10. When the leather on the under hammer is rough.

How remedied.

(1.) File the mortice carefully. (2.) Weaken the spring by straining it a little from the hopper. (3.) Black lead it, and rub the inner edge with a hard stick. (4.) First consider whether the pins are in a proper position; if so, plane a little off where the keys touch; or if a key is considerably warped, bend it back with a warm iron; press it very gently, in case the mortice is weak. (5.) Incline the slip outwards by putting a piece of paper or card between that and the frame. (6 and 7.) The defects here mentioned can be remedied without directions. (8.) Hollow out carefully a large space.

Great care must be used in all these operations, particularly in opening the mortices or pin-holes. For the latter, a very fine key-file must be used—a flat one for the square hole, and a round or rat-tail file for the round hole under the key. In taking out a key, great caution must be used. Draw the front block or blade of the hopper forward with your finger, to prevent its touching the under hammer, while with your other hand you gently lift up the key and pull it out. The same care is requisite in replacing it.

The Clicking or Rattling of the Keys

Takes place from the following causes :—1. When the pin-holes are too large. 2. By friction of one key against another. 3. By friction of the key against the front slip. 4. By friction of the key against one of the pillars that support the hammer-rail. 5. When the key touches the balance-rail. 6. When the ivory or ebony is loose. 7. When the lead with which the key is loaded is loose. 8. When the key is unsound. 9. When the cloth or baize under the key is not sufficiently soft. 10. When some hard detached substance lies between the key and the cloth or baize. 11. When the key-frame is not firmly attached to the bottom. 12. When a loose splinter is in the pin-hole. 13. When a pin is rough, at or near the head. 14. When the metal of a pin has communicated itself to the hole which has become too hard or corroded. 15. When the further end of the key touches two damper levers. 16. When a key touches a cheek of the hammer-rail. 17. When a key touches a cheek of the case. 18. When a key touches the name-board. 19. When the ivory or ebony touches that of the next key. 20. When the leather at the further end of the key is too hard, causing it to rattle against the damper lever. 21. When the further end of the ebony touches the front of the name-board. 22. When a key touches any hard substance at the further end near the damper lever. 23. When any hard detached substance is on a key. 24. When a hopper or hopper-guard is loose.

How remedied.

(1.) Wedge the key on one or both sides of the mortices; when this defect occurs in all the keys, it is better to introduce thicker pins. An extremely thin chisel, bevelled on both sides, is necessary for this purpose. (2.) Plane a little off where the keys touch. (3.) Incline the slip outwards, and place a piece of paper or card between that and the frame. (4.) Hollow out carefully a large space. (5.) Hollow it underneath. (6.) Carefully remove it and clean away the glue, and reglue it with strong glue, and a small quantity. (7.) Hammer it till firm. (8.) Glue it. (9.) Renew it. (10.) Remove it. (11.) First examine the screws; if they are tight, place some brown paper betwixt the rail and bottom, where the vacancy occurs. The screws may require to be replaced by larger ones. (12.) Remove it. (13.) Polish off the roughness. (14.) File the mortice and clean the pin. (15.) Reduce the key. (16 and 17.) Reduce the parts touching. (18.) Raise the latter and place some cloth under it. (19.) File it very smoothly, or perhaps the key may require wedging. (20.) Renew the leather.

(21.) Saw or file it off very carefully. (22 and 23.) Remove the causes; most likely accidental. (24.) The hopper may require a new hinge, or to be reglued.

An unpleasant Sound in the Hoppers.

The chief causes are as follows:—1. A looseness of the spring. 2. The friction of the spring against the groove. 3. A looseness of the hinge. 4. A looseness of the check. 5. A looseness of the tennant. 6. A roughness in that part which touches the under-hammer. 7. A sudden blow against a hard under-hammer. 8. By touching the next hammer. 9. By touching the next hopper. 10. When the regulating screw is loose. 11. When the cloth is too hard.

These defects can easily be remedied without any particular directions.

A Noise in the Upper Hammers.

Produced by—1. Looseness or unsoundness of the hinges. 2. Hardness of the leather under the block. 3. Looseness or unsoundness of the head. 4. Friction of the head against the damper socket. 5. Unsoundness of the shank. 6. Friction of loose glue against the hammer-rail near the hinge. 7. Looseness or unsoundness of the block. 8. Looseness of the leather under the block. 9. The upper coat of the hammer being too hard. 10. A hammer in the box action touching the wrest-plank at the back, or the sound-board.

In upright pianofortes, the upper hammer rattles occasionally at the centre. This occurs from various causes—when the hole is too large, or badly clothed—when the head or shank is unsound—when the shank is loose—when the bed of the centre wire is broken or gulled. The hammers occasionally stick when the centre wire is too tight in the hole, or when the butt is confined in the notches, or when the hammer is caught between two wires, or when it catches the damper in its return.

How remedied.

The only causes requiring directions are the following:—(9.) Prick the upper coat with a marking awl. If there is no substance in the leather to admit of this being done, it must be replaced by new leather. (10.) The part of the hammer touching should be marked, the action taken out, and the part reduced, to free it.

A Noise in the Dampers

Happens in various ways:—1. When a damper wire is too close to the string. 2. When the damper is loose in the head. 3. When the damper wire is loose in the button, or detached from it.

APPENDIX III. 383

4. When the whole or chief part of the socket-holes are misplaced. 5. When the socket-hole is not well lined, or the cloth too hard. 6. When the socket-hole is broken. 7. When the damper head touches the top. 8. Or, in grands, when it touches the iron arches.

How remedied.

(1.) Bend the wire, or loosen the cloth from the socket-hole, on that side of the damper wire that touches the string. Perhaps the string may require to be removed from the damper wire, by bending the bridge pins. Both operations require the greatest care. (2.) Plug up the hole, and bore a fresh one. (3.) If the wire does not hold properly, plug up the button-hole, and bore a new one, or introduce another damper wire. (4.) The socket must be detached and placed in a better position, by planing or other means, as may seem best. (5.) Prick the cloth with a marking awl, or unscrew the damper, and line the socket-hole with new cloth, removing the old. Paste, or very thin glue, is best for this purpose. (6.) Glue some cloth or leather round it. (7 and 8.) Screw the damper further in.

A Noise in the Damper Levers

Frequently occurs from the following causes:—1. When the lever touches any hard substance. 2. When the last lever touches the frame-cheek. 3. When the hinge is loose or unsound. 4. When one lever touches another from being badly hinged. 5. When the leather, if any, is too hard. 6. When the wood touches the slip. 7. When the wood is unsound. 8. When there is glue betwixt the hinge and the edge of the slip.

These defects are easily remedied, and require no particular directions.

Defects in the Damping

Are likely to occur—1. When the damper is not sufficiently screwed down. 2. When the damper cloth is too hard. 3. When the damper cloth does not bear equally on two strings. 4. When the damper cloth touches the next string. 5. When two wires are not of the same height under the damper. 6. When two wires are of different thicknesses. 7. When the damper wire does not play in the socket-hole. 8. When the pedal-wire is too long, or other obstructions prevent the damper-action falling to its place.

The remedies suggest themselves.

The Sticking of a Damper

Occurs sometimes—1. In the socket-hole. 2. When the lever does not descend. 3. When the pedal-wire does not act properly. 4. When the pedal-foot sticks.

How remedied.

(1.) Open it, or unscrew the damper-wire, and rub the wire with leather. The other remedies require no directions.

The Sticking of a Hopper

Occurs sometimes—1. Against the under-hammer. 2. When the top of the hopper is rough. 3. When the hopper-spring does not operate in the groove. 4. When it is displaced to one side of the hammer. 5. When the spring is too strong. 6. When the regulator touches the hole of the front block. 7. When any part of the hopper is loose.

How remedied.

(1.) Examine the leather and hopper-spring. (2.) Black lead it, and rub with a hard stick. The other remedies suggest themselves.

The Sticking of a Damper Lever.

1. Against another. 2. Against the key frame. 3. Against any detached substance.

The Sticking of a Hammer.

1. Against the wrest-plank. 2. Against the damper-socket. 3. Against the next hammer head. 4. Against a damper-wire. 5. Against the sound-board. 6. From any glutinous substance adhering to it.

How remedied.

(1.) When this is the case, pare off as much leather from the hammer as it may seem to require; alter the position of the hammer, or press it with a warm iron. The other causes are easily remedied.

The Blocking of a Hammer.

1. When the hopper-spring is too weak. 2. When the hopper-cheek is too high. 3. When the top of the hopper is not smooth, particularly on the inner edge. 4. When any part of the hopper is loose. 5. When the hopper strikes but one side of the under-hammer. 6. When the hopper is too far under the hammer. 7. When the leather of the under hammer is not firm. 8. When the regulating-button is turned too far in.

How remedied.

All the directions required are :—(1.) Bend it, to give it strength. This is done by removing it from its place to the side of the hopper, and bending it downward in a curve; then replace it and try its strength. (2.) Reduce it. (3.) Black lead it, and rub the inner edge with a hard stick. (5.) Place it in its right position. (6.) Unscrew it till the hammer falls from the string, about a quarter of an inch.

The Jarring of the Wires

Takes place from the following causes. 1. When two or more strings touch each other. 2. When a string is not firm on the bridges. 3. When the damper-wire is too close to the string. 4. When a string touches a wrest-pin. 5. When the centre bridge is loose. 6. When the sound-board is unglued. 7. When the barring is loose. 8. When the instrument is not firmly placed on the floor. 9. When any hard detached substance is on the sound-board. 10. When one string is thinner than the other. 11. When a string is confined by the pins on the sound-bridge. 12. When there is not sufficient side bearing. 13. When a bridge-pin is loose. 14. When a covered string is loose. 15. When the vibration of the strings is not sufficiently damped by the cloth betwixt the sound-bridge and right block. 16. When a damper-cloth is too hard. 17. When a wire is unsound. 18. When a wire touches the break of the treble string. 19. When a wire touches the name-board.

The remedies suggest themselves.

Hammers touching the wrong Strings.

When this occurs, it is from the following causes. From the hammer-head being too large. 2. From its not being properly hinged. 3. When, from the action not being properly adjusted, the majority of the hammers strike in a wrong place.

How remedied.

(1.) Cut it; this is done by removing the action, or holding up firmly the hammer with a loop of wire while cutting. (2.) Rehinge. (3.) The hammers will generally require to be wedged to the right from left-hand cheek of the hammer-rail.

Defects in the Wrest-pins.

1. When the wrest-pin starts or jumps. 2. When too close to another, thereby hindering the proper use of the tuning-hammer. (3.) When the wire is twisted too high or too low on the wrest-pin. 4. When a wrest-pin is too close to the next string. 5. When the wrest-pin is too small for the hole.

How remedied.

(1.) Probably caused by an unseasoned wrest-plank; or perhaps by the wire having been wound on the pin with a damp hand. A little chalk filled in the hole, will sometimes remedy this. The other defects are easily removed.

Defects in the Pedal.

1. When the pedal wire is too short to raise the dampers to their proper height. 2. When, by being too long, it raises them too high. 3. When the pedal foot is too light. 4. When the pedal foot-pin is too tight. 5. When the pedal foot is too close to the floor. 6. When a rattling is caused by the pedal foot being too loose.

The remedies suggest themselves.

How to alter the Touch.

1. When the touch is too shallow, place brown paper under the balance-rail, near the screws, till you obtain the requisite depth. If the hoppers are too near the under hammers, plane the bottom of the front rail. When the alteration in touch is accomplished, reduce the hopper cheeks if too high. 2. When the touch is too deep, place some paper under the front rail, near the screws. If the hopper cheeks should be found too low, glue some thicker leather on them. 3. When any part of a key is deeper or shallower in touch than the rest, you must operate as directed above, on that particular part of the key alone. 4. When one key is higher than the rest, reduce it on the balance-rail, with sand-paper. 5. When any key is shallower in touch than the rest, raise it on the balance-rail by placing a thin piece of paper on the balance-pin under the cloth. 6. When the hoppers are too short, raise them by putting another piece of cloth under the end rail. 7. When the hammer falls off too far from the strings, rectify it by turning the hopper-pin to the right. 9. When the hopper is high, and the front of the key too low, plane off a little under the further end of the key.

In grand pianofortes the touch is generally altered by moveable blocks or brackets under the balance-rail, screwed up and down, as required; or by placing pieces of paper, or card, under the blocks.

New Leathering the Hammers.

The result of this process is very uncertain. When the hammers have become hard merely by much use, new leathering will succeed. When they are hardened by imbibing damp, the instrument will be found to have suffered irremediable injury from the same cause, and any attempt to restore the tone by new leathering the hammers, will be unsuccessful. It is rather a difficult matter to ascertain which of these two causes may have affected a pianoforte; but by careful inspection we may discover small blue specks upon the sounding-board of the instrument, which are sure indications of damp. If the sounding-board be free from these marks, and the hammers be deeply sulcated with the wires, it is probable that new leathering will, in a considerable degree, restore the tone.

APPENDIX IV.

A GLOSSARY OF THE PRINCIPAL TERMS USED IN THE MANUFACTURE OF THE PIANOFORTE.

ACTION (The). The key-frame, with all its apparatus of hammers, hoppers, keys, &c. In other words, the machinery through which the impulse given by the finger of the performer is transmitted to the string. It is this part of the pianoforte that taxes the ingenuity of various makers.

ÆOLIAN ATTACHMENT. An addition to the pianoforte, the object of which is to sustain and graduate the tone, without the assistance of reeds, pipes, or any vibrating bodies, other than the string. The principle (an invention of M. Isoard, an engineer and mechanician) consists in causing a current of air to act on the string, which prolongs its vibration somewhat on the principle of an æolian harp. For this purpose there is an opening opposite to each string, through which a stream of air passes from a bellows, when a valve, corresponding to the given note, is opened by the key. The bellows are moved by pedals, in the same manner as those of the seraphine or harmonium.

ALBION GRAND PIANOFORTE. The peculiarity of this instrument is that it has a *down-striking* action. It has no metallic bracing, and affords a good example of how much the introduction of the down-striking principle would cheapen the instruments of this form. It was patented by Wornum in 1842.

BEARING (The). The direction the strings take from pin to pin; that from the bridge to the long block is called the *side* bearing.

BELLY—*i. e.* the sounding-board of the pianoforte. See SOUNDING-BOARD.

BELLY-BRIDGE. The bridge on the sounding-board.

BICHORD PIANOFORTE. Any instrument with two strings to each note.

BOUDOIR COTTAGE PIANOFORTE. A name given to those small instruments extending in width at the back, the bass strings of which run obliquely, thereby increasing the richness of the bass.

BOUDOIR GRAND PIANOFORTE. A small horizontal grand piano, generally with two strings to each note.

BRASS OPEN COVERED STRINGS. First introduced for the bass notes of square and other pianofortes.

BRASS WIRE. Formerly used (and still by the French) for the higher portion of the bass notes: by some makers, throughout the instrument.

BRIDGES. There are two bridges: that on the sounding-board varies in form, according to the scale of the different makers. It is glued and screwed to the sounding-board, with wooden nuts underneath, before the latter is fixed on the case. That on the long block is glued and pinned, and sometimes screwed to it. Some pianofortes, not having the metallic plate, have a third bridge—that is, a slip of wood near the hitch-pin.

BUTTON. A circular piece of leather or wood, moving upon a screw wire; for regulating purposes.

CABINET PIANOFORTE. A form of upright instrument, invented and patented by William Southwell, in 1807. The name still remains; but the invention has long since been superseded and laid aside.

CHECK. Only used in grand and double-action instruments. It is a small projection fixed at the back end of the key, serving to prevent the reiteration of the hammer, by catching and firmly holding it when freed from the string.

CLOSE-COVERED STRINGS. These strings, lately introduced in England, for the entire bass are of steel, covered with copper. The largest of them are now, for the extreme low notes, double lapped with thick copper wire. The wrapping too is close, like that of the fourth string of the violin; whereas, formerly, it was open, like the worm of a corkscrew. The best pianoforte wire is made, expressly for the purpose, by Mr. Webster, of Penn's Mills, near Birmingham.

COMPACT SQUARE PIANOFORTE. An instrument six or eight inches shorter than the ordinary square; hence the name. The action is "down-striking," and exceedingly simple. Stodart introduced the inverted mechanism into square pianofortes some ten or twelve years ago. The present invention was by Greiner, who exhibited it in 1851.

Compensation Grand Pianoforte. This instrument has a frame-work of metal tubes, extending from end to end, to withstand the tension of the strings, which have always a tendency to depress the sounding-board and curve the frame-work upward. This invention, patented by Stodart in 1820, was an appliance to prevent the tendency referred to.

Console Pianoforte. A small upright instrument, a little more than three feet high; the top projecting only a few inches above the box enclosing the key-frame. It has the appearance of a cheffonier, and is very effective for its size. The sound-board is made to extend over the whole vertical area of the instrument; whereas, in ordinary uprights, it is of necessity limited to the area occupied by the strings alone. On this account, the tone of the console piano is remarkable for so small an instrument. It is the invention of M. Pape, of Paris.

Copper Wire. At one time used by Broadwood, and some other makers, for a few notes in the bass.

Cottage Pianoforte. The original name of the short upright pianoforte.

Damper. A silencing agent to stop the vibration of the strings when the fingers are lifted from the keys. It consists of several folds of soft cloth, which press against the strings when at rest, but are lifted off by the back end of the key when the front end is pressed down. The grand pianoforte damper originally consisted of a simple rod, headed with cloth, and rising vertically between the strings. But little alteration has been made in this, except that, as the strings were made heavier, and the vibration became stronger, the force with which the damper was held against the strings required to be increased, and the damping surface of cloth extended. The damper movement is variously disposed by different makers, sometimes *above* the strings, sometimes *beneath* them.

Damper-crank. A hinged or centred lever, raised by the key, and connected with the damper-head by a fine wire.

Damper-slip. The slip to which the damper is hinged.

Damper-stick. A stick running through a rack-rail, simply raised by the end of the key; formerly made of wood, latterly of wire; also connected or unconnected with the damper-lever.

Double-grand Pianoforte. An instrument consisting of two grands, enclosed in one large oblong rectangular case—the players sitting at the two opposite ends, facing each other. One string-plate serves for both instruments, the short strings of one coming in a line with the long strings of the other. Invented by Mr. Pirsson, of New York, and shown in the Great Industrial Exhibition of 1851.

ESCAPEMENT. That part of the hopper which, moving on a hinge or centre, is pressed to its raising power by a spring, and by means of the regulating screw (acting upon a bevelled point) is nicely adjusted to cause the hammer to leave the string at the instant of impact. It is in this particular part of the action that makers, who claim invention, so widely differ.

EUPHONICON PIANOFORTE. An upright pianoforte invented by J. Steward, Esq. in 1841. The compass is seven octaves, and its frame, wholly of iron, highly japanned, beautifully ornamented with pearl and gold pencilling on black, blue, or crimson grounds, and embellished with exquisitely chased ormoulu designs, produces an extremely light and elegant appearance. The left portion of the instrument is much higher than the right. To the upper part of the former are attached the three lower octaves of the strings, which are exposed to view; thus combining the appearance of harp and piano. It has three sounding-boards—treble, tenor, and bass,—corresponding to the violin, tenor, and violoncello. It is not now under manufacture.

GRAND PIANOFORTE. The largest sized horizontal instrument, with *three* strings to each note.

GRAND SQUARE PIANOFORTE. Similar to the common square, but having the sounding-board the whole length of the instrument, and the action the same as the grand. Generally made a few inches wider, from back to front, than the common square.

HAMMER. The striking lever, moving upon a centre. The covering of the face of the hammer was formerly of buff leather; now it is made of a fine kind of felt, prepared expressly for the purpose, which gives a much superior quality of tone, and is much more regular in its structure.

HAMMER-BUTT. The part of the hammer-lever which is centred, and the point upon which the hopper acts.

HAMMER-RAIL. A rail extending from end to end of the action, into which the butts of the hammer-lever are centred or hinged.

HARMONIC BAR. A metallic bar firmly attached to the edge of the wrest-plank, through which the treble strings pass, in lieu of over the solid pin-bridge. By this means a bearing *upwards*, instead of *downwards* (as formerly), is attained, giving a more firm and clear tone to the grand pianoforte.

HITCH-PIN. The pin in which the eye or noose of the string is hitched.

HITCH-PIN BLOCK. The block in which the hitch-pin is inserted, at the opposite end or side to the wrest-plank, now generally covered with a metal plate.

HOPPER. A spring medium between the key and hammer, with an escapement to let the hammer fall from the string. It is well explained by Mr. Pole:—" It was a jointed upright piece, attached to the back end of the key, and used to lift the hammer, in place of the stiff wire and button of the former mechanism. When the key was pressed down, the hopper, engaging in a notch on the under side of the hammer, lifted it to within a very short distance of the string—so near, in fact, that almost the slightest pressure would cause it to strike; but at this moment, while the key was still pressed down, the jointed part of the hopper coming in contact with a fixed button as it rose, escaped from, or 'hopped' out of, the notch, and let the hammer fall clear away from the string. This mechanism, as applied with trifling variation to the square pianoforte, was called the ' double action,' and is extensively in use for this and the upright form at the present day."

HOPPER-LEVER. A delicately adjusted lever, with double centres, upon which the hopper action is centred; acting upon the damper action by reverse motion. It is used in Erard's action.

HOPPER-SPRING. A fine brass spring to keep the hopper to its bearing.

JEU CÉLESTE. A soft pedal, interposing cloth between the hammers and the strings. It is used in many of the French pianos, in addition to the ordinary soft and loud pedals.

KEY (CLAVIER). The lever upon which the finger acts, giving motion to all other parts of the action.

KEY-FRAME. The frame upon which the keys act (moveable in grands), made always of wainscot, formed of three rails; the front and centre to receive the key-pins, the back (lined with green baize) to receive the balanced end of the key. In grands, and usually in Broadwood's upright instruments, this frame is made to slide to the right by means of the left pedal. In many transposing pianos, the key-frame is made to move to the right or left by some simple mechanism. See TRANSPOSING PIANOFORTE.

KIT-GRAND PIANOFORTE. The smallest size of grand-shaped instruments.

LYRA PIANOFORTE. An instrument of the upright shape, the back of which is intended to be turned towards the centre of the room, and is formed like a lyre, with openings covered with silk; the object being to throw the sound outwards. The piano stands on a raised platform or sound-conductor, into which the bass strings descend, and which also elevates the stool for the player. It has three pedals, the additional one being a soft one on the French principle, viz. introducing a thickness of soft cloth between the hammer and the string. Invented by Messrs. Hund and Son, and exhibited in 1851.

MICROCHORDON PIANOFORTE. An upright instrument, in size between the piccolo and cottage.

OBLIQUE COTTAGE PIANOFORTE. A small upright instrument, having the strings placed obliquely, thereby obtaining greater length and power of vibration. These pianos are generally wider than ordinary piccolos, and usually with three strings through the upper part of the compass. A very superior and powerful description of small-class piano.

PÉDALIER (The). A kind of *armoire*, placed upright against the wall, and played by means of a pedal-board under the feet of the performer. The instrument has its own strings, hammer, and peculiar mechanism, and is totally independent of the pianoforte, which is placed before it. Its height allows its strings to be unusually long and thick; while the dimensions of the sounding-board, proportionably large for a pedal-board of two octaves and a half, imparts a peculiar richness and power to its tones. The gravity of the thick strings is modified by their being united with finer strings, which produce at the same time the octave next above. This valuable instrument, so desirable for playing a pedal obbligato, is the recent invention of M. Auguste Wolff, of the house of Pleyel and Co. Paris.

PEDALS (The). The forte pedal, usually on the right side of the instrument, is used to lift off the dampers from the strings. By touching the pedal-foot, a wire or stick, is set in motion, which raises the damper frame. The piano pedal moves the entire action along the strings, causing the hammer to strike on one of two, or on two of three strings.

PICCOLO ACTION. The double or 'piccolo action' was the invention of Mr. Wornum. It is now universally used on the Continent for upright pianofortes.

PICCOLO PIANOFORTE. A very small upright instrument, generally 3 feet 9 inches high, 4 feet wide, and 2 feet 2 inches deep.

PINS. There are six sorts of pins:—the *wrest*-pins, or tuning-pins; the *bridge*-pins; the *hitch*-pins, on which the strings are hooked; the *key*-pins; the *hopper*-pins; and the *pedal*-pins.

PIN-BRIDGES. Either single or double: the latter, generally used in the grand pianoforte and harpsichord, has a reversed bearing. These bridges serve to give the *sounding* length of the string; one placed near where the string is struck, on the edge of the wrest-plank solid; the other on the most sonorous point of the sound-board.

PITCH. The acuteness or gravity of any particular sound, or of the tuning of any instrument. Any sound less acute than some other sound, is said to be of lower *pitch* than that other sound, and *vice versâ*.

POCKET GRAND PIANOFORTE. A small semi-grand instrument, generally with two strings to each note.

RAIL AND SOCKET. A rail of wood covered with cloth, extending from end to end of the action, under the hammers, midway, as a fixed point of rest to which the hopper is regulated.

REGULATING SCREW. Variously used to adjust the point of escapement of the hammer in the hopper movement.

REPETITION ACTION. "In the ordinary action," says Mr. Pole, "after the hammer has fallen, the key must rise to its position of rest before the hopper will engage again in the notch of the hammer, so as to be ready for another stroke; and hence a note cannot be repeated without not only requiring the finger to be lifted through the entire height of the key's motion, but also demanding a length of time between the repetitions, sufficient to allow of its full rise. The contrivances by which this inconvenience has been overcome, are of various kinds, according to the fancy or the ingenuity of the makers; but they all act on the same principle,—namely, by holding up the hammer at a certain height while the key returns; by which means the hammer is allowed to engage itself under the hopper earlier, and to reproduce the note in less time, and with less labour to the finger, than before."

ROYAL ALBERT TRANSPOSING PIANOFORTE. The invention of Messrs. Addison and Co. A "Piccolo upright," capable of transposing music upwards or downwards. For instance, if a song be played on the keys as if in C, it can be made to sound either in the key of C sharp, D, E flat, B, B flat, or A; i. e. in any key within a range of three semitones above or below the original one.

RULER. A rail lined with cloth, used in the old actions, as also in harpsichords, spinets, &c. to prevent the jacks and dampers from jerking out.

SCALE (The). The distance between each wire; in fact, the general plan of the instrument. Each maker has his particular scale. Formerly the wires were much thinner than they are at present; consequently the distance from one bridge to the other was greater; for the longer the measure, the thinner the wire must be, and *vice versâ*.

SEMI-COTTAGE PIANOFORTE. A somewhat shorter instrument than the ordinary Cottage Piano.

SEMI-GRAND PIANOFORTE. The next size smaller to the grand instrument, and with a somewhat different action.

SOSTINENTE. The application of a cylinder and silk loops to an upright pianoforte. The loops were attached to the strings and the cylinder, which, being moved by the foot, bowed them: the tones came forth somewhat like the tones of a seraphine. It was the invention of Mr. Mott.

SOUNDING-BOARD. Often called the "belly." It is that smooth thin board over which the strings are distended, and which, by its vibrations, greatly contributes to the tone of the instrument. It is analogous to the belly of the violin, and is composed of the best Swiss pine, perfectly free from knots or imperfections, cut in a particular direction of the grain, and thoroughly seasoned.

SQUARE PIANOFORTE. The shape of the first pianoforte introduced into this country. Its inferiority, even in its present improved state, to the grand instrument, consists in the comparative weakness of its tones, consequent to its having only two, instead of three sets of strings, and the body of the instrument being so much smaller than that of the latter. Very few instruments of this shape are now made in this country.

SQUARE SEMI-GRAND PIANOFORTE. This instrument, invented by the Messrs. Collard, has precisely the same action as that used for semi-grands; whereas the ordinary grand-square has only an adaptation of the peculiarities of the grand action to that of the square.

STEEL ARCHES. Used in old grand pianos to counteract the tension.

STEEL SPUN-WIRE. Used for the lapped strings of the lower part of the pianoforte.

STEEL WIRE. Used, of various thicknesses, for the upper four and a half octaves of the pianoforte.

STICKER. A medium of communication between the *under*-hammer and the butt of the hammer; used in the action of the upright pianofortes.

STRING-PLATE. A metal plate, partially extending over the hitch-pin block, to obviate the fault of the hitch-pin's tendency to draw out. It was first introduced by the Messrs. Broadwood.

STRINGS. Of various metals, substance, and manufacture. See STEEL WIRE, BRASS WIRE, COPPER WIRE, BRASS OPEN COVERED STRINGS, CLOSE COVERED STRINGS.

STUD. A metallic application to grand and other superior pianofortes, screwed into the wrest-plank to obtain an upward bearing of the string, instead of a downward one over the pin-bridge, by which clearness of tone is attained.

TABLE PIANO. An instrument having the size and appearance of an ordinary drawing-room table; one end being lifted up, the keys slide out in a sort of drawer, and the table is converted at once into a pianoforte. The action is down-striking, and the hammers are directly under the front end of the keys; the strings are brought up to the front, and cross each other in two different planes, by which the necessary length for the lower notes is obtained. The sounding-board extends over the whole instrument. It was invented by M. Pape, of Paris.

TENNANT. A small groove in the middle of the key, into which the hopper is inserted.

TENSION. The force employed in stretching a string to the required degree.

TEMPERAMENT. A small, and to the ear almost imperceptible, deviation from the absolute purity of intervals. In its more limited sense, it denotes that arrangement of a system of musical sounds by which a minute quantity is abstracted from the original purity or magnitude of some or most of the intervals which may be formed by them.

396   APPENDIX IV.

TRANSPOSING PIANOFORTE. The object of this instrument is to transpose music to suit voices of different compasses. The key-board and action, or the strings and framing, are shifted laterally, so as to make one hammer strike different strings, according to its position. See ROYAL ALBERT TRANSPOSING PIANO.

TRANSVERSE BAR. Part of the bracing so called.

TUNING FORK. A steel utensil, about three inches long, consisting of two prongs and a handle, and which, being struck against a table or any other substance, produces the tone to which itself was originally set. There are various tones or pitches; but the A and C forks are most generally used.

TUNING HAMMER. A steel or iron utensil used by pianoforte tuners. It is about four inches long, and formed like a common hammer. With the head of the hammer the pegs round which the ends of the wires are twisted are driven into the sockets; and the bottom of the handle is furnished with a square or oblong hole, in a longitudinal direction, which, being of a size to fit the tops of the pegs, enables the hand to turn them, and thereby to relax or extend the wires.

UNACHORD. Any instrument with one string to each note.

UNDER-HAMMER. A hinged lever, similar to the damper lever, to which the hopper is adjusted; used in upright pianofortes.

UNDER-HAMMER SLIP. The slip to which the under-hammer is hinged.

UTILITARIAN BOUDOIR PIANO. A small piccolo upright instrument, with one string to each note. The keys are shorter and project less, by which the legs or scrolls usually put under the key-frame are saved. The action consists of a simple projection at the end of the key, which lifts the tail of the hammer directly, without the intervention of any hopper. It is, in short, a return to the old single action, with which the pianoforte was first made; the only difference being the variation in form necessary to adapt it to the upright instrument.

WREST-PIN. Iron pins upon which the strings are strained. They are not screws, but have sufficient tendency to draw themselves in tightly, when turned to the right. They protrude about an inch from the wrest-plank, having an oblong or square upper end, by which they are turned.

WREST-PLANK. Usually formed of two or more kinds of wood, joined together in the flat, with the grains running in opposite directions; the upper one of wainscot oak endwise, to resist the great tension of the strings, usually veneered with holly or other white wood. It receives the wrest-pins, on which the wires are stretched to their necessary tension. Its situation differs according to the kind of pianoforte. In the *grand*, it is placed in the front of the instrument, immediately above the keys; in the *upright*, at the top of the instrument, above the action; in the *square*, (originally at the right end) latterly at the back, behind the keys.

ADDITIONAL NOTES AND ILLUSTRATIONS.

Page 15. In summing up our information upon the musical acquirements of those extraordinary people, the ancient Egyptians, we extract the following passage from Sir J. Gardner Wilkinson's recent volume on *The Egyptians in the time of the Pharoahs*, 8vo. 1857.—"Their bands were often composed of a harp, lyre, and *guitar*, a double pipe, and tambourine; of a fourteen-stringed harp, a double pipe, and a lyre of seventeen chords, with voices; of two harps, a flute, and voices; of a harp, a *guitar*, and a double pipe or of two flutes; of harp and two *guitars*, with a double pipe, and the clapping of hands; of two harps, and a jingling instrument which may correspond to the crescent-crowned bells of our military bands; besides many other combinations.   *   *   To discover, rather than to invent, these simple instruments, required little skill; but, before they could devise the means of obtaining various notes from a small number of strings, by shortening them on a neck, as in our modern guitar and violin, considerable experience was required; and this could only have resulted from an attentive study of musical sounds. The three-stringed guitar, therefore, proves that the Egyptians had acquired a knowlege of music at a very remote time, for, though not represented in a band of music earlier than the eighteenth dynasty, it is found among the hieroglyphics upwards of 600 years before that period as the initial of the word *nofr*, 'good." The guitar had a long neck, about twice the length of its oval body, which last was a hollow case of wood with leather or parchment strained over it, having small holes to allow the sound to escape. It was played with the *plectrum;* and as the *cithara* of Greece was smaller than the other Greek lyres, the guitar of the Egyptians was of less power than their lyre. Women generally played it; men rarely. It was supported on the right arm, and even by a strap over the shoulder, like the Spanish guitar; while the strings were shortened by the left hand; and the performer occasionally danced to its sound."

Page 28, line 18. *Catgut* is the name applied to strings made from the peritoneal covering of the intestines of sheep. The greatest care is necessary in preparing these strings for musical instruments, to secure the strength necessary for the great tension required for the high notes. The best strings are made at Naples, because the sheep, from their leanness, afford the best raw material; it is a well-ascertained fact that the membranes of lean animals are much tougher than those of animals in high condition.

Page 33, line 1. Du Sommerard, in his *Album of Archæology*, engraves a Clavichorde with "*cordes de laiton,*" which belonged to one of the *dames d' honneur* of Catherine de Medicis, and was preserved in the Hotel Richelieu till 1791. The "strings of brass" strongly favour our theory.

Page 34, line 15. We are not quite clear upon the point that the monochord of the middle ages was not used in the *performance* of music. Since writing the passage in the text, we have noticed in the second volume of Gerbert's *De Cantu et Musicâ Sacrâ*, plate 34, the figure of a man evidently playing upon an instrument of this description. See also plate 26, of the same work.

Page 48, line 22. Gold and silver compounded and rendered elastic would undoubtedly produce beautiful tones. A gold string or wire will sound stronger than a silver one; those of brass and steel give feebler sounds than those of gold and silver. Silk strings were made of the single threads of the silk worm, a sufficient number of them being taken to form a chord of the required thickness; these were smeared over with the white of eggs, which was rendered consistent by passing the threads through heated oil. The string was exceedingly uniform in its thickness, but produced a tone which the performer called tubby.

It seems probable that when Josephus speaks of the musical instruments belonging to the Temple as being "made of a composition between *gold and silver*," he alluded to the strings or wires.

Page 48, line 11.—The following advertisement appeared in *The Times* newspaper, July 8, 1858:—

"A MUSICAL CURIOSITY.—A magnificent and historical HARPSICHORD may be seen, for a few days, at No. 6, Arundel Street, Haymarket. It has belonged to the old and princely house of De Medicis, Dukes of Florence, and is the great work of Marco Sadre, who flourished in the sixteenth century. There are five octaves and a half, and the keys still have their original sweetness. In front of the keys are three authentic portraits chiselled in gold, surrounded with the following relative inscriptions:—" Francis Medices Florent Senaraum; the other " Carolus Galliorum Rex Cristianis, 1565 " (who was the son of Henry IV and Catherine de Medicis); and the last, " Joanna Princ, Florent, Senar, Arcid " (who was the wife of Francis de Medicis). Besides, there is the name of the great manufacturer, and the year (1565) in which he made this work."

Upon inspecting this "musical curiosity," it proved to be a very small virginal, of sweet tone, and in the most perfect state of preservation; its compass, from E below the bass staff to F in alt, four octaves and one note. The maker's name is Marco *Jadrae* (not Sadre as printed in the *Times*), concerning whom nothing seems to be known. After making considerable research for some particulars of this early maker without success, we wrote to Count Pepoli upon the subject, and were favoured with the following answer:

"I believe that 'Opus Marci Jadræ,' id est, 'Opera di Marco Jadra,' or di Jadra, is the name of the artist Marco dai Cembali, or Marco dalle Spinette; and that Jadra or Jadera was the name (being the latter one) used very often instead of Zara. And it was the fashion to call the artistes after the names of their towns: Coreggio, Bassano, D'Arpino, &c. This is my opinion; but '*valeat quantum valere* potest."

This interesting instrument was purchased in Rome, by the present possessor, from an old monk of the Cornaro family. The price put upon it by the advertiser was £500!

A small virginal of German make, bearing date 1600 (called a spinet in the description), was lately exhibited in the Art Department of the South Kensington Museum; its compass was from G, the lowest note of the bass staff, to A above the treble staff, three octaves and one note.

Page 57, line 16—" A man whose facultie in profession is a maker of Virginalls, going to the brick kilns, at the upper end of Golding Lane, to seek *Ravens feathers*, which he putteth to some use in his handy craft," &c.—Anthony Munday's *View of Sundry Examples*, 1580, 4to. (*Shakespeare Society's* reprint, p. 93.)

Page 58, line 19. Queen Elizabeth's virginal was purchased at Lord Spencer Chichester's sale at Fisherwick, by Mr. Jonah Child, a painter, of Dudley in Worcestershire. Shaw, in his *History of Staffordshire*, article Fisherwick (vol i, p. 369), gives a minute description of the instrument.

Page 64, line 10. Among the Howard papers, Lady Arabella Stuart, writing to the Earl of Shrewsbury from Broad Street, June 17, 1609, says:—" But now from doctrine to miracles; I assure you within these few dayes I saw a paire of virginalles make good musick without help of any hand, but of *one* that did nothing but warme, not move, a glass some five or six foote from them. And if I thought these great folkes invisibly and farre off worke in matters to tune them as they please, I pray your Lordship forgive me; and I hope God will, to whose holy protection I humbly recommend your Lordship," &c. How was this virginal made to play without the " help of hand "? The passage affords an early example of scientific knowledge. We have in vain searched for a more minute account of this wonder.

Page 65, line 2. The following extracts from the *Obituary of Richard Smyth* (printed by the Camden Society in 1848), relate to a virginal-maker whose name had escaped our notice:

"1660. Janua. 5. Tho. White, virginal maker in Old Jury, buried."

"1665. Septem. 2. Mary White, ye relict of Thom. White, virginall maker, my late tennant in Old Jury, buried, *ex peste*."

Page 65, *note*. The interesting virginal mentioned in the note as being in the possession of T. Mackinlay, Esq. is now the property of the author of the present volume. It was made in the year 1666, by Adam Leversidge, and is in an excellent state of preservation. The painting, embossing, and gilding, are all as fresh as if they had recently come from the hands of the manufacturer.

Page 69, line 8. Baker Harris was an eminent maker of spinets in the latter half of the eighteenth century. We saw one by this maker at a broker's shop in Great St. Andrew's Street, Seven Dials, in April 1858. It had white keys, and was dated 1776.

Page 77, line 29. A book very little known and imperfectly described by Forkel and Lichtenthal, in their Musical Bibliographies, contains some singular descriptions of musical instruments constructed in the seventeenth century, upon principles which, after having been lost and forgotten, were brought forward again as new at a later period. This book is entitled *Dichiaratone della Galeria Armonica eretta in Roma da Michele Todini*, *Pièmontese di Saluzzo, nella sua habitatione, posta all arca della Ciàmbella*, printed at Rome by Francesco Tizzoni, 1676, ninety-two pages, 12mo. Forkel and Lichtenthal mention this book only by the abridged title of *La Galeria Armonica*, and do not appear to have been aware of its real contents; for they cite it merely as a description of an ingenious organ which had cost Todini eighteen years to complete; whereas it is not only a description of the organ, but of several other musical instruments and curious pieces of mechanism, which Todini had constructed and placed in those apartments of his dwelling-house to which he gave the designation of an *Harmonic Gallery*. In the first room were some curious and complicated specimens of clocks; in the second, a mechanical representation of the story of Polypheme and Galatea, in which tritons and sea gods played several tunes on a harpsichord, and Polypheme himself performed on a kind of bagpipe, the sounds of which were produced by a key-board under that of the harpsichord.

It was in the third chamber that the most curious of Todini's inventions in the construction of musical instruments were deposited; and these, considering the period at which they were manufactured, are really astonishing. Amongst them were two violins, the pitch of one of which could, by an ingenious mechanical contrivance, be at once heightened a whole tone, a third, or even a fifth; the other, under the usual strings, had a second set of strings, like those of a kit, tuned in the octave above, and was so contrived that the violin and kit might either be played separately or both together, at the pleasure of the performer.

In the twenty-third chapter of this tract is a description of a viol-di-gamba, so contrived that, without shifting the neck, all the four kinds of violins, namely, the treble violin, the contralto (or *viola bastarda*), the tenor, and bass viol, could be played upon it. Todini had originally given the bass of this instrument an unusual depth; but he abandoned that when he invented the double bass, which instrument he was the first to introduce and play upon in oratorios, concerts, and serenades.

Todini also invented and manufactured two harpsichords; on one of which, by an ingenious contrivance, the three genera of the ancients, the diatonic, chromatic, and enharmonic, could be played without any multiplied or inconvenient division of the keys.

In this third room of the gallery was also his grand organ, which had cost so many years' labour, and in the construction of which were many contrivances that have since been revived and called new inventions. This organ contained seven instruments of different kinds, any number of which might be played on separately or united, at the pleasure of the performer. The organ had numerous stops, which could be adjusted, combined, or separated, without the necessity of the player taking his hands off the keys. There were an harpsichord, an octave spinet, a small theorbo, a violin, and a kind of bass violin with fifteen strings, then in use, and called the lyra or accordo. Todini had invented a mechanism by which the effect of the bow on these instruments was perfectly produced. It is well known how many attempts were made to produce this effect, a detailed account of which has been given in our earlier pages; but what is worthy of notice in Todini's instrument is, that the same key-board served for the organ with all its stops, the harpsichord, spinet, theorbo, and violins; and that they might not only all be played, as above mentioned, either separately or united at pleasure, but without the performer being at any time obliged to lift his hands from the keys.

Todini wrote his book when all these inventions of his were completed, and invites all musicians to satisfy themselves, by ocular inspection and examination, of their advantages. There can be no doubt, therefore, of their reality, even if Lichtenthal had not expressly said that the organ was still in existence, at Rome, in his time.

Page 84, line 12. The earliest harpsichord made in England which we have seen was lately exhibited in the Art Department of the South Kensington Museum. It consisted of a mere shell, the inside being entirely gone, with the inscription on the name-board, "Johannes Asard, 1622."

Page 91. To the note on this page add the following:
"The Harpsichord, an instrument of power and compass, is now going out of use. The guitar, a trifling instrument in itself, and generally now taught in the most ignorant and trifling manner, is adopted in its place; while the theorbo and lute, the noblest because the most expressive and pathetic of all accompaniments, are altogether laid aside. What is the reason of this? Because the guitar is a plaything for a child, the harpsichord and lute require application."
—Dr. Brown's *Estimate of the Manners and Principles of the Times*, vol. ii, p. 77, edit. 1758.

Page 93, line 32. In addition to the English makers of the middle of the eighteenth century which we have noticed, we may add the names of "Mr. Mahoon, Harpsichord-maker to His Majesty," and "Mr. Sells, Harpsichord-maker," both of which appear among the subscribers to *Travers's Canzonets*.

Page 147, line 17. In the *Quarterly Musical Register*, edited by A. F. C. Kollman (of which we believe only two numbers were published), No. 1, January 1, 1812, is an interesting article, giving a "Retrospect of the state of Music in Great Britain, since the year 1789," from which we extract what relates to the various inventions which have been introduced in the pianoforte:

"1. *Additional Keys*, above the former high F, three lines and a space over the treble stave; and below the former low F, four lines under the bass stave. In regard to these, it is certain that, though any rational extension of the compass of the scale is an improvement in an instrument, the modern rage for additional keys *without end* seems to carry the art of invention too far in that respect. For no great composer for keyed instruments, or great performer on them, has reason to complain of their limited compass, even when they contained but five octaves, from F to F; and to them a good tone, with a mechanism that admits of a highly finished, as well as an expressive performance, always will remain the first consideration. To this must be added, that too great an extension of the scale of keyed instruments renders their construction precarious in regard to an equality of tone throughout; as well as the instruments themselves too unwieldy for a removal, and too large for a room of moderate size. It might therefore be wished that the compass of pianofortes would not be enlarged beyond six octaves.

"2. Hammers with different sorts of *double actions*. These have been universally considered as real improvements of the pianoforte.

"3. Varieties of *dampers*. In regard to these, every good player knows how much there depends on dampers which take away the sound perfectly and promptly without occasioning a noise or jarring. Every *improvement* of this kind, therefore, ought also to be considered as very useful and desirable.

"4. Square pianofortes, with the sound-board extending over the whole instrument, have been made for some years by Messrs. Broadwood; and they seemed to depend on the principle of giving a firmness to the instrument *at the top*, where it is particularly wanted; but their unremitted attention to the improvements of those instruments seems to have made them discover a method by which that support at the top can be dispensed with, for which reason they have discontinued making them in the above manner.

"5. Other sorts of square pianofortes, apparently on a similar principle to the above, have also been made by other manufacturers; one of which were those with a slender wooden beam *at the top* along the lowest bass string, similar to that in front of the harp. This invention greatly improved the firmness of the instrument, without injuring its tone. But it has not been generally adopted.

"A variation of the same principle seemed to be Mr. Hawkins's pianoforte, with a *metal frame* all around the strings, as well as with a metal supporter along the midst of them; which, however, appeared as being too stiff for the necessary vibration, and as spoiling the tone.

"And, as another variation of the principle, we consider the square pianoforte by Mr. Scott, which were equally firm and closed up in front, as behind; and the keys to be pulled out, in a manner as at some organs. This construction seemed to be very natural, and not disadvantageous to the sound of the instrument; but the required sliding of the keys apparently rendered the mechanism of the action less certain than otherwise. And we are not sure whether this kind of instrument is still manufactured.

"6. A few years ago, a Mr. Riley, of Hull, brought out a patent pianoforte, constructed so that the whole set of keys could be shifted towards the right or left, in order to transpose the same keys into a higher or lower scale. This was very useful for the accommodation of singers, though it conld be of no advantage to good players; but we have also not heard of these instruments lately.

"7. Upright grand pianofortes have been brought to a great perfection by several of the first makers, and they are very useful for saving room; but, we must confess, that, though in regard to a fullness of tone, we think them highly preferable to square pianofortes, we cannot, for several reasons, consider them as equal to horizontal grand pianofortes.

"8. A smaller sort of upright pianoforte, with only two strings to each key, called *cabinet* pianofortes, have lately been brought forward by Messrs. Wilkinson and Wornum, but are also manufactured by the other makers. Whether they will be adopted as preferable to the square pianoforte, time must show."

Page 159, line 18. The New York Exhibition, of 1853, brought into notice a number of pianoforte makers, whose names deserve to be placed on record; viz. William Hall and Son; Hazelton and Brother; Bennett and Co.; Grovesteen and Co.; Lighte and Newton; Charles J. Holden; Jean Lankota; A. Bassford; Firth, Pond and Co.; John Ruck; and W. H. Bowden; all of New York. Hallet, Davies and Co.; George Hews, and Gilbert; all of Boston. Schomaker and Co. of Philadelphia; and Knare, and Gahele and Co. of Baltimore.—*Science and Mechanism; illustrated by Examples in the New York Exhibition*, 1853-4. Edited by C. R. Goodrich, Esq. 4to. Putnam, New York, 1854, p. 250.

Page 171, line 10. "Some philosophers have imagined that there are certain fibres in a sounding-board which vibrate to one tone, and others which vibrate to another, and that in no case the entire board can be made to sympathise with any particular sound. From M. Savart's experiments it is evident that the board in every instance becomes a part of a vibratory system, and acts in unison with every note, although much more perfectly with some than with others. To this philosopher much honour is due for the accurate and ingenious manner in which his experiments were made, as well as for the splendid results he obtained; but it ought in fairness to be stated that the fact here alluded to was first observed by M. Perrole."

In stringed instruments the sound is not produced by the vibration of the strings alone, but by the communication of these vibrations to the substances that surround them; and experiments have been made to prove the absolute vibration of the entire body of an instrument. See Mr. Higgins's charming volume on *The Philosophy of Sound*, 12mo. 1838.

Page 188, line 9. The old way of producing the soft tone was to shift the action so that the hammers would strike two strings instead of three, or òne instead of two; the French method is now often adopted of interposing a piece of soft cloth between the hammer and the string, which deadens the blow, and produces a very pleasing effect, without the risk of putting the instrument out of tune by striking upon only one string.

"One of the recent American improvements is the "dolce campana" pedal, by which the sound is prolonged and the quality changed to that of sweet bells or harps. The mechanism is simple, being merely a number of weights arranged, by a lever pedal, to fall, when required, upon an equal number of screws fixed in the sounding-board; this, of course, alters the vibrations, and, in connexion with the other pedals, produces great brilliancy and delicacy of tone, like the chimes of distant bells, whence its name."—*Science and Mechanism*, 4to. Putnam, New York, 1854, p. 250.

Page 206, line 11. A more minute account of Hohlfeld's claims to having perfected an instrument for noting down music is given in Professor Beckmann's *History of Discoveries, Inventions, and Origins*, edit. 1846, vol. i, p. 12, from which we extract the following:

After noticing Creed's proposition, he goes on to say, "In the year 1745, John Frederic Unger, then land-bailiff and burgomaster of Einbec, and who is known by several learned works, fell upon the same invention without the smallest knowledge of the idea published in England. This invention, however, owing to the variety of his occupations, he did not make known till the year 1752, when he transmitted a short account of it, accompanied with figures, to the Academy of Sciences at Berlin. The Academy highly approved of it, and it was soon celebrated in several gazettes; but a description of it was never printed.

"A few days after Euler had read this paper of Unger's before the Academy, M. Sulzer informed Hohlfeld of the invention, and advised him to exert his ingenuity in constructing such a machine. In two weeks this untaugh mechanic, without having read Unger's paper, and even without inspecting the figures, completed the machine, which Unger himself had not been able to execute, through want of an artist capable of following his ideas.

"Unger's own description of his invention was printed with copper-plates at Brunswick, in the year 1774, together with the correspondence between him and Euler, and other documents. A description of Hohlfeld's machine, illustrated with figures, was published after his death by Sulzer, in the New Memoirs of the Academy of Berlin, 1771, under the title of '*Description of a machine for noting down pieces of music as fast as they are played upon the harpsichord.*' Sulzer there remarks that Hohlfeld had not followed the plan sketched out by Unger, and that the two machines differed in this—that Unger's formed one piece with the harpsichord, while that of Hohlfeld could be applied to any harpsichord whatever.

"When Dr. Burney visited Berlin, he was made acquainted with Hohlfeld's machine by M. Marpurg, and has been so ungenerous, or rather unjust, as to say, in his 'Musical Travels,' that it is an English invention, and that it had been before fully described in the Philosophical Transactions. This falsehood M. Unger has fully refuted. Without repeating his proofs, I shall here content myself with quoting his own words in the following passage: 'How can Burney wish to deprive our ingenious Hohlfeld of the honour of being the sole author of that invention, and to make an Englishman share it with him, because our German happened to execute successfully what his countryman, Creed, only suggested? Such an attempt is as unjust in its consequences as it is dishonourable to the English nation and the English artists. When we reflect on the high estimation in which music is held in England, the liberality of the English nobility, and their readiness to spare no expenses in bringing forward any useful invention—a property peculiar to the English, it affords just matter of surprise that the English artists should have suffered themselves to be anticipated by a German journeyman lace-maker. To our Hohlfeld, therefore, will incontestibly remain the lasting honour of having executed a German invention; and the Germans may contentedly wait to see whether Burney will find an English mechanic capable of constructing this machine from the information given by his countryman Creed.'"

INDEX.

See also the *Glossary of Terms used in the Manufacture of the Pianoforte* (p. 387), the references to which are not included in the present *Index*.

A.

	Page.
Action, explanation of the	184 *et seq.*
———— various diagrams of the	187 *et seq.*
Actions, downward, of various makers	194 *et seq.*
Adam, G. pianoforte maker	220
Addison, R. pianoforte maker	217
Additional keys to the pianoforte	141, 401
Aerts, F. G. pianoforte maker	218
Aggio, G. H. pianoforte maker	218
Agricola, Martin, his *Musica Instrumentalis*	49
Akerman, W. H. pianoforte maker	217
Allen, William, pianoforte maker	152, 154, 158
Allison, Messrs. pianoforte makers	217
Alwood, an early composer for the virginals	228
Amphion, adds three strings to the lyre	5
Ancients, knowledge of counterpoint possessed by the	11
Anemochorde	203
Anne, Queen, her spinet bequeathed to the Chapel Royal	68
Apollodorus, his account of the lyre	2
Archicembalo, a harpsichord with six rows of keys	77
Artusi, his *Imperfettioni della moderna Musica*	67, 77
Asard, John, harpsichord maker	401
Ashúr, an instrument of the Jews	13, 15
Aston, Hugh, an early composer for the virginals	228
Athenæus, his notice of the *simicum* and the *epigonium*	35
Aucher and Son, pianoforte makers	219

B.

	Page.
Bach, Carl Philip Emanuel, his pianoforte works	232, 235
———— his performance on the clarichord	31
—— John Christian, his arrival in England	131
—— Sebastian, his visit to Frederick the Great	113
———— his opinion of the clavichord	31
———— Capriccio by	235
Backers, Americus, an early pianoforte maker	89, 131
Balbastre, M. his Ruckers harpsichord	76
Ball, James, pianoforte maker	150, 157
Barbitos, a name for the lyre	3
Barbetta, Giulio Cesare, an early performer on the harpsichord, &c	228
Bartholomeus, his *de Proprietatibus Rerum*	20, 29
———— his description of the cithara	29

	Page.
Barton, William, an improver of the harpsichord	86, 149
Baudin, a maker of spinets, &c	69, 85
Bauer, his transposing piano	207
Beck, pianoforte maker	147
Becker, John Conrad, musical instrument maker	151
Bemetzrieder, Antonius, patent for improvements in the pianoforte	151
Berden, Messrs. F. and C. pianoforte makers	218
Berlin Museum, ancient lyre preserved in the	5
Bessalié, H. P. pianoforte maker	159, 220
Bindella of Treviso, a celebrated performer on the harpsichord, &c	228
Blanchets, family of the, eminent musical instrument makers of Paris	81
Blitheman, William, his compositions for the virginals	59, 228, 233
Boccaccio's *Decameron*, important passage in	36
Bochet, Henry du, patent taken out by	156
Bologna, Jacopo di, an early composer	42, 226
Bonanni, his *Gabinetto Armonico*	34, 67, 77
Bord, pianoforte maker	219
Boulogne-sur-mer, ancient MS. in the library of	19
Bow-shaped harps	8
Bowman, Robert, virginal player in the Courts of Edward VI, and Queen Mary	55
Brass tongues used in the place of quills	82
Breitkhopf and Härtel, pianoforte makers	220
Breton, Nicholas, his *Flourish upon Fancie*	60
Brewer, Dr. on *Sound and its Phenomena*	171, 174
Brickler, Miss, her benefit at Covent Garden Theatre	133
Bridge, uses of the, explained	182
Brinsmead, J. pianoforte maker	217
British Museum, MSS. quoted	25
Broadwood, John, the founder of the eminent firm	139, 150, 157
———— James Shudi, his Son	140, 153, 154
———— his *Practice of Tuning*	375
———— Henry Fowler, grandson of John Broadwood	156
———— Messrs., Ruckers harpsichord in their possession	74
———— their metallic bracing	167
———— number of instruments made by them annually	211
———— their pianofortes in the Great Exhibition	217

INDEX.

	Page.
Bruce, his account of the harps in the tomb of Bibàn el Moloók	9, 10, 11
Buchner, Johann, a famous performer on the harpsichord, &c.	228
Buff leather, a substitute for quill	81
Buff, stop in the harpsichord	81
Bull, Dr. John, his virginal compositions	59, 233
Bull, harpsichord maker	74
Buntebart (or Buntlebart), pianoforte maker	132
Buntlebart and Sievers, pianoforte makers	147
Burel, his account of the Queen of James VI entering Edinburgh	611
Buret, a writer of harpsichord music	231
Burkinyoung, Frederick Handell, patent taken out by	156
Burney, Dr. his account of the Theban harps	11
——— Reflections on the construction of ancient Musical Instruments	17
——— his notice of the *difficulties* of Queen Elizabeth's virginal book	59
——— his notice of the spinet	69
——— his account of the harpsichord makers of Antwerp	73
——— account of his visit to M. Balbastre	76
——— account of his visit to Farinelli	83
——— his notice of Tschudi and other contemporary harpsichord makers	89
——— on the excellence of English harpsichords	93
——— his account of the progress of the pianoforte in Germany	120
Burney, Mr. *pianist* to Drury Lane Theatre	139
Buttery, George, pianoforte maker	151, 157
Byrd, William, his virginal compositions	59, 233

C.

Cabinet Pianoforte	157
Cadby, C. pianoforte maker	173, 217
Calanson, Giraud de, his *Conseils au Jongler*	36
Camden, his account of Queen Elizabeth's love of music	55
Canareggio, Andrea de, an early performer on the harpsichord, &c.	228
Canticum or psaltery	18
Caracci, Annibal, his painted harpsichord	75
Carreyre, M. inventor of a melographic piano	206
Carleton, Richard, an early composer for the virginals	228
Carli, Count G. R. his account of Cristofali's invention of the pianoforte	94
Castel, Louis Bertrand, the inventor of the *Ocular Harpsichord*	82
Castello, Paulo de, an early performer on the harpsichord, &c.	228
Catgut strings	398
Catgut used for the Egptian harps	9
Catherine of Spain, entertainment to	43
Caxton, his *Knyght of the Toure*	42
Cazalet, Rev. W. W. his *Lecture on the Musical Department of the Great Exhibition*	211
Celestina	199

	Page.
Celestina stop	158
Celestial harp	93
Celestinettes	199
Cembalo, Boccaccio's mention of the	36
——— the term explained	38
Chambers's Edinburgh Journal, article on the *Pianoforte*	161
Chambonnières, his harpsichord works	230, 234
Champion, Jacques, an early composer for the harpsichord, &c.	230
Chapel Royal, old spinet belonging to the	68
Chaucer, his *Knight's Tale*	26
Check action	185
Chelys, a name for the lyre	3
Chetham Library, Manchester, curious broadsides in	86, 88
Chichering, Messrs. of Boston, pianoforte makers	159, 217
——— their metallic framing	168
Choron, A. his notice of the *difficulties* of Queen Elizabeth's virginal book	59
Chorley, H. F. his article on the *Pianoforte Composers*	232
Chounter, Anthony, virginal player in the Courts of Edward VI and Queen Mary	55
Cithara, a name for the lyre	3
——— described by Bartholomeus	29
——— of the middle ages	19
Citole, description of the	25
Ckánóon, an instrument used in modern Egypt	24
Clariodus and Meliades, a MS. romance	41
Clarion	33
Clark, Joseph, patent taken out by	155
Clavecin d'Amour	82
Clavecin viole	197
Clavecins à Maillets, invented by Marius	103
Clavichord, notice of the	29
——— its mechanism	31, 41, 399
——— origin of the name	31
——— its distinction from the clarichord	32
Clavicymbal, the origin of the harpsichord	33
Clavicytherium	28, 29, 79
Clementi, Muzio, biographical notice of	143
Clementi and Collard, their bridge of reverberation	182
——— their *self-acting* pianoforte	206
Cloth used in place of the quill in harpsichords	79
Coleman, Obed. Mitchell, patent taken out by	156
Collard, Frederic William, the founder of the house of Collard and Collard	146, 152, 153, 158
——— Messrs. their mode of stringing	178
——— their patent grand action, diagram of	190
——— number of instruments made by them annually	211
——— their instruments in the Great Exhibition	217
Collin, pianoforte maker	219
Cologne, Johann von, a celebrated performer on the harpsichord, &c.	228
Concerts, Bach and Abel's (*note*)	132
Confessio Amantis, Gower's	26

INDEX.

	Page.
Conrad of Spire, a famous performer on the harpsichord, &c.	228
Cornish, William, his *Treatise between Trouth and Informacion*	44
Correggio, Claudio di, an early performer on the harpsichord, &c.	228
Corrie, pianoforte maker	147
Cortecia, Francesco, an early clavichord performer	227
Cottage pianoforte	157
Couchet, a maker of spinets	68
Counterpoint, whether known to the ancients (*note*)	11
Couperin, François, his harpsichord works	231, 235
Coxe, Archdeacon, his *Anecdotes of Handel and Smith*	74
Creed, Rev. Mr. his plan for a *Melographic* piano	205, 402
Crisp, Samuel, Esq. biographical notice of (*note*)	130
Cristofali, Bartolommeo, the inventor of the pianoforte	94 *et seq.*
Cromwell, Samuel Thomas, patent taken out by	156
Cropet, pianoforte maker	219
Crotone, an Italian harpsichord maker	79
Cuijpers, J. F. pianoforte maker	220
Custom House rates in 1545	49
Cymbals, the ancient, described	38, 40
—— their use in churches	41
Cymbal octave, and *cymbal regal*, ancient stops in the organ	41

D.

Danchell, Frederick Ludwig Hahn, musical instrument maker	154
D'Anglebart, a writer of harpsichord music	231
Davie, Adam, his metrical *Life of Alexander*	25
Davis, John, organ builder	150
—— Samuel, musical instrument maker	151
Day, Francis, his patent for improvements in the pianoforte	154
—— John, improves musical instruments	152, 157
Deacon, pianoforte maker	217
Deakin, Francis, improves musical instruments	153
Debain, Alexandre, pianoforte maker	157, 219
—— his contrivance to supersede barrels	207
Deffaux, pianoforte maker	218
Dell' Anima e del Corpo, an oratorio performed in 1600	78
Dennis, Jean, a celebrated maker of spinets	68
Denon, his drawings of the Theban harps	9
Détis and Co. pianoforte makers	219
Dibdin, Charles, biographical sketch of	133
—— his notice of Garrick's old virginals	65
Diettmar, William, pianoforte maker	154
Dieudonné and Bladel, pianoforte makers	220
Dietz, M. inventor of the *Polyplectron*	202
Dimoline, A. pianoforte maker	218
Diruta, Geronimo, his *Il Transilvano*	228
Dodd, his article on the pianoforte	177
—— Edward, musical instrument maker	154, 155
Dolce Campana pedal	402
Domeny, L. F. pianoforte maker	219

	Page.
Done, Joshua, pianoforte maker	147
Dörmer, F. pianoforte maker	159, 220
Douce, Francis, his description of the clavichord	30
Douglas, Gawain, his *Palace of Honour*	22
Downward actions	194 *et seq.*
Dreaper, pianoforte maker	171
Dreschke, Theophile Auguste, patent taken out by	156
Driggs, Messrs. of New York, pianoforte makers	159
—— Spencer, his newly-constructed square pianoforte	169
Dulcimer	23, 24 38
Dulcino	23
Dulcken, J. Dan, harpsichord maker	73
Dulsacordis	23
Dumont, H. his virginal compositions	234
Dulzain	23

E.

Early composers for instruments of the pianoforte class	223
East, Peter, instrument maker	149
Edward the Sixth's virginal players	55
Edwards, Richard, his compositions for the virginals	228
Egyptians, Ancient, their knowledge of music	15, 398
Elizabeth, Queen, her love of music	55
—————— virginals belonging to	58
—————— her virginal book, in the Fitzwilliam Museum, Cambridge	58
Elizabeth, of York, her Privy Purse Expenses	43
Elsche, Vanden, harpsichord maker	74
Elwick, pianoforte maker	147
English action	159
English harpsichords, the excellence of	93
Ennever and Steedman, pianoforte makers	217
Epigonium, Athenæus's description of the	35
Erard, Sebastian, Memoir of	122 *et seq.*
—— Patents for improvements on the pianoforte	151, 152, 157
—— Diagram of his patent grand action	190
——Pierre, patents taken out by, &c.	153, 155, 157, 217, 219
——Messrs. their metallic bracing	168
Euler, Dr. his account of a melographic pianoforte (*note*)	205
Eurydice, a drama performed at Florence in 1600	78
Evelyn, John, his account of a harpsichord	198

F.

Faber, Daniel, clavichord maker	47
Faggia, Enrico Rodesca da, an early performer on the harpsichord, &c.	228
Farinelli's harpsichords	83
Farini, an Italian harpsichord maker	79
Farnaby, Giles, composer of the virginals	59
Farrant, Richard, his compositions for the virginals	228
Fattorini, an early clavichord performer	227
Fenton, a maker of spinets, &c	69, 85
Fetis, F. J. his *Sketch of the History of the Pianoforte*, &c.	28
—— his description of the *Cembalo*, mentioned by Boccaccio	37

INDEX.

Fetis, F. J. ceremony in honour of, at Brussels (*note*) ... 38
——— on the origin of the virginal 48
——— on Italian harpsichords 79
——— his notice of Cristofali (*note*) 95
——— his *La Musique Misé à la Portée de tout le Monde* 208
——— his remarks on C. P. E. Bach 232
Fiebeg, inventor of an instrument to sustain the sounds 203
Fisher, Pierre Frederic, patent taken out by 154, 155
Florence, drawing of harps preserved in the museum of 813
Flügel, the German name for the harpsichord 72
Forkel, Dr. his *Life of Bach* 113
Forte, stop in the harpsichord 81
Franche, C. pianoforte maker 219
Frederici, Christian Ernest, the maker of the *first* square pianoforte 119
Frescobaldi, Girolamo, the celebrated organist of St. Peter's at Rome 229, 233
Froberger, the celebrated organist 229

G.

Gabrielli, Andrea, composer and performer on the harpsichord 227, 229
Galilei, Vincenzio, his *Dialogo della Musica Antica e Moderna* 35, 71
Gama, M. inventor of the *Plectroeuphon* 202
Ganer, pianoforte maker 147
Garbrecht, inventor of a piano to sustain the sound 203
Garcka, John, pianoforte maker 150, 157
Gardiner, William, of Leicester 138
Garrick's "old virginals" 65
Gautier, a writer of harpsichord music 231
Gebauhr, pianoforte maker 220
Gerbert, the Abbé, biographical notice of 19
German mechanics arrive in England 131
German mechanism of the pianoforte 118
Gerli, a machinist of Milan 200
Geronimo, of Florence, pianoforte maker 129
Gherardi, of Parma, pianoforte maker 129
Gibbons, Orlando, composer for the virginals 59
Gieb, John, the inventor of the *grasshopper* action 140, 150, 157
Gilbert and Co. pianoforte makers 218
Gillespy, Samuel, harpsichord maker 150
Giornale de' Litterati d' Italia 95
Gluck's pianoforte, described by Thalberg (*note*) 133
Godwin, John, pianoforte maker 155
Gower's *Confessio Amantis* 26
Graces used in old harpsichord music 231
Grainer, inventor of a piano to sustain the sound 203
Grassineau, his Musical Dictionary 21
——— his description of the *cymbal* 39
Greeks, musical instruments of the 6
Greff, Valentine, a celebrated performer on the harpsichord, &c 228

Greiner, Frederick George, pianoforte maker 154
Greiner, J. F. pianoforte maker 217
Greville, Fulke, Esq. biographical notice of 130
Guami, Giuseppe, an early composer for the harpsichord 229
Guido, said to have invented the *Clavier* or key-board... 35
Guitar, favour of the, in this country 91, 401
Gunter, John Henry Anthony, pianoforte maker 154
Gurike, B. pianoforte maker 220
Guynemer, Charles, patent taken out by 155

H.

Hackbret drawing of the 24
Hackel, inventor of a piano to sustain the sounds 203
Halliwell, J. O. Esq. his Collection of Proclamations, Broadsides, &c. in the Chetham Library 86
Hamilton's *Art of Tuning* 373
Hancock, pianoforte maker 147
Hancock, John Crang, organ builder 150, 150
Handel, Capriccio by 235
Handel's harpsichord 74
Hardelle, a writer of harpsichord music 231
Harmonic Chambers 171
Harp 7
—— drawings of the, in the tomb of Bibàn el Moloók 9, 10
Harpsichord 70
——— its use in the public theatres of London 85
——— belonging to Salvator Rosa 75
——— belonging to Handel 74
——— pedal 84
——— vertical 79
Harpsichords, painted 75
——— with three rows of keys 80
——— transposing 84
Harris, Baker, a maker of spinets 400
Harris, John, a celebrated harpsichord maker ... 85, 86, 149
Harrison, J. pianoforte maker 217
Harwar, J. pianoforte maker 217
Hattersley, William, pianoforte maker 156
Haward, Charles, a maker of spinets and harpsichords 68
Hawes, Stephen, his *Pastime of Pleasure* 43
Hawkins, John Isaac, pianoforte maker 168, 402
Hawkins, inventor of a piano to sustain the sounds 203
Hawkins, J. S. his MS. on the Troubadours and Provençal Poets 226
Hawley, John, patent taken out by 155
Hayward, John, harpsichord maker 84
Haxby, Thomas, harpsichord maker 149
Heath, an early composer for the virginals 228
Hebrew musical instruments 7, 12
Heitermeyer, T. pianoforte maker 159, 220
Helmingham Hall, Suffolk, ancient virginals at 58
Hengrave Hall, ancient inventory of musical instruments at 60
Henry the Seventh's Privy Purse Expenses 43
Henry the Eighth 51

INDEX.

Henry the Eighth, the Venetian Ambassador's account of the Court of 52
———— Privy Purse Expenses of 53
Herberth and Co. pianoforte makers 218
Herculaneum, representations of musical instruments found at................ 4, 6
Herding, pianoforte maker...................... 219
Hermes, see MERCURY
Herz, H. pianoforte maker 159, 219
Hews, G. pianoforte maker........................... 218
Heyden, John, inventor of the "Geigen Clavycymbal" 197
Heywood, John, the virginal player 55
Higgins, J. M. his work on *Sound* 18
Hildebrand, John Godfrey, a famous maker of musical instruments................ 119, 122
Hitchcock, John, a maker of spinets and harpsichords 68
Hoffhaimer, Paul, organist to the Emperor Maximilian 227
Hogarth, George, his *History of the Pianoforte* 95
Hohlfeld, of Berlin, his *bowed* harpsichord................ 198
———— his melographic piano 206, 402
Holderness, C. pianoforte maker 217
Holland, his poem of *The Houlate*............................ 22
Hollinshed, his notice of Henry the Eighth's fondness for music................ 51
Hopkinson, an improver of the harpsichord.............. 82
———— John, pianoforte maker.................. 157, 158
———— Messrs. their repetition and tremolo action 186
———— their pianofortes in the Great Exhibition................. 217
Hopper, explanation of the...................... 184
Horn, clavichord maker......................... 47
Hornung, C. C. pianoforte maker................. 159, 168, 219
Houston and Co. pianoforte makers........................ 147
Hoxa, of Vienna, pianoforte maker 159, 218
Hullmandel, N. J. his article *Clavecin*, in the *Encyclopédie Méthodique*................ 41
Hund, F. and Son, pianoforte makers........................ 217
Hüni and Hubert, pianoforte makers....................... 219
Hunt, F. pianoforte maker 217

I.

Il Desiderio, curious notice of musical instruments in a work so called............. 77
Inglott, William, composer for the virginals.............. 59
Isoard, M. the engineer and mechanician.................. 203
Italian harpsichords of the 16th century................... 76
———— of the 18th century.................... 93
Italian Orchestra as shown in *Festa, fatta in Roma, alli 25 di Feb.* 1634................ 79

J.

Jack, description of the....................... 57, 72
———— Lord Oxford's allusion to the........................ 57
———— allusions to the, by the old dramatists............. 57
———— alluded to by John Strangways 58
Jadra, Marco, an early virginal maker...................... 399

Jastrzébski, F. pianoforte maker............................. 218
Jaulin, J. pianoforte maker 219
Jebb, Rev. John, his *Literal Translation of the Book of Psalms*................ 12, 15
Jenkins, W. & Son, pianoforte makers..................... 217
Johnson, Edward, composer for the virginals............. 59
———— Richard, his compositions for the virginals.... 228
———— Robert, composer for the virginals............... 59
Jones, Griffith, pianist to Covent Garden Theatre 139
———— J. C. and Co. pianoforte makers....................... 217
Joyce, George, instrument maker 149
Julyan, F. J. his pianoforte with sustained sounds 204
Juvenal, his notice of musical instruments 7

K.

Kalkbrenner... 129
Keen, Stephen, virginal, spinet, and harpsichord maker 63, 69, 85
Kelly, Michael 139
Kenilworth Castle, the Earl of Leicester's musical instruments at................ 60
Kircher, Father, his *Musurgia Universelle* 13, 198
Kirk, William, pianoforte maker............................ 155
Kirkman, Jacob, the eminent harpsichord maker 89, 140 *et seq.*
———— Abraham, his nephew.................. 91, 140, 147
———— Joseph, his grand nephew... 91, 140, 152, 156, 158
Kirkman and Son, pianoforte makers....................... 217
Kinnór, a form of lyre 3, 13
Kirnberger, John Philip, his performance upon the clavichord 121
Kitarus, or cithara.................................. 13
Kleinjasper, J. F. pianoforte maker 219
Klems, J. B. pianoforte maker................................ 220
Knight's Tale 26
Koch, H. C. his *Musikalisches Lexikon* (*note*)................ 110
Kollman, George Augustus, his improved pianofortes 153, 155
Kotter, Johann, a famous performer on the harpsichord, &c.......................... 228
Krämer, of Göttingen, clavichord maker................... 47
Kühmst, G. pianofore maker................................. 220
Kuhnau, Johann, his harpsichord works 234
Kützing, pianoforte maker 219

L.

La Barre, a writer of harpsichord music 231
Lambert, Thomas, musical instrument maker....... 156, 217
Lampe, Frederic Adolph, his work *De Cymbalis Veterum* 39
Landini, Francesco, alias *Francesco Cieco*, an early composer 226
Landreth, John, musical instrument maker......... 150, 157
Lange, M. his invention of the *Æolodikon*................. 201
Lardner, Dr. his *Popular Essays on Scientific Subjects* 186, 193, 209

	Page.
Lasz, Roland Von, Chapel Master to Duke Albert of Bavaria	47
Launfal, the romance of	26
Layard, Dr. his discoveries at Nineveh	15
Lemme, Carl, clavichord maker	47
Lenkler, Christopher Michael, of Rudolstadt, an ingenious pianoforte maker	120
Leversidge, Adam, virginal maker	400
Lichtenthal, M. pianoforte maker	159, 220
Lidel, Joseph, patent taken out by	155
Lipp, R. R. pianoforte maker	220
Livy, his notice of musical instruments	7
Loeschman, David, pianoforte maker	152, 180
Longman and Broderip, Clementi's predecessors in the pianoforte trade	145, 147, 158
Loosemore, John, virginal maker	63, 64
Lorris, Guillaume de, his *Roman de la Rose*	25
Loud, Thomas, musical instrument maker	152
Loulié, Francis, his *Nouveau Système de Musique*	378
Luff and Son, pianoforte makers	217
Lully, Jean Baptiste, his harpsichord lessons	234
Luscinius, Ottomarus, his *Musurgia seu Praxis Musicæ* described	23
Luthiers, makers of musical instruments of Paris	124
Luzaschi, an early composer for the harpsichord, &c.	229
Lydgate, his Poem on *Reson and Sensualitié*	26
Lyre	2
—— Egyptian	1, 4
—— preserved in the Berlin Museum	5
—— figure of a Theban	5
—— Greek	5
Lyres, drawings of, copied from vases found at Herculaneum	6
Lyrichord	88, 199
Lytton, Sir E. Bulwer, ancient virginals in his possession	58

M.

	Page.
Mace, Thomas, his "pedal harpsicon"	84
Mack, clavichord maker	47
Mackinlay, Thomas, Esq. virginals in his possession	64, 399
M'Culloch, pianoforte maker	218
Maffei, Scipione, his account of Cristofali's invention of the pianoforte	95
Mahoon, harpsichord maker	401
Manichord, description of the	45, 46
Marius, M. his claim to the invention of the pianoforte	102 et seq.
—— his *clavecin vielle*	198
Marot, Clement, his mention of the spinet	67
Mary, Queen, her love of music	54
—— her Privy Purse Expenses when Princess	55
Mason, William, biographical notice of	134
—— description of the mechanism said to be invented by	137

	Page.
Mason, William, his celestinettes	199
Materials used in the construction of pianofortes.	215 et seq.
Mathews, W. pianoforte maker	218
Matheson, John, his harpsichord works	234
Mechanical contrivances to obtain sustained sounds.	197 et seq.
—————— pianos	205 et seq.
Medieval Instruments that preceded the invention of the key-board	17
Melographic pianos	205 et seq.
Melville, Francis, pianoforte maker	153
Melvil, Sir James, his account of Queen Elizabeth's virginal playing	56
Mercier, Sebastien, pianoforte maker	156, 219
Mercury, legend of the lyre concerning	2
Merlin, Joseph, a celebrated harpsichord maker and mechanist	93, 138, 150, 157
Mersennus, Marin, biographical notice of	13
—————— his description of the manichorde	46
—————— his description of the spinet	66
—————— his description of the harpischord	72
Merulo, Claudio, an early clavichord performer	227, 229
Metallic bracing	165
Metals, used in place of the quill, in harpsichords	87
—— used in the manufacture of pianofortes	216
Metzler, George, pianoforte maker	217
Meyer, Conrad, pianoforte maker	132, 218
—————— inventor of a piano to sustain the sounds	203
Milleville, Alessandro, an early performer on the harpischord, &c.	228, 229
Moigno, the Abbé, his discoveries in musical science	379
Mondonville, De, Toccata by	235
Monochord of the middle ages	35, 398
—————— of the 16th and 17th centuries	34
Monocórdo, an instrument of the clavichord kind	31
Montal, C. pianoforte maker	219
Moore and Co. pianoforte makers	217
Morley, Thomas, composer for the virginals	59
Montfaucon, his examination of the ancient musical instruments	17
Montgomery, James, patent taken out by	157
Mott, Isaac Henry Robert, pianoforte maker	156, 217
—————— inventor of the *sostinente* pianoforte	152, 158, 200
Mozart, his notices of Stein's pianofortes	115
—— his early performance on the pianoforte (*note*)	117
—— correspondence relative to his pianoforte, in the *Neue Berliner Musik-Zeitung* (*note*)	117
Muffat, Teofilo, his compositions for the harpsichord	235
Mulcaster, Richard, his eulogy of Queen Elizabeth	57
Müller, inventor of a piano to sustain the sound	203
Mulliner, Thomas, his *Book for the Virginals*, MS. temp. Henry VIII	228
Mundy, John, his compositions for the virginals	59, 228
Mürshhauser, F. X. A. his harpsichord works	234
Musical Directory for 1794	147
Musick's Hand-maid	63

INDEX.

N.

	Page.
Nabulum of the middle ages	21
Naubauer, Frederick, harpsichord maker	88
Nebel, the Hebrew	8, 13, 15
Newman, an early composer for the virginals	228
Neysidler, Melchier, a celebrated performer on the harpsichord, &c.	228
Nickels, Benjamin, patent taken out by	156
Nineveh, recent discoveries at	15
Nunns and Clark, pianoforte makers	159, 218

O.

Octave stop to the pianoforte	158
Ocular harpsichord	82
Oetzman and Plumb, pianoforte makers	217
Oldfield, Thomas, composer for the virginals	59
Orchestra of the London Theatres in 1667	85
Orfeo, an opera performed in 1607	78
Organi, Francesco degli, an early performer on the clavichord	42
Overberg, Van, pianoforte maker	219

P.

Pace, Richard, his Letter to Cardinal Wolsey	45
Painted harpsichords	75
Palace of Honour, quotation from	22
Pandoron, a musical instrument of the lute kind	30
Panormo, Francis, the first suggester of additional keys to the pianoforte	141
Pape, M. pianoforte maker	158, 159, 172, 194, 219
Paris, MS. in the Imperial library of	19, 21
Parker, William Phillip, patent taken out by	157
Parthenia Inviolata, or Mayden Musicke for the Virginalls and Bass Viol	63
Parthenia, or the Maydenhead of the first musicke that ever was printed for the Virginalls.	50, 62
Paston, Mr. Princess Mary's teacher on the virginals	54
Pasquino, Bernard, a writer of harpsichord music	231
——— Ercole, a writer of harpsichord music	231
Patents, list of, chronologically arranged	149 *et seq.*
Paulmann, Conrad, an early organ performer	227
Pausanius, his notice of music	5
Peachey, George, pianoforte maker	217
Pedals of the pianoforte	188, 402
Peerson, Martin, composer for the virginals	59
Pepys, his notice of the virginals at the fire of London	64
Perne, M. de, inventor of the *Organon-Lyricon*	200
Perronard, a French harpsichord maker	81
Pesarese, Domenico, an early spinet and harpsichord maker	68
Pether, George, pianoforte maker	147
Petzold, pianoforte maker	159
Pfeiffer, pianoforte maker	159
Philips, J. B. pianoforte maker	218
Phillips, Peter, composer for the virginals	59
Pianoforte, claimants to the invention of the	94 *et seq.*

	Page.
Pianoforte, its progress on the Continent	112 *et seq.*
——— its introduction and progress in England	130
——— its first introduction on the public stage	133
——— its construction	162 *et seq.*
——— Framing	162
——— Stringing	162
——— Action	168
——— original scale of the	141
——— to regulate defects in its mechanism	380 *et seq.*
——— how to place it for effect	370
——— how to prevent its sounds from penetrating into an adjoining chamber	370
Pianofortes, hints to those who have the care of	369
——— in the Great Exhibition of 1851	217
——— annual estimate of those made in London	211
Piccolo pianoforte	157
Pietri, Giovanni, composer for the virginals	59
Pirsson, James, pianoforte maker	159, 218
Player, a maker of spinets, &c.	69, 85
Plectrum described (*note*)	4
Plenius, Rutgerus, a celebrated harpsichord maker	87, 131, 149
Pleyel, Ignace, biographical Notice of	127 *et seq.*
——— Camille, pianoforte maker	129, 159
Pohlman, John, an early pianoforte maker	133
Pole, William, Esq. on the Musical Instruments in the Great Exhibition of 1851	162, 166, 168, 170, 179, 184, 196, 212, 221
Poli-Toni-Clavichordium, a musical instrument invented by Stein (*note*)	115
Polythongum, an instrument of the lyre kind	17
Pottje, J. pianoforte maker	218
Pouleau, M. inventor of the *Orchestrina*	200
Prætorius, his description of the monochord or clavichord	34
——— his *Syntagma Musicum* described (*note*)	34
Prices of pianofortes	212
Proposto, Nicolo del, an early composer	42, 226
Provençal poets	225
Proverbs at Leckingfield	44, 49
Psaltery of the Jews	15
——— of the middle ages	18, 19
——— of a later period, described by *Bartholomeus*	20
——— of the fourteenth and fifteenth centuries	21
Purcell, Henry, his harpsichord works	234
Pythagorean Monochord	35

Q.

Quagliati, an early composer for the virginals	229
Quilling a harpsichord (*note*)	82
Quintilian, his notice of ancient musical instruments	17

R.

Rafael d' Urbino, Farinelli's pianoforte so called	83
Redford, John, an early composer for the virginals	228
Repetition action	158, 185

	Page.
Reverberation, the bridge of	182
Richard, a French harpsichord maker.	79
Richard, a writer of harpsichord music	231
Richardson, Ferdinand, composer for the virginals	59
Rigoli, a Florentine harpsichord maker	79
Rimbault, Dr. E. F. his *Little Book of Songs and Ballads from Ancient Musick Books*.	226
Rolfe, William, musical instrument maker... 151, 154,	157
———— and Son, pianoforte makers	217
Roller, M. his transposing piano	207
Roller and Blanchet, pianoforte makers	219
Roman de la Rose.	25
Romans, musical instruments of the.	6
Rosa, Salvator, his harpsichord.	75
Rosellini, harps copied from	8, 14
———— his *Description de l' Egypte*	9
Roussier, The Abbè, his account of Erard's mechanical harpsichord	123
Royal Albert transposing piano.	208
Ruckers family of Antwerp	68
——— Hans	72, 76
——— Jean.	73
——— Andreas	73, 74
Rühms, H. pianoforte maker	159, 219
Rüst, pianoforte maker	170
Ryley, Edward, pianoforte maker	151, 403

S.

Sambuc, or *Sambuca*, a musical instrument of the Jews,	13, 15, 17, 23
Sautry, mentioned by Chaucer (*note*)	21
Sautter, Charles Maurice Elizée, patent taken out by	156
Savart, M.	403
Scaliger, Julius Cæsar, his description of the *Simicum*...	33
Scarlatti, Domenico, his harpsichord works	232, 234
———— his harpsichord given to Farinelli	83
Schachinger, a celebrated organist at Padua	228
Scheel, C. pianoforte maker	220
Scheibler, his apparatus for tuning pianofortes	379
Schiedmayer and Son, pianoforte makers.	220
Schmidt, pianoforte maker.	200
Schneider, J. pianoforte maker.	218
Schnell, pianoforte maker	203
Schobert, his harpsichord with a *double bottom*	81
Schott and Son, pianoforte makers	220
Scholtus, pianoforte maker	219
Schröter, Christopher Gottlieb, his claim to the invention of the pianoforte	108 *et seq.*
Schröder, C. H. pianoforte maker,	220
Schroeter, J. S. an early *pianoforte* player, mistakes concerning	142
Schwieso, John Charles, musical instrument maker	154
Scotland, Lord High Treasurer's Accounts quoted	42
Scott, Robert, John, and Alexander, pianoforte makers	151, 402
Self-acting pianos, &c.	206 *et seq.*

	Page.
Sells, harpsichord maker	401
Seuffert, Francis Ignace, eminent pianoforte maker	120
———— E. pianoforte maker.	218
Shakespeare, his Sonnet on the virginal	62
———— his *Tempest* as acted in 1667	85
Shelbye, an early composer for the virginals	228
Sheminith, a harp of eight strings	12
Shepperd, John, an early composer for the virginals	228
Shudi, Burkat.	147, 149
Shudi, see Tschudi.	
Silbermann, Godfrey, of Freyberg, pianoforte maker	81, 82
Silbermann, Godfrey, the invention of the pianoforte erroneously ascribed to him	112
Simicum, description of the	33, 35
Simmons, William, an improver of musical instruments	152
Skelton's poem, *A Comely Caystrowne*	44
Slade, a maker of spinets, &c.	69
Smart, Henry, pianoforte maker	153
Smith, Joseph, improves the *bracing*	151
———— J. S. his *Musica Antiqua*	226
Smith and Roberts, pianoforte makers	218
Snetzler, the eminent organ builder	89
Soft stop in the harpsichord	81
Soufleto, pianoforte maker	219
Sounding-board	171, 402
Southwell, William, pianoforte maker. 151, 152, 153, 155,	157, 189, 217
Späett, or Spaeth, John Adam, a celebrated maker of musical instruments	119
Spear, John, patent taken out by	157
Spenser, his allusion to the virginal	61
Sperling, Rev. Mr. ancient virginals in his possession...	58
Spinet, description of the	33, 66
Sprecher and Beer, pianoforte makers	219
Squarcialupi, Antonio, surnamed *Antonio degli Organi*..	227
Squire of Lowe Degree	22
Stanhope, Lord, his method of stringing	179
Statistics of pianoforte manufacturing	209
Steel wire	183
Stein, John Andrew, of Augsburg, harpsichord and pianoforte maker	82, 115, 120
Sternberg, L. pianoforte maker	218
Stewart, James, pianoforte maker	153, 154, 155, 156
Stodart, Robert, the founder of the firm. 140, 147, 150, 151,	157
———— Messrs. their metallic bracing	165 *et seq.*
———— and Son, their pianofortes in the Great Exhibition	217
Stops in harpsichords	81
Streicher, John Andrew, pianoforte maker	115, 120
Striggio, Alessandro, an early clavichord performer	227
String, stretched, *first* canon of the	175
———————— *second* canon of the	176
———————— *third* canon of the	177
Stringed instruments, the particular names of which are unknown	12

INDEX.

	Page.
Stringing	174
——— Messrs. Collard's method of	179
——— Lord Stanhope's method of	179
——— Erard's improved method of, for grand horizontal pianos	183
Strings of Egyptian harps	9
——— of the clavichord	30
——— thin wire, of the old pianofortes	178
——— of one size and tension	180
——— gold and silver	398
Strogers, Nicholas, composer for the virginals	59
Stumpff, Johann Andreas, musical instrument maker	155
Summary of pianofortes in the Great Exhibition of 1851.	220
Swellinck, J. P. composer for the virginals	59

T.

Tabel, harpsichord maker	88
Table of pianofortes in the Great Exhibition of 1851	217
Tallis, his compositions for the virginals	59, 228
Taskin, Paschal, harpsichord maker of Paris	81
Taverner, his compositions for the virginals	228
Taxis, Count, his *transposing* harpsichord	83, 84
Tension, equal, of strings	180 *et seq.*
Terpander adds several strings to the lyre	5
Testudo, a name for the lyre	3
Thalberg, S. his *Remarks upon the Pianofortes* in the Great Exhibition of 1851	110, 159, 192
——— his Description of Gluck's pianoforte (*note*)	133
Theban lyre, drawing of	5
——— harps, drawings of	8
Theophilus, *De Mensura Cymbalorum*	40
Thom, James, pianoforte maker	152, 158
Thompson, Simon, his improvements in the pianoforte	154
Tisdall, W. composer for the virginals	59
Todd, Thomas, organ builder	153
Todini, Michele, musical instrument maker	77, 400
Tomkins, Thomas, composer for the virginals	59
Tortoise, the origin of the lyre	2
Towns and Packer, Messrs. pianoforte makers	217
Transposing harpsichords	84
Transposing pianos	204 *et seq.*
Trentia, Abbe Gregorio, inventor of the *Violicembalo*	201
Trevisa, his translation of *Bartholomeus*	20
Trumpet Marine of the 16th and 17th centuries	34
Troubadours	223
Trouflant, M. his letter on the inventions of M. Paschal Tasquin (*note*)	81
Tschudi, Burkat or Burckhardt, the founder of the house of Broadwood and Sons	88
Tuning explained	372 *et seq.*
——— An Essay on the Theory and Practice of	373, 379
Twining, Mr., Ruckers harpsichord in the possession of	74
Tye, Dr. his compositions for the virginals	228
Tympanum, or timpano, of the Italians	37

U.

	Page.
Unachord instruments	180
Unger, John Frederick, inventor of a melographic piano	205, 403
Upright grand pianoforte	157
——— pianofortes, diagrams of the framing of	169

V.

Valle, Pietro della, his *Discourse on the Music of his own Time*	67
Vander-Noodt, his *Theatre for Voluptuous Worldlings*	56
Vensky, clavichord maker	47
Verhasselt, pianoforte maker	218
Verospi Palace at Rome, musical instruments in the.	77, 401
Vertical harpsichord	79
Viasky, J. pianoforte maker	218
Viator, an early pianoforte maker	131
Vienna Action	159, 192
Vincentino, Don Nicola, famous harpsichord made by	77
Violine-éolie	203
Virbes, the Sieur, his "harpsichord imitating fourteen wind and chorded instruments"	80
Virginal or Virginals	48, 399
——— etymology of the name	51
——— made "harp fashion"	53
——— Queen Elizabeth's	58
——— self-acting	64
——— painted, Mary Queen of Scots'	75
Vis-à-vis harpsichord	82
Vittoria of Bologna, an early performer on the harpsichord, &c.	228
Vogelsang, Messrs. pianoforte makers	218

W.

Wace, his *Brut d' Angleterre*	21, 86
Walesby, Mr. his trumpet marine	84
Walker, Adam, his *Celestina*	149, 158, 199
——— Edward Lesley, patent taken out by	156
Wallace Pianoforte Company	169
Walton, Humphrey, musical instrument maker	150, 157
Warren, Ambrose, his *Tonometer*	379
Warrock, Thomas, composer for the virginals	59
Webster's steel wire	183
Westermann and Co. pianoforte makers	220
Wheatstone, William, patent taken out by	153
——— and Co. pianoforte makers	217
White, Thomas, virginal maker	399
Wiegleb, musical instrument maker	82
Wilder, Philip Van, Biographical notice of (*note*)	54
——— musical instruments in the charge of, on the death of Henry VIII,	45, 53
Wilhelm, of Cassel, clavichord maker	47
Wilkinson, Sir J. Gardner	2, 3, 9, 13
Wire, steel and brass	183
——— Berlin	183

	Page.
Wood, Father, the maker of the first pianoforte seen in England	130
Woodcroft, Professor, his Indexes to the Patents (note)	148
Wood, James S. pianoforte maker	218
Woods, George, improves musical instruments	152
Woods used in pianoforte manufacture	215
Woollen fabrics used in pianoforte manufacture	215
Woolley, F. pianoforte maker	218
Woolley, Thomas, pianoforte maker	165
Wolf, Robert, pianoforte maker	155
Workmen employed in the manufacture of pianofortes	213, et seq.

	Page.
Wornum, Robert, pianoforte maker	152, 153, 154, 156, 157, 180, 190, 191, 217, 402
Wrest pins	163

Z.

Zanetti, a Venetian harpsichord maker	79
Zarlino, his spinet with quarter tones	68
Zeiger, pianoforte maker	219
Zeitter, Jacob Frederick, pianoforte maker	154, 191
Zeitter and Winkelmann, pianoforte makers	220
Zipoli, a writer of harpsichord music	232
Zumpé, John, a celebrated pianoforte maker	132

INDEX TO THE SPECIMENS OF MUSIC.

B.

Bach, C. P. E. Rondo in E flat	357
———— Fantasia	363
Bach, J. S. Capriccio	332
Blitheman, William, Gloria Tibi, Trinitas	237
Bull, Dr. John, The King's Hunting Jigg	245
———— Les Buffons	248
———— Courante Jewell	253
Byrd, William, Sellenger's Round	240

C.

Chambonnières, Suite de Pièces	265
Couperin, François, Suite de Pièces	316

D.

Dumont, H. Suites de Pièces	262

F.

Frescobaldi, Girolamo, Capriccio del Soggetto sopra l'Aria di Roggiero	257

H.

Handel, G. F. Capriccio in G	340

K.

Kuhnau, Johann, Sonata	292

L.

Lully, Jean Baptiste, Suite de Pièces	268

M.

Mattheson, John, Suite de Pièces	299
Mondonville, De, Introduction and Toccata	351
Muffat, Teofilo, Fantaisie	344
———— Air	348
———— Allemand	350
Mürshhauser, F. X. A. Variationes super Cantilenam	284

P.

Purcell, Henry, Prelude and Airs	278

S.

Scarlatti, Domenico, Sonata in A minor	306
———— Sonata in G	310

FINIS.

SUBSCRIPTION LIST.

Allison, Ralph, Jun. Esq.   108, Wardour Street, Soho.
André, Gustave, and Co.   Philadelphia, U. S.   6 Copies.
André, Wm. Esq.   Islington.
Andrews, Mr. Thomas, Music Warehouse, Guildford.
Ashpitel, Arthur, Esq. F.S.A.   Poet's Corner.
Atkins, R. A. Esq. Organist of the Cathedral, St. Asaph.
Augener and Co. Messrs.   Newgate Street.

Banister, Henry C. Esq. Professor at the Royal Academy of Music.
Barry, Mr. W.   12, College Street, Belfast.
Beaumont, J. F. Esq.   Whaddon, near Royston.
Beevor, Charles, Esq.   41, Upper Harley Street.
Bennett, W. Esq. Organist, Andover.
Blackshaw, Edward, Esq. Professor of Music, 8, Lansdowne Terrace, South Lambeth.
Browne, Mr. R. Music Warehouse, Lowestoft.
Bunnett, E. Esq. Mus. Bac. Cantab. Assistant Organist of Norwich Cathedral, Upper Close, Norwich.

Caldecutt, Thomas, Esq.
Causton, W. S. Esq, Professor of Music, Woodbridge.
Chappell, Wm. Esq. F.S.A.   3, Harley Place.
Chippendale, A. Esq.   10, John Street, Adelphi.
Clarke, Mr. Joseph, Musicseller, next Reynolds's Mill, Skirbeck, Boston.
Cole, J. Parry,   Arundel, Sussex.
Collard and Collard, Messrs.   16 and 17, Grosvenor Street, W. and 26 Cheapside.
Cooper, Rev. Allen T.   University Club, Suffolk Street, Pall Mall.
Cooper, J. Thomas, Esq. F.R.A.S.   13, Canonbury Square, N.
Corbett and Son, Messrs. Music Warehouse, 108 and 109, Georges Street, Limerick.

Cotton, Wm. Esq. Mus. Bac. Cantab. Organist of Trinity Church, Kentish Town.
Cramer, J. B. Esq. Organist, Loughborough.
Crossley, G. J. Esq. Professor of Music, Bowdon, near Manchester.
Crowe, Richard, Esq. Professor of Vocal Music, Liverpool Collegiate Institution.
Cruse, Edward, Esq. Organist of St. Barnabas' Church, Pimlico.
Curtis, Lambert, Esq. St. Giles's, Norwich.

Darken and Colsey, Messrs. Music Warehouse, London Street, Norwich.
Dawes, Albert, Esq. Organist of The Holy Trinity Church, Hastings.
Dimoline, Mr. A. Music Warehouse, Bristol.
Dixon, Wm. Esq. Organist, Grantham.
Duncan, James, Esq. Professor of the Pianoforte, Perth, N. B.
Dyer, J. P. Esq. Organist, Warminster.

Emery, J. Jun. Esq. Professor of Music, High Street, Hanley.
Ennever and Co. Messrs. Soho Square.

Favarger, Réné, Esq.
Field, Mr. George, Music Warehouse, Bath. 3 Copies.
Foulkes, William, Esq. Organist, Whitchurch, Salop.
Fowler, C. Esq. Professor of Music, Torquay.
French, Thomas, Esq. 2 Copies.

Gardner, C. Jun. Esq. Pimlico.
Gilbert, Messrs. S. and T. Booksellers, 4, Copthall Buildings, City.
Gilbert, Bennett, Esq. 13, Berners Street.
Gilmore, Mr. George, Musicseller, Clones, Co. Tyrone.
Glover, Professor, Royal Irish Institution, College Street, Dublin.
Gordon, Sir Henry, Chelsea College.
Gough, James, Esq. 37, Prospect Place, Hull, Yorkshire.
Green, William, Esq. 1, Foley Place, Gloucester.
Griffiths, George R. Esq. Organist, St. Paul's, Hammersmith.
Grosvenor, S. Esq. Mus. Bac. Oxon. Organist, Dudley.

Hall, R. W. Esq. Professor of Music, Hull.

Hamilton, Adams, and Co. Messrs. Paternoster Row.   4 Copies.

Hammond, Alfred W. Esq. Organist of St. Mary's, Lombard Street;   Fox Lodge, North Brixton.

Harcourt, Mr. T. Music Warehouse, Rochester.

Harraden, Messrs. S. and Co.   3, Chapel Place, Poultry.   3 Copies.

Harris, Mr. Edwin,   Bradford, Yorkshire.

Harrison, John, Esq. Professor of Music, Deal.

Hayden, Henry, Esq. Professor of Music, St. Leonard's.

Haynes, Wm. Esq. Organist, Abbey and Trinity Churches, Malvern.

Holst, Matthias von, Esq. Professor of Music, Worcester.

Hopkins, J. Esq. Organist, Rochester

Hopkinson, Mr. James,   Leeds.

Hopkinson, Mr. John, Pianoforte Manufacturer, Regent Street, London.

Howard, The Honourable Miss, Oatlands Park, Surrey.

Howell, Miss, Professor of Music, Chippenham, Wilts.

Huchtin, Madame Louise,   Madison, Wisconsin, United States, America.

Hyde, Major T. C. S.   Twickenham, Middlesex.

Inglis, Mr. James, Music Warehouse, Greenock.

Jackson, Miss Monymia,   Onslow Square, Bromptonia, London.

Jackson, Mr. Musicseller, Bradford.

Jacob, F. K. Esq. Professor of Music, St. Leonard's-on-Sea.

Jewson, Frederick Bowen, Esq. London.

Jewson, Mr. Musicseller, Stockton-on-Tees.

Jones, Mr. C. 21, Soho Square.

Jungenfeld, Anna Fraeulein von,   Mayence.

King, Mr. H. Bookseller, 8, Spring Street, Hyde Park.

Kinkee, F. Esq. Organist and Choir-master, St. Paul's, Knightsbridge; 38, Sloane St.

Kippax, Mr. J. Retford.

Kraus, Conrad, Esq. Architect,   Mayence.

Kurtz, A. G. Esq.   Liverpool.

Longley, George, Esq. Organist of Fitzwilliam Street Church, Huddersfield.

Marie Agnèse, Mademoiselle la Sœur, de l'Ordre de Saint Vincent de Paul, à Metz.
Marshall, James, Esq. Professor of Music, Full Street, Derby.
Martin, J. U. Esq. Organist, East Dereham.
Mason, Mr. Joseph, Music Warehouse, Glossop.   2 Copies.
May, Miss, Professor of Music, Jersey.
Meller, Mr. Professor of Music, Blackburn.
Meller, Mr. Richard, Huddersfield.
Mellor, Mr. John H. Organist of Trinity Church, and Dealer in Pianofortes, Pittsburgh, Pennsylvania, U. S. America.
Mellor, Mr. Charles C. Organist of St. James's Church, Pittsburgh, Pennsylvania, U. S. America.
Mellor, Mr. James, Dealer in Pianofortes, Wheeling, Virginia, U. S. America.
Mellor, Mr. Joseph S. Teacher of the Pianoforte, Wheeling, Virginia, U. S. America.
Mellor, Mr. Levi, Pittsburgh, Pennsylvania, U. S. America.
Mellor, Mr. Samuel C. Pittsburgh, Pennsylvania, U. S. America.
Messiter, A. Esq. Organist, Worthing.
Monk, W. H. Esq. Glebe Field Houses, Stoke Newington ; and King's College, Strand.
Moore, Messrs. John and Henry, Pianoforte Manufacturers, 104, Bishopsgate Street, Within.
Moore, Mr. J. General Music Repository, Huddersfield.

Norbury, John, Jun. Esq.   5, Finsbury Square.
Norwood, Mr.   Professor of Music, Preston.
Nunn, R. Esq. Organist, Bury St. Edmunds.

Oakeley, H. S. Esq.
Ouseley, Sir Frederick A. Gore, Bart. M.A. Mus. Doc. Præcentor of Hereford, and Professor of Music in the University of Oxford.

Pearce, George, Esq.   Pau, Basses-Pyrénées.
Pech, Dr. James (è Coll. Nov. Oxon.), Pianist and Composer to the Countess of Darnley,   St. Saviour's, Paddington.

Phillips, Messrs. George and Co. 1, Peninsular and Oriental Buildings, and 21, Bernard Street, Southampton.
Pickering, Mr. T. Musicseller, Royston.
Pietsch, Mademoiselle Thadea, Mayence.
Pringle, George, R. G. Esq. Professor of Music, Melbourne, Victoria.
Prior, George, Esq. Professor of Music, Wantage.

Rhodes, Jeremiah, Esq. Organist, Pontefract.
Rhodes, John, Esq. Organist and Director of the Choir, Parish Church, Croydon.
Richards, Brinley, Esq. Member of the Royal Academy of Music, London.
Robinson, George, Esq. Professor of Music, Gainsborough.
Roe, John, Esq. Pianoforte Tutor to the French Royal Families, Claremont; 52, Stanhope Street, N. W.
Rogers, J. Esq. Organist, Doncaster.
Russell, James, Esq. Mus. Bac. Oxon. Elford Barton, Topsham, Devon.
Rüst, R. Anderson, Esq. 4, Great Marlborough Street.

Sacred Harmonic Society (The), Exeter Hall.
Salaman, Charles, Esq. 36, Baker Street.
Salter, Edward, Esq. Professor of Music, St. Andrews, Fife.
Sapio, A. Esq. Professor of Music, Chester.
Savory, Douglas, Esq. 22, Lower Lyon Street, New Town, Southampton.
Schnegelsberg, — Esq. Chalcot Terrace, Primrose Hill.
Schœlcher, Victor, Esq. Wellington Square, Chelsea.
Shargool, Edwin, Esq. Organist, Stafford.
Simms, E. Esq. Organist, Coventry.
Simpkin, Marshall, and Co. Messrs. 6 Copies.
Smith, Mr. Philip, Music Warehouse, Bristol. 3 Copies.
Spark, Edward J. Esq. Bury, Lancashire.
Steggall, Dr. 27, Grafton Square, Clapham.
Stephens, Charles E. Esq. 2, Howley Place, Maida Hill, W.
Stephenson, Mr. Professor of Music, Bishopton, Ripon.
Stirling, Miss, 1, Charlton Terrace, East India Road, Poplar.
Stodart, Messrs. W. and Son, 1, Golden Square, W.

Stone, J. T. Esq. 40, Berners Street, W.
Stonex, H. Esq. Organist, Great Yarmouth.
Suggate, Mr. Musicseller, Lowestoft.

Taylor, Edward, Esq   Gresham College.
Taylor, James, Esq. Professor of Music, Gloucester.
Taylor, Mr. Musicseller, The Quay, Bristol.
Thurnam, Edward, Esq. Professor of Music, Reigate.
Toms, C. J. Esq. Professor of Music, Liverpool.
Turner, Mr. James, Stockport.
Turner, John, Esq. Professor of Music, Halifax.

Vernon, Madame, Tunbridge Wells.
Vincent, Charles J. Professor of Music, Sunderland.

Walker, Mrs. 1, Scroop Terrace, Cambridge.
Watts, Mr. J. Organist, Ormskirk.
Weisbecker, Charles, Esq. 12, Connaught Terrace, Connaught Square.
Wetter, Conrad, Esq. 67, Myddelton Square, London.
Wetter, J. Esq. Architect, Mayence.
Wetter, Miss Madelina, Mayence.
Wetter-Taillefer, Madame, Savannah, Georgia, United States, America.
Wheatley, Mr. W. K. Musicseller, Evesham.
Wheeler, R. B. Esq. Organist of St. Ann's Church, Wandsworth.
Winn, Mr. Thomas, Jun. Music Warehouse, Rochdale.
Wood, Samuel, Esq. Professor of Music, Clitheroe.
Woodward, Mr. Musicseller, Cheltenham.
Wornum, A. N. Esq. Music Hall, Store Street, London.
Wrenshall, W. Esq. 6, Sandon Terrace, Upper Duke Street, Liverpool.
Wrighton, A. J. Esq. Dundee, N. B.
Wrigley, Mr. F. Organist, Kettering
Wrigley, John, Esq. Professor of Music, Ardwick, Manchester.

Yeomans, A. Esq. Professor of Music, Stourbridge.

Titles published by Travis & Emery Music Bookshop:

Bathe, William: A Briefe Introduction to the Skill of Song
Bax, Arnold: Symphony #5, Arranged for Piano for Four Hands by Walter Emery
Burney, Charles: An Account of the Musical Performances in Westminster-Abbey
Burney, Charles: The Present State of Music in France and Italy
Burney, Charles: The Present State of Music in Germany, The Netherlands …
Crimp, Bryan: Dear Mr. Rosenthal … Dear Mr. Gaisberg …
Crimp, Bryan: Solo: The Biography of Solomon
Frescobaldi, Girolamo: D'Arie Musicali per Cantarsi. Primo Libro & Secondo Libro.
Geminiani, Francesco: The Art of Playing the Violin.
Hawkins, John: A General History of the Science and Practice of Music (5 vols.)
Herbert-Caesari, Edgar: The Science and Sensations of Vocal Tone
Herbert-Caesari, Edgar: Vocal Truth
Isaacs, Lewis: Hänsel and Gretel. A Guide to Humperdinck's Opera.
Isaacs, Lewis: Königskinder (Royal Children) A Guide to Humperdinck's Opera.
Lascelles (née Catley), Anne: The Life of Miss Anne Catley.
Mainwaring, John: Memoirs of the Life of the Late George Frederic Handel
Malcolm, Alexander: A Treaty of Music: Speculative, Practical and Historical
Mellers, Wilfrid: Angels of the Night: Popular Female Singers of Our Time
Mellers, Wilfrid: Bach and the Dance of God
Mellers, Wilfrid: Beethoven and the Voice of God
Mellers, Wilfrid: Caliban Reborn - Renewal in Twentieth Century Music
Mellers, Wilfrid: François Couperin and the French Classical Tradition
Mellers, Wilfrid: Harmonious Meeting
Mellers, Wilfrid: Le Jardin Retrouvé, The Music of Frederic Mompou
Mellers, Wilfrid: Music and Society, England and the European Tradition
Mellers, Wilfrid: Music in a New Found Land: … … American Music
Mellers, Wilfrid: Romanticism and the Twentieth Century (from 1800)
Mellers, Wilfrid: The Masks of Orpheus: …… the Story of European Music.
Mellers, Wilfrid: The Sonata Principle (from c. 1750)
Mellers, Wilfrid: Vaughan Williams and the Vision of Albion
Playford, John: An Introduction to the Skill of Musick.
Purcell, Henry et al: Harmonia Sacra … The First Book, [1726]
Purcell, Henry et al: Harmonia Sacra … Book II [1726]
Quantz, Johann: Versuch einer Anweisung die Flöte traversiere zu spielen.
Rastall, Richard: The Notation of Western Music.
Rimbault, Edward: The Pianoforte, Its Origins, Progress, and Construction.
Rubinstein, Anton : Guide to the proper use of the Pianoforte Pedals.
Simpson, Christopher: A Compendium of Practical Musick in Five Parts
Spohr, Louis: Grand Violin School
Tans'ur, William: A New Musical Grammar; or The Harmonical Spectator
Tosi, Pier Francesco: Observations on the Florid Song.
Van der Straeten, Edmund: History of the Violoncello, The Viol da Gamba …
Van der Straeten, Edmund: History of the Violin, Its Ancestors… Vol.1.
Van der Straeten, Edmund: History of the Violin, Its Ancestors… Vol.2.

Travis & Emery Music Bookshop
17 Cecil Court, London, WC2N 4EZ, United Kingdom.
Tel. (+44) 20 7240 2129

© Travis & Emery 2009

ADDENDA TO SUBSCRIPTION LIST

(*Omitted by Oversight*).

Broadwood, Messrs. John and Sons.

Reid, John, Esq.

William H. Callcott, Esq. the Mall, Kensington.

Burkinyoung and Co. Messrs. Calcutta,

The following Erratum has been kindly pointed out by Mr. ROBERT STODART.

PAGE 140, line 9, instead of "John, William and Matthew Stodart," read "Matthew and William Stodart," omitting the name John.

www.ingramcontent.com/pod-product-compliance
Lightning Source LLC
Chambersburg PA
CBHW082014220426
43671CB00014B/2580